Unfolding Cluster Evolution

Various theories have been put forward as to why business and industry develop in clusters. However, despite good work being carried out on path dependence and dynamics, this is still very much an emerging topic in the social sciences. To date, no overarching theoretical framework has been developed to show how clusters evolve.

Unfolding Cluster Evolution aims to address this gap by presenting theoretical and empirical research on the geography of innovation. This contributed volume seeks to shed light on the understanding of clusters and their dynamic evolution. The book provides evidence to suggest that traditional perspectives from evolutionary economic geography need to be wedded to management thinking in order to reach this point. Bringing together thinking from a range of disciplines and countries across Europe, this book explores a wide range of topics, from the capability approach to network dynamics, to multinational corporations, to firm entry and exit, and social capital.

This book will be of interest to policy makers and students of urban studies, economic geography, and planning and development.

Fiorenza Belussi is Professor at the University of Padova, Italy. Her areas of interest include management of innovation and creativity; creative industries; theoretical models on innovation diffusion through gatekeepers; studies of open innovation; international business; and the impact of globalisation on local economies.

Jose Luis Hervás-Oliver is Full Professor of Strategy and Innovation at the Polytechnic University of Valencia, FADE, Spain. His research interests lie at the intersection between innovation and economic geography.

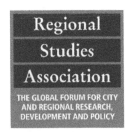

Regions and Cities

Series Editor in Chief
Susan M. Christopherson, *Cornell University, USA*

Editors
Maryann Feldman, *University of Georgia, USA*
Gernot Grabher, *HafenCity University Hamburg, Germany*
Ron Martin, *University of Cambridge, UK*
Martin Perry, *Massey University, New Zealand*
Kieran P. Donaghy, *Cornell University, USA*

In today's globalised, knowledge-driven and networked world, regions and cities have assumed heightened significance as the interconnected nodes of economic, social and cultural production, and as sites of new modes of economic and territorial governance and policy experimentation. This book series brings together incisive and critically engaged international and interdisciplinary research on this resurgence of regions and cities, and should be of interest to geographers, economists, sociologists, political scientists and cultural scholars, as well as to policy makers involved in regional and urban development.

For more information on the Regional Studies Association visit www.regionalstudies.org

There is a **30 per cent discount** available to RSA members on books in the **Regions and Cities** series, and other subject related Taylor and Francis books and e-books including Routledge titles. To order just e-mail cara.trevor@tandf.co.uk, or phone on +44 (0) 20 7017 6924 and declare your RSA membership. You can also visit www.routledge.com and use the discount code: **RSA0901**

Unfolding Cluster Evolution

**Edited by Fiorenza Belussi and
Jose Luis Hervás-Oliver**

Routledge
Taylor & Francis Group

LONDON AND NEW YORK

First published 2017 by Routledge

2 Park Square, Milton Park, Abingdon, Oxfordshire OX14 4RN

52 Vanderbilt Avenue, New York, NY 10017

Routledge is an imprint of the Taylor & Francis Group, an informa business

First issued in paperback 2019

British Library Cataloguing in Publication Data
A catalogue record for this book is available from the British Library

Library of Congress Cataloguing in Publication Data
Names: Belussi, Fiorenza, editor. | Hervás-Oliver, Jose Luis, editor.
Title: Unfolding cluster evolution / edited by Fiorenza Belussi and Jose Luis Hervás-Oliver.
Description: Abingdon, Oxon; New York, NY : Routledge, [2017]
Identifiers: LCCN 2016011823 | ISBN 9781138123687 (hardback) | ISBN 9781315648712 (ebook)
Subjects: LCSH: Industrial location. | Industrial districts. | Diffusion of innovations. | Economic geography.
Classification: LCC HD58.U54 2017 | DDC 338.8/7–dc23
LC record available at https://lccn.loc.gov/2016011823

ISBN: 978-1-138-12368-7 (hbk)
ISBN: 978-0-367-87625-8 (pbk)

Typeset in Times New Roman
by Out of House Publishing

Contents

Figures

Tables

Contributors

Gregorio Gonzalez Alcaide is Associate Professor at Valencia University, Spain.

Alexander Auer is Associate Professor at Vienna University of Economics and Business Austria.

Jose A. Aznar-Sanchez is Professor at University of Almeria, Spain.

Jonathan Beaverstock is Professor at the University of Bristol, UK.

Luis J. Belmonte-Urena is Associate Professor at University of Almería, Spain.

Fiorenza Belussi is Professor at Padova University, Italy.

Francesco Capone is Associate Professor at University of Florence, Italy.

Anselmo Carretero-Gómez is Professor at University of Almeria, Spain.

Gary Cook is Professor at University of Liverpool, UK.

Aitziber Elola is Associate Professor at ORKESTRA, Deusto University, Spain.

Raquel Rubio Fernández is Associate Professor at University of Castilla-la-Mancha, Spain.

Susana Franco is Associate Professor at ORKESTRA, Deusto University, Spain.

Renato Garcia is Professor at University of Campinas, Brazil.

Markus Grillitsch is Associate Professor at CIRCLE, Lund University Sweden.

Robert Hassink is Professor at Kiel University, Germany.

Jose Luis Hervás-Oliver is Full Professor at Polytechnic University of Valencia, Spain.

Arne Isaksen is Professor at the Department Of Working Life And Innovation, University Of Agder, Norway.

Luciana Lazzeretti is Professor at University of Florence, Italy.

Santiago M. López is Associate Professor at Orkestra, Deusto University, Spain.

Edoardo Mollona is Professor at University of Bologna, Italy.

Andrea Morrison is Associate Professor at Utrecht University, the Netherlands.

Flávio Nunes is Associate Professor at University of Minho, Portugal.

Maria Jose Ruiz Ortega is Assocaite Professor at University of Castilla La Mancha, Spain.

Christian R. Østergaard is Associate Professor at Aalborg University, Denmark.

Naresh Pandit is Professor at Norwich Business School, UK.

Eunkyung Park is Associate Professor at Aalborg University, Denmark.

Manuela Presutti is Associate Professor at University of Bologna, Italy.

Kristian H. Reinau is Associate Professor at Aalborg University, Denmark.

Gloria Parra Requena is Associate Professor at University of Castilla La Mancha, Spain.

Francisca Sempere Ripoll is Associate Professor at Polytechnic University of Valencia, Spain.

Gonzalo Rodríguez-Rodríguez is Associate Professor at University of Santiago de Compostela, Spain.

Patricia Romeiro is Associate Professor at University of Porto, Portugal.

Maria Francesca Savarese is Researcher at University of Verona, Italy.

Gabriela Scur is Associate Professor at FEI University, Brazil.

Silvia Rita Sedita is Associate Professor at Padova University, Italy.

Tanja Sinozic is Researcher at Institute For The Environment and Regional Development, Vienna.

Franz Tödtling is Professor at Vienna University of Economics and Business, Austria.

Michaela Trippl is Associate Professor at CIRCLE, Lund University Sweden.

Rodrigo Troncoso-Ojeda is Associate Professor at University of Santiago de Compostela, Spain.

Jesús M. Valdaliso is Associate Professor at Orkestra, Deusto University, Spain.

Pedro Manuel García Villaverde is Professor at University of Castilla La Mancha, Spain.

Foreword

Since Becattini's (1979, 1990) 'rediscovery' of the Marshallian industrial district and Porter's (1990) popularisation and transformation of the industrial district into a cluster, clusters have become one of the most studied phenomena in economic growth, development, and innovation research. These geographical agglomerations of firms in the same or in closely related sectors, eliciting constant interaction among its constituent firms, have been considered as essential drivers of firm competitiveness, knowledge diffusion, and innovation. Moreover, following the work of Porter (1990), clusters have become an often recommended recipe for policy intervention the world over (e.g. Feser, 2005; Davies, 2006; Borrás and Tsagdis, 2008; Zeng, 2008; Ketels 2013). Many countries, regions, and cities have actively pursued the identification or outright development of new clusters as a means to improve firm-level competitiveness, innovation, and to produce local employment and improve well-being (Roelandt and Den Hertog, 1999). Clusters have also not been without detractors. Martin and Sunley (2003) have challenged their viability as a policy figure on the basis of the ambiguity in their definition, their weak theorisation, selective empirics and, most importantly, their shaky political models and intervention. The nature of networking within clusters – or 'co-operative competition' – has also been frequently questioned (e.g. Markusen, 2003).

However, despite the massive exposure of clusters to academic and policy scrutiny, they, somewhat surprisingly, still remain poorly understood. We know relatively little about why certain clusters succeed and others do not; about why some clusters are innovation hotbeds, while others rarely innovate; and about why some of them constantly create new firms and employment, while others struggle to survive. This is probably because the analysis of clusters in the past has suffered – and, to a large extent, still suffers – from a number of shortcomings. First, clusters have tended to be considered as static entities, neglecting their internal capacity to evolve (Hervás-Oliver and Albors-Garrigós, 2014). Our understanding of how clusters change and reinvent themselves is still limited due to what can be still be considered as relatively weak theoretical frameworks and limited empirical evidence. Second, most of the literature on clusters has tended to focus on the role of interaction within the cluster (e.g. Leydesdorff and Fritsch, 2006; Asheim *et al.*, 2007). External networks, regularly covering vast geographical spaces, have tended to play second fiddle to the analysis of the relationships developed within the cluster and/or connections in the immediate vicinity of the cluster (i.e. in close geographical proximity). Third, and related to the previous point, the dominant perception of clusters has been as organisations (e.g. Waits, 2000), rather than as systems. And when they have been considered as systems, the examination of the systems has generally been constrained to the boundaries of the cluster, largely overlooking the connections of individual actors and agents of the cluster to the outside world.

Yet, there is increasing evidence that the economic dynamism of clusters is related to the capacity of individuals and firms in the clusters to evolve and change and to constantly renew internal knowledge by reaching out well beyond cluster boundaries. This implies generating complex networks in which physical proximity counts for little (e.g. Fitjar and Rodríguez-Pose, 2011; Tödtling *et al.*, 2012; Grillitsch and Nilsson, 2015). Clusters which remain geographically constrained and rely on interaction with other agents and the cluster often suffer from lock-in (Boschma, 2005) and, as a consequence, commonly experience limited progress. Reaching out outside the cluster means the establishment of pipelines which channel new knowledge and ideas into the cluster. Hence, cluster openness is essential for the competitiveness of local firms and, consequently, the overall dynamism of clusters.

Unfolding Cluster Evolution edited by Fiorenza Belussi and Jose Luis Hervás-Oliver addresses precisely the issue of clusters as dynamic and complex systems, whose evolution and success greatly depend on their capacity to reach out to the outer world in order to reap and diffuse new knowledge. In the book, a rich collection of authors – all at the forefront of the analysis of clusters – explore the external sources of new knowledge within clusters, focusing chiefly in the role of multinational enterprises. Many of the contributions assess how the external flow of knowledge affects not just the evolution of clusters as a whole, but also the capabilities of their constituent firms. The book dwells on how cluster openness and the constant flow of knowledge generated by reaching out to the wider world affect the transformation of clusters at different stages of their life cycle. In this respect, the clusters are considered in a much more realistic way than in most traditional research. From the case of the City of London to the Galician turbot industry or the Brazilian ceramic tile industry, clusters are conceived as dynamic, living systems in constant transformation because of both the channelling and absorption of knowledge from outside, as well as the diffusion and use of this new knowledge in the networks internal to the cluster. The book, hence, stands out not only for its wide geographic coverage, but also for the detailed case studies it contains, as for the carefully crafted theoretical chapters located at the beginning and at the end of the book.

Overall, the book represents a significant step forward in our understanding of a phenomenon which, in spite of the massive attention garnered over the last decades, remains in many respects as much a mystery as it was when it first emerged. No success of a cluster can be understood without properly grasping how new knowledge is generated and assimilated and across most successful clusters in the world this has only happened through openness, 'pipelines', and networking outside the cluster. *Unfolding Cluster Evolution* understood this from the beginning and portrays a different angle to the analysis and comprehension of clusters, making it enthralling and entertaining reading even for those who, like me, thought that everything there was to know about clusters had already been written.

Andrés Rodríguez-Pose
London School of Economics

References

Asheim, B., Coenen, L. and Vang, J. (2007) Face-to-face, buzz, and knowledge bases: Socio-spatial implications for learning, innovation, and innovation policy. *Environment and Planning C: Government and Policy* 25(5), 655–670

Bathelt, H., Malmberg, A. and Maskell, P. (2004) Clusters and knowledge: local buzz, global pipelines and the process of knowledge creation. *Progress in Human Geography*, 28, 31–56.

Becattini, G. (1979) Dal 'settore' industriale al 'distretto' industriale. Alcune considerazione sull'unita d'indagine dell'economia industriale. *Rivista di Economia e Politica Industriale* 5(1), 7–21.

Becattini, G. (1990) The Marshallian industrial district as a socio-economic notion. In F. Pyke, W. Sengenberger and G. Becattini (eds) *Industrial districts and inter-firm co-operation in Italy* (pp. 37–51). Geneva: International Institute for Labour.

Borrás, S. and Tsagdis, D. (2008) *Cluster policies in Europe*. Cheltenham: Edward Elgar Publishing Limited.

Boschma, R. (2005) Proximity and Innovation: A Critical Assessment. *Regional Studies* 39(1), 61–74.

Davies, A. (2006) Why are they popular, again? In OECD, *A review of national cluster policies* (pp. 23–38). Paris: Organisation for Economic Cooperation and Development.

Feser, E. (2005) Industry cluster concepts in innovation policy: A comparison of U.S. and Latin American experience. In G. Maier and S. Sedlacek, *Spillovers and innovations: Space, environment, and the economy* (pp. 135–155). Vienna/New York: Springer.

Fitjar, R. D. and Rodríguez-Pose, A. (2011) When local interaction does not suffice: Sources of firm innovation in urban Norway. *Environment and Planning A*, 43, 1248–1267.

Grillitsch, M. and Nilsson, M. (2015) Innovation in peripheral regions: Do collaborations compensate for a lack of local knowledge spillovers? *Annals of Regional Science* 54, 299–321.

Hervás-Oliver, J. L. and Albors-Garrigós, J. (2014) Are technology gatekeepers renewing clusters? Understanding gatekeepers and their dynamics across cluster life cycles. *Entrepreneurship and Regional Development* 26(5–6), 431–452.

Ketels, C. (2013) Recent research on competitiveness and clusters: What are the implications for regional policy? *Cambridge Journal of Regions, Economy and Society*, 6, 269–284.

Leydesdorff, L. and Fritsch, M. (2006) Measuring the knowledge base of regional innovation systems in Germany in terms of a triple helix dynamics. *Research Policy*, 35, 1538–1553.

Markusen, A. (2003) Fuzzy concepts, scanty evidence, policy distance: the case for rigour and policy relevance in critical regional studies. *Regional Studies*, 37(6–7), 701–717.

Martin, R. and Sunley, P. (2003) Deconstructing clusters: chaotic concept or policy panacea? *Journal of Economic Geography*, 3(1), 535.

Porter, M.E. (1990) *The Competitive Advantage of Nations* (p.857). New York: The Free Press.

Roelandt, T. J. and Den Hertog, P. (1999) Cluster analysis and cluster-based policy making in OECD countries: an introduction to the theme. In OECD (eds) *Boosting innovation: the cluster approach* (pp. 9–23). Paris: OECD.

Tödtling, F., Grillitsch, M. and Höglinger, C. (2012) Knowledge Sourcing and Innovation in Austrian ICT Companies – How Does Geography Matter? *Industry and Innovation*, 19, 327–348.

Waits, M. J. (2000) The added value of the industry cluster approach to economic analysis, strategy development, and service delivery. *Economic Development Quarterly*, 14(1), 35–50.

Zeng, D. (2008) *Knowledge, technology, and cluster-based growth in Africa*. Washington DC: The World Bank.

Preface

The understanding of phenomena related to the dynamics of the geography of innovation constitutes a promising debate in academia. So far, most research has been devoted to studying static representations of the agglomeration phenomenon. In the new global economy, however, longitudinal and dynamic analysis covering the evolution of clusters/industrial districts and their firms turns out to be necessary. In addition, the entrance of new knowledge from outside the cluster, along with the presence of multinationals that bridge and connect the cluster to other territories and knowledge domains, are quintessential factors to be considered in a new, and more open, paradigm capturing key facts of clusters and industrial districts. This book, overall, presents an attempt to bring those different factors to the debate among scholars.

For this reason, this book focuses on those different yet related themes. We tackle them in three distinct sections, offering a novel empirical evidence of the present agglomeration phenomenon: a) the role played by MNEs and their interaction with local firms; b) the triggering factors or drivers explaining the evolution of clusters and industrial districts (C/ID) life cycle and; c) the evolution of capabilities, or the dynamic firm heterogeneity, in cluster firms.

The first section, addressing multinationals and C/IDs, starts with Chapter 1 which explores the common roots of the literature studying the MNEs phenomenon, throughout the *bibliometric* analysis, in the intersection between international business (IB) and economic geography/regional science (EG). Because IB typically refers to localisation at the national level, usually dismissing the local dimension, we need a new theoretical approach for better evaluating the influence of agglomerations in local space, but also considering the globalisation process. The remaining chapters of this section are mainly empirical. As such, Chapter 2 tries to measure the importance of C/ID efficiency among firms in the financial district of London. Positive externalities (knowledge sharing, and close contacts with local specialised suppliers) are shown to be related to social interactions, more important than negative ones (like congestion costs). Interestingly, despite the fact that ICT has moved financial transactions on the web, the advocated 'dead of distance' did not occur, and the co-location in the City of London of financial services is still a major observable trend. Chapter 3 discusses the positive and negative aspect of the foreign entry of MNCs in a cluster. Clearly the entry of MNCs with a competence-creating mandate brings resources, new knowledge, and external networks to the cluster. It also helps to legitimise the cluster, strengthening its identity. In contrast, MNC subsidiaries with a competence-exploiting mandate might reduce local interactions, limiting local firms' technological search and constraining possibilities to react to disruptive technologies, restricting the adaptability of the overall cluster. In order to show this, Chapter 3 presents the important example of the Wireless Communications Cluster in North Jutland (Denmark). Chapter 4 contributes to the current understanding of the interwoven evolution of C/IDs and MNEs, presenting the case of the marble-cluster of Macael in Spain, characterised by the emergence of the 'home-grown MNE', Cosentino. A very similar theoretical perspective is adopted in Chapter 5, where the authors describe the long-term evolution of the tannery ID of Arzignano in Italy. Despite the external 2008 economic shock, Arzignano ID has successfully reconverted its past manufacturing capabilities throughout the emergence of a small group of very innovative 'home-grown MNES' (*Mastrotto Group, Dani*, and *Rino Mastrotto*). In Chapter 6, another important phenomenon is illustrated: the entry of foreign firms in the historical old ID of Prato, where Chinese firms have now substituted the old declining textile district. Chapter 7 deals with the evolution of the Toy Valley cluster in Alicante, in Spain, analysing the continuous transformation of the local C/ID through the entry of foreign MNEs. A process of 'smart specialization' is presented, showing the openness and insertion into global value chains along the cluster evolution. Chapter 8 studies the entry of foreign MNEs in a typical textile Italian district, *Val Vibrata*, where national clients have been substituted by large foreign MNEs.

The second section, at the heart of C/ID evolution, starts with Chapter 9. It describes the emergence and evolution of six industrial clusters of the Basque Country, in Spain, in the nineteenth and twentieth centuries. Cluster origins are explained by a mix of local and global factors, although the former ones predominate. Among the local factors, demand, factor conditions and entrepreneurship, plus historical preconditions, play a triggering role, while entry of MNCs and/or inflow of external knowledge and technology appear as the most important global factors. As clusters evolved from development to maturity, it seemed that former local factors no longer provided sources of competitive advantages to the firms and to the cluster as a whole, and that both the firms and the cluster had to 'reinvent' themselves to differentiate in a global market. At this stage, firms needed to set up global pipelines to other clusters in order to escape from lock-in situations and to drive the cluster to a renewal phase.

Chapter 10 compares the triggering factors of two advanced C/ID: the New Media cluster in Vienna and the Environmental Technology cluster based in Upper Austria. Overall, the authors reject the *Porterian* view, that cluster competitiveness and growth is mainly based on local and regional factors, because national and international factors may appear of overwhelming importance, although the regional setting indeed matters more in the early stages. A similar analysis, stressing the importance of external factors in C/ID dynamics, is presented in Chapter 11, where a Spanish aquaculture cluster is studied: the Galician turbot cluster of Spain. Chapter 12 reflects on cluster decline and political lock-in. It tries to analytically answer the question: to what extent do the characteristics of an industry affect the strength of political lock-in? investigating if political lock-ins are stronger or not in clusters with high stocks of social capital and trust. Lastly, Chapter 13 studies the case of educational and entertainment software cluster in the Porto City Region, in the northwest of Portugal.

The third section applies the approach of dynamic capabilities to cluster studies and, in particular, to cluster firms. Chapter 14, using a combination of the micro- and the meso-level approach, integrates the process of firms' capabilities development by using (as an illustrative empirical example) the Castellon cluster in Spain. Then, the analysis of the development of the footwear industrial districts in Spain is the focus of Chapter 15. The empirical study was carried out using a cohort of 165 companies located in different Spanish C/ID. The study, combining various factors, identifies a typology of five specific organizational configurations. The accumulation of technological capabilities among local producers in Brazilian tiles clusters in Santa Catarina and San Paulo is described in Chapter 16. This accumulation was mainly driven by three key actors, two were external (Italian machinery suppliers and Spanish suppliers of glaze materials), and one was internal (the Center of Technological Innovation in Ceramics (Citec/CCB)). This catalysed an important process of interactive learning between Italian machinery suppliers, Spanish glaze chemical producers, local researchers, and Brazilian C/ID firms. The last chapter, Chapter 17, is a critical review article which discusses the various theories of C/ID change. The literature on industrial districts, innovative milieus and regional innovation systems is all simultaneously analysed and confronted within the discussion on the heterogeneity of C/ID new path creation or path modification.

The editors

Padova and Valencia, April 2016

Acknowledgements

This book has received support from a large project (SMARTSPEC) funded by the European Union under the FP7 Cooperation Programme: Social Sciences and the Humanities. Grant number 320131. This book has also received support from the *Spanish Ministry of Economics and Competitiveness*, under the grant ECO2015-63645-R, *Open Innovation in Clusters*, directed by Dr. Jose Luis Hervás-Oliver.

Introduction

Unfolding cluster and industrial district evolution: into the future

Fiorenza Belussi and Jose Luis Hervás-Oliver

Why this contributed volume?

Clusters are of the utmost importance for economic growth and fostering innovation. Openness of territories and their connection to the global value chain remains an imperative for triggering competitiveness, to the extent that Horizon 2020 by the EU has emphasized the importance of clusters. This volume attempts to discuss and serve as a forum for theoretical and empirical debates on current topics challenging and shaping the clusters' and industrial districts' research agenda.

First, despite observations that clusters and industrial districts (IDs)[1] are path-dependent (Martin and Sunley, 2006) and should be addressed as dynamic phenomena (e.g. Pouder and St John, 1996; Brenner, 2004), cluster dynamics have been largely overlooked in the literature (Hervás-Oliver and Albors-Garrigós, 2014; Wang *et al.*, 2014; Martin and Sunley, 2011; Boschma and Fornahl, 2011; Crespo, 2011; Belussi and Sedita, 2009). In fact, the broad and comprehensive understanding of cluster evolution still constitutes an emerging topic in evolutionary economic geography and other related disciplines (management, innovation and technological change, etc.). There still does not exist a comprehensive theoretical framework, nor ample empirical evidence, capable of fully explaining why and how clusters and IDs evolve. One of the reasons for this is that most empirical works on clusters have examined a 'static' rather than longitudinal picture. Another reason possibly lies in the complexity involved in integrating the diverse set of intellectual disciplines required for building a comprehensive theoretical framework capable of addressing all actors and micro-processes involved in the functioning of clusters. For example, in order to fully understand cluster micro-processes an evolutionary economic geography perspective must be integrated with a management perspective (e.g. Pouder and St John, 1996; Wang *et al.*, 2014). The understanding of the meso unit of analysis also needs to consider the micro-level and, especially, the cluster firms' capabilities and strategies recombining existing and new knowledge from and beyond the territory. Hence, the need to cross-fertilize between different fields makes research on cluster dynamics particularly difficult because of the necessary integration of the micro and meso aspects in tandem.

On this chain of thought, literature shows that there exist different but complementary approaches to addressing cluster evolution. Each has highlighted a different actor or element to explain the phenomenon. For example, Belussi and Sedita (2009) pointed out a need to consider individual firm strategies and firms' capabilities for understanding cluster dynamics. They showed there is not a single standard life cycle pattern for Italian IDs, and that each cluster's growth pattern can vary, with individual firm strategies being of utmost importance for shaping cluster evolution. Also, Klepper (2007) introduced the idea of the role in cluster dynamics of inherited capabilities which new firms (spinoffs) acquire from their spinners. Thus, clusters are formed and evolve through an organizational reproduction or spinoff process in which new firms' development is influenced by knowledge brought to them from parent firms, complementing the available externalities in a synergistic way. This process of capability inheritance plays a vital role in the ongoing construction of a cluster, a phenomenon understood as an evolving capability-based dynamic concentration of companies. Again, evidence on the latter is rather scarce (e.g. Boschma and Wenting, 2007). Last but not least, other key aspects have been brought into the picture of understanding how clusters evolve. For example, it has been found that the evolution of networks and of technology gatekeepers (Hervás-Oliver and Albors-Garrigós, 2014), and their dynamics, can affect development processes in clusters. Also, multinational companies have been highlighted as an important element in cluster evolution (Sedita *et al.*, 2013), as well as the cluster firms' capabilities (e.g. Ter Wal and Boschma, 2011). The latter, also named the micro-level, has been less studied. All in all, this book embraces three main sections: cluster and ID evolution, multinational companies in clusters, and cluster firms' capabilities and cluster evolution.

The key to understanding why, and how, a cluster evolves throughout its life cycle is the variation of knowledge heterogeneity among the cluster's organizations (Menzel and Fornahl, 2010). This idea is not new, based as it is on evolutionary economics (e.g. Nelson and Winter, 1982), on how routines in organizations evolve and are diffused through innovation and imitation. In fact, this is in line with the Belussi and Sedita (2009) approach to the cluster life cycle, based on the understanding of the cluster firms' capabilities (and strategies) and their interplay with the formation of cluster capabilities, integrating the micro and macro levels and opening the black box of the cluster's central actor: firms.

Variation, selection and retention processes by cluster firms diffuse routines, while spatial clustering fosters cluster evolution through the accumulation of new cluster-level routines. In order to provide a full picture of this process, it is necessary to construct an integrated conceptual framework through which to understand the evolutionary process of clusters. Assuming that clusters evolve through a process of accumulation of capabilities which start in individual firms and networks, before, eventually, being transferred to the whole cluster level implies understanding how cluster firms' capabilities are evolving. Despite previous attempts to use managerial or organizational theory to describe the creation of knowledge in clusters (Tallman *et al.*, 2004), and the description of the process of knowledge creation and diffusion in clusters by multinationals (Tallman and Chacar, 2011), managerial theories tackling firms' capabilities, like the resource-based view or the dynamic capabilities perspective (e.g. Teece *et al.*, 1997), have not been applied to the cluster evolution phenomenon. This is a major challenge we intend to cover in this book.

In short, both the economic geography (EG) (e.g. Brenner, 2004; Belussi and Sedita, 2009; Menzel and Fornahl, 2010; Crespo, 2011; Boschma and Fornahl, 2011; Martin and Sunley, 2011; Hervás-Oliver and Albors-Garrigós, 2014) and the strategic management perspectives (e.g. Pouder and St John, 1996; Klepper, 2007; Wang *et al.*, 2014) have generated explanatory models and empirical evidence for the topic of cluster dynamics and its differing sub-fields of inquiry, with each intellectual field following its own particular research agenda. Within the general cluster evolution field there now exists much theoretical and conceptual diversification and even fragmentation, with different discourses and communities of practice focusing on particular topics and methods and drawing on varying intellectual foundations.

Thus, various models through which to understand cluster evolution have been proposed. Menzel and Fornahl (2010) assert that central to understanding why and how a cluster evolves through its life cycle is the variation of knowledge heterogeneity among the cluster's organizations. A complementary approach is that of Martin and Sunley (2011), who reject the idea of a single model of cluster evolution and suggest that overly deterministic ideas of the life cycle should be replaced by thinking of clusters as complex systems (e.g. Belussi and Samara, 2010: xviii; Martin and Sunley, 2011). The debate is still inconclusive. What other models can framework cluster evolution? How deterministic can it be? What other factors and moderators could influence and shape evolution?

Second, the idea of cluster openness and cluster evolution is of the utmost importance in this volume, being associated with cluster MNEs and foreign direct investment (FDI) and/or global value chains. Focusing on clusters and IDs, those topics have been less researched, with some exceptions (e.g. Hervás-Oliver and Boix-Domènech, 2013). The study of MNEs and their associated FDI has not been linked to the topic of life cycles, Sedita *et al.* (2013) and Mudambi and Santangelo (2015) being two remarkable exceptions. Sedita *et al.* (2013) analyse the implications of the multinational enterprises' (MNEs) entry into clusters throughout different stages of the life cycle. We posit that better and extended elaboration on the cluster openness idea and its relation to the cluster life cycle can provide in-depth insights to help to advance that evolutionary phenomenon. The consideration of the MNEs and the cluster life cycle in tandem constitutes a promising research avenue. In this vein, Harrison (1994) argues against the self-sufficiency implicit in IDs, that is, the local endogenous model may suffer from lack of openness and for this reason emphasizes the importance of external forces such as the presence of MNEs.

In this chain of thought, Eisingerich *et al.* (2010: 252) find out that high-performing clusters are underpinned by network openness, the latter being defined as: 'We are connected to a range of firms, differing in size, age, capabilities, and industry; this organization readily accepts new members to its network of exchange partners in the cluster; we are well-connected with actors outside this cluster; linkages with actors in this cluster are very difficult to reconfigure.' Eisingerich *et al.* (2010) conclude that superior performance in clusters is likely to depend on the diversity of actors, openness to new members and extent of linkages to organizations operating outside the cluster, facilitating thus the detection of inventions outside the cluster and avoiding lock-in. As Adams (2011: 377) evidenced, the emergence and consolidation of Silicon Valley as a formidable high-tech region came about mainly because of the actions of multilocational/multinational firms based elsewhere, that is, due to the openness to attract new firms and knowledge from outside the cluster. Similarly, in the management literature the search for new knowledge beyond local search has received increased attention which can be useful for our topics (e.g. Rosenkopf and Nerkar, 2001). Literature has recognized the necessity to open territories and connect them to global value chains (Bathelt *et al.*, 2004; Hervás-Oliver and Boix-Domènech, 2013; Iammarino and McCann, 2013), pointing out the key role played by MNEs, which are recognized to be central actors connecting and shaping clusters and IDs[2] (Hervás-Oliver and Boix-Domènech, 2013; Sedita *et al.*, 2013; Narula, 2014). In fact, the international business (IB) perspective also claims that it is necessary to shed light on that intertwined phenomenon intersected by different yet related disciplines, such as EG and IB.

In line with this chain of thought, MNEs have been referred mainly to foreign and large companies, disregarding those MNEs that are home grown and thanks to a cluster's vibrant local buzz. These are the homegrown MNE (Seditta *et al.*, 2013) or indigenous MNEs (Hervás-Oliver and Albors-Garrigós, 2008). These were once small, family-run firms extending their operations overseas but maintaining deep embeddedness in their home cluster. These firms foster competitiveness to their local milieus and coordinate local networks, connecting them to global value chains and orchestrating innovation in local agglomerations, feeding small sub-contractors with new knowledge, technology and techniques to keep up with the latest changes. Key questions remain unanswered in that particular topic: what is the connection between IB and EG perspectives? What is the role of those foreign and indigenous MNEs? How do MNEs enter clusters and industrial districts and what role do they perform?

While MNEs benefit local firms in clusters (Mariotti *et al.*, 2014), there is no consensus on the fact that some MNEs may avoid entering clusters, due to the potential knowledge leakages that can occur. Thus, while benefits overcome losses, feeding local knowledge to new MNEs through agglomerations (e.g. Birkinshaw and Hood, 2000; Mariotti *et al.*, 2014; Rugman and Verbeke, 2011), different empirical evidence contradicts those gains (Shaver and Flyer, 2000), a fact strongly confirmed in the strategy literature but less researched in the EG strand (e.g. Canina *et al.*, 2005; Gilbert *et al.*, 2008; Kukalis, 2010; Stuart and Sorenson, 2003). This double-edged sword, with pros and cons, reflects the fact that not all firms gain from agglomerations, a debate also inconclusive and embedded in the strategy literature connecting agglomerations and firm performance (e.g. Canina *et al.*, 2005; Chung and Kalnins, 2001; Gilbert *et al.*, 2008; Kalnins and Chung, 2004; Shaver and Flyer, 2000). All in all, this effect between entrance/agglomeration and firm performance is moderated by diverse factors, mainly related to the type of agglomerations and firms' own knowledge capabilities, as Alcacer and Chung (2014) have explained.

Clusters offer a growing opportunity to disaggregate value-chain activities into fine-sliced parts due to their competitive advantage, which arises from their agglomerations. The literature about the MNE learning process from locally embedded knowledge pools (McCann and Mudambi, 2004; Dunning, 2009; Tallman and Chacar, 2011) is scant and recent. Cluster openness to external actors permits new knowledge to circulate and thus cluster capabilities could be renewed. The rationale of co-locating in clusters, in general, is that firms, both indigenous and foreign MNEs, can capture knowledge spillovers, improving their products or processes. As Hervás-Oliver and Albors-Garrigós (2008) have debated, are both types of MNEs performing the same way in clusters? Which is their role? How do they influence life cycles?

All things considered, the following question requires further research: who gains and who loses from co-location? While more knowledge-intensive firms have more to lose and less to gain (Rigby and Brown, 2013; Alcacer and Chung, 2007; Shaver and Flyer, 2000), it is also said that firms with higher knowledge stocks benefit more from agglomeration (McCann and Folta, 2011). The debate is inconclusive and nascent. In other words, it can be said that agglomerations do matter but their influence on firms' performance varies asymmetrically (Hervás-Oliver and Albors-Garrigós, 2009).

Acknowledgements

This chapter has received support from (SMARTSPEC), FP7 Grant number 320131 and MINECO/FEDER EU ECO2015-63645-R.

Notes

1 We recognize differences between clusters and industrial districts (see more details in Asheim, 2000). In this book we refer to and use both terms and literatures indistinctively for the purpose of developing a comprehensive framework.
2 See also works by Cantwell, Mudambi, Porter or Dunning.

References

Adams, S.B. (2011) Growing where you are planted: exogenous firms and the seeding of *Silicon Valley, Research Policy*, 40(3): 368–379.

Alcacer, J. and Chung, W. (2007) Location strategies and knowledge spillovers. *Management Sciences*, 53: 760–776.

Alcacer, J. and Chung, W. (2014) Location strategies for agglomeration economies, *Strategic Management Journal*, 35(12): 1749–1761.

Asheim, B. (2000) Industrial districts, in Clark, G.L., Feldman, M.P. and Gertler, M.S. (eds) *The Oxford Handbook of Economic Geography*, Oxford: Oxford University Press.

Audia, P. and Rider, C.H. (2010) Close, but not the same: locally headquartered organizations and agglomeration economies in a declining industry, *Research Policy*, 39(3): 360–374.

Bathelt, H., Malmberg, A. and Maskell, P. (2004) Clusters and knowledge: local buzz, global pipelines and the process of knowledge creation, *Progress in Human Geography*, 28(1): 31–56.

Belussi, F. and Samarra, A. (2010) *Business Networks in Clusters and Industrial Districts*, London: Routledge.

Belussi, F. and Sedita, S. (2009) Life cycle vs multiple path dependency in industrial districts, *European Planning Studies*, 17(4): 505–528.

Birkinshaw, J.M. and Hood, N. (2000) Roles of foreign subsidiaries in industry clusters, *Journal of International Business Studies*, 31(1): 141–154.

Boschma, R. and Fornahl, D. (2011) Cluster evolution and a roadmap for future research, *Regional Studies*, 45(10): 1295–1298.

Boschma, R.A. and Wenting, R. (2007) The spatial evolution of the British automobile industry: does location matter? *Industrial and Corporate Change*, 16(2): 213–238.

Brenner T. (2004) *Local Industrial Clusters: Existence, emergence and evolution*, London: Routledge.

Brenner, T. and Schlump, C. (2011) Policy measures and their effects in the different phases of the cluster life cycle, *Regional Studies*, 45)10): 1363–1386.

Canina, L., Enz, C. and Harrison, J. (2005) Agglomeration effects and strategic orientations: evidence from the US lodging industry, *Academy of Management Journal*, 48(4): 565–581.

Chung, W. and Kalnins, A. (2001) Agglomeration effects and performance: a test of the Texas lodging industry, *Strategic Management Journal*, 22(10): 969–988.

Clark, G.L., Feldman, M.P. and Gertler, M.S. (eds) (2000) *The Oxford Handbook of Economic Geography*, Oxford: Oxford University Press, pp. 413–431.

Crespo, J. (2011) How emergence conditions of technological clusters affect their viability? Theoretical perspectives on cluster life cycles, *European Planning Studies*, 19(12): 2025–2046.

Dunning, J.H. (2009) Location and the multinational enterprise: John Dunning's thoughts on receiving the JIBS 2008 Decade Award, *Journal of International Business Studies*, 40: 20–34.

Eisingerich, A.B., Bell, S.J. and Tracey, P. (2010) The role of network strength, network openness, and environmental uncertainty, *Research Policy*, 39(2): 239–253.

Frenken, K., Van Oort, F.G. and Verburg, T. (2007) Related variety, unrelated variety and regional economic growth, *Regional Studies*, 41: 685–697.

Gilbert, B.A., McDougall, P.P. and Audretsch, D.B. (2008) Clusters, knowledge spillovers and new venture performance: an empirical examination, *Journal of Business Venturing*, 23(4): 405–422.

Harrison, B. (1994) Concentrated economic power and Silicon Valley, *Environment and Planning*, 26: 307–328.

Hervás-Oliver, J.L. and Albors-Garrigós, J. (2008) Local knowledge domains and the role of MNE affiliates in bridging and complementing a cluster's knowledge, *Entrepreneurship and Regional Development*, 20(6): 581–598.

Hervás-Oliver, J.L. and Albors-Garrigós, J. 2009. The role of the firm's internal and relational capabilities in clusters: when distance and embeddedness are not enough to explain innovation, *Journal of Economic Geography*, 9(2): 263–283.

Hervás-Oliver, J.L. and Albors-Garrigós, J. (2014) Are technology gatekeepers renewing clusters? Understanding gatekeepers and their dynamics across cluster life cycles, *Entrepreneurship & Regional Development: An International Journal*, 26(5–6): 431–452.

Hervás-Oliver and Boix-Domènech (2013) The economic geography of the meso-global spaces: integrating multinationals and clusters at the local-global level. *European Planning Studies*, 21(7): 1064–1080.

Huggins, R. (2008) The evolution of knowledge clusters: progress and policy, *Economic Development Quarterly*, 22(4): 277–289.

Iammarino, S. and McCann, P. (*2013*) *Multinationals and Economic Geography: Location, technology and innovation*, Cheltenham: Edward Elgar.

Jensen, P.D.Ø. and Pedersen, T. (2011) The economic geography of offshoring: the fit between activities and local context, *Journal of Management Studies*, 48(2): 352–372.

Kalnins, A. and Chung, W. (2004) Resource-seeking agglomeration: a study of market entry in the lodging industry, *Strategic Management Journal*, 25(7): 689–699.

Klepper, S. (2007) Disagreements, spinoffs, and the evolution of Detroit as the capital of the U.S. automobile industry, *Management Science*, 53(4): 616–631.

Kukalis, S. (2010) Agglomeration economies and firm performance: the case of industry clusters, *Journal of Management*, 36(2): 453–481.

Mariotti, S., Picitello, L. and Elia, S. (2014) Local externalities and ownership choices in foreign acquisitions by multinational enterprises, *Economic Geography*, 90(2): 187–211.

Martin, R. and Sunley, P. (2006) Path dependence and regional economic evolution, *Journal of Economic Geography*, 6(4): 395–437.

Martin, R. and Sunley, P. (2011) Conceptualizing cluster evolution: beyond the life cycle model? *Regional Studies*, 45(10): 1299–1318.

McCann, B.T. and Folta, T.B. (2011) Performance differentials within geographic clusters, *Journal of Business Venturing*, 26(1): 104–123.

McCann, P. and Mudambi, R. (2004) The location decision of the multinational enterprise: some theoretical and empirical issues, *Growth & Change*, 35(4): 491–524.

Menzel, M. and Fornahl, D. (2010) Industrial and Corporate Change, 19(1): 205–238.

Mudambi, R. and Santangelo, G. (2015) From shallow resource pools to emerging clusters: the role of multinational enterprise subsidiaries in peripheral areas (with G.D. Santangelo), *Regional Studies*, 1–15.

Mudambi, R. and Venzin, M. (2011) The strategic nexus of offshoring and outsourcing decisions, *Journal of Management Studies*, 47(8): 1510–1533.

Narula, R. (2014) Exploring the paradox of competence-creating subsidiaries: balancing bandwidth and dispersion in MNEs, *Long Range Planning*, 47(1–2): 4–15.

Neffke, F., Henning, M. and Boschma, R. (2011) How do regions diversify over time? Industry relatedness and the development of new growth paths in regions, *Economic Geography*, 78(3): 237–265.

Nelson, R. and Winter, S. (1982) *An Evolutionary Theory of Economic Change*, Cambridge, MA: Harvard University Press.

Pouder, R. and St John, C. (1996) Hot spots and blind spots: geographic clusters of firms and innovation, *Academy of Management Review*, 21(4): 1192–1225.

Rigby, D.L. and Brown, W.M. (2013) Who benefits from agglomeration? *Regional Studies*, 1–16.

Rosenkpof, L. and Nerkar, A. (2001) Beyond local search: boundary-spanning, exploration, and impact in the optical disk industry, *Strategic Management Journal*, 22(4): 287–306.

Rugman, A., Verbeke, A. and Yuan, W. (2011) Re-conceptualizing Bartlett and Ghoshal's classification of national subsidiary roles in the multinational enterprise, *Journal of Management Studies*, 48(2), 253–277.

Sedita, S., Caloffi, A. and Belussi, F. (2013) Heterogeneity of MNEs entry modes in industrial clusters: an evolutionary approach based on the cluster life cycle model, DRUID 2013. Barcelona (Spain), available at www.druid.dk

Shaver, J.M. and Flyer, F. (2000) Agglomeration economies, firm heterogeneity, and foreign direct investment in the United States, *Strategic Management Journal*, 21(12): 1175–1194.

Sorenson, O. and Audia, P.G. (2000) The social structure of entrepreneurial activity: geographic concentration of footwear production in the United States, 1940–1989, *American Journal of Sociology*, 106(2): 424–462.

Stuart, T. and Sorenson, O. (2003) The geography of opportunity: spatial heterogeneity in founding rates and the performance of biotechnology firms, *Research Policy*, 32(2): 229–253.

Tallman, S. and Chacar, A. (2011) Knowledge accumulation and dissemination in MNEs: a practice-based framework, *Journal of Management Studies*, 48(2): 278–304.

Tallman, S., Jenkins, M., Henry, N. and Pinch, S. (2004) Knowledge, clusters, and competitive advantage, *Academy of Management Review*, 29(2): 258–271.

Teece, D., Pisano, G. and Shuen, A. (1997) Dynamic capabilities and strategic management, *Strategic Management Journal*, 18(7): 509–533.

Ter Wal, A. and Boschma, R. (2011) Co-evolution of firms, industries and networks in space, *Regional Studies*, 45(7): 919–933.

Wang, L., Madhok, A. and Li, S.X. (2014) Agglomeration and clustering over the industry life cycle: toward a dynamic model of geographic concentration, *Strategic Management Journal*.

1 Crossing economic geography and international business to understand the collocation of multinationals in agglomerations

An analysis of its inception

Jose Luis Hervás-Oliver and Gregorio Gonzalez Alcaide

1.1 Introduction

The intersection between international business (IB) and economic geography (EG) is very recent and still represents an emerging debate, which is rather inconclusive. The turn towards outward-looking global value chains has provoked the necessity to get more insights about Multinationals (MNE) collocating or connecting local clusters. Despite the intensive focus on global value chains from EG (e.g. Amin and Thrift, 1992; Bathelt *et al.*, 2004), MNEs are said to be much more studied within the IB strand. Assuming that IB needs to learn the subtleties of territories and the nuances of agglomerations from EG, while EG needs to borrow knowledge on MNEs from the IB perspective, as stated by scholars (e.g. McCann and Mudambi, 2004; Hervás-Oliver and Boix-Domènech, 2013), this study seeks to explore the common roots or fundamentals shared by the inception of that intersection between IB and EG/regional science literatures. Because IB refers to localization as the national level, dismissing local properties found in agglomerations and thus does not explicitly recognize the subtleties of the local space (e.g. Dunning, 2009; McCann and Mudambi, 2004; Narula, 2014), both constitute relevant theoretical exceptions; while EG tackles MNEs as a minor construct within agglomerations by emphasizing the meso-level connections through global value chains or global pipelines (e.g. Bathelt *et al.*, 2004; Hervás-Oliver and Boix-Domènech, 2013 and Sedita *et al.*, 2013 are interesting exceptions). As a result of this dual yet intertwined perspective, knowledge about that phenomenon remains fragmented and incomplete. Integration of literatures and exploration of their potential intersection, addressing a similar phenomenon from different perspectives, require a more in-depth and systematic analysis of their literatures and, specifically, of their fundamentals or foundations.

This study's objective consists of analysing the fundamentals of the intersection between EG and IB literatures addressing the collocation of MNEs in agglomerations. This study applies a bibliometric analysis in order to understand and extend knowledge on the collocation of MNEs in agglomerations. In doing so, it sheds light on the inception studies that, from different approaches, started to tackle that phenomenon.

1.2 Crossing IB and EG: a short overview

EG literature, along with innovation and technological change, has traditionally taken account of localization advantages (Marshall, 1890), emphasizing the local nodes in global networks (e.g. Amin and Thrift, 1992) or global pipelines (e.g. Bathelt *et al.*, 2004) and even recognizing the leading role of MNEs in agglomerations opening networks and fostering knowledge exchange (Harrison, 1994; Eisingerich *et al.*, 2010; Hervás-Oliver and Boix-Domènech, 2013; Sedita *et al.*, 2013). Following Hervás-Oliver (2015) those inter-cluster or external linkages (Cooke, 2005; Hervás-Oliver and Albors-Garrigós, 2008) are usually connected through MNE subsidiaries which operate in a cluster and convey knowledge in a two-way street through their internal MNE channels (e.g. Cooke, 2005). From this perspective, opening clusters/industrial districts is a way to reduce lock-in (Bathelt *et al.*, 2004; Hervás-Oliver and Albors-Garrigós, 2008; Eisingerich *et al.*, 2010). EG and technical change literature, however, have failed to encompass the role of MNEs, which remain as black boxes within agglomerations, Cooke (2005) being a formidable exception.

On the contrary, IB literature has mainly focused on MNEs throughout countries, giving less importance to the local specificities of agglomerations, also with remarkable exceptions (e.g. Alcácer and Chung, 2014; Majocchi and Presutti, 2009; Meyer *et al.*, 2011; Nachum and Keeble, 2003a, 2003b) that have paved the way to explore the agglomeration construct in order to enrich MNEs' decisions from an IB perspective. The latter body of literature has pioneered the intersection between EG and IB, but, unfortunately, it has received less attention in the IB literature as there are few works on that topic. Besides, it has not impacted on the EG, nor has it opened new research lines. Despite this fragmentation, there are major coincidences in respect of diverse topics within both strands. First, the importance of embeddedness and inter-firm interaction is recognized in both literatures (from IB, e.g. Narula, 2014; Narula and Santangelo, 2012; Meyer *et al.*, 2011; Rugman *et al.*, 2011; Pla-Barber and Puig, 2009; Nachum and Keeble, 2003a, 2003b; from EG, e.g. Hervás-Oliver and Boix-Domènech, 2013; Sedita *et al.*, 2013). Second, the integration-responsiveness or fit between subsidiaries' activities and agglomerations depends on the specific host location (from IB, e.g. Rugman *et al.*, 2011; Mudambi and Venzin, 2010), especially in the case of clusters (Tallman and Chacar, 2011; Nachum and Keeble, 2003a, 2003b; from EG, Hervás-Oliver and Boix-Domènech, 2013), subsidiaries' internal resources notwithstanding.

1.3 Bibliometric application: crossing EG and IB

Crossing both disciplines requires a deep understanding of the relationship and commonalities between those views addressing different, yet intertwined, topics. Bibliometrics consist of analysing knowledge diffusion and generation through the study of scientific publications. For example, the identification of the literature that aggregates the highest citation index in a given discipline or theme permits us to determine which are those authoritative publications or seminal studies (those most used and diffused) that have established the fundamentals or cornerstones of that discipline or topic (Shibata *et al.*, 2007; Zupic and Cater, 2014). See more in Tu (2011).

Bibliometrics have recently been applied to EG in different works (e.g. Hervás-Oliver *et al.*, 2015; Lazzereti *et al.*, 2014), producing a systematic, quantitative, objective and complete coverage of that literature within EG. Following a similar approach as the one used in those studies, we explore the intersection between IB and EG literatures, analysing their focus on similar phenomena: the intersection of agglomerations and MNE collocation. For this purpose, we searched within the *Social Sciences Citation Index* (SSCI) by Thomson Reuters, using a search strategy depicted in the field named *TOPIC* (title, abstract, key words). After testing different 'topics' (clusters, agglomerations, MNEs, off-shoring, FDI, etc.) representing the phenomenon (the intersection of localization and multinationals), checking journals, relevant authors and so forth, a search in the SSCI was undertaken through the TOPIC criteria that follow: [(Cluster* OR Agglomeration* OR Industrial district*) AND (Multinational* OR Multi-national* OR MNC* OR MNE* OR 'global value chain' OR offshore* OR transnational*)], and by then further restricting the output to the *BUSINESS, ECONOMICS, ENVIRONMENTAL STUDIES, GEOGRAPHY, MANAGEMENT, PLANNING DEVELOPMENT* and *URBAN STUDIES* fields within the SSCI. Then, after cleaning the dataset obtained we listed a sample composed of 475 journal articles, which included 28,620 references, covering the 1957–2014 period. Our procedure assigned a numeric code to every document, so that they could all be identified throughout the study. Every document contained references. We focused on analysing those most cited out of the 475 documents. There were 203 documents (>9 citations) that concurrently researched the intersection between MNEs and agglomerations that were the most cited. Our analysis was centred around 143 documents. We named those 143 the inception documents (203 but only 143 available for study) and their analysis revealed vital knowledge on the intersection between IB and EG addressing concurrently the intersection between agglomerations and the collocation of MNEs. See Figure 1.1 for an explanation of the process.

First, the key studies (out of those 203, each of them being more than 28 cited) on that intersection of disciplines listed in Table 1.1. Diverse seminal contributions from those three basic strands stand out: Porter (1990) from IB/strategy, Head *et al.* (1995) from international economics, or Bathelt *et al.*

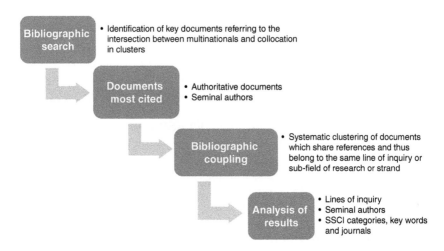

Figure 1.1 Explanation of the processes followed to study multinationals and collocation intersection.

Source: Authors.

Table 1.1 Top cited references crossing IB and EG (> 28 citations)

Reference	Frequency
Porter, M. 1990, Competitive Advantag	72
Head, K. 1995, V38, P223, J Int Econ	65
Bathelt, H. 2004, V28, P31, Prog Hum Geog	53
Krugman, P. R. 1991, Geography Trade	45
Humphrey, J. 2002, V36, P1017, Reg Stud	45
Dunning, J. H. 1993, Multinational Enterp	42
Markusen, A. 1996, V72, P293, Econ Geogr	40
Marshall, A. 1920, Principles Ec	36
Gereffi, G. 1999, V48, P37, J Int Econ	34
Dunning, J. H. 1998, V29, P45, J Int Bus Stud	34
Gereffi, G. 2005, V12, P78, Rev Int Polit Econ	34
Porter, M. E. 1998, V76, P77, Harvard Bus Rev	34
Krugman, P. 1991, V99, P483, J Polit Econ	34
Cohen, W. M. 1990, V35, P128, Admin Sci Quart	33
Coughlin, C. C. 1991, V73, P675, Rev Econ Stat	30
Head, C. K. 1999, V29, P197, Reg Sci Urban Econ	30
Vernon, R. 1966, V80, P190, Q J Econ	29
Martin, R. 2003, V3, P5, J Econ Geogr	29
Guimaraes, P. 2000, V47, P115, J Urban Econ	29

Source: Author.

(2004) from EG. Krugman, Dunning, Markusen or Gereffi follow, among many others such as Marshall. Second, those inception references are published from the 1990s onwards, with the exception of Marshall (1920) and Vernon (1966). The debate about that phenomenon concurrently addressing MNEs and localization is very recent, basically starting in the 1990s. This fact confirms the figure revealing that 83 per cent of those 28,620 references date from the 1990s.

These documents basically represent three main strands or literatures: international/general economics (e.g. Head *et al.*, 1995; Krugman 1991), IB and strategy (e.g. Porter, 1990; Dunning, 1998; Shaver and Flyer 2000) and EG (e.g. Bathelt *et al.*, 2004; Humphrey and Schmitz 2002). The segmentation within those three lines of inquiry or sub-fields of knowledge is achieved by applying a technique named bibliographic coupling.[1] This technique consists of analysing shared references by those 203 documents: those documents sharing references belong to the same line of inquiry. Only 143 of those 203 documents were available in SSCI, due to the fact that 51 documents are books or book chapters, and 9 articles were published in outlets that were not part of SSCI at that specific time.

Third, regarding the importance of authors/seminal contributions, we observe in Figure 1.2 that, relatively, the IB strand presented by seminal authors such as Cantwell, Mudambi or Kogut, EG emphasizes Markussen, while economics mostly cites Venables or Glaeser *et al.* (1992). Besides, Figure 1.2 also confirms the previous fact about the three main intertwined disciplines covering that phenomenon.

Then, in Figure 1.3 it is observed how the seminal inception references, which constitute the pillars of the phenomenon, are also classified in the same three blocks of literatures, with Almeida (2004) standing out [Almeida and Phene (2004)], Rugman (2004) [Rugman and Verbeke (2004)], Birkinshaw (2000) [Birkinshaw and Hood (2000)], Dunning (1998) in IB/strategy; Storper (2004) [Storper and Venables (2004)], Bell (1999) [Bell and Albu (1999)], Gereffi (2005) [Gereffi *et al.* (2005).], Bathelt (2004) [Bathelt *et al.* (2004)] and Amin (1992) [Amin and Thrift (1992)] in EG; and Glaeser *et al.* (1992) or Coughlin *et al.* (1991) in economics.

Information from Figure 1.3 is analysed by crossing it with the Thomson Reuters SSCI domains, showing that the EG strand (red) is mainly framework in SSCI Economics (26), Geography (21), Planning (8) and Environment Studies (7); IB/strategy (green) is set in SSCI Management and Business sections (35 and 28, respectively), while economics (blue and yellow) belongs mainly to SSCI Economics (46 in total). See Table 1.2.

Then, in Table 1.3, we show the different key words most used in each literature. As such, EG contains mainly the words *clusters, innovation* or *networks*, while IB contains mostly *multinational corporations and subsidiaries*, and economics reflects *foreign direct investment, agglomeration economies* or *trade*. Obviously, each strand refers to the principal and mostly used subtopics within the phenomenon.

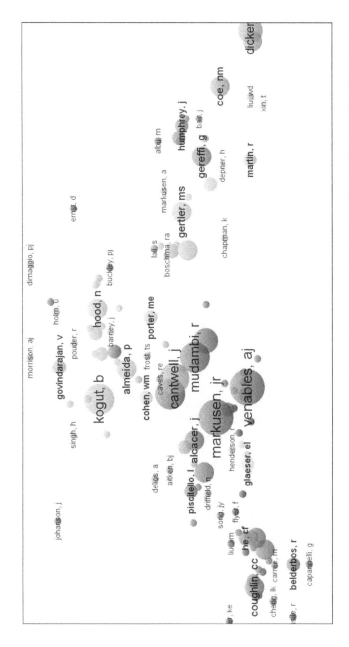

Figure 1.2 Author bibliographic coupling of top cited references crossing IB and EG (visualization using Vosviewer).

Source: Authors.

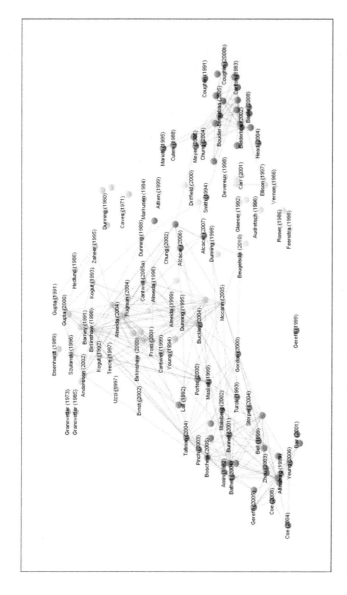

Figure 1.3 Bibliographic coupling of top cited references crossing IB and EG (visualization using Vosviewer).

Note: Only first author from each study is represented.

Source: Authors.

Table 1.2 Information from Figure 1.2 related to the SSCI domains

Literature	Web of Science category	Frequency
EG (red)	Economics	26
	Geography	21
	Planning & Development	8
	Environmental Studies	7
IB/Management (green)	Management	35
	Business	28
	Economics	8
	Planning & Development	5
International economics (blue)	Economics	23
	Management	8
	Environmental Studies	7
	Urban Studies	5
General economics (yellow)	Economics	23

Source: Author.

Table 1.3 Key words across different groups

Literature	Key words	Frequency
EG	clusters	10
	innovation	7
	networks	6
	value chains	3
	agglomeration economies	3
	institutions	3
	industrial districts	3
	globalization	3
IB/Management	multinational corporations	11
	subsidiaries	5
	innovation	3
	knowledge	3
International economics (blue)	foreign direct investment	11
	agglomeration economies	7
	location choice	4
	China	3
General economics (yellow)	multinational corporations	3
	trade	2

Source: Author.

Table 1.4 Main journals throughout different lines of inquiry

Literature	Journal	Frequency
EG	*Journal of Economic Geography*	7
	World Development	6
	Economic Geography	4
	Regional Studies	4
IB/Management	*Journal of International Business Studies*	11
	Strategic Management Journal	9
	Academy of Management Review	5
International economics	*Journal of International Economics*	3
	Journal of Urban Economics	3
	Review of Economics and Statistics	3
General economics	*American Economic Review*	5
	Journal of Political Economy	3
	Quarterly Journal of Economics	3

Source: Authors.

In Table 1.4 the leading journals within each strand are shown: *Journal of Economic Geography* in EG, *Journal of International Business Studies* in IB, *Journal of International Economics* in international economics and the *American Economic Review* in general economics.

1.4 Content analysis

As regards the content and knowledge published in those inception references from diverse literatures, it is observed that each strand follows its own agenda and uses its own constructs and key words. First, from the EG, Bathelt *et al.* (2004) emphasize the key importance of global pipelines connecting territories, taking up once more the outward-looking debate initiated by the neo-Marshallian nodes in global networks from Amin and Thrift (1992) or trade theories by Krugman (1991). Then, Harrison (1994) specifically points to the role of MNEs connecting clusters, and Markusen (1996) also uses MNEs to explain agglomeration typologies. Related to the EG but more focused on development literature, Humphrey and Schmitz (2002) argue that clusters are inserted into global value chains in different ways, paying particular attention to the position of developing country firms selling to large global buyers. Storper and Venables (2004) elaborate on the importance of localizations based on face-to-face encounters and interactions for organizing networks. Bell and Albu (1999) refer to gatekeepers as those firms that connect the cluster with non-cluster sources of knowledge. Nevertheless, from the EG the specific exploration of the role of MNEs is not addressed but only the openness of clusters to global value chains and inter-cluster connections.

Second, from the IB and strategy perspective, Dunning (1998) elaborates about the (L) location construct, Birkinshaw and Hood (2000) and Nachum and Keeble (2003a, 2003b) being significant performers by subsequently elaborating on the specific *Location* idea. Birkinshaw and Hood (2000) examine the characteristics of foreign-owned subsidiaries in clusters, showing that those subsidiaries are more embedded, autonomous and internationally orientated than subsidiaries in other industry sectors, emphasizing the role of the local environment for subsidiaries and the heterogenous character of clusters. Nachum and Keeble study the collocation of American MNEs in the Soho cluster in London, connecting Hollywood and London for media and entertainment products. Then, Almeida and Phene (2004) analyse US MNEs and their innovation performance from interacting with regional organizations when collocating, and thus complementing the internal MNE networks, to the extent that those contexts positively influence subsidiary technological innovation depending on the characteristics of the knowledge network (technological richness and diversity) and the knowledge linkages of the subsidiary with other entities. Similarly, Cantwell and Mudambi (2005) analyse foreign MNEs in the UK, finding that the level of subsidiary research and development (R&D) depends on MNE group-level and subsidiary-level characteristics as well as locational factors, emphasizing the key importance of location for competence-creating mandates from headquarters.[2]

Third, from urban and international economics, Coughlin *et al.* (1991) examine the attraction of foreign direct investment (FDI) for US states, showing a common pattern of decision to invest in a given state depending on the density of manufacturing activities, unemployment rate or level of wages. It is not done following clusters or collocation, it is the local environment that conditions the decision of MNEs to invest in specific states. Head *et al.* (1995) insert MNEs and collocation in agglomeration, finding positive and significant effects. Lastly, combining also urban and international economics, Guimeraes *et al.* (2000) study the spatial choices for newly created foreign-owned plants in Portugal, showing that agglomeration economies are decisive location factors.

All in all, we can state that the differing blocks of literatures were rather isolated from each other and only Krugman (1991) and Porter (1990) were the more fundamental ones nurturing all different strands, starting with analysing geography and international trade and national competitiveness. Results should be interpreted, however, by taking into account the fact that we are describing the origins or inception references addressing the intersection between MNEs and collocation in agglomerations, a phenomenon taken up again in the early 1990s.

1.5   Conclusions

This study's objective consists of analysing the fundamentals of the intersection between EG and IB literatures addressing the concurrent collocation of MNEs in agglomerations. This study has applied a bibliometric analysis in order to understand and extend knowledge on the topic which combines the collocation of MNEs in agglomerations. In doing so, this study analyses qualitatively and quantitatively the common roots and foundations of both disciplines. Searching through SSCI we obtained 475 documents belonging to three main strands: IB, EG and international economics. By conducting a co-citation bibliometric analysis, we obtained those documents most concurrently cited in those 475 documents. The latter constitute the fundamentals or intellectual structure of the cross-fertilization of that conversation. Subsequently, analysing the 203 documents most cited out of those 475, through bibliographic coupling, we can also explore the differing strands concurrently analysing MNEs and collocation. Then, the study of those 203 documents, in a very special retrospective analysis, permits us to better understand the origin of the divergence and the convergence between the main strands, i.e. EG, IB and international economics.

In short, as shown throughout this study, three main conclusions can be drawn in order to summarize our findings: (i) there is a clusterization of different literatures, that is, IB, EG and economics, addressing in parallel the concurrency of MNE collocation in agglomerations and reflecting a diverse and complex set of views, communities of scholars and assumptions; (ii) the integration between localization and MNEs is nascent and scholars are becoming conscious of its importance, taking up once again the debate initiated in the early 1990s; (iii) in respect of the content analysed, it can be stated that each sub-discipline has its inception or seminal studies. In our view, it is the IB strand (being Birkinshaw and Hood (2000), Nachum and Keeble (2003a, 2003b) or Cantwell and Mudambi (2005) the most significant pioneers of the Location idea, following Dunning (1998)), together with studies positioned in international economics (Coughlin *et al.*, 1991; Head *et al.*, 1995), that start the study of the intersection of MNEs and collocation. EG, however, represents the strand that has put less emphasis on that phenomenon, despite the early reference to global value chains (Amin and Thrift 1992) and subsequent discussions (e.g. Bathelt *et al.*, 2004), almost overlooking the role of MNEs. In any case, that diverse literature encompassing different strands is very recent, as discussion started in the 1990s.

This study presents limitations. First, the selection of a database (Web of Science) and key words using English might exclude important works written, or listed in journals, or indexed in a different language. Second, the search strategies utilized in this work may prevent us from finding different conversations. Third, our study is mainly retrospective and based on past foundations of the literature. Fourth, our own processes treating data, along with our personal interpretations, also influence results. For future studies, the study of the 28,000 plus references constituting those 475 documents can expand our knowledge on the topic.

Acknowledgements

This chapter has received support from (SMARTSPEC), FP7 Grant number 320131 and MINECO/FEDER EU ECO2015-63645-R.

Notes

1 See more at Hervás-Oliver *et al.* (2015).
2 Others such as Rugman and Verbeke (2004) use regional concepts in conjunction with multinationals but referring to the triad, that is, regions as supranational groups of countries (NAFTA, EU and Asia). Kogut and Zander (1993) elaborate on the internal transfer of knowledge within multinationals, not referring to the regional or collocation concept.

References

Alcácer, J. and Chung, W. 2014. 'Location strategies for agglomeration economies.' *Strategic Management Journal* 35(12):1749–1761.

Almeida, P. and Phene, A. 2004. 'Subsidiaries and knowledge creation: the influence of the MNC and host country on innovation.' *Strategic Management Journal* 25(8–9):847–864.

Amin, A. and Thrift, N. 1992. 'Neo-Marshallian nodes in global networks.' *International Journal of Urban and Regional Research* 16(4):571–587.

Bathelt, H., Malmberg, A. and Maskell, P. 2004. 'Clusters and knowledge: local buzz, global pipelines and the process of knowledge creation.' *Progress in Human Geography* 28(1):31–56.

Bell, M. and Albu, M. 1999. 'Knowledge systems and technological dynamism in industrial clusters in developing countries.' *World Development* 27(9):1715–1734.

Birkinshaw, J. and Hood, N. 2000. 'Characteristics of foreign subsidiaries in industry clusters.' *Journal of International Business Studies* 31(1):141–154.

Cantwell, J. and Mudambi, R. 2005. 'MNE competence-creating subsidiary mandates.' *Strategic Management Journal* 26(12):1109–1128.

Cohen, W. M., and Levinthal, D. A. 1990. 'Absorptive capacity: a new perspective on learning and innovation.' *Administrative Science Quarterly* 35(1):128–152.

Cooke, P. 2005. 'Regional knowledge capabilities and open innovation: regional innovation systems and clusters in the asymmetric knowledge economy.' In *Clusters, Networks, and Innovation*, edited by S. Breschi and F. Malerba, Oxford: Oxford University Press, 80–109.

Coughlin, C., Terza, J. and Arromdee, V. 1991. 'State characteristics and the location of foreign direct-investment within the United States.' *Review of Economics and Statistics* 73(4):675–683.

Dunning, J. H. 1993. *Multinational Enterprises and the Global Economy*. Reading, MA: Addison-Wesley.

Dunning, J. H. 1998. 'Location and the multinational enterprise: A neglected factor?' *Journal of International Business Studies* 29(1):45–66.

Dunning, J. H. 2009. 'Location and the multinational enterprise: a neglected factor?' *Journal of International Business Studies* 40(1):5–19.

Eisingerich, A. B., Bell, S. J. and Tracey, P. 2010. 'How can clusters sustain performance? The role of network strength, network openness, and environmental uncertainty.' *Research Policy*, 39(2):239–253.

Gereffi, G. 1999. 'International trade and industrial upgrading in the apparel commodity chain.' *Journal of International Economics* 48(1):37–70.

Gereffi, G., Humphrey, J. and Sturgeon, T. 2005. 'The governance of global value chains.' *Review of International Political Economy* 12(1):78–104.

Glaeser, E., Kallal, H., Scheinkman, J. and Shleifer, A. 1992. 'Growth in cities.' *Journal of Political Economy* 100(6):1126–1152.

Guimaraes, P., Figueiredo, O. and Woodward, D. 2000. 'Agglomeration and the location of foreign direct investment in portugal.' *Journal of Urban Economics* 47(1):115–135.

Harrison, B. 1994. *Lean and Mean: The changing landscape of corporate power in the age of flexibility*. New York: Basic Books.

Head, K., Ries, J. and Swenson, D. 1995. 'Agglomeration benefits and location choice: evidence from Japanese manufacturing investments in the United States.' *Journal of International Economics* 38(3–4):223–247.

Head, C. K., Ries, J. C. and Swenson, D. L. 1999. 'Attracting foreign manufacturing: investment promotion and agglomeration.' *Regional Science and Urban Economics*, 29(2):197–218.

Hervás-Oliver, J. L. 2015. 'How do multinational enterprises co-locate in industrial districts? An introduction to the integration of alternative explanations from international business and economic geography literatures.' *Investigaciones Regionales* 32:115–132.

Hervás-Oliver, J. L. and Albors-Garrigós, J. 2008. 'Local knowledge domains and the role of MNE affiliates in bridging and complementing a cluster's knowledge.' *Entrepreneurship and Regional Development* 20(6):581–598.

Hervás-Oliver, J. L. and Boix-Domènech, R. 2013. 'The economic geography of the meso-global spaces: integrating multinationals and clusters at the local-global level.' *European Planning Studies* 21(7):1064–1080.

Hervás-Oliver, J. L., Gonzalez, G., Caja, P. and Sempere-Ripoll, F. 2015. 'Clusters and industrial districts: where is the literature going? Identifying emerging sub-fields of research.' *European Planning Studies* 23(9):1827–1872.

Humphrey, J. and Schmitz, H. 2002. 'How does insertion in global value chains affect upgrading in industrial clusters?' *Regional Studies* 36(9):1017–1027.

Kogut, B. and Zander, U. 1993. 'Knowledge of the firm and evolutionary theory of the multinational corporation.' *Journal of International Business Studies* 24(4):625–645.

Krugman, P. 1991. 'Increasing returns and economic geography.' *Journal of Political Economy*, 99(3):483–499.

Lazzeretti, L., Sedita, S. R. and Caloffi, A. 2014. 'Founders and disseminators of cluster research.' *Journal of Economic Geography* 14(1):21–43.

Majocchi, A. and Presutti, M. 2009. 'Industrial clusters, entrepreneurial culture and the social environment: the effects on FDI distribution.' *International Business Review* 18(1):76–88.

Markusen, A. 1996. 'Sticky places in slippery space: a typology of industrial districts.' *Economic Geography* 72(3):293–313.

Marshall, A. 1890. *Principles of Economics*. London: Macmillan.

Marshall, A. 1920. *Principles of Economics* (Revised edition). London: Macmillan.

Martin, R. and Sunley, P. 2003. 'Deconstructing clusters: chaotic concept or policy panacea?' *Journal of Economic Geography* 3(1):5–35.

McCann, P. and Mudambi, R. 2004. 'The location behavior of the multinational enterprise: some theoretical and empirical issues.' *Growth & Change* 35(4):491–524.

Meyer, K. E., Mudambi, R. and Narula, R. 2011. 'Multinational enterprises and local contexts: the opportunities and challenges of multiple embeddedness.' *Journal of Management Studies* 48(2):235–252.

Mudambi, R. and Venzin, M. 2010. 'The strategic nexus of offshoring and outsourcing decisions.' *Journal of Management Studies* 47(8):1510–1533.

Nachum, L. and Keeble, D. 2003a. 'Neo-Marshallian clusters and global networks: the linkages of media firms in central London.' *Long Range Planning* 36(5):459–580.

Nachum, L. and Keeble, D. 2003b. 'MNE linkages and localised clusters: foreign and indigenous firms in the media cluster of Central London.' *Journal of International Management* 9(2):171–192.

Narula, R. 2014. 'Exploring the paradox of competence-creating subsidiaries: balancing bandwidth and dispersion in MNEs.' *Long Range Planning* 47(1–2):4–15.

Narula, R. and Santangelo, G. D. 2012. 'Location and collocation advantages in international innovation.' *Multinational Business Review* 20(1):6–25.

Pla-Barber, J. and Puig, F. 2009. 'Is the influence of the industrial district on international activities being eroded by globalization?: Evidence from a traditional manufacturing industry.' *International Business Review* 18(5):435–445.

Porter, M. E. 1990. *The Competitive Advantage of Nations*. New York: Free Press.

Porter, M. E. 1998. 'Clusters and the new economics of competition.' *Harvard Business Review* 76(6):77–90.

Rugman, A. and Verbeke, A. 2004. 'A perspective on regional and global strategies of multinational enterprises.' *Journal of International Business Studies* 35(1):3–18.

Rugman, A., Verbeke, A. and Yuan, W. 2011. 'Re-conceptualizing Bartlett and Ghoshal's classification of national subsidiary roles in the multinational enterprise.' *Journal of Management Studies* 48(2):253–277.

Sedita, S., Caloffi, A. and Belussi, F. 2013. *Heterogeneity of MNEs entry modes in industrial clusters: an evolutionary approach based on the cluster life cycle model* (paper presented at the 35th DRUID Celebration Conference 2013, Barcelona, Spain, June 17–19), accessed 30 December 2015, http:www.druid.dk.

Shaver, M., and Flyer, F. 2000. 'Agglomeration economies, firm heterogeneity, and foreign direct investment in the United States.' *Strategic Management Journal* 21(12):1175–1193.

Shibata, N., Kajikawa, Y. and Matsushima, K. 2007. 'Topological analysis of citation networks to discover the future core articles.' *Journal of the American Society for Information Science and Technology* 58(6):872–882.

Storper, M. and Venables, A. J. 2004. 'Buzz: face-to-face contact and the urban economy.' *Journal of Economic Geography* 4(4):351–370.

Tallman, S. and Chacar, A. S. 2011. 'Knowledge accumulation and dissemination in MNEs: a practice-based framework.' *Journal of Management Studies* 48(2):278–304.

Tu, P. P. 2011. 'A study of influential authors, works and research network of consumer behavior research.' *African Journal of Business Management* 5(23):9838–9854.

Vernon, R. 1966. 'International investment and international trade in the product cycle.' *Quarterly Journal of Economics* 80(2):190–207.

Zupic, I. and Cater, T. 2014. 'Bibliometric methods in management and organization.' *Organizational Research Methods* 18(3):429–472.

2 Economies and diseconomies of clusters

Financial services in the City of London

Naresh Pandit, Gary Cook and
Jonathan Beaverstock

2.1 Introduction

Geographical clusters are agglomerations of industry that have been variously referred to as 'industrial districts' (Pyke *et al.*, 1990), 'new industrial spaces' (Scott, 1988), 'milieus' (Camagni, 1991) and 'nodes' (Amin and Thrift, 1992). The study of clusters is not new, dating back at least to the work of Marshall (1890). The recent revival of interest in the phenomenon has three important sources. The first is a growing body of empirical work showing high and rising levels of clustering across a wide range of industries (e.g. Kim, 2007). The second is another growing body of empirical work, which shows that clustering can be associated with high economic performance: 'buzz' and knowledge spillovers (e.g. Malmberg and Maskell, 2002; Storper and Venables, 2004); that firms in strong clusters grow faster than average and that strong clusters attract a disproportionate number of new entrants (e.g. Pandit *et al.*, 2008); and that productivity and innovation (e.g. Swann, 2009) are higher within strong clusters. The third is the influential work on the relationality of clusters, linked through distinctive ties, 'pipelines' and cross-border economic practice through co-presence in global (urban) networks (e.g. Bathelt and Turi, 2011; Bathelt *et al.*, 2004). Importantly, the concept of the cluster has firmly put the mantra (and role) of 'location' back on the agenda for economic growth, performance and longevity in the spatialisation of the knowledge and 'real' economy (e.g. Martin and Sunley, 2003).

In response to this renewed interest, new attempts have been made to explain clustering by elucidating the general link between the geographical concentration of production and superior economic performance (Karlsson, 2008). Many reasons that underpin the rationality of clustering have been advanced. Much of this work builds on the classic three-part explanation offered by Marshall (1890): that firms in clusters benefit from (1) access to specialised suppliers; (2) access to a large pool of specialised labour; and (3) access to knowledge that has the characteristics of a public good because it is, as Marshall famously stated, 'in the air'. Clustering does also have its costs and these relate to the congestion that naturally arises when economic activity is geographically dense. These costs can reduce the productivity of a cluster and can even lead to its decline (Swann *et al.*, 1998).

A more specific attempt to explain clustering is being made in the international business literature. Here the interest is in why multinational enterprises (MNEs) may be disproportionately attracted to clusters (Cook *et al.*, 2013; Hervás-Oliver, 2015; Narula, 2014). A re-evaluation of the spatial organisation of MNE activities and foreign direct investment (FDI) has been under way since Dunning's (1998) call for more research on location, and in particular, location in clusters, as a determinant of FDI.

Although there is a wealth of theorising about clusters, evidence is scarce (Karlsson, 2008). The aim of this chapter is to rise to this empirical challenge by shedding further light on the benefits and costs of clustering, drawn from an empirical study of banking and professional services transnational and small and medium-sized firms located in London's financial district, referred to here as the City of London.

Following this introduction, the remainder of this chapter is structured in four main sections. Section 2.2 briefly elucidates the clusters concept, which is necessary as it is much misunderstood, drawing on both business and management and economic geography literatures. In section 2.3 we detail the research design of the study by describing its unit of analysis (the City of London spatial cluster) and its method of data collection and analysis. Section 2.4 presents findings on the benefits and costs of a cluster location and these are discussed in relation to the previous clusters literatures. In the final section, we conclude by relating the findings more specifically to the financial services literature and to the 'end of geography' debate in financial services thesis (Agnes, 2000; O'Brien, 1991).

2.2   Cluster definition

There is significant variation in how clusters are defined and this has led to some unwarranted criticism of the clusters concept (Martin and Sunley, 2003). Although there is no standard definition (Swann, 2009), a popular starting point is provided by Porter (1998, pp. 197–198):

> Clusters are geographic concentrations of interconnected companies, specialised suppliers, service providers, firms in related industries, and associated institutions (for example, universities, standards agencies, and trade associations) in particular fields that compete but also cooperate.

This definition captures four important elements of a cluster. First, it does not relate to a single industry; rather, it merely requires that companies in a cluster are interdependent in some way. Second, a cluster is defined in terms of not just companies but also supporting institutions. Third, market and non-market linkages are stressed. Finally, it encourages the conceptualisation of clusters as complex systems of industrial organisation that confer sustainable

Table 2.1 Swann's clusters ladder

Phenomenon	Richness of cluster	Difficulty of measurement
Co-location	Shallow	Easy
Co-location and technological proximity		
Co-location and superior performance		
Companies interdependent in a value chain		
Network firms		
Marshallian externalities		
Labour mobility		
Explicit collaboration		
Informal knowledge exchange	Rich	Difficult

Source: Adapted from Swann (2009: 149).

competitive advantage to incumbents. A weakness of the definition is that it is imprecise in at least two important ways: it provides little guidance on the required quantity or quality of incumbents and linkages in a cluster, and it provides no guidance on the geographic scope of a cluster. These weaknesses are beginning to be addressed in the most recent literature, which recognises cluster heterogeneity ranging from rich 'strong clusters' associated with high economic performance, to shallow 'weak clusters' with low to average economic performance. Swann (2009) distinguishes between the two extremes by way of a clusters 'ladder' (see Table 2.1).

It is fair to say that much criticism of the clusters concept is levelled at studies of shallow/weak clusters (Martin and Sunley, 2003) and that scholarly, practitioner and policy-maker interest in clusters increases with cluster richness/strength (Swann, 2009). It is not our intention to unravel these debates or intervene in the conceptual discussions about 'cluster theory' as this has been done extensively elsewhere (e.g. Cook *et al.*, 2011; Gordon and McCann, 2000; Maskell and Malmberg, 2007).

2.3 Research design

2.3.1 *Unit of analysis*

This study's cluster, or unit of analysis, needs to be a strong or rich cluster in terms of Swann's (2009) clusters 'ladder' (Table 2.1). The unit of analysis chosen, that meets this criterion, is the City of London financial services cluster. Swann (2009, p. 151) states: 'Probably the strongest cluster in the UK is the financial services cluster in the City of London.' Similarly, Dunning (1998, p. 61) states: 'Perhaps the best illustration of a spatial cluster, or agglomeration, of related activities to minimise distance-related transaction-costs, and to exploit the external economies associated with the close presence of related firms is the Square Mile of the City of London.'

Although the City has historically referred to the 'square mile' around the Bank of England, developments to the east, west and north have extended the centre to the extent that the term 'the City' is now used to refer to the cluster as a whole and not just the square mile (Golding, 2001).

Much has been written in the field of economic geography on the City and wider financial cluster (including Canary Wharf and the 'West' End). Pertinent to our study is the collective works of commentators such as Clark (2002), Cook *et al.* (2007) and Thrift (1994), who have written extensively on the economic competitiveness and agglomeration economies of the City in international financial marketplaces. Setting aside the economic factors accounting for the City's prominence as a global financial centre (e.g. Z/Yen, 2015), a significant competitive advantage of its milieu in the world is the functioning of its 'epistemic communities' (Thrift, 1994), where proximity and sheer co-location are reproduced through distinctive codes of face-to-face contact, trust relations and traded and untraded interdependencies (e.g. Clark, 2002; Cook *et al.*, 2007; Thrift, 1994). The close proximity of these 'epistemic communities' creates the conditions for 'global-local' buzz (Bathelt *et al.*, 2004; Storper and Venables, 2004), both tacit and codified knowledge production *in situ* and, importantly, drives the economic competitiveness of the City in the network of international financial centres.

The 'square mile' and Canary Wharf's place in the world of international finance is also strengthened by its position as a global hub or 'node' (Amin and Thrift, 1992), where many 'pipelines' meet and originate, stretching out to North America, Europe and Asia. London's financial cluster benefits from the replenishment of knowledge, innovation and skills, where its global-local 'buzz', focused in a very small geographical space (nominally the 'square mile'), packed with global financial institutions and professional services, produces significant competitive advantages which further enhance the productivity of this rich cluster. The 'node' function of the City as a beneficiary of 'pipelines' from other centres such as New York, Frankfurt, Paris, Mumbai, Singapore, Hong Kong, Shanghai and Tokyo cannot be under-estimated in its place as the global financial centre (e.g, Z/Yen, 2015). As Bathelt *et al.* (2004, p. 31) note: 'The co-existence of high levels of buzz and many pipelines may provide firms located in outward-looking and lively clusters with a string of particular advantages not available to outsiders.'

Returning to the City's economic profile, it is best understood as a wholesale financial services centre with core activities in (global investment) banking, insurance and fund management supported by a panoply of activities including legal services, accounting, management consultancy, advertising, market research, recruitment, property management, financial printing and publishing, and the provision of electronic information. The City remains strong, despite the financial services downturn beginning in 2007. A recent Global Financial Centres Index (Z/Yen, 2015) shows that the cluster is ranked number two globally.

2.4 Method

Data on perceived cluster benefits and costs in the City of London financial services cluster were collected via a postal questionnaire survey. In order to ascertain the reach of *prima facie* important clustering forces, a focus group study of senior financial services executives was conducted. This revealed that the appropriate area was up to 500 metres beyond the boundaries of the City of London and Canary Wharf. The sample of financial services companies (engaged in banking, investment banking, insurance, fund management, legal services, accounting, management consultancy, advertising, market research, recruitment, property management, financial printing and publishing, and the provision of electronic information) was therefore drawn from this area from the Market Locations database. Sampling was stratified with 100 per cent of the largest 350 financial services firms included and 1,150 firms drawn at random. Accordingly, a total of 1,500 questionnaires were posted. A total of 310 usable questionnaires were returned, a response rate of just over 20 per cent. We tested to see whether our sample was representative. In 294 cases it was possible to classify the response to a specific line of activity (a small number of questionnaires were returned anonymously and could not be assigned to a particular line of activity). These 294 returns were found to be distributed across lines of activity in very much the same proportions as the 1,500 firms to which the questionnaire was issued. We are therefore confident that we have a random and representative sample from the population of interest. In almost all cases, respondents were asked to rank the importance of a potential benefit or cost from 1 (not important) to 5 (very important), with an option of 0 if not applicable.

The data were subjected to exploratory principal factor analysis. The main method used to determine the number of factors to use was the scree plot (Cattell, 1966), which indicated six factors at the point of inflection. According to Stevens (1992), the scree plot method is reliable provided there are more than 200 observations. The scree plot is preferred to Kaiser's criterion of retaining all factors with an eigenvalue greater than one as neither of the rules for Kaiser's criterion being accurate is satisfied: the average communality value is less than 0.6, even though there are 294 observations. In any case, Kaiser's criterion indicated that six factors should be extracted. Extracting additional factors was not informative.

The method of rotation used was varimax, which has the benefit of producing more interpretable groups of variables on each factor, important because the factors themselves are of independent interest in this analysis (Field, 2009). In principle, there is a case for oblique rotation as there are theoretical grounds for suspecting the factors to be correlated with one another. Oblimin rotation was used as a robustness check. Essentially, the substantive interpretation of the factors extracted was the same, although the factors themselves were not quite so distinct. For this reason the results using varimax rotation are reported. Nothing important hinges on this choice.

Stevens (1992) suggests that with at least 200 observations, any variable that has a loading of 0.512 or more on a factor is important, and with at least 300 observations the relevant criterion is a factor loading of 0.364 or more. Based on this rule, only factor loadings after rotation in excess of 0.37 are reported.

Having approximately 300 observations and more than 10 observations per variable in the final analysis, the analysis satisfies the general criteria that various researchers have proposed for factor analysis to deliver stable and reliable solutions (Field, 2009). Communalities are all in the 0.5 range or greater, therefore the factors may be regarded as reliable given the sample size.

Initially forty variables were entered in the analysis. This set of variables needed to be reduced as problems of multicollinearity were indicated by a determinant of the R-matrix well below 0.00001. Variables were identified for removal based on two criteria. First, the anti-image correlation matrix was inspected. No items had small correlations, all being above 0.7, but off-diagonal elements were inspected to identify pairs of variables which had the largest correlations and/or correlation substantially greater than zero with several variables. Second, theoretical priors regarding which variables ought to be included in any subsequent analysis were used. Some robustness analysis was applied by deleting slightly different sets of variables where alternative borderline judgements were used. This did not materially affect the substantive conclusions regarding factor structures.

Regarding the validity of the factor analysis, the Kaiser-Meyer-Olkin measure of sampling adequacy is very good at 0.846, indicating reliable factors will be extracted. The correlations in the anti-image matrix all lie between 0.776 and 0.918, indicating good sampling adequacy. Cronbach's α is generally satisfactory, as reported in Table 2.2, with all values apart from factor six lying above the 0.7 threshold. The value of α in each case was not sensitive to deletion of items in each sub-scale. This indicates that the scales are reliably measured.

2.5   Results and discussion

The factor loadings in Table 2.3 show how strongly each variable correlates with the factor onto which it loads. It is not unusual nor a problem if one variable loads onto more than one factor.

Table 2.2 Cronbach's α measure of scale reliability

Factor	Cronbach's α
1	0.871
2	0.793
3	0.738
4	0.728
5	0.706
6	0.654

Table 2.3 Rotated factor matrix

Variable	Factor 1	Factor 2	Factor 3	Factor 4	Factor 5	Factor 6
Proximity promotes trust	0.734					
Proximity aids easy communication	0.712					
Proximity makes it easier to build and maintain personal contacts	0.839					
Proximity makes it easier to assemble multi-disciplinary teams	0.451					
Proximity makes it easier to have face-to-face contact	0.730					
Our location makes it easier to take market share		0.390			0.607	
We benefit from proximity to market-leading customers		0.382			0.568	
Our location has the advantage of access to real-time information about market trends		0.522				0.424
Local rivalry among competitors is a powerful spur		0.740				
We are able to benchmark against competitors		0.758				
We benefit from proximity to an exchange or physical marketplace		0.436				
Poor infrastructure is a disadvantage			0.512			
Poor availability of staff with language skills is a disadvantage			0.478			
Environmental quality is a disadvantage			0.527			
Poor national transportation links are a disadvantage			0.602			
Poor international transport links are a disadvantage			0.631			
Government regulation is a problem			0.466			
We benefit from access to a strong, skilled labour supply				0.433		
A pool of talented labour with innovative skills helps innovate				0.542		
Labour mobility helps spread knowledge and good practice				0.608		
A fluid labour market helps attract good staff				0.689		
Our address is important to being conceived as credible					0.648	
Customers external to London find it easier to interact with us						0.415
We benefit from being able to find firms that will supply bespoke services						0.729

The factors have a ready interpretation in the light of the extant literature on the benefits and costs of cluster location.

The first group of variables loading highly onto factor one represents what can be labelled *social capital*. Considerable importance has been placed in the literature on building trust and personal relationships in clusters (Hendry and Brown, 2006). This leads to a higher degree of knowledge generation and diffusion, which enhance innovation and productivity. Of course, the most valuable knowledge is tacit knowledge, which Gertler (2003, p. 79) argues is 'the most important basis for innovation-based value creation'. Specifically, the argument is that it is the effective generation and diffusion of tacit knowledge that leads to superior economic performance in clusters. Tacit knowledge is sticky in geographical space because its acquisition can occur only through social interaction (observation, demonstration, imitation, correction, repetition, etc.), which is greatly aided by geographical proximity, especially when such proximity is coupled with the contextual homogeneity or 'common culture' that exists within clusters. Pinch *et al.* (2003, p. 375) state: 'Tacit knowledge is often context dependent, being facilitated by a common language, culture and value system.' Codifiable knowledge, meanwhile, can be acquired without social interaction (for example, it can be communicated in the form of an instruction manual). Amin and Thrift (2002) point out that the two types of knowledge should not be viewed as mutually exclusive as they often work in a reinforcing manner. Pinch *et al.* (2003, p. 376) corroborate, stating: 'Not only is codified knowledge effective when interpreted through a variety of tacit measures, but tacit knowledge often relies on codified knowledge in forms such as instruction manuals.' Recent work in economic geography has elaborated on the generation and diffusion of tacit knowledge by focusing on the role of face-to-face contact. In line with Gertler, who argues that 'the production of tacit knowledge occurs *simultaneously* with the act of transmission primarily through the mechanism of user-producer interaction .... The end product arising from this close interaction benefits both users and producers, and embodies within it new tacit knowledge that could not have been produced by either party working in isolation' (2003, pp. 84–85, emphasis in original), Storper and Venables (2004) unpack four main knowledge and learning benefits of face-to-face contact: (1) that it can be an efficient communication technology; (2) that it can enhance trust and incentives in relationships; (3) that it can improve screening; and (4) that it can motivate extra effort. Let us briefly look at each in turn. When important knowledge is tacit, face-to-face contact works well as a communication technology because it allows uniquely rich exchange (including intentional and non-intentional visual clues) and instant feedback between parties. With respect to the second benefit, improving relationships, the better observation and interpretation of another person's behaviour that face-to-face contact allows reduces information asymmetry, with the result that parties are more likely to be honest and trustworthy and less likely to free-ride. This is particularly important when teamwork between firms is necessary. Trust between parties engaging in face-to-face contact is further enhanced because such contact is expensive and is a sunk cost. The simple act of attending a face-to-face meeting signals a person's commitment to the relationship and so enhances parties' trust in each other. Repeated meetings strengthen this signal. With respect to the third benefit, face-to-face contact improves screening because it involves loss of anonymity, allows judging and being judged, and facilitates the acquisition of shared values. Successfully screened individuals are admitted to 'the loop' in which certain tacit knowledge is shared. Finally, with respect to the fourth benefit, face-to-face contact can motivate extra effort because such contact is a type of performance (Goffman, 1982) for which considerable effort is needed. Storper and Venables (2004, p. 365) collectively label the four benefits of face-to-face contact as 'buzz' and conclude: 'To be able to reap these benefits in full almost invariably requires co-location, rather than occasional interludes of face-to-face contact. It is unsurprising that people in a buzz environment should be highly productive.'

The second group of variables loading onto factor two relate to benefits of local competition. It is notable that the spur of rivalry and the ability to benchmark load most heavily onto this factor, supporting one of Porter's (1998) leading contentions. Malmberg and Maskell (2002) propose a theory in which the mechanisms through which clusters are able to create and sustain knowledge and learning are central to explaining the superior productivity and innovation that empirical work has detected. They categorise clustering processes that occur horizontally and vertically and argue that it is lamentable that the horizontal dimension has been neglected, with Marshall (1890) and Porter (1998) being notable exceptions, as it is at this level that many knowledge and learning processes occur which enable a group of firms at a location to outperform a single larger firm or a network of small but geographically disparate firms. First, horizontal co-location allows for superior observability:

'Just as people in a residential area simply cannot help noticing what their next-door neighbours do ... business firms often have remarkably good knowledge of the undertakings of nearby firms even if they do not make any dedicated efforts at systematic monitoring. If those neighbouring firms are in a similar business, it is more likely that the observing firm will understand, and learn from, what it observes' (Malmberg and Maskell, 2002, p. 439).

Second, horizontal co-location allows for superior *comparability*:

'The sharing of common conditions, opportunities, and threats make the strengths and weaknesses of each individual firm apparent to the management, the owners, the employees, and everyone else who cares to take an interest. Each firm in the horizontal dimension to the cluster is provided with information about the possibilities to improve and the incentives to do so ... If the firms of the cluster were to be spread throughout a large city among many unrelated businesses their ability to learn from each other's mistakes and successes would be severely restricted' (Malmberg and Maskell, 2002, p. 439).

As already mentioned, Porter (1998, p. 219) has long emphasised the rivalrous benefits of horizontal co-location:

'Rivalry with locally based competitors has particularly strong incentive effects because of the ease of constant comparison and because local rivals have similar general circumstances (for example, labour costs and local market access), so that competition must take place on other things. In addition, peer pressure amplifies competitive pressure within a cluster, even among indirectly competing or non-competing firms. Pride and the desire to look good in the local community motivate firms in their attempts to outdo each other.'

The third group of variables loading onto factor three represent classic congestion costs, which have been widely suggested as forces which slow cluster growth or even lead to cluster decline. This finding on the importance of clustering costs supports the cluster life cycle (CLC) concept, which explains the demise of once highly productive and innovative clusters: when clustering benefits are greater than costs, a cluster grows; when costs are greater than the benefits, a cluster declines (Hervás-Oliver and Albors-Garrigós, 2014; Menzel and Fornhal, 2009).

Cost of premises lay slightly below the threshold value for reporting of 0.367 with a loading of 0.321. The concerns over lack of availability of staff with language skills indicate competition for skilled labour, language skills being particularly important in this highly globalised industry. Perhaps the odd one out among these factors is government regulation, which is not so obviously related to congestion and competition in factor markets. It is, nevertheless, perceived as a friction on doing business.

The fourth factor reflects classic advantages of labour market pooling. There is an emerging recognition in the literature that access to labour is a prime attraction for firms and central to the dynamics of clustering (Cook *et al.*, 2007). A pool of talented labour attracts successful firms, and these firms in turn attract yet more labour. As the labour pool deepens, so workers become increasingly incentivised to invest in both higher levels of human capital and more specialised forms of human capital. This is a critical resource and a source of abiding regional advantage for firms located in the cluster.

Churn in the labour market pool is also recognised as an important means through which knowledge diffuses in a cluster (Florida, 2002). Finally, there is a flexibility advantage that comes with a large labour pool. In line with other industries, demand for financial services is cyclical and the industry benefits from the ability to recruit quickly and cheaply when demand picks up after a decline. Outside of a cluster this ability would be much curtailed.

The fifth factor reflects the importance of local demand, a neglected benefit in the clusters literature generally. Three aspects are important. First, similar to a shopping mall, the cluster represents a place where many customers shop and so provides the opportunity for suppliers to win market share from rivals. Relatedly, the clustered firm may also benefit from reduced consumer search costs. The idea here is that the firm is more likely to be found by customers when it is located in a cluster. This is particularly important when consumers have specific requirements (and so explains why antique shops tend to cluster). Second, the clustered firm benefits from proximity to market leading customers. Such customers can encourage innovation by being demanding and by alerting suppliers of new trends and innovations. Such knowledge exchange between customers and suppliers can be problematic because the value of knowledge is difficult for users to gauge before they have acquired or absorbed it. Accordingly, it is difficult for a market for the exchange of knowledge to arise. Clusters allow for the development of reputation and of networks of trust between the parties involved and so provide a solution to this problem. Third, information externalities on the demand side may also exist, that is, a cluster's reputation rubs off on the company that is located in it. This can be a major benefit when a cluster has a high reputation (e.g. Harley Street and Savile Row in London for medical and tailoring services respectively). This finding on the reputational benefits of a location, 'a credible address', is surprising as there is little mention of it in the general theoretical literature on clusters. However, the benefit is well understood by scholars of the City. For example, Allen and Pryke (1994, p. 459, emphasis in original) find that 'in the case of finance, the abstract space of the City of London has secured its dominance over time through its ability continually to mould the space around it in its own image. The City *is* finance'. Similarly, on the basis of extensive interview evidence, Clark (2002, p. 440) finds that, 'a firm's reputation may depend upon the reputation of its financial centre as much as its own competence'. By way of explanation, it is possible that the general literature on clusters fails to emphasise the reputational advantage of location because it has focused on manufacturing industries (Sjoberg and Sjoholm, 2002). In service industries, not only is it more difficult to evaluate the quality of the product provided in advance, to some extent even after the product has been provided, it may be rational for customers to rely heavily on a projected image (partly created by the right address).

The variable loading most heavily on the sixth factor, the ability to find firms able to supply bespoke services, is a classic Marshallian externality. As the cluster deepens, so a greater array of specialised suppliers emerges. This sophisticated supplier base is a foundation for innovation and efficiency. In financial services, information is a key resource, therefore it is perhaps not surprising to find access to real-time information being coupled with specialised suppliers.

2.6   Conclusion

In addition to contributing to the general literature on clusters, our findings contribute to the limited literature on financial services clustering. In their seminal work, Eccles and Crane (1988) identify five firm-level production characteristics in investment banking that benefit from clustering. Thrift's (1994, p. 333) summary of these characteristics is worth quoting at length:

> 'First, much of the production of financial products and services takes place at the boundaries of the firms. Firms tend to be client-rather than task-centred and to rely on repeat business. Second, firms tend to be flattened and non-hierarchical. Responsibility is often diffuse and vague with results coming from the efforts of small teams of relationship and product specialists .... Third, as a matter of course, firms need to cooperate with one another as well as compete, for example in syndicated lending or the placement of securities. Fourth, firms often find it difficult to judge their performance accurately. They can only be sure of how they are doing through comparison with other firms' successes and failures .... Fifth, it is difficult for financial services firms in international financial centres to build up the equivalent of inventories to buffer the firm. The result is that the employees of these firms have to be constantly 'on the go' to find new business. They must be able to work in a crisis mode, dropping everything to complete a task on time or to get work'.

Our findings support this analysis and therefore concur with those of Thrift, who concludes that the building of relationships between firms is crucial and that this is aided by geographical proximity. Our findings also concur with Agnes's (2000, p. 348) analysis of the Australian interest-rate swaps industry, which concludes that 'dealing by necessity involves the revelation of proprietary trading information, so the formation of relationships characterised by trustworthiness, rapport, and confidence assumes great significance; these features develop through face-to-face meetings and social interaction, facilitated by spatial proximity' Finally, our findings echo those of Tickell (2003). His review of the literature concludes that 'Despite the phenomenal transformations in the nature of finance in the latter third of the twentieth century ... the business of finance still thrives upon close inter-firm and inter-personal relationships' (Tickell, 2003, p. 236). Regarding the 'end of geography thesis', our study supports the argument that this is at best exaggerated (Martin, 1994; Tickell, 2003) and at worst also diametrically incorrect (Gertler, 2003; Porter, 1998). This thesis argues that advances in information and communication technologies, increasing globalisation, increasing deregulation, lower trade barriers, lower transport costs, and the emergence of English as the *de facto* world language all contribute to a new economic reality in which production can be footloose. O'Brien (1991, pp. 1–2) applies this thesis to financial services thus:

'The end of geography, as a concept applied to international financial relationships, refers to a state of economic development where geographic location no longer matters in finance, or much less than hitherto .... For financial firms, this means that the choice of geographical location can be greatly widened, provided that an appropriate investment in information and computer systems can be made .... There will be forces seeking to maintain geographical control ... Yet, as markets and rules become integrated, the relevance of geography and the need to base decisions on geography will alter and often diminish.'

If we follow the best-case argument that the thesis is exaggerated, our findings support Tickell's (2003) observation that, although these changes have impacted on the location of financial services production, the impact has been limited, applying more to low-value, back-office activities and less to the high-value knowledge-intensive activities of the City that critically benefit from clustering. Corroborating, Martin (1994, p. 262) first states that:

'In principle, modern telecommunications technologies render the need for financial centres increasingly obsolete: new banking and trading technologies, such as local area networks (LANs), on-line transaction processing (OLTP) and electronic data interchange (EDI), not only increase the range of financial services, but also confer considerable locational freedom on institutions. Market participants no longer have to be in the same centre, the same country or even the same continent for trading to take place.'

He then continues to observe that such developments have indeed led to the dispersal of financial services activity away from established clusters, but concludes that 'Much of this, however, has been of back offices, leaving the head offices and primary business within the national capital' (Martin, 1994, p. 263). If we follow the worst-case argument that the end of geography thesis is not only exaggerated but also diametrically incorrect, our findings support Gertler (2003, p. 83), who argues that 'in a world in which access to codified knowledge is becoming ever easier, a firm's ability to produce, access and control tacit knowledge is most important to its competitive success'. This resonates with Porter's (1998) 'location paradox': 'Now that companies can source capital, goods, information and technology from around the world, often with the click of a mouse ... more open global markets and faster transportation and communication should diminish the role of location in competition' (p. 77), but, paradoxically, 'The enduring competitive advantages in a global economy lie increasingly in local things ... that distant rivals cannot match' (p. 78). Ultimately, our findings concur with those of Nigel Thrift, who concludes: 'International financial centres will continue because they satisfy essential communicative/interpretive needs that cannot be met through electronic communication. There will be no 'end of geography"' (Thrift, 1994, p. 352).

References

Agnes, P. (2000) The 'end of geography' in financial services? Local embeddedness and territorialisation in the interest rate swap industry, *Economic Geography*, 76(4): 347–366.

Allen, J. and Pryke, M. (1994) The production of service space, *Environment and Planning D*, 12(4): 453–75.

Amin, A. and Thrift, N. (1992) Neo-Marshallian nodes in global networks, *International Journal of Urban and Regional Research*, 16(4): 571–587.

Amin, A. and Thrift N. (2002) *Cities: Reimagining the Urban*. Cambridge: Polity Press.

Bathlet, H., Malmberg, A. and Maskell, P. (2004) Clusters and knowledge: local buzz, global pipelines and the process of knowledge creation, *Progress in Human Geography*, 28(1): 31–56.

Bathelt, H. and Turi, P. (2011) Local, global and virtual buzz: the importance of face-to-face contact in economic interaction and possibilities to go beyond it, *Geoforum*, 42(5): 520–529.

Camagni, R. (1991) *Innovation Networks: Spatial perspective*. London: Belhaven Press.

Cattell, R. B. (1966) The scree test for the number of factors, *Multivariate Behavioral Research*, 1(2): 245–276.

Centre for Economic Business Research (2012) City jobs down by 90,000 during recession. News release 9 May, available from www.cebr.com.

Clark, G. L. (2002) London in the European financial services industry: locational advantages and product complementarities, *Journal of Economic Geography*, 2(4): 433–454.

Cook, G. A. S., Pandit, N. R., Beaverstock, J. V., Taylor, P. J. and Pain, K. (2007) The role of location in knowledge creation and diffusion: evidence of centripetal and centrifugal forces in the City of London financial services agglomeration, *Environment and Planning A*, 39(6): 1325–1345.

Cook, G. A. S., Pandit, N. R. and Beaverstock, J. V. (2011) *Environment and Planning A*, 43(12): 2918–2933.

Cook, Gary A. S., Pandit, Naresh R., Lööf, H. and Johansson, B. (2013) Clustering, MNEs and innovation: who benefits, and how? *International Journal of the Economics of Business*, 20(2): 203–227.

Dunning, J. H. (1998) Location and the multinational enterprise: A neglected factor?, *Journal of International Business Studies*, 29(1): 45–66.

Eccles, R. G. and Crane, D. B. (1988) *Doing Deals. Investment banks at work*. Boston, MA: HBS Press.

Field, A. (2009) *Discovering Statistics Using SPSS*. London: Sage.

Florida, R. (2002) The economic geography of talent, *Annals of the American Association of Geographers*, 92(4): 743–755.

Gertler, M. S. (2003) Tacit knowledge and the economic geography of context, or The undefinable tacitness of being (there), *Journal of Economic Geography*, 3(1): 75–99.

Goffman, E. (1982) *Interaction Rituals: Essays on face-to-face behaviour*. New York: Pantheon.

Golding, T. (2001) *The City: Inside the great expectation machine*. London: Prentice Hall.

Gordon, I. and McCann, P. (2000) Industrial clusters: complexes, agglomeration and/ or social networks, *Urban Studies*, 37(3): 513–532.

Hendry, C. and Brown, J. (2006) Organizational networking in UK biotechnology clusters, *British Journal of Management*, 17(1): 55–73.

Hervás-Oliver, J. L. (2015). How do multinational enterprises co-locate in industrial districts? An introduction to the integration of alternative explanations from international business and economic geography literatures, *Journal of Regional Research*, 32: 115–132.

Hervás-Oliver, J. L. and Albors-Garrigós, J. (2014). Are technology gatekeepers renewing clusters? Understanding gatekeepers and their dynamics across cluster life cycles, *Entrepreneurship and Regional Development*, 26(5–6): 431–452.

Karlsson, C. (2008) (ed.) *Handbook of Research on Cluster Theory*. Cheltenham: Elgar.

Kim, S. (2007) Changes in the nature of urban spatial structures in the United States, 1890–2000, *Journal of Regional Science*, 47(2): 273–287.

Malmberg, A. and Maskell, P. (2002) The elusive concept of localisation economies: towards a knowledge-based theory of spatial clustering, *Environment and Planning A*, 34(3): 429–449.

Marshall, A. (1890) *Principles of Economics*. London: Macmillan.

Martin, R. (1994) Stateless monies, global financial integration and national economic autonomy: the end of geography? In: S. Corbridge, R. L. Martin and N. Thrift (eds) *Money, Power and Space*, Oxford: Blackwell, pp. 253–278.

Martin, R. and Sunley, P. (2003) Deconstructing clusters: chaotic concept or policy panacea? *Journal of Economic Geography*, 3(1): 5–35.

Maskell, P. and Malmberg, A. (2007) Myopia, knowledge development and cluster evolution, *Journal of Economic Geography*, 7(5): 603–618.

Menzel, M. and Fornahl, D. (2009) Cluster life cycles – dimensions and rationales of cluster evolution, *Industrial and Corporate Change*, 19(1): 205–238.

Narula, R. (2014). Exploring the paradox of competence-creating subsidiaries: balancing bandwith and dispersion in MNEs, *Long Range Planning*, 47(1–2): 4–15.

O'Brien, R. (1991) *Global Financial Integration: The end of geography*. London: Pinter.

Pandit, N. R., Cook, G. A. S. and Swann, G. M. P. (2008) Financial services clustering. In C. Karlsson (ed.) *Handbook of Research on Clusters*, Cheltenham: Edward Elgar, pp. 249–260.

Pinch, S., Henry, N., Jenkins, M. and Tallman, S. (2003) From 'industrial districts' to 'knowledge clusters': a model of knowledge dissemination and competitive advantage in industrial agglomerations, *Journal of Economic Geography*, 3(4): 373–388.

Porter, M. E. (1998) Clusters and competition. In M. E. Porter (ed.) *On Competition*, Cambridge, MA: HBS Press, pp. 197–271.

Pyke, F., Becattini, G. and Sengenberger, W. (eds) (1990) *Industrial Districts and Inter-firm Cooperation in Italy*. Geneva: International Institute for Labour Studies.

Scott, A. J. (1988) *New Industrial Spaces: Flexible production organisation and regional development in North America and Western Europe*. London: Pion.

Sjoberg, O. and Sjoholm, F. (2002) Common ground? Prospects for integrating the economic geography of geographers and economists, *Environment and Planning A*, 34(3): 467–486.

Stevens, J. P. (1992) *Applied Multivariate Statistics for the Social Sciences*. Hillside, NJ: Erlbaum.

Storper, M. and Venables, A. J. (2004) Buzz: face-to-face contact and the urban economy, *Journal of Economic Geography*, 4(4): 351–370.

Swann, G. M. P. (2009). *The Economics of Innovation*. Cheltenham: Elgar.

Swann, G. M. P., Prevezer, M. and Stout, D. (eds) (1998) *The Dynamics of Industrial Clustering: International comparisons in computing and biotechnology.* Oxford: Oxford University Press.

Thrift, N. (1994) On the social and cultural determinants of international financial centres: the case of the City of London. In S. Corbridge, R. L. Martin and N. Thrift (eds) *Money, Power and Space*, Oxford: Blackwell, pp. 327–355.

Tickell, A. (2003) Finance and localities. In G. L. Clark, M. P. Feldman and M. S. Gertler (eds) *The Oxford Handbook of Economic Geography*, Oxford: Oxford University Press, pp. 230–247.

Z/Yen (2015) Global Financial Centre Index 17. March (available from www.zyen.com).

3 The dual role of multinational corporations in cluster evolution

When you dance with the devil, you wait for the song to stop

Christian R. Østergaard, Kristian H. Reinau and Eunkyung Park

3.1 Introduction

The role of multinational corporations in clusters is a growing topic in the literature (Santangelo 2009; Mudambi and Swift 2012; Sedita *et al.* 2013; Mudambi and Santangelo 2015). MNCs are increasingly locating their activities within clusters in various countries and thereby affecting the dynamics of the clusters (Birkinshaw and Hood 2000). The entry of MNC subsidiaries is often seen as something positive, since they bring in new resources to the cluster and provide access to global networks (Giuliani *et al.* 2005; De Propris and Driffield 2006). The MNC subsidiaries especially allow the cluster as a whole to be connected to other clusters in a similar field across the world, which is becoming increasingly important for achieving global competitiveness (Mudambi and Swift 2012). However, MNCs could also have negative influences on the cluster. For one thing, they are well known for being footloose in times of crisis (Görg and Strobl 2003; Østergaard and Park 2015). In addition, the MNC subsidiaries' participation in local networks and their ability to choose their own technological search depend on the mandates that the subsidiaries have (Cantwell and Mudambi 2005; Østergaard and Park 2015; Mudambi and Santangelo 2015). This suggests that MNCs might have a dual role in cluster evolution in that they could exert both positive and negative impact over time.

The increasing focus on MNC subsidiaries in clusters is linked to a growing awareness that clusters also participate in global value chains, not only in the local value chain (Humphrey and Schmitz 2002; Giuliani *et al.* 2005). In this line of literature, the focus is placed on the possible upgrading of the cluster through insertion into the value chain, mainly from the perspective of developing economies (Humphrey and Schmitz 2002). However, the participation in the global value chain might have an effect on clusters regardless of their position in the value chain, and it is the intention of this chapter to shed light on how a cluster with firms in the higher end of the value chain is influenced by relations in the global value chain in the course of its evolution.

In cluster evolution literature, other clusters in the same field and the global value chains are seen as a part of the external environment that affects cluster evolution (Menzel and Fornahl 2010; Martin and Sunley 2011). It is recognised that clusters might change their development path by diversifying into other parts of the value chain, but surprisingly little attention is given to the effect of the global value chain and to the role of MNC subsidiaries in cluster evolution. Thus the impact of the individual MNC strategies, subsidiary mandates and subsidiary capabilities on cluster evolution has not been discussed sufficiently. Consequently, it is often neglected that, when clusters face changes in technological trajectories or in industry boundaries, the response of the MNC subsidiaries depends on their strategic independence given by the MNCs. When the subsidiary has limited strategic independence, the direction of technological search is determined by the headquarters of the MNC located elsewhere, which indicates that the technological evolution of the cluster can largely be influenced by the MNC strategies, depending on the importance of the MNC activities in the cluster. Metaphorically, the cluster will continue to dance to the song chosen by the MNCs. Therefore it is necessary to study the micro-dynamics of interactions within and between firms in clusters to understand the benefits and hidden costs of MNCs in clusters and their effect on cluster evolution.

The purpose of this chapter is to analyse the changes that occur on a micro-level when MNCs enter a cluster and how the MNC subsidiaries affect cluster evolution. Using detailed case studies of cluster companies during the life cycle of a wireless communications cluster in northern Denmark and an analysis of patent data, this chapter illuminates the impact of MNCs on cluster evolution, specifically their dual role in changing the network within and outside the cluster and affecting the technological heterogeneity of the cluster.

3.2   Theories on cluster evolution, global value chains and MNCs

The literature on clusters has often focused on the role of internal factors, such as Marshallian externalities and spin-off activities, when explaining cluster evolution. Some authors have made limited remarks on the role of external linkages in relation to the evolution of clusters. Menzel and Fornahl (2010) argue that cluster evolution depends on changes in the diversity and heterogeneity of knowledge in the cluster. They mention that cluster firms' networks with outside firms are important in bringing new knowledge to the cluster. In explaining the adaptive cycles of clusters, Martin and Sunley (2011) point out that the firms' connection to competitors or collaborators outside the cluster could be an important source of innovation. Bathelt *et al.* (2004) also argue that external linkage to firms located outside the cluster is necessary for cluster development. These external 'pipelines' bring new knowledge to the cluster that can be diffused to other firms through local 'buzz'. Local 'buzz' is the information flow within the cluster through various types of formal and informal networks, which is a key source of knowledge spillover (Bathelt *et al.* 2004). Although some authors have made remarks on how external linkages may enhance the adaptability of the cluster and increase the heterogeneity of knowledge, external relations still do not receive enough attention as the driver for changes in cluster evolution (Humphrey and Schmitz 2002; Bathelt *et al.* 2004; Giuliani *et al.* 2005).

3.2.1   Global value chain

The concept of the global value chain illustrates how firms and regions are involved in the global division of labour for producing certain products and services (Mudambi 2008). It explains that, as firms become more specialised in their activities, the production processes are more finely divided and allocated to firms located in different parts of the world. Firms in clusters are also connected to other firms located outside the cluster through buyer–supplier relations in the global value chains. External relations created by the global value chain are one of the channels through which cluster firms can get access to external knowledge and thereby increase the heterogeneity of knowledge.

In literature on global value chains, it is also acknowledged that clusters' insertion in global value chains may allow the clusters to realise 'upgrading', which is defined as 'innovating to increase value added' (Giuliani *et al.* 2005, 552). This suggests that clusters with firms that have global buyers get opportunities for gaining knowledge that can be used for innovation. According to Humphrey and Schmitz (2002), firms can achieve four types of upgrading through their participation in the global value chain: process, product, functional and intersectoral upgrading. The authors also note, however, that the governance mode in buyer–supplier relationships affects possibilities for firms to learn from their customers. Depending on the governance mode, which can take the form of arm's-length market relations, networks, quasi hierarchy or hierarchy (Humphrey and Schmitz 2002), the extent of a key firm's control and thereby the interdependence of suppliers in the value chain will vary. This will in turn influence the possibilities of firms and clusters to upgrade. Certain buyers will try to keep the supplying firms in a specific part of the value chain to avoid the erosion of the firms' position in the value chain (Humphrey and Schmitz 2002).

The literature on upgrading in global value chains has mostly focused on production-intensive, low-tech clusters in less developed countries and the possibilities for manufacturing firms to become more innovative and R&D intensive. However, mechanisms for upgrading and learning in buyer–supplier relations can also be applied to the high-tech clusters that need to sustain and increase the competitiveness of the cluster. For these clusters, the challenge is not moving up the value chain but keeping the inflow of knowledge from other actors in the value chain.

3.2.2   *Multinational corporations*

MNCs in clusters play an important role in creating global pipelines as well. By design, MNCs can be understood as networks of organisations that are connected through organisational pipelines across national borders. Through these pipelines, MNCs are able to bring new knowledge to the cluster and also connect it to other clusters. Organisational proximity among the entities within the MNCs facilitates knowledge transfer over geographical distances (Boschma 2005).

The entry of MNC subsidiaries in clusters has recently gained attention in the cluster literature (Santangelo 2009; Mudambi and Santangelo 2015). When MNCs enter a cluster, they bring resources, such as technology, investments and networks, but they also increase wages and poach skilled employees from other cluster firms (Østergaard and Park 2015). In some cases, they legitimise the cluster, thereby strengthening the cluster's identity (Mudambi and Santangelo 2015), which might attract other MNCs or other firms that have buyer–supplier relations with the MNC.

Whether or not MNC subsidiaries become an integrated part of local networks depends on their entry mode (Mudambi and Santangelo 2015). Some MNCs enter a cluster through acquisitions of local firms to gain access to local knowledge and networks, while others enter through greenfield investments. The development phase of the cluster also affects the types of MNC entry (Sedita *et al.* 2013). Mudambi and Santangelo (2015) argue that the timing of the entry is important in an emerging cluster in regions characterised as shallow resource pools. First movers often achieve a competence-creating mandate and benefit from local knowledge resources. Second movers find that these resources are 'taken' and therefore often are competence-exploiting. However, the first and second movers gradually transform and build local resources, which create agglomeration externalities and make the location more attractive. Therefore late movers might enter through acquisitions of local firms to enter local networks with a competence-creating motive or with a greenfield investment if the agglomeration externalities are still weak (Mudambi and Santangelo 2015).

How the subsidiaries of MNCs influence cluster dynamics depends much on their mandate. Cantwell and Mudambi (2005) describe how some MNC subsidiaries are given a competence-creating mandate that allows them to adapt to local needs, network with local actors and develop new technologies, while others are given a competence-exploiting mandate and are focused on exploiting the MNCs' existing knowledge. Santangelo (2009) shows how competence-creating/knowledge-seeking subsidiaries are more embedded in the local economy and collaborate with local universities, while the competence-exploiting/market-seeking subsidiaries do not collaborate with local universities, local suppliers or buyers. If the MNCs are co-located with market rivals, then the competence-creating subsidiaries are even more active in establishing linkages with local firms. The opposite reaction occurs in competence-exploiting subsidiaries due to the fear of unintended knowledge spillover to competitors.

Similarly, the decision power and autonomy of the subsidiaries impact how these firms influence cluster evolution. Reinau (2011) argues that local cooperation between firms in a cluster becomes much more difficult if it is between two MNC subsidiaries than if it is between indigenous firms because of differences in the extent of local decision power. The subsidiary mandate and its autonomy are related constructs that still need be understood separately. Cantwell and Mudambi (2005) do not find evidence that the strategic independence (autonomy) of a subsidiary increases the likelihood of firms achieving competence-creating mandates, but they find that once firms are mandated, the autonomy increases the intensity of R&D.

Being part of an MNC, and therefore being dependent on external decision making, not only affects interaction patterns within the cluster but also affects how these firms react when they face disruptions and changes in the cluster. Clusters are typically defined within a certain industry boundary, which also determines the technological specialisation of the cluster. However, this technological specialisation is not constant; it develops continuously over time, following the technological trajectory of the industry (Dosi 1982). The main technological trajectory in a cluster might converge with other technological trajectories, forming a new trajectory, meaning that the cluster may go through a transformation in terms of its technological focus. When this happens, foreign firms are more footloose compared with indigenous firms and are more prone to leave a cluster if the direction of the change does not follow their own technological focus (Görg and Strobl 2003; Østergaard and Park 2015). Decision making regarding an MNC's entry and exit lies typically in the hands of entities high up in the hierarchy; therefore, subsidiaries have limited decision power in these matters.

In summation, the entry of foreign MNCs in a cluster clearly affects the cluster's evolution. The entry of MNCs with a competence-creating mandate brings resources, new knowledge and external networks to the cluster. It also helps to legitimise a cluster, strengthen its identity, create possible agglomeration externalities and attract other firms. However, they also increase wages and poach human capital. In addition, MNC subsidiaries with a competence-exploiting mandate might limit local interaction in the cluster. Furthermore, even for competence-creating subsidiaries, there are limits to their technological search and their possibilities to react to disruptions in the market or technologies. Therefore, although an MNC's entry into a cluster may create positive impact for cluster evolution, it may also limit the adaptability of the cluster.

3.3   Method and data

This chapter is based on a detailed case study of the wireless communications cluster in northern Denmark from its emergence to its decline. This cluster is a critical case of a high-tech cluster in an advanced economy, and the role played by MNCs in this cluster is likely to resemble the role of MNCs in other high-tech clusters (Flyvbjerg 2006). The data used in this chapter are both qualitative and quantitative in nature. First of all, this chapter presents a detailed account of all the firms that have existed in the cluster from 1963 to 2011, noting the entry, exit, merger and acquisition of the firms and documenting the number of firms and employees in the cluster over the years. Several researchers have followed the general history and some specific events of the firms and the cluster based on personal interviews with the firms and the cluster organisation. This chapter also draws on nine interviews with the eight largest cluster firms and the local university conducted in 1992. These interviews were originally conducted by Bent Dalum for an EU FAST project (see also Dalum 1993). This paper additionally draws on forty interviews and observations in cluster firms from 2006 to 2011 conducted by Reinau (2011). A part of the empirical data was supplemented by information found in the public and private archives, including newspaper articles and material used in older studies of the cluster (see also Østergaard and Park 2015). Second, data on patents are used to analyse innovation activities in the cluster. Patents granted by the US Patent Office (USPTO) within computer and communication technology[1] with at least one inventor located in the cluster region are identified as patents created in the cluster. For those patents, information on inventors and assignees was collected to study global connections in terms of inventor networks in both local and foreign firms.

3.4   Analyses

3.4.1   *Evolution of the mobile communications industry*

For many years changes in the mobile phone industry followed a rather stable technological development trajectory with jumps between different generations of mobile communication standards. These generations evolved from the first analog, country-based standards (1G) in the 1980s, such as NMT and AMPS, to the continent-based, digital communications standards (2G) in the 1990s, such as GSM, D-AMPS and CDMA, as well as the worldwide communications standards (3G) in the 2000s, such as CDMA2000, W-CDMA and TS-CDMA, and finally the newer 4G standards, such as LTE. Each of these constituted important technological shifts that posed a major disruptive challenge to firms in the industry. They allowed for new entrants in the industry but also marked industry shake-outs, and the firms in the industry became very large. Although the introduction of these new standards was planned and expected as it was based on international cooperation and competition between the players of the industry and public authorities, it still created disruptive changes every time the transition took place from one generation to another. Of all the transitions, the rollout of 3G in 2006 proved to be a disruptive innovation that changed the entire industry.

The technological development with different standards shadows a fast technological development and improvement of performance in the different components of the mobile phone, such as antennas, RF technology, FM radio, speakers, headphones, base bands, protocol stacks, screens, mechanical interfaces, batteries, cameras, menu systems, user interfaces, power management and other software (e.g. games and apps). The underlying technological development of mobile phones combined with the new possibilities of high-speed data communications in the 3G network constituted complementary innovations. These changed the industry's technological trajectory and subsequently redefined industry boundaries as focus shifted to users and applications rather than connectivity and speed. Thus, new types of complementary assets, such as app stores and music services, became a key competitive feature. At the same time, former key competitive features, such as radio frequency (RF) solution hardware and antennas, had nearly become standard commodities and no longer core competitive technology. As a result, the entry of Apple and Google with the iOS and Android systems in 2007 and 2008 introduced new business models, which transformed the mobile communications industry and caused the decline of former giants Nokia, Motorola, Ericsson, LG and Siemens.

The disruption to the industry and the subsequent decline of these large MNCs also changed the global value chains and linkages in the industry. Subsequently, the spatial configuration of the industry changed, and the clusters in which the declining MNCs were present suddenly faced significant challenges.

3.4.2 MNCs in the wireless communications cluster in North Jutland

The first company in the cluster was established in the early 1960s and became successful in producing and selling maritime communication equipment. During the first two decades after its establishment, this company became the seedbed for spin-offs as some of its employees created new firms in the related field of wireless communication. These companies were mainly specialised in technologies for Nordic standard mobile telephony (NMT), which represented the 1G technology standard in Nordic countries. In the late 1980s, when the technology generation shifted to 2G, a joint venture (DC Development) by two cluster firms (Dancall and Cetelco) succeeded in developing some basic modules of pan-European GSM phones, which was one of the dominant technology standards for 2G phones. However, the development work left both companies drained financially, and as a consequence, both were acquired by MNCs (Amstrad and Hagenuk). Another outcome of joint venture was that a local identity emerged in the cluster, where a generation of electrical engineers worked together within the GSM field. Furthermore, a strong competence in radio frequency technology was created in the cluster, stemming from the joint venture. This became apparent when a number of companies specialised in RF, for example ATL Technology, a spin-off from Cetelco, which later was acquired by Texas Instruments (TI) and grew to become one of the most successful companies in the region.

During the 1990s, more spin-offs and other new entrants were established based on the leadership in GSM technologies. During this period, foreign firms began to enter the cluster through either greenfield investments or acquisition of local firms. Examples of MNCs that entered the cluster in the 1990s included Analog Devices, Lucent, Bosch Telecom, Maxon, Texas Instruments, L.M. Ericsson and Nokia. From 2000 onwards, the list of foreign firms expanded with the entry of Flextronics, Siemens, Infineon, Motorola and Intel, among others. While some foreign firms were involved in manufacturing activities, the majority of them focused on R&D activities, exploiting the world-leading research at the local university and the highly skilled engineering graduates from the university. The entry of MNCs and the general growth of the cluster had an effect on the local labour market. In the late 1990s the increasing demand for engineers led to rapidly increasing wages but also attracted engineers to the cluster. It became difficult for non-cluster firms to hire electrical engineers because the cluster firms paid higher wages. In many instances, the MNCs' subsidiaries, which upscaled very fast, paid the highest wages and also offered other benefits, such as stock options.

The number of foreign MNCs in the cluster and their contributions to the total employment in the cluster from 1992 to 2010 are shown in figures 3.1 and 3.2. Although MNCs make up less than half of the firm population (the highest share was 43.5 per cent in 2006), their contribution to employment is much higher. In the early 2000s, foreign MNCs employed almost 80 per cent of the labour force in the cluster.

After the turn of millennium, the mobile communication industry went through another technology shift from 2G to 3G. This disruption was a game changer for many in the industry, affecting both foreign and local firms in the cluster. As many cluster firms subsequently lost their technology leadership, the cluster began to decline, primarily due to a lack of cluster adaptive capability, mainly caused by a technological and cognitive lock-in (Østergaard and Park 2015). We show that, among other factors, the existence of MNC subsidiaries influenced the adaptive capability of the cluster over time. The role of the MNCs is discussed further in the next section. As the figures show, firm population and especially employment decreased starting in 2003. In the course of the downturn, the two core MNCs, Motorola and Texas Instruments, ceased their R&D activities in the cluster, which led to many highly skilled engineers being laid off in 2009.

3.4.3   The role of MNCs in cluster evolution

The entry of MNCs in the emergence phase was positive for the evolution of the cluster. The two main companies were in financial trouble because of high development costs related to the GSM technology. An interview with the founder of Cetelco revealed that the company needed financial support from

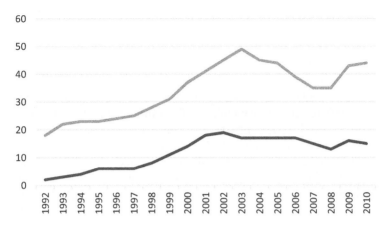

Figure 3.1 Number of firms in the cluster.
Note: The blue line shows the total number of firms in the cluster, while the red line shows the number of MNCs subsidiaries.

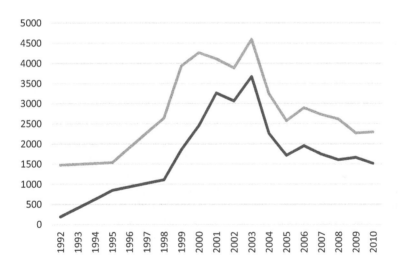

Figure 3.2 Level of employment.
Note: The blue line shows the total number employment in the cluster, while the red line shows the number of employees in MNCs subsidiaries.

Hagenuk to develop GSM competences, while Hagenuk needed Cetelco to gain these competences. The MNCs mainly entered through the acquisition of local firms and brought in important financial resources that allowed their subsidiaries to expand their production and R&D activities. They also brought new technological competences and access to new markets. In this phase the mobile communications industry was becoming increasingly international, but the markets were small and fragmented by different technological standards. The market was growing, and capabilities related to the mass production of electronics were becoming more important. In an interview from 1992, the head of Cetelco (owned by German Hagenuk) explained that the ownership offered financial stability, access to the large German market, access to the economics of scale in the sourcing of components, and help in improving the company's production capabilities. The rationale for the entry of MNCs in the growth and decline phases was somewhat similar to their rationale in the emergence phase. The MNCs still entered to exploit existing local competences and brought in financial resources, networks and knowledge.

In the emerging phase of the cluster, most cluster firms were involved in all activities in the value chain, from R&D to design, manufacturing, logistics, marketing and after-sales services. However, some of the early firms (e.g. T-COM and RRI) introduced a new business model in the cluster. They focused on R&D and design and sold turnkey solutions to other firms, which then manufactured and sold the mobile phones as their own brand. Cetelco also offered OEM products for other firms (e.g. Hitachi and Philips). The MNCs that entered the cluster in the early 1990s also focused on R&D and design. Most of them entered by acquiring local firms to access their knowledge and competences. Many local firms collaborated with the MNCs before they were acquired by them.

During the growth phase the cluster was increasingly located in the high end of the value chain, since the new entrants were only doing R&D. The manufacturing and also marketing activities gradually moved away from the cluster, and in 2004 the last mobile phone manufacturing activities in the cluster shut down. The cluster firms positioned themselves in the high end of the value chain, and the subsidiaries became more focused on R&D in very specific technologies. This distributed R&D effort of the MNCs resulted in the rapid growth of the subsidiaries, but it also made them even more detached from the market and limited their options to explore other technologies and business opportunities. Therefore, it became difficult to see major changes in the market in the mid-2000s. In the cluster, the key to survival was seen as additional 3G and 4G development work. However, the introduction of the iPhone and the Android system changed the key competitive features in the industry. The focus on 3G and 4G technology rather than the new competitive features made the cluster unable to adapt to the disruption.

MNCs entered the cluster to exploit local knowledge and the subsidiaries were given development mandates, but the degree of strategic independence became limited. After the successful introduction of a first-generation GSM phone by the joint venture DC Development, the local managers of the two companies behind the joint venture (Dancall and Cetelco) wanted to expand the mandate to also include the development of a second-generation GSM phone in order to stay on the technological frontier. However, this move was eventually blocked by Hagenuk. One of the reasons for this action was that

Dancall had begun a formal collaboration with Philips and Hagenuk did not want to collaborate with Philips. A manager of a cluster company that had been acquired by Korean Maxon explained that he had to ask Maxon whenever his company wanted to collaborate with other companies. Thus the subsidiaries' strategic independence was limited. However, the development engineers in the various companies continued to have widespread, local, informal networks through which they shared knowledge. In the later stages of the cluster evolution, local interaction between cluster firms became increasingly limited because the subsidiaries were focused on the internal MNC networks and markets.

As most foreign firms established R&D centres in the cluster, they were deeply involved in innovation activities in the cluster. An analysis of the patenting activities of the cluster firms reveals the positive influence of MNCs on innovation in the cluster. First, foreign MNCs contributed significantly to the level of innovation activities in the cluster. Table 3.1 shows the number of patents granted by the USPTO within the field of computers and communication, with at least one inventor located in the region of North Jutland. A comparison of the number of patents owned by local and foreign firms shows that patenting activities in this region were mostly driven by foreign firms.

Furthermore, foreign firms allowed the cluster to gain access to knowledge outside the cluster by encouraging global collaboration on innovation activities through their organisational pipeline. Table 3.2 shows that foreign firms engaged in a higher degree of global collaboration in innovation activities. Patents granted to local firms include only three inventors located outside

Table 3.1 Number of patents granted to the cluster firms, 1992–2008

	Local	*Foreign*	*Total*
1992	1	0	1
1993	0	0	0
1994	0	1	1
1995	0	1	1
1996	0	0	0
1997	2	3	5
1998	3	1	4
1999	2	12	14
2000	2	5	7
2001	4	11	15
2002	2	27	29
2003	4	5	9
2004	2	2	4
2005	1	6	7
2006	0	10	10
2007	1	5	6
2008	0	3	3
Total	24	92	116

Table 3.2 Global collaboration in patenting activities

	Local firm	*Foreign firm*	*Total*
Local inventor	44	180	133
Foreign inventor	3	130	224
Total	47	310	357

Denmark, while the number of foreign inventors in the patents granted to foreign firms is much higher. Foreign multinationals are likely to have a network of R&D centres distributed around the world, which allows international collaboration within the organisational boundary. Figures 3.3 and 3.4, by mapping the locations of co-inventors in foreign firms and local firms, illustrate the stark contrast of the degree of international collaboration on innovation.

The dual role of the MNCs was also seen in the cluster decline phase. Many of the MNCs were footloose and chose to close their subsidiaries in the cluster as a response to the disruption in the industry rather than make efforts to adapt to the disruption in the cluster. However, a few MNCs also entered the cluster seeking specific competences – for instance, Molex hired seven former Motorola employees working with antenna technology and also bought equipment from Motorola when it closed down in 2009.

3.4.4   An example of the role of an MNC in the evolution of the cluster

The story of ATL Research illustrates in more detail the role of MNCs in the evolution of the cluster. ATL Research was a local spin-off company with thirty employees, which was acquired by Texas Instruments in 1999 and renamed TI Denmark. It became a success story, reaching around 250 employees at its peak in 2006 before a downturn and its closure in 2009. ATL Research was acquired by TI because of its specific competences in making RF solutions and ability to integrate them with base-band processors.

Interviews with the founders of ATL Research revealed that, from their perspective, the driver for the acquisition was changes in the market that made it increasingly difficult for them to survive. The big players either developed their own RF competences or acquired those competences through acquisitions of companies such as ATL Research. From a cluster perspective, acquisitions by MNCs were not only about getting access to the resources and networks of the MNCs but also about survival.

The acquisition gave access to both resources and a global R&D network, but the subsidiary did not have much strategic independence. The former CEOs were 'just' managers and the decision power lay in remote headquarters, which was made clear from the beginning. R&D engineers in TI Denmark felt the MNC's control even in their daily work. They went from having virtually no rules for how to approach solutions to being part of a system in which

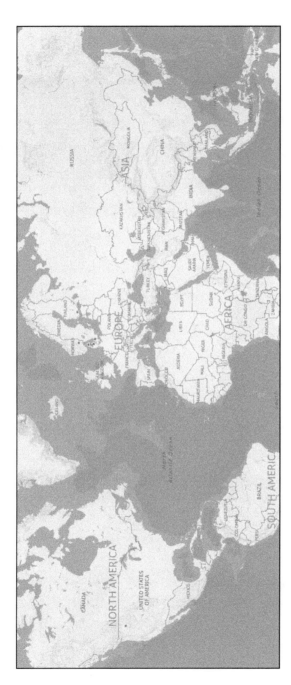

Figure 3.3 Co-inventor location of patents granted to local firms in communication in North Jutland.

Note: The dots represent the locations of co-inventors of patents assigned to firms located in the cluster.

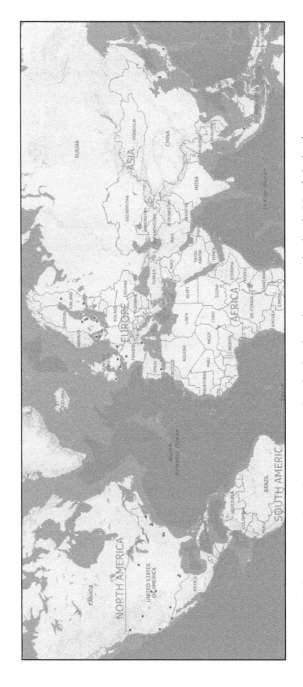

Figure 3.4 Co-inventor location of patents granted to foreign firms in communication in North Jutland.
Note: The dots represent the locations of co-inventors of patents assigned to firms located in the cluster.

different agendas from different parts of the MNC had a significant impact on R&D work. The R&D workers also experienced increased bureaucracy in decisions on technical solutions.

It also became apparent to the local management in TI Denmark that they were exposed to competition from other TI subsidiaries. More specifically, other TI sites started to build competences and gain work tasks and responsibilities in the RF areas too. Therefore, to survive, the subsidiary had to constantly work on getting new work tasks and building new competences. As GSM technology matured and GSM development had less and less value, there were many internal discussions about what new wireless technologies should be worked on in the future. Despite the concern, the GSM solutions that TI Denmark was working on became low-cost solutions for phones aimed at the third world rather than newer smartphones and 3G technologies. Towards the end, it became unclear what unique RF tasks, knowledge and competences TI Denmark possessed. TI Denmark closed down in 2009.

3.5   Conclusions

This chapter shows that MNC subsidiaries can play an important role for the evolution of a high-tech cluster in an advanced economy. The MNCs enter with knowledge-seeking behaviour to exploit local knowledge and competences. They also give their subsidiaries a development mandate, but the degree of the subsidiaries' strategic independence varies. MNCs bring resources to the cluster, such as financial resources, technology, knowledge, innovation networks and access to new markets. The financial resources help the cluster companies survive and boost the expansion of the subsidiaries. MNCs internationalise the innovation networks in the cluster and allow for collaboration on patents across vast geographical distances. MNCs also bring production technology and provide easy access to foreign markets. As a result, MNCs enter in the cluster's emergence phase and actually support the survival and growth of the cluster. This positive effect of MNCs on cluster evolution has often been overlooked in literature that focuses on internal factors in clusters.

However, there is also a dark side to MNCs' entry in a cluster, which includes changes in local interaction, lack of strategic independence and a narrowed scope of activities in the value chain. The fine slicing of the value chain and the specialisation in R&D activities of the subsidiaries leads to a lack of market knowledge and increasing dependence on auxiliary competences in the MNC organisations. The lack of strategic independence also decreases the scope of the subsidiaries' technological search and possibilities for exploring new business areas. The cluster thus becomes more vulnerable to market disruptions. As the subsidiaries get more involved in internal competition for development projects within the MNC networks and do not have much decision power and strategic independence, their interaction and collaboration with other local actors is less prioritised over time.

This study argues that MNCs should be treated differently compared with indigenous companies in the cluster literature due to their specific characteristics described above. MNCs contribute with much more complex dynamics to cluster evolution than their role as potential sources of external knowledge suggested by Menzel and Fornahl (2010) and Martin and Sunley (2011). Instead, studies need to include detailed analyses of the subsidiaries' mandates and their strategic independence.

Note

1 Classification by Hall *et al.* (2001).

References

Bathelt, H., A. Malmberg and P. Maskell. 2004. 'Clusters and knowledge: local buzz, global pipelines and the process of knowledge creation.' *Progress in Human Geography* 28 (1): 31–56.

Birkinshaw, J. and N. Hood. 2000. 'Characteristics of foreign subsidiaries in industry clusters.' *Journal of International Business Studies* 31 (1): 141–54.

Boschma, R. 2005. 'Proximity and innovation: a critical assessment.' *Regional Studies* 39 (1): 61–74.

Cantwell, J. A. and R. Mudambi. 2005. 'MNE competence-creating subsidiary mandates.' *Strategic Management Journal* 26 (12): 1109–28.

Dalum, B. 1993. 'North Jutland: a 'technology district' in radio communications technology?' In EC/Monitor-Fast, *FAST Dossier: Continental Europe: Science, Technology and Community Cohesion.* Volume 26. Brussels.

De Propris, L. and N. Driffield. 2006. 'The importance of clusters for spillovers from foreign direct investment and technology sourcing.' *Cambridge Journal of Economics* 30 (2): 277–91.

Dosi, G. 1982. 'Technological paradigms and technological trajectories.' *Research Policy* 11 (3): 147–62.

Flyvbjerg, B. 2006. 'Five misunderstandings about case-study research.' *Qualitative Inquiry* 12 (2): 219–45.

Giuliani, E., C. Pietrobelli and R. Rabellotti. 2005. 'Upgrading in global value chains: lessons from Latin American clusters.' *World Development* 33 (4): 549–73.

Görg, H. and E. Strobl. 2003. '"Footloose" multinationals?' *The Manchester School* 71 (1): 1–19.

Hall, B. H., A. B. Jaffe and M. Trajtenberg. 2001. 'The NBER Patent Citation Data File: lessons, insights and methodological tools.' NBER Working Paper No. 8498. The National Bureau of Economic Research.

Humphrey, J. and H. Schmitz. 2002. 'How does insertion in global value chains affect upgrading in industrial clusters?' *Regional Studies* 36 (9): 1017–27.

Martin, R. and P. Sunley. 2011. 'Conceptualizing cluster evolution: beyond the life cycle model?' *Regional Studies* 45 (10): 1299–318.

Menzel, M. P. and D. Fornahl. 2010. 'Cluster life cycles – dimensions and rationales of cluster evolution.' *Industrial and Corporate Change* 19 (1): 205–38.

Mudambi, R. 2008. 'Location, control and innovation in knowledge-intensive industries.' *Journal of Economic Geography* 8 (5): 699–725.

Mudambi, R. and G. D. Santangelo. 2015. 'From shallow resource pools to emerging clusters: the role of multinational enterprise subsidiaries in peripheral areas.' *Regional Studies*, published online.

Mudambi, R. and T. Swift. 2012. 'Multinational enterprises and the geographical clustering of innovation.' *Industry and Innovation* 19 (1): 1–21.

Østergaard, C. R. and E. Park. 2015. 'What makes clusters decline? A study on disruption and evolution of a high-tech cluster in Denmark.' *Regional Studies* 49 (5): 834–49.

Reinau, K. H. 2011. *Local Clusters in a Globalized World*. Aalborg, Denmark: Aalborg University Press.

Santangelo, G. D. 2009. 'MNCs and linkages creation: evidence from a peripheral area.' *Journal of World Business* 44 (2): 92–205.

Sedita, S., A. Caloffi and F. Belussi. 2013. 'Heterogeneity of MNEs entry modes in industrial clusters: an evolutionary approach based on the cluster life cycle model.' Barcelona: DRUID Society Conference.

4 Multinational corporations and cluster evolution

The case of Cosentino in the Spanish marble cluster

Jose A. Aznar-Sanchez, Anselmo Carretero-Gómez and Luis J. Belmonte-Ureña

4.1 Introduction

Most traditional cluster studies follow a static approach (Martin and Sunley, 2003). In fact, the broad and comprehensive understanding of cluster evolution still constitutes an emerging topic in different disciplines (Hervás-Oliver, 2015). Clusters are dynamic units which emerge, transform themselves and reconvert or disappear. It is necessary to adopt a dynamic perspective for the cluster study in order to know the reasons why the cluster evolves, how these evolution mechanisms work and the role the different cluster actors play (Wang *et al.*, 2014). To study the genesis and evolution of clusters, the analytical framework of the so-called life cycle model can be used though the prevailing discussion over its validity (Boschma and Fornahl, 2011; Martin and Sunley, 2011). The ideal-type phases of cluster life cycle described by the literature are three: origin, development and maturity (Menzel and Fornahl, 2010). In the origin stage (emergence), cluster-specific conditions are not present, but the cluster can host some historical sediment of knowledge and competencies. The development stage is characterised by the emergence of a set of cluster-specific institutions, knowledge and competencies. It shows a progressive increase in the number of local firms, and a thickening of the web of relations among them and the external context. In the maturity stage, the growth rate of local firms gradually slows down, as does the virtuous cycle of semi-automatic reproduction of cluster-specific conditions (Belussi and Sedita, 2009).

In order to understand the heterogeneity of cluster life cycles, it is important to analyse the triggering factors which intervene in their genesis and evolution. These factors are mechanisms that generate novelty and thus characterise evolutionary path-dependent systems. One of the main triggering factors for the emergence and development of cluster is the presence of multinationals. In some cases, MNEs are the main actors responsible for the rise of the local cluster, while in others they enter (or emerge in) the local cluster in one of the subsequent phases of its life cycle (development or maturity). 'Homegrown' MNEs in clusters are formed when small firms invest strategic resources in innovation and expansion and progressively transform themselves into MNEs (Sedita *et al.*, 2013). The literature on cluster has explicitly recognised the role played by MNEs in promoting cluster innovativeness and competitiveness (Belussi and Sammarra, 2010; Belussi and Sedita, 2012). In fact, the emergence of MNEs has been decisive in order to improve many clusters since they introduce new technologies and organisation skills and open up new markets. It also affects the structure of the internal cluster organisation (competitiveness way, cooperation, access to inputs and foreign markets, etc.). It can be a key actor in the cluster evolution due to its bigger size, higher growth capacity and introduction of improvement strategies.

Sedita *et al.* (2013) have considered MNEs and the cluster life cycle together and introduced a cluster typology derived from the modelling of industrial clusters presented by Markusen (1996). They present a typology in relation to the moment in which MNEs entered the analysed cluster and the role played by MNEs. They propose four types of clusters: 'satellite cluster' (the MNEs' entry in the origin phase of the cluster which evolved only thanks to external investments); 'evolving satellite cluster' (MNEs' entry in the origin phase of the cluster but in the process of development also act as local firms); 'evolutionary Marshallian cluster' (the evolution of clusters is linked to the emergence of local homegrown MNEs in the development/maturity phase); and 'multinationalised Marshallian cluster' (the external MNEs enter the cluster in a development/maturity phase).

The analysis of the marble cluster of Macael in Spain contributes to the current understanding of the interwoven evolution of cluster and MNEs. This chapter analyses the evolution of this cluster by adopting an evolutionary approach based on the cluster life cycle model and the role played by the emergence of the homegrown MNE, Cosentino, in shaping the cluster. The chapter is structured as follows. The next section is devoted to identifying the cluster life cycle and the triggering factors that influenced its origin, development and maturity stages. Section 3 focuses on the analysis of the emergence of a homegrown MNE (Cosentino) and the factors that explain its success. Section 4 is devoted to show, through an exploratory analysis, the interwoven evolution of Cosentino and the cluster. Finally, Section 5 offers some concluding remarks.

The research integrates qualitative and quantitative data collection methods in a two-stage case study design (Yin, 1989). At the first stage, we reviewed secondary data and previous studies. At the second stage, we conducted in-depth semi-structured open-ended interviews (five of them) with key informants and local institutional actors. We also selected a stratified sample of fifteen firms in order to represent the different phases of the cluster production chain (extraction, elaboration and sales). Interviewed companies included final firms, subcontractors and the leading firm (Cosentino). Sampled firms were identified using institutional information sources. The authors carried out the survey and questions were addressed to the firm owner or manager. Field work was conducted during spring 2015.

4.2   The cluster evolution

The marble cluster of Macael is located in the southern Spanish province of Almería. In this region, half of the Spanish marble quarries are to be found and they account for 45 per cent of the national marble production. Furthermore, Almería has the biggest marble reserve in Spain in terms of both quantity and quality. The cluster surface is relatively small (it covers 228 km^2) with a 15 km radius of action, including five municipalities in the Province of Almería (Macael, Olula del Río, Fines, Cantoria and Purchena). The cluster has a long historic trajectory. Since its formation, the Macael marble cluster has gone through different phases. Table 4.1 offers a list of specific triggering factors for the cluster origin, development and maturity phases.

4.2.1   Origin

The availability of a high-quality natural resource (white marble) in the Macael region meant extraction activities had already taken place in early times. Along the centuries, marble extraction experienced many highs and lows. During these centuries there were also periods of inactivity. Until 1834 mountains hosting marble quarries were communal goods and later on they were goods with municipal management. Due to this institutional peculiarity, marble quarries were owned mainly by local inhabitants and their dimensions were quite reduced. In 1837 the first regional factory was set up and many then followed until in 1905 there were twenty-five marble factories. Until the beginning of the twentieth century, marble exploitation and elaboration were quite rudimentary. For instance, sawmills in the county worked in winter only when they could profit from the waterfalls. From 1950 on, many improvements were introduced (lorry transport, gasoil compressors, electrification, etc.) but relevant structural deficiencies in the field of extraction, transformation and trading prevented expansion (Carretero Gómez, 1995).

Nevertheless, the number of firms located in this region grew significantly despite these problems. In 1983 there were 241 firms which employed 1,708

Table 4.1 Triggering factors in the life cycle stages of Macael marble cluster

Origin (1834–1983)	Development (1984–2000)	Maturity (2001–)
Natural resources endowment	Local institutions	Local institutions
	Technological innovation	Differentiation Internationalisation Homegrown multinational

Source: Own elaboration.

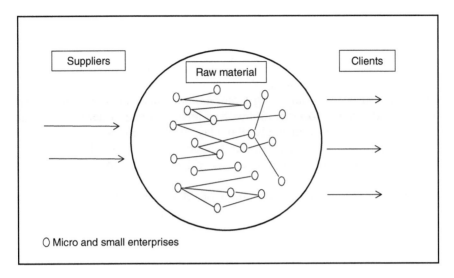

Figure 4.1 Macael marble cluster in 1983.
Source: Markusen (1996) and own elaboration.

workers. Firms were small (around 80 per cent were microfirms) and most of them had old technology resources. The firms were specialised in three different activities within the cluster: extraction, elaboration (building materials, handicrafts and by-product exploitation) and delivery of services and equipment goods. The main cluster activity was the local marble extraction. Almost all equipment goods and spare parts needed for maintenance were delivered by external suppliers (mainly from Italy). Sales went to the domestic market; marble was sold as stone or tables, with scarce introduction of added value (Carretero Gómez, 1995). Cluster firms showed a high degree of homogeneity in terms of size and ownership-control structure (Figure 4.1). The cluster was made up of a large number of micro and small enterprises. Only a few firms integrated all tasks since they owned quarries, could transform products and sell them. In some instances, firms reached agreements in order to satisfy some big orders, but this was not the norm since the differing technologies used at each firm made it impossible to offer a homogenous product. Within the cluster there were no medium or large enterprises or foreign-owned companies. The prevailing governance structure was based on the family business model.

4.2.2 Development

The start-up phase of the cluster took place with the measures introduced by regional and local public institutions to boost and modernise the sector.

In 1983, the *Instituto de Promoción Industrial de Andalucía* (Andalusia Institute for Industrial Promotion) launched the *Plan de Actuación Global de la Zona del Mármol de Macael* (1983–1992), with the aim at studying the general cluster problems and proposing solutions. The involvement of local firms was relevant during all development phases of the Plan. In fact, they were present and took actively part in all working meetings of the Plan and in the Monitoring Commission. This Plan stimulated social capital and brought together all involved local agents in order to overcome obstacles and reach joint goals (Barzelay, 1991). Some measures focused on the mechanisation of quarries and elaboration factories; bigger marble blocks therefore could be extracted and a final product of higher quality could be obtained.

Later on, the Province Association of Marble Enterprises (Asociación Provincial de Empresarios del Mármol de Almería) promoted the *Plan Estratégico de Macael* (1996–2000). This Macael Strategic Plan continued with the previous actions and set the foundations for the cluster to become a transformation centre, as well as an extraction place. The involvement of local enterprises continued to be very important. Thanks to this Plan, elaboration and transformation activities increased notably. The added value given to the local product, as well as to other products coming from Spain and foreign markets, improved constantly. In fact, marble importations from other countries (mainly Turkey) started to grow spectacularly. Foreign marble elaborated in the cluster began to become more and more important. In the elaboration process, the contribution of craft firms stands out since they generated the greatest added value. Furthermore, industrial craftsmanship had become more important than the traditional one. This trend provoked a higher level of technification and the employment of highly qualified workers. All this generated a relevant competitive advantage.

At the beginning of the twenty-first century, the sector was already well established and its competitiveness has grown thanks to technology improvements and the promotion of elaboration activities. The number of firms grew notably, reaching 397, with 5,471 employees. There were already more elaboration firms (135) than extractive ones (95). Within the cluster, some enterprises emerged producing machinery; they contributed to reduce the dependency on foreign suppliers.

In the development phase, the cluster still had an endogenous character since almost all firms were set up by entrepreneurs from the region. The exception to this trend was the existence of some firms devoted to the exploitation of by-products with French and Catalan capital, attracted to the region by the calcium carbonate purity. In the cluster configuration, micro and small firms (Figure 4.2) continued to predominate. Nevertheless, a group of local firms emerged to integrate the whole productive process (extraction, elaboration and sales); they also sold a considerable amount of their production in foreign markets through their own distribution channels.

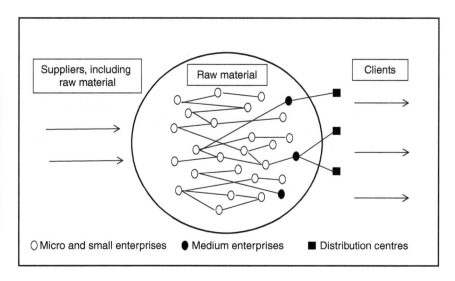

Figure 4.2 Macael marble cluster in 2000.
Source: Markusen (1996) and own elaboration.

4.2.3 *Maturity*

With the new century, new institutions were created within the cluster in new fields of work with public support which would strengthen and provide a qualitative change to the cluster. In 2002, the *Centro Tecnológico Andaluz de la Piedra* (the Andalusia Technology Centre for Stone) was inaugurated. It was set up to boost quality, promote research and development projects, offer entrepreneurs quick information about activities related to the natural stone, and enable technology transfer among the sector enterprises, firm cooperation, market analysis and studies. In 2006 the *Fundación Marca Macael* (Foundation for Macael brandname) was established as a platform to design and implement promotion campaigns of the brandname 'Mármoles de Macael' (Marble from Macael).

The international economic crisis which started in 2007 and which seriously affected the Spanish construction sector from 2008 on had a negative impact on the cluster: firms and workforce were reduced to 50 per cent. Between 2007 and 2013, the cluster lost about 169 firms and 3,118 workers (Asociación de Empresarios del Mármol de Andalucía, 2014). The crisis was more severe for small local firms executing the most labour-intensive phases such as extraction and the elaboration firms that obtained low-quality products and which kept the same strategies focused on low-cost advantages and price competitiveness supplying the national market exclusively (Escuela del Mármol de Andalucía, 2013).

In order to face the strong impact of the crisis and the increase in competition pressure from a large number of low-labour-cost countries (especially Turkey and China), the most dynamic firms followed a twofold strategy. On the one hand, a new product differentiation strategy was launched, as well as specialisation in high-quality exclusive products. These new products had a considerable added value and were directed to design and decoration businesses. Hence, promotion campaigns addressed to architects and designers were carried out. The participation at specialised trading fairs was reinforced, as well as inverse trading missions. A new strategy based on the brandname 'Mármol Blanco de Macael' (White Marble from Macael) was programmed. The district also aimed to achieve the designation of origin of the raw material (protected geographical indication – PGI) (Escuela del Mármol de Andalucía, 2013). This PGI is a quality label, which would strengthen the marble brandname from Macael. This would also improve the cluster firm position at international markets through a higher degree of differentiation. On the other hand, the cluster firms have opted for internationalisation. The most frequent and successful formula is the search for a local dealer in the target market. A contract of exclusivity is signed to ensure the distribution of products from the district enterprises. In other cases, the formula is the implantation of a trading agent in the target country (Analistas Económicos de Andalucía, 2013). A third path, which is also working well, is to establish direct contact with the end client and offer an integral service. This includes assessment, manufacturing, elaboration, installation and after-sale customer service. The cluster business tissue, made up mainly of small and medium enterprises, was aware that cooperation between local firms was the most adequate way to deal with internationalisation. Although they continue to compete among themselves in the domestic market, they collaborated in foreign markets to carry out specific projects. These cooperative relationships require a clearer division of work and enable specialisation so that subcontracting enterprises can improve their competitiveness and productivity. Moreover, they are able to meet requirements of bigger projects and place themselves in international markets (Aznar Sánchez *et al.*, 2015a).

Despite the decline of local firms and employment, the cluster strategy of differentiation and internationalisation has increased cluster competitiveness. In the last few years the cluster's turnover and exports have shown a general trend of expansion and growth. The output of the cluster went from €1,570 million in 2012 to €1,657 million in 2014. Meanwhile, sales in foreign markets increased dramatically, from €54 million in 2012 to €345 million in 2014, accounting for 53.1 per cent of total sales (Asociación de Empresarios de Andalucía, 2015). Furthermore, there has also been diversification in foreign markets, with the strong dependence on the North American market being reduced.

Changes in the cluster configuration have been notable; we should highlight two decisive facts. The first interesting change is the emergence of several driving enterprises, which start to show leadership skills over the rest. On

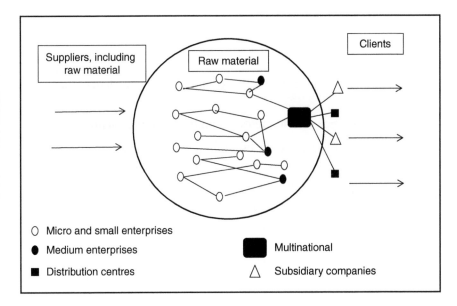

Figure 4.3 Macael marble cluster in 2014.
Source: Markusen (1996) and own elaboration.

the one hand, we can find medium productive enterprises devoted to marble elaboration, which have achieved a relevant competitive advantage thanks to their distribution channels. Most of them own quarries, many of which are also abroad, so that they can achieve raw materials at a good price, as well as considerable availability of supply. They have a significant production capacity, a sophisticated production system and an outstanding logistic capacity with own stores in different regions. They are developing a brandname policy together with important communication strategies. On the other hand, we can find the exporting craftsmanship group made up of enterprises which followed a product differentiation strategy and reached new market niches. They produce mainly industrial crafts on stone. Some of these firms carry out integral projects where they combine crafts and industrially elaborated products which used to be outsourced to other manufacturing firms. These driving enterprises have experienced great development in a short period of time and they already number more than ten (Agencia de Innovación y Desarrollo de Andalucía, 2014).

The second relevant change is the spectacular increase of a medium enterprise in the cluster (Cosentino). This enterprise was a pioneer opting for innovation, differentiation and internationalisation. It followed its own path within the cluster and has become a multinational enterprise with many branch firms abroad. Nowadays it is an international leader in the artificial stone market. At the moment, cluster firms show a high degree of heterogeneity, not only in terms of product and technical specialisation but also with respect to size (Figure 4.3). The Macael cluster is marked by the presence of an important multinational company in the artificial stone sector, around ten medium locally owned enterprises, and a core of small and micro family-owned firms. The emergence of a multinational has changed the nature of the old Marshallian cluster, which is now an 'evolutionary Marshallian cluster'.

4.3   The emergence of a homegrown multinational Cosentino

The key factor that has allowed Cosentino to become an international leader in the artificial stone sector has been its strategy for technological innovation, differentiation and internationalisation. At first, the history of this enterprise was similar to the many others in the cluster. The Cosentino family began to work with the marble in the 1940s, focusing mainly on quarry exploitation and the elaboration of basic marbles. Then in 1979 the second generation founded Mármoles Cosentino S.A. with seventeen employees. However, the Martínez-Cosentino brothers became aware that if they wanted to increase their business volume, their activities should go beyond mere local marble extraction and transformation. Their own limits conditioned the stone trading opportunities. They considered their strategy of depending on a unique local natural resource and addressing sales to the Spanish construction sector only to be a risky one (Martínez-Cosentino, 2010). Thus, they decided to launch a strategy of differentiation and international expansion based on research and innovation.

In order to have a sound basis for its differentiation strategy, the enterprise focused on the search for new materials that performed better than marble. After failure and near-ruin, the company developed a new product, Silestone, in 1990, adding to the natural stone properties some physical and mechanical qualities, unique in the market. After some trials to trade the product in traditional market niches, the company opted for a new market segment (kitchen working surfaces) where it has become the international leader.

Constancy in research and innovation has allowed the enterprise to develop new materials which have also become international references within their markets. In order to face up to the competition from manufacturers in other countries which offer similar products to Silestone but at a lower price, in 2004 the 'antibacterial Silestone' was put on the market, with relevant differentiating improvements. With this innovation, Cosentino offered a unique quartz surface with antibacterial protection. This surface was the most secure and hygienic within the kitchen worktop market. Furthermore, it could be introduced in exclusive segments such as hotels and catering establishments, hospitals and laboratories. The group continued to introduce new materials to its product portfolio (Eco, Sensa, Prexury, etc.), but the most valuable is the one termed 'Dekton'. Its launch into the market took place in 2013. This material is an ultra compact surface with higher technical properties than Silestone; it is made up of inorganic raw materials. Dekton has allowed the group to increase its activity in the architecture and design field, as well as strengthen its position in fields such as facades, external applications and decoration.

The second growth factor for Cosentino was its decisive action for internationalisation. Silestone opened up the doors to a regular exporting activity in some foreign markets and was the first big step to internationalisation. The availability of a differentiated product with the highest quality level and a secure service was the foundation for the internationalisation process. At the beginning of the 1990s, the enterprise started to sign exclusivity agreements with suppliers to introduce Silestone in several foreign markets. In 1997, Cosentino set up its first subsidiary company in the United States with a local partner. Cosentino was in charge of manufacturing the quartz surfaces, whereas its local partner was responsible for the exclusive distribution of Cosentino products in the United States, Canada, Mexico and Puerto Rico. With this subsidiary company, Cosentino entered the most important distribution channel of kitchens in the US. Furthermore, Cosentino made a great investment in promotion and publicity to generate a brandname image among the end clients. The Silestone kitchen worktop experienced huge success and sales increased dramatically, leading to it becoming the world leader within this market segment (Martínez Mendiara, 2012). In 2010, Cosentino acquired the whole share capital and incorporated completely the subsidiary company into the group structure.

Building on this experience, Cosentino followed some patterns in its internationalisation process. It established trading contacts with the desired markets through participation at specialised international trade fairs and reached exclusive distribution agreements with local partners. When regularity of sales in those markets was reached, a trading subsidiary company was grounded and headed by an expert in the specific market. Cosentino offered shares to its local partners, but it always kept more than 50 per cent of the shares, with the aim of developing its control policy over distribution. If the business volume was high, production centres and transformation workshops were set up, where Cosentino offered its knowhow and designed training plans for employees. Regarding management and marketing, the subsidiary company was quite autonomous, but positive results were always required (Llano Irusta, 2008). This flexible model of trading organisation enables a quick and systematic adaptation to the continuous changes in the markets and to its particularities. Within each market, the preferred products and the distribution channels may vary greatly. Following this concept, Cosentino increased its trading infrastructure. Nowadays it controls more than seventy suppliers all over the world and owns fifteen subsidiary companies (Aznar-Sánchez *et al.*, 2015b).

As far as distribution and trading are concerned, Cosentino has innovated constantly. From 2008 on, the enterprise developed a new trading model based on its stores, labelled 'Cosentino Centres'. They were no longer mere stores for marble workers; they started to be the place to approach new clients (architects, designers, kitchen and bathroom furniture sellers, installers, etc.). These centres founded an integrated organisation unit for delivery, exhibition and sales. They were responsible for the development and service of a territory. This model presents some advantages. The costs of the value chain are reduced since scale economies are captured from the existing material distribution and the promotion channel. Moreover, a better service is offered to users and the real needs of the market can be better understood. The centres are also training and updating institutions for different collectives (Martínez Mendiara, 2012). The business model worked really well and the enterprise started to spread this practice widely. Nowadays it owns 94 centres around the world. In 2013 the group took a step forward with the creation of the so-called 'Cosentino City'. An exhibition site is located in the town centre of big cities such as Milan, Sydney, Singapore and New York. They are specially designed to welcome architects and designers.

Cosentino's differentiation and internationalisation strategy were a success from the beginnings. Since 1990, Cosentino has enjoyed uninterrupted growth. Increases in sales have been spectacular: €10 million in 1990, €70 million in 2000, €305 million in 2010 and €560 million in 2014; the number of employees has also multiplied: 200 in 1990, 630 in 2000, 1,950 in 2010 and 2,645 in 2014. At the time of writing, the Cosentino Group is the international leader in quartz surfaces and is the biggest enterprise in the sector of ornamental stones. It has seven manufacturing sites (six in Spain – Almería – and one in Brazil), fifteen bathroom and kitchen worktop elaboration sites (fourteen in the United States and one in Almería), an intelligent logistic platform in Spain, two dealing hubs in the US and more than ninety Cosentino Centres all over the world. More than 90 per cent of the group turnover comes from international markets. The group owns subsidiary companies in fifteen countries and works directly with employees, producing and trading agents in twenty-nine countries around the five continents. It sells its products in over eighty countries (Grupo Cosentino, 2015).

4.4   Cosentino's role in the cluster dynamics

The constant development of improvement strategies from its beginnings has allowed Cosentino to grow and increase progressively. These dynamics made Cosentino more and more relevant within the cluster until it became the leader enterprise with an overwhelming weight. The number of employees and turnover of Cosentino factories located in the region of Macael accounts for 50 per cent of the total sum of the cluster; this reaches over 90 per cent if we consider the whole group.

Cosentino is the largest worldwide multinational manufacturing artificial stone. It also leads many distribution channels in the US and the EU. Although it owns fifteen subsidiary companies abroad, the feeling of belonging to the cluster makes the group keep its headquarters located in the region where the high-added-value and strategic activities such as prototyping, R&D, design, marketing, logistics and distribution are also to be found. The whole value chain of the company remains deeply rooted in its original territory. However, the fidelity to its territory makes less and less sense since the advantages obtained from its location within the cluster are shrinking. The Cosentino option for research led it to develop a radical innovation in the 1990s (a new product). This innovation had a 'disruptive' character since it placed the enterprise in a different sector (artificial stone) to that of the rest of the cluster firms. From that moment, Cosentino separated itself from the other cluster firms. The raw material to elaborate the new products (Silestone, Dekton) comes from other regions outside the county of Macael. The manufacturing machinery is different to that used for marble products and the workforce need very different skills. Thus Cosentino was forced to search for a high percentage of the most qualified workforce (computer specialists, engineers, etc.) out of the cluster and created its own R&D and training centres.

These different requirements in technology, inputs, know-how and working skills, as well as the creation of specific training institutions, knowledge and competencies, considerably reduced the potential positive spillovers to the rest of the cluster firms. Few capacities are shared. In fact, many of those capacities are exclusive to Cosentino. They are private goods since they were internally generated and the other firms cannot access them. In some aspects, such as recruitment, small and medium cluster enterprises can be disturbed. Working for Cosentino has become one of the biggest ambitions for the young people of the region; it reduces the labour offered to other cluster firms. Furthermore, Cosentino actively looks for the most qualified people in the county since its location in a rural area makes it difficult to attract professionals who live in different cities. In contrast, there are very few cases of employees who leave Cosentino to work in a different firm of the cluster. All production phases are executed by Cosentino so that we cannot find outsourcing with other cluster firms and there is no interaction between them.

Although economic relations between Cosentino and the cluster firms are weak, the multinational contributes to improve the competitive repositioning of the local cluster. Cosentino has fostered the infrastructure improvement of the cluster (communications, natural gas, etc.), participates in and supports the cluster institutions (Asociación de Empresarios del Mármol de Andalucía, Centro Tecnológico Andaluz de la Piedra, Escuela de Andalucía del Mármol, etc.). Cosentino also assesses and helps the cluster firms with technical and financial means in the processes of differentiation and internationalisation. It has become a benchmark for the most dynamic firms of the cluster which try to copy some of its competitive strategies.

4.5 Conclusions

The economic activity around marble extraction was relevant from the beginning of the twentieth century but the cluster did not really take off until the 1980s. The growth was driven mainly by the actions of local public institutions to foster the modernisation of marble production. The cluster changed from its original specialisation in the extraction of marble from Macael to become a centre of elaboration and transformation of local and foreign marble. Therefore, cluster development in the maturity stage was associated with the implementation of a strategy of differentiation and internationalisation. This strategy was based on cooperation between the cluster firms (unions and outsourcing) and on the availability of a highly qualified and specialised labour force. A remarkable fact in the cluster evolution is that in its maturity phase a leader firm (Cosentino) emerged. This enterprise was a pioneer opting for innovation, differentiation and internationalisation in the 1990s. For this reason it has become a worldwide benchmark as an MNE. The different dynamics followed by the cluster firms have modified its configuration, leading to a more hierarchical and heterogeneous structure so that nowadays it can be termed as an evolutionary Marshallian cluster.

The fact that Cosentino placed itself in a different sector to the rest of the cluster firms due to the creation of artificial products makes the positive contributions of a homegrown MNE to the cluster rather limited compared with other clusters in terms of know-how transfer, availability of qualified labour force and the presence of suppliers. Nevertheless, Cosentino's decision to keep its headquarters and its main added-value activities within the cluster is very positive, as is the support and collaboration given to other cluster firms for its competitive repositioning.

Regarding cluster resilience, the role played by small and medium enterprises, which are becoming driving firms within the cluster, is more decisive. These firms follow a strategy focused on the most added-value and immaterial activities and strengthen the benefits of being integrated within the cluster. On the one hand, the development of this strategy is possible due to the presence of some assets within the cluster (specialised workforce, high-quality raw materials, specialised supply of inputs, etc.). On the other hand, the cluster is being reinforced due to the different collaboration and outsourcing schemes followed by firms which need support within the cluster. This allows high flows and interactions between cluster firms and helps increase the degree of resilience.

This twofold trend (Cosentino versus driving small and medium enterprises) with different impacts on the cluster renovation and resilience should be taken into account by policy makers when designing and implementing intervention and supporting measures. Public administrations should give priority to those initiatives that improve competitiveness of the cluster small and medium enterprises. We should highlight the measures that foster R&D, training, financing and the achievement of an own trademark. Attention should also be paid to driving enterprises due to the important influence over the rest of the cluster firms.

Acknowledgements

The research in this chapter is framed under the Spanish Research Project titled 'Marco institucional y externalidades en la minería ibérica (siglos XVIII a XXI)', reference HAR2014- 56428-C3-2, financed by the Spanish Science and Innovation Ministry.

References

Agencia de Innovación y Desarrollo de Andalucía (2014). *Impulso de los clusters. Plan de Actuación del cluster de la piedra*, Sevilla: Agencia de Innovación y Desarrollo de Andalucía.

Analistas Económicos de Andalucía (2013). *Diagnóstico del sector del mármol de Macael: iniciativa estratégica para la cooperación y la internacionalización*, Málaga: Analistas Económicos de Andalucía.

Asociación de Empresarios del Mármol de Andalucía (several years). *Datos económicos del sector del mármol en Macael*, Almería: Asociación Provincial de Empresarios del Mármol.

Aznar Sánchez, J.A., Carretero Gómez, A. and Velasco Muñoz, J.F. (2015a). La internacionalización del cluster del mármol de Almería y la multinacional Cosentino, *Economía Industrial*, 397: 143–154.

Aznar-Sánchez, J.A., Carretero-Gómez, A. and Velasco-Muñoz, J.F. (2015b). An industrial district around a mining resource: the case of marble of Macael in Almería, *Investigaciones Regionales – Journal of Regional Research*, 32: 133–148.

Barzelay, M. (1991). Managing local development: lessons from Spain, *Policy Sciences*, 24(3): 271–290.

Belussi, F. and Samarra, A. (2010). (eds) *Business Networks in Clusters and Industrial Districts*, Oxford: Routledge.

Belussi, F. and Sedita, S.R. (2009). Life cycle vs. multiple path dependency in industrial districts, *European Planning Studies*, 17(4): 505–528.

Belussi, F. and Sedita, S.R. (2012). Industrial districts as open learning systems: combining emergent and deliberate knowledge structures, *Regional Studies*, 46(2): 165–184.

Boschma, R. and Fornahl, D. (2011). Cluster evolution and a roadmap for future research, *Regional Studies*, 45(10): 1295–1298.

Brenner, T. (2004). *Local Industrial Cluster: Existence, emergence and evolution*, London: Routledge.

Carretero Gómez, A. (1995). *La industrial del mármol en Almería*, Almería: Universidad de Almería.

Escuela del Mármol de Andalucía (2013). *Eurostone, la lucha por la supervivencia de la piedra*, Sevilla: Escuela del Mármol de Andalucía.

Grupo Cosentino (varios años). *Informe Annual del Grupo Cosentino*, Almería: Grupo Cosentino.

Hervás-Oliver, J. L. (2015). How do multinational enterprises co-locate in industrial districts? An introduction to the integration of alternative explanations from international business and economic geography literatures, *Investigaciones Regionales – Journal of Regional Research*, 32: 115–132.

Llano Irusta, M. A. (2008). *Grupo Cosentino. Un caso de internacionalización exitoso*, Madrid: Instituto Español de Comercio Exterior.

Markusen, A. (1996). Sticky places in slippery space: a typology of industrial districts, *Economic Geography*, 72(3): 293–313.

Martin, R. and Sunley, P. (2003). Deconstructing clusters: chaotic concept or policy panacea? *Journal of Economic Geography*, 3(1): 5–35.

Martin, R. and Sunley, P. (2011). Conceptualizing cluster evolution: beyond the life cycle model? *Regional Studies*, 45(10): 1299–1318.

Martínez Mendiara, F. (2012). La creación de una empresa familiar líder mundial, *Boletín de Estudios Económicos*, 207: 505–516.

Martínez-Cosentino, F. (2010). De la innovación a la internacionalización, *Mediterráneo Económico*, 17: 223–230.

Menzel, M.P. and Fornahl, D. (2010). Cluster life cycles: dimensions and rationales of cluster development, *Industrial and Corporate Change*, 19(1): 205–238.

Sedita, S., Caloffi, A. and Belussi, F. (2013). Heterogeneity of MNEs entry modes in industrial clusters: an evolutionary approach based on the cluster life cycle model, DRUID, Barcelona.

Wang, L., Madhok, A. and Li, S. (2014). Agglomeration and clustering over the industry life cycle: toward a dynamic model of geographic concentration, *Strategic Management Journal*, 35(7): 995–1012.

Yin, R. K. (1989). *Case Study Research, Design and Methods*, Beverly Hills, CA: Sage.

5 Reverse relocation, off-shoring and back-shoring in the Arzignano tannery district

Moving labour and capital in the global economy

Fiorenza Belussi, Maria Francesca Savarese and Silvia Rita Sedita

5.1 Introduction

In this chapter we discuss the global evolutive paths of an industrial district: the leather tanning district of Arzignano, localised in the north of Italy. We aim to describe here the specific case that illustrates an 'anomalous' path of internationalisation. At the beginning, at the end of the Second World War, it was composed of small artisanal firms, but intense development of new technologies in machinery and in new methods of tanning led to a process of growth.

Firms became competitive and successful. During the 1970s and 1980s, this district followed the growth path of the majority of Italian clusters/industrial districts, enjoying success in international markets in terms of export flows. Nevertheless, its 'replicability' was at risk at the end of the period, due to the difficulty of finding sufficient blue-collars workers in the area. Instead of off-shoring those manufacturing activities in countries where the availability of labour was guaranteed, and less costly, such as in Asian or Eastern countries, local firms made the strategic decision to employ immigrants. Hence, during the 1990s, the share of foreign workers out of the total number of workers in the district rose to about 50 per cent (while nowadays, after the 2008 crisis, it is no more than 30–35 per cent). The majority of local actors favoured a developmental model, which we have called 'reverse relocation'. However, local leading firms also followed a more traditional pattern of manufacturing off-shoring, but very soon they back-shored the main production at home.

Our research, based both on meta-analysis techniques and on qualitative research, organised throughout several interviews with entrepreneurs and local consultants, showed that the deep local embeddedness of firms (and their accumulated tacit knowledge, difficult to transfer to other locations) had dissuaded them from pursuing the path of international relocation. Instead, they preferred to open the local labour market to non-EU workers (thereby solving problems connected with institutional labour market hyper-rigidity). This case is emblematic, because it confirms the existence of different (more or less efficient and/or effective) strategies of internationalisation. The choice of 'reverse relocation', as we will discuss below, can be considered a second best solution because it does not yield a net reduction of costs as would the relocation to low-wage countries (the first best solution). However, it was at the basis of the district resilience to the global 2008 crisis.

During the 2000s, four important groups emerged from the overlapping networks of firms constituting the district of Arzignano: the Rino Mastrotto Group, the Mastrotto Group, the Concerie Montebello spa and the Dani Conceria. We can call these firms 'homegrown MNEs'. In one sense, they followed a more traditional path of internationalisation, developing new FDI in Brazil, Indonesia, Tunisia and China, without hollowing out the most significant high-value tasks. In 2014 the leather-tanning Arzignano district recovered completely from the 2008 slow-down, showing a trend towards consolidation. An entrepreneurial discovery process was based on a path renewal based on a) the development of numerous new market niches, such as the automotive industry (leather chairs) and consumer electronics (skin pockets), b) a strategic choice towards sustainable products and process technologies, and c) the introduction among the leading firms of advanced 'just in time' organisational innovations related to customers' demand in logistics.

The remainder of the chapter is structured as follows. In the following two sections, a theoretical framework is presented. Then, the methodology and data analyses are discussed. In the final sections, results are discussed and commented on, and some conclusions are drawn.

5.2   A global 'Marshallian' district

The literature on industrial districts since the seminal studies of Marshall (1919, 1920) has highlighted the institutional and social aspects that favour the embeddedness of social networks of small specialised firms (Maskell, 2001; Grabher, 1993; Sorenson, 2005) and the mechanism determining the inter-firm division of labour. The approach of Porter (1998; 2000), which has popularised the concept of 'cluster' (see also Lazzeretti et al., 2014), has also stressed the importance of geographically clustered interconnected companies and associated institutions in a particular field, linked by commonalities and complementarities. Clusters are characterised by the co-presence of cooperation and coordination within the various phases of the production chain, and by the existence of competitive relations among the local firms operating in the same phase of the production process (You and Wilkinson, 1994). This theoretical model assumes that the clustering process (Martin and Sunley, 2003) develops mainly in sectors able to benefit from the transmission and sharing of knowledge made possible by spatial proximity (Amin and Cohendet, 2000; Loasby, 1998; Lombardi, 2000). This process typifies: 1) sectors where the knowledge possessed by the various actors must constantly and flexibly be recombined (e.g. traditional sectors characterised by high fashion content), or 2) sectors which benefit from knowledge spillovers deriving from local relationships with partners possessing highly specialised skills (Cooke, 2004; Saxenian, 1994; Zeller, 2001). Since the mid-1990s, Italian districts have undergone new evolutionary paths (Markusen, 1996; Belussi *et al.*, 2003; Belussi and Sedita, 2009), including a process of verticalisation (Lazerson and Lorenzoni, 1999; Cainelli and De Liso, 2005 Mariotti *et al.*, 2008), and the international relocation of many activities previously carried out by local sub-contractors (Guerrieri and Iammarino, 2001; Zucchella, 2006; Sammarra and Belussi, 2006) – following a more general pattern of international fragmentation of production (Arndt and Kierzkowsky, 2001).

5.3 'Reverse relocation', off-shoring/back-shoring and the birth of homegrown MNEs

The classical globalisation pattern of Italian clusters/districts has mainly been driven largely by a 'mercantile' path of export flows. During the 1990s and the 2000s off-shoring and relocation have characterised the new trends. Thus, there has been an objective convergence of the neo-district model with the global expansion of multinational companies (Bair and Gereffi, 2001).

Many Italian cluster/district firms have maintained their international competitiveness through large-scale international outsourcing of labour-intensive manufacturing activities to low-cost countries (Moon and Roehl, 2001; Calvet, 1981). Despite the 'liability of foreignness' (Zaheer, 1995), small firms have also frequently used international subcontractors. This process has favoured the growth of 'satellite' districts in developing countries, such as Romania or Hungary (Belussi and Sammarra, 2010). Whereas the Marshallian theory conceived an industrial district as a 'self-contained' territorial area, the Italian clusters and districts of the 1990s became 'open systems', able to contrast the international competitiveness of low labour-cost countries (Belussi and Caldari, 2011; Belussi and De Propris, 2013). Carabelli *et al.* (2006), studying the evolutionary dynamics of Italian industrial clusters/districts, have shown that tertiary and service activities are now predominant, while the specialisation sector has often changed. Some districts, in fact, have become producers of technologies: for example, the district of Vigevano switched from producing footwear to producing machines for footwear manufacture. Economic theory suggests that globalisation eliminates imbalances in growth rates and resource endowments in two ways: a) by developing international trade, and b) by moving production factors (labour and capital). Flows of FDI and the migration of skilled workers from the underdeveloped countries appear to be interchangeable (Kluger and Rapoport, 2005). Migratory flows are often associated with the dynamics of international trade (Carbaugh, 2007). In the neoclassical paradigm, production factors are mobile, and it must be assumed that the economy will react to an imbalance in costs (related to labour and/

or capital), or to the availability of some factors (abundance or shortage), by stimulating the migration of labour or capital. In the long term, the prices of the inputs will converge, reducing wage inequalities and capital endowments. Hence, international trade and migration are substitutes. However, a second-best alternative is available, which consists of moving workers by encouraging migration from countries with low-cost and abundant labour supplies. Therefore, instead of moving capital, it is labour that is moved (even if it is employed in conditions of relatively higher costs than in the country of origin). In Europe, migration processes have traditionally been intense (Trebilcock and Sudak, 2006), because the more developed countries needed to reduce their labour demand gaps.

Behind some migratory flows, there are social and/or business networks that may stimulate the formation of strong ties between countries through labour circulation, the birth of new entrepreneurship, and inward and outward FDI flows, as discussed by Saxenian (2000) and Albertoni *et al.* (2015). Off-shoring initiatives but also re-shoring have characterised the global economy in the past decade (Ancarani *et al.*, 2015; Frattocchi *et al.*, 2014).

Clusters/district dynamics can be intrinsically interlinked with the presence of MNEs. While in some cases MNEs are the main actors responsible for giving rise to the local cluster (Mudambi and Santangelo, 2015), in others they entered from outside in the development or maturity of the cluster life cycle (Iammarino and McCann, 2013). 'Homegrown' MNEs in clusters are formed when small firms invest strategic resources in innovation and expansion, and progressively transform themselves into MNEs (Oliver *et al.*, 2008).

5.4   Methodology

In order to deepen our knowledge of the internationalisation of clusters/industrial districts, we focused on a specific case study. Our research asks for an explorative method more than a confirmatory one. Therefore we applied a qualitative rather than a quantitative approach (Doz, 2011; Welch *et al.*, 2011). A qualitative case study research design is particularly recommended when the boundaries between phenomenon and context are not clearly defined (Eisenhardt, 1989; Yin, 1994; Glaser and Strauss, 1967). We used some interviews we had conducted to entrepreneurs or top managers of the main firms of the cluster/district. Our selection was not random but information-oriented, guided by the principle of having in our sample the most important cases. The interviews were conducted in two steps: during 2009 (with entrepreneurs of fifteen firms and fifty employees) and at the beginning of 2015 (eight with entrepreneurs and managers and one with the president of the Arzignano district). Each interview (lasting one hour or more) was conducted by the authors with entrepreneurs or top managers on the basis of a semi-structured questionnaire. Financial data were collected through the Aida database (Bureau van Dijk). We conducted a meta-analysis study. Our approach is based on a literature review of previous empirical research, following the guidelines for qualitative analysis suggested by the grounded theory (Glaser and Strauss, 1967). The search strategy consisted of the collection of relevant publications in the field, including previous research from the authors (Belussi and Sedita, 2010). Considering all the literature which appeared in academic journals, books and the local press, we systematise all information in the following section. Information from textual reports was synthesised (Eisenhardt, 1989) by creating some categories for meta-analytical review. These categories were derived from our initial research questions: why and how the district developed; how the small district firms approach the international markets; how they develop new environmentally clean technologies and new machinery; which were the factors that triggered the emergence of a small group of leaders; why firms choose or not to invest abroad. Using the information gathered in texts and interviews, we were able to address the issue of district origin and development pattern.

5.5 Birth, growth, decline and resilience of the district of Arzignano

The Arzignano district represents about 40 per cent of total employment in the national leather-tanning industry, which in 2013 was estimated at 18,000 units (Unic, 2013). The district's main market originally was the furniture industry, while now the dominant segments are the automotive industry and the production of leather covering for consumer electronics firms (such as Apple). Footwear accounts for approximately 25 per cent of production and clothing for only 7 per cent.

The first historical evidence of the presence of the leather-tanning industry at Vicenza dates back to 1366 (Zampiva, 1997). It was under the Republic of Venice that trade by the leather-tanning industry began, especially between Venice and Milan. In that period, intense marine traffic with the Middle East led to the diffusion of the most advanced tannery techniques. This benefited the industry not only around the Venice lagoon but also in its hinterland, and particularly in the Valle del Chiampo near Vicenza, which could rely on large amounts of clean water and trees from which to extract tannin, an essential element in the tanning process. During 1800, the Valle del Chiampo became industrialised, first in wool manufacturing (Signori, 1980) and then, when the latter slumped, in silk products. During the two world wars, the silk industry declined: demand diminished and Japanese competition increased (Patto per lo Sviluppo del Distretto Vicentino della Concia, 2004). The development of the district took place after the 1950s (see Table 5.1).

At the beginning of the 1990s, the bankruptcy of an important local mechanical engineering company, Pellizzari, triggered a diffused process of new firms start-up in electro mechanics sectors; thereafter, a flourishing tanning-machinery industry also developed in the area. In the beginning, local firms copied some German technology, but very soon numerous original innovations were introduced in machinery and tumblers (Banca Intesa,

Table 5.1 Main historical trends of the district

| Year | Tannery industry | | Other connected manufacturing industries | |
	Local units	Number of employees	Local units	Number of employees
1951	19	361	63	2068
1961	100	1929	91	2765
1971	161	3209	191	3228
1981	602	6358	230	2606
1991	615	8017	227	2590
2001	649	7988	222	2514
2002	658	8105	218	2567
2004	600	10426	200	2100
2013	468	8272	180	1500

Source: Authors' elaboration on ISTAT data.

2006, p. 17). Initially, the district's birth was not based on small firms, but on the expansion of a few large Fordist firms. Spin-offs from existing firms by technicians or blue-collar workers supported the formation of today's district model. The largest firms, instead of satisfying the increased demand by expanding their internal organisation, activated a stable subcontracting system. This modality was widely followed by all Italian clusters/districts because it enables firms to be more flexible and to become more specialised. Figure 5.1 illustrates the main stages of the district's development and the birth of collective initiatives (training, urban planning and environmental improvement) supporting the co-development of firms and local institutions in the area. The district's consolidation has been due to the activity of support institutions in the provision of training and infrastructures, as well as to numerical growth in the population of firms. In 1965 a leather-tanning chemistry school – Istituto Tecnico Industriale per la Chimica Conciaria 'Galileo Galilei' – was established so that the district no longer had to hire specialised personnel from Germany and other countries.

Between 1976 and 1985 the municipality of Arzignano created three industrial areas with an expenditure of €6 million, inducing firms to transfer to the industrial park and modernise their equipment. The most inefficient firms were expelled from the market and the largest companies took over the failed firms. In those years, the Arzignano district 'industrialised' its production, in contrast with the craft cluster of Santa Croce sull'Arno (Gjerdåkers, 2006). In order to promote clean technologies, the government supported the installation of a downstream purification plant, which was inaugurated in 1985 at a cost of €50 million. This plant now serves about 300 firms. In the early 1980s, a second purifier was built at Montebello to serve a further forty firms. During the 2000s the district of Arzignano has absorbed a large inflow of

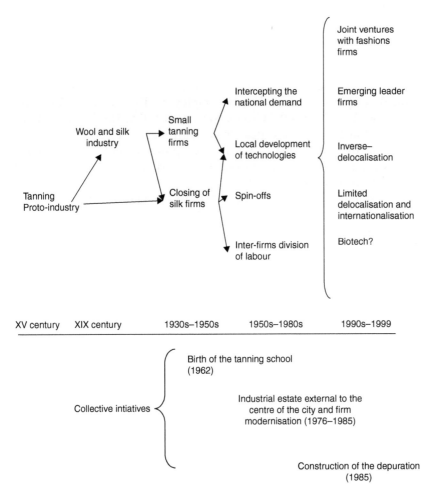

Figure 5.1 Evolution of firm population in the Arzignano district and co-evolution of local institutions.

Source: Belussi and Sedita, 2010.

immigrants, showing a 'reverse relocation' pattern. The main migratory flows are those involving workers from Asia and Africa. At Arzignano, non-EU immigrant workers are mainly employed in tanning activities. Official sources estimate their total number at about 5,000 units (Poster, 2005).

During the 2000s Arzignano has transformed itself into a heterogeneous district, characterised by the presence of leader enterprises. Actually there are only 100 final producers and no more than 60 firms in which the entire value chain is complete; 200 subcontracting firms are specialised in the various laundering phases (raw hide treatment to obtain wet-blue, semi-processed and semi-finished skins treated with chromium but not dyed or refined). About 100 firms carry out mechanical and/or auxiliary processes, and about 40 firms are focused on commercial activities. In the period 2008–2013 the number of firms and employees declined and some small or inefficient firms were expulsed from the market (Table 5.2). Recent data (Table 5.3) show that about 50 per cent of employment is now concentrated in firms with more than 100 employees. There are now four large groups (the Rino Mastrotto Group, Mastrotto Italia, Dani Conceria and Conceria Montebello) in the area which control about forty-five complete-cycle firms (from raw hide to the finished product) and which account, directly or indirectly through subcontracted work, for about 60 per cent of the district's turnover (Table 5.3).

From our interviews, we could highlight three main factors influencing the strategy of embeddedness adopted by the Arzignano firms which have slowed down the relocation processes: 1. the existence of a high local level of expertise in firms and technicians, 2. the presence of a collective depuration plant, and 3. the social embeddedness of the local entrepreneurs, which prevented them from going abroad because of the costs of export. Tacit knowledge

Table 5.2 Performance indicators of the district of Arzignano

Year	Firm	Number of employees	Sales (€)	Export (€)
2001	760	11900	4,500,000	1,685,000
2002	736	12154	4,479,000	1,670,000
2003	720	11644	4,223,000	1,461,337
2004	721	11504	4,257,000	1,391,400
2013	468	8272	2,732,00	1,350,000

Source: Authors' elaboration on the entrepreneurial local association.

Table 5.3 The main tannery firms of the district of Arzignano

	2004		2013	
	Revenue (millions of €)	Number of employees	Revenue (millions of €)	Number of employees
Gruppo Mastrotto*	209,5	619	261,5	1800
Rino Mastrotto Group	238,7	521	250	1100
Dani Leather srl	40,3	149	220	900
Conceria Cristina**	96,2	182	126	213
Conceria Montebello spa	48,6	188	60	200

Note: *Since 2013 this includes Duma and Conceria Mastrotto; **Since 1988 it is part of Peretti Group.

Source: Authors' elaboration on the Aida database.

is rooted in the professional skills of workers employed by local firms. The difficulty of codifying these skills makes any greenfield investment abroad risky. The processing of hides requires great experience and artistic sensitivity. Transforming hides from the raw to the finished state involves about eighty different operations, each of which requires specific machinery and actions by 'intermediate' qualified personnel, such as chief machine operators, pickers and product controllers, or professionals (such as dyeing and refining technicians) who possess key skills in the use of the chemicals to be added to the process. Re-tanning and dyeing – wet operations, which take place in the tumblers – are based on more or less secret 'company recipes'. Those workers are usually over fifty years old and are not inclined to move. Mismanagement of the process would be extremely costly for the firms because raw materials account for 60 per cent of the total cost.

The few large local firms that have relocated their activities often do not re-import products into Italy for final checks but sell them directly abroad. High-quality production is again entirely carried out at Arzignano.[1] The second factor explaining the slow dynamics of internationalisation of the tannery district concerns the so-called external economies. Innovation in the mechanisation of tanning processes by the local machine producers has always provided Arzignano firms with a formidable competitive advantage, which has offset their higher labour costs (Conejos *et al.*, 1997). The existence of a collective water purifier binds firms to the local district. The third factor is the scarce propensity of local entrepreneurs to transfer abroad. When small firms internationalise, they suffer greatly from the liability of foreignness. Small family-run enterprises are not in a position to amortise the costs of a new investment in the short term, given the numerous risks that they may encounter without knowledge of either the language or the local culture.

The large international clothing, leather and footwear brands produce in the East, but they acquire their raw materials from Vicenza. The largest production area for buyers is now Guangdong, in China, which produces 20 per cent of leather furniture in the world and 30 per cent of the footwear related to the lower segment of the market. The district of Arzignano, however, seems able to maintain its leadership in the medium-to-high segment. The important shift towards the automotive market has supported the consolidation of the major groups that now are offering to their clients the final cover sitting for the car (cut and sewn). These operations are organised outside Italy (in MNEs' subsidiaries units located in Tunisia or Serbia). A small part of the production is manufactured by the MNEs of the district in Brazil and China, but it covers mainly the less valuable products, and the direct demand coming from Brazil, the US and China.

The recent reorganisation of the Mastrotto Group saw the opening of a large logistic hub using the just-in-time technique with global clients, and a big warehouse with more than 800 colours, and leader pieces available to be sent to clients in about 48 hours). This confirms, once again, the centrality of the district in Arzignano as a productive site. Another important common feature that characterises the homegrown MNEs, but also the small companies of the district, is their continuous attention to environmental problems. Interestingly, Mastrotto Group and Dani Conceria, which are direct competitors, are now collaborating on a specific project related to environmental sustainability and green technologies (investing in R&D for research on new leather material as a substitute for plastic). Another company, Conceria Montebello, concluded a project in 2014 sponsored by the European Union, called 'nanoleather', focused on the application of nanotechnologies for making the leather soft.

To sum up, the main MNEs of the district present some common and important characteristics that, differently from other MNEs, have been the main drivers of their growth and success. Their internationalisation is not driven by the need for cutting costs but from the need for a strong presence in a specific market and their physical proximity to raw materials. In some cases, we also assist in some back-shoring of the production process within the district where it is easier to find specific skills and competencies.

5.6 Conclusions

The process of globalisation has significantly involved the Italian industrial clusters/districts, mainly through a process of global relocation (involving global value chains), boosting their export flows, and the building of international distributive channels (Sammarra and Belussi, 2006). In the leather-tanning district of Arzignano, the 'classic' model of internationalisation through FDIs has been pursued by only a few large firms, the homegrown local MNEs (and particularly by Rino Mastrotto, Gruppo Mastrotto and Dani). In Arzignano, most of the firms adopted the 'second-best solution', which we call 'reverse relocation', moving labour and not capital in the district, and absorbing a large inflow of unskilled labour (which involved almost one-third/one quarter of the total workforce hired in the district). The positive aspects of this phenomenon concern the district's growth model, which appears able to redistribute more income to local factors. The model of labour circulation has characterised the development of the high-tech American districts, a case in point being Silicon Valley (Saxenian, 1994; 2000). In Prato, new Chinese firms have repopulated the district (Becattini, 2003). Our analysis has shown that internationalisation can occur together with territorial embeddedness of firms, combining 'reverse relocation' and re-shoring or back-shoring. The existence of and the need to transmit 'practical knowledge' have dissuaded small local firms from undertaking the traditional relocation route. Arzignano has progressively become a leading global district by developing specific expertise in the treatment of hides and finishing. It has followed a distinctive path by resisting the strong competition that emerged in the 1990s, relying on embeddedness, high production-cycle industrialisation, and developing small homegrown MNEs. The adoption of a 'reverse relocation' strategy has acted as a significant barrier against the leakage of tacit local knowledge to new industrialising countries. This is an interesting – and involuntary –collective process of protecting innovation (as an alternative way to the standard strategy of diffused patenting activity). Our study raises several important issues concerning the international trajectories of Italian industrial clusters/ districts. The heterogeneity of firms' strategies prevents the predominance of a single 'optimal route' and generates numerous evolutionary paths. The model of 'reverse relocation' seems to be a major factor in local development which prevents the activation of de-industrialisation mechanisms and induces local actors to invest in higher value-added production phases. A final consideration concerns the integration of immigrants into the district's social context. Attracting and keeping a foreign labour force also means endowing the local community with the social, educational and religious institutions which guarantee immigrants an adequate lifestyle.

To conclude, the Arzignano district has activated a new model of internationalisation based on moving both labour and capital in the global economy.

Note

1 The Mastrotto Group, which derives from Conceria Mastrotto founded in 1958, has been present in Brazil since 1998, where it has built a new tannery with Bertin Ltd, Bermas, which specialises in the low end of the market. In 2001 the Gruppo Mastrotto launched a joint venture in Brazil – at Cachoeira in the state of Bahia – with Mastrotto Reichert Sa. Its global expansion started in 1998 with the opening of a new manufacturing plant in Brazil, followed by two other production plants in Tunisia and Indonesia, thus leading to it becoming one of the key world players in the leather industry and the first tanning company in Europe. In 2000 the group acquired a tannery specialising in processing raw hide up to the wet-blue stage, situated in Croatia, near Zagreb. In 2005 Mastrotto opened a tannery in Indonesia, Mastrotto Indonesia Pt. Today it employs more than 2,000 people throughout the world and has an annual turnover of more than €450 million. In 1994 the Beschin tannery started up a joint venture factory in China to serve the Asian market. Rino Mastrotto Group was born in the mid-1950s and, as Gruppo Mastrotto, it started its expansion in 1998 with the opening of manufacturing plants in Brazil, China and Australia. In recent years, the Rino Mastrotto Group has shifted from investment in the Chinese distribution network to the operation of a tannery. Another recent small MNE is Dal Maso Group Hong Kong Limited, which markets leather goods and controls Dal Maso Leather Co. Ltd, which has opened a factory in the Chinese province of Guangdong. Conceria Dani was born in 1950, but differently from the other two companies it started its global expansion only in 2005 when it opened manufacturing plants in the US, China, Slovenia and Tunisia. In the US it manufactures the leather of deer, and recently it has opened numerous showrooms in China and in the US. In Conceria Dani we can count twenty-two nationalities; only 40 per cent are Italian, with the remaining being from other European countries (21 per cent), Asia (19 per cent), Africa (18 per cent) and America (2 per cent).

References

Albertoni, F., Elia, S. and Piscitello, L. 2015. Reconfiguration of the value chain: the back shoring of business services, paper presented at the XXVI Riunione scientifica annuale AiIG, Vicenza, Italy.

Amin, A. and Cohendet, P. 2000. Organisational learning and governance through embedded practices, *Journal of Management and Governance*, 4(1–2), 93–116.

Ancarani, A., Di Mauro, C., Fratocchi, L., Orzes, G. and Saror, M. 2015. A survival analysis of offshore initiatives, paper presented at the XXVI Riunione scientifica annuale AiIG, Vicenza, Italy.

Arndt, S. and Kierzkowsky, H. 2001. *Fragmentation. New Production Patterns in the World Economy*, Oxford University Press, Oxford.

Bair, J. and Gereffi, G. 2001. Local clusters in global chains: the causes and consequences of export dynamism in Torreon's blue jeans industry, *World Development*, 29(11), 1885–1903.

Banca Intesa. 2006. *Il distretto della concia di Arzignano*, internal publication.

Becattini, G. 2003. *From Industrial Districts to Local Development*, Edward Elgar, Cheltenham.

Belussi, F. 2006. In search of a theory of spatial clustering: agglomeration vs active clustering, in B. Asheim, P. Cooke and R. Martin (eds) *Clusters in Regional Development*, Routledge, London, pp. 69–89.

Belussi, F. 2015. The international resilience of Italian industrial districts/clusters (ID/C) between knowledge re-shoring and manufacturing off (near)-shoring, *Investigaciones Regionales – Journal of Regional Research*, 32, 89–113.

Belussi, F. and Caldari, K. 2011. The Lancashire industrial district: its rise, prosperity and decline in the analysis of British economists, in T. Raffaelli, T. Nishizawa and S. Cook (eds) *Marshall, Marshallians, and Industrial Economics*, Routledge, Oxford, pp. 135–162.

Belussi, F. and De Propris, L. 2013. They are industrial districts, but not as we know them!, in P. McCann, F. Giarratani and G. Hewings (eds) *Handbook of Economic Geography and Industry Studies*, Elgar, Cheltenham, pp. 479–492.

Belussi, F., Gottardi, G. and Rullani, E. (eds) 2003. *The Technological Evolution of Industrial Districts*, Kluwer, Boston, MA, pp. 1–600.

Belussi, F. and Sammarra, A. (eds) 2005. *Industrial Districts, Relocation, and the Governance of Global Value Chain*, Cleup, Padova.

Belussi, F. and Sammarra, A. (eds) 2009. *Business Networks in Clusters and Industrial Districts: The governance of the global value chain*, Routledge, London.

Belussi, F. and Sammarra, A. 2010. The international fragmentation of the industrial districts and clusters (IDs&Cs) value chain between relocation and global integration, in F. Belussi and A. Sammarra (eds) *Business Networks in Clusters and Industrial Districts. The governance of the global value chain*, Routledge, London, pp. 3–23.

Belussi, F. and Sedita, S.R. 2009. Life cycle vs. multiple path dependency in industrial districts, *European Planning Studies*, 17(4), 505–528.

Belussi, F. and Sedita, S.R. 2010. Moving immigrants into Western industrial districts: the 'inverse' delocalisation of the leather tanning district of Arzignano, in, F. Belussi and A. Sammarra (eds) *Business Networks in Clusters and Industrial Districts. The governance of the global value chain*, Routledge, London, pp. 136–145.

Cainelli, G. and De Liso, N. 2005. Innovation in industrial districts: evidence from Italy, *Industry and Innovation*, 12(3), 383–398.

Calvet, A.L. 1981. A synthesis of foreign direct investment theories and theories of the multinational firm, *Journal of International Business Studies*, 12(1), 43–59.

Caniato, F., Elia, S., Luzzini, D., Piscitello, L. and Ronchi, S. 2014. Location drivers, governance model and performance in service offshoring, *International Journal of Production Economics*, 163, 189–199.

Carabelli, A., Hirsh, G. and Rabellotti, R. 2006. Italian SMEs and industrial districts on the move: where are they going? *Quaderno SEMeQ*, 13, Università degli Studi del Piemonte Orientale.

Carbaugh, R. 2007. Is international trade a substitute for migration? *Global Economy Journal*, 7(3), 113.

Conejos, J., Duch, E., Fontrodona, J., Hernández, J.M., Luzárraga, A. and Terré, E. 1997. Canvi estratègic i clusters a Catalunya. Dep. Indústria. *Generalitat de Catalunya*, Barcelona.

Cooke, P. 2004. Regional knowledge capabilities, embeddedness of firms and industry organisation: bioscience megacentres and economic geography, *European Planning Studies*, 12(5), 625–641.

Doz, Y. 2011. Qualitative research for international business, *Journal of International Business Studies*, 42(5), 582–590.

Eisenhardt, K.M. 1989. Building theories from case study research, *Academy of Management Review*, 14(4), 532–550.

Fratocchi, L., Di Mauro, C., Barbier, P., Nassimbeni, G. and Zanoni, A. 2014. When manufacturing moves back: concepts and questions, *Journal of Purchasing and Supply Management*, 20(81), 54–59.

Gjerdåkers, A. 2006. Green innovation and leather tanning: an Italian industrial district, its global commodity chain and distributed knowledge base, PhD thesis, Oslo University.

Glaser, B. and Strauss, A. 1967. *The Discovery of Grounded Theory: Strategies of qualitative research*, Weidenfeld and Nicolson, London.

Grabher, G. 1993. *The Embedded Firm: On the socio-economics of industrial networks*, Routledge, London.

Guerrieri, P. and Iammarino, S. 2001. The dynamics of Italian industrial districts: towards a renewal of competitiveness, in P. Guerrieri, S. Iammarino and C. Pietrobelli (a cura di), *The Global Challenge to Industrial Districts: Small and meduim-sized enterprises in Italy and Taiwan*, Edward Elgar, Cheltenham.

Iammarino, S. and McCann, P. 2013. *Multinationals and Economic Geography*, Edward Elgar, Northampton, MA.

Kluger, M. and Rapoport, H. 2005. Skilled immigration, business networks and foreign direct investment, CESifo Working Paper, n. 14555.

Lazerson, M. and Lorenzoni, G. 1999. The firms that feed industrial districts: a return to the Italian source, *Industrial and Corporate Change*, 8, 36–47.

Lazzeretti, L., Sedita, S.R., Caloffi A. 2014. Founders and disseminators of cluster research. *Journal of Economic Geography*, 14(1): 21–43.

Loasby, B. 1998. Industrial districts as knowledge communities, in M. Bellet and C. L'Harmet (eds) *Industry, Space and Competition. The contribution of economists of the past*, Edward Elgar, Cheltenham.

Lombardi, M. 2000. The cognitive approach to the study of local production systems, in F. Belussi and G. Gottardi (eds) *Evolutionary Patterns of Local Industrial Systems*, Ashgate, Aldershot.

Mariotti, S., Mutinelli, M. and Piscitello, L. 2008. The internationalization of production by Italian industrial districts' firms: structural and behavioural determinants, *Regional Studies*, 42(5), 719–735.

Markusen, A. 1996. Sticky places in slippery space: a typology on industrial districts, *Economic Geography*, 72(3), 293–313.

Markusen, J. 1983. Factors movements and commodity trade as complements, *Journal of International Economics*, 14(3–4), 341–356.

Marshall, A. 1919. *Industry and Trade*, Macmillan, London.

Marshall, A. 1920. *Principles of Economics*, 8th edn, Macmillan, London; 1st edn [1891] Macmillan, London.

Martin, R. and Sunley, P. 2003. Deconstructing clusters: chaotic concept or policy panacea? *Journal of Economic Geography*, 1, 5–35.

Maskell, P. 2001. Towards a knowledge based theory of the geographical cluster, *Industrial and Corporate Change*, 10(4), 921–943.

Moon, H.C. and Roehl, T.W. 2001. Unconventional foreign direct investment and the imbalance theory, *International Business Review*, 10(2), 197–215.

Mudambi, R. and Santangelo, G. 2015. From shallow resource pools to emerging clusters: the role of multinational enterprise subsidiaries in peripheral areas, *Regional Studies*, published online.

Mundell, R. 1957. International trade and factor mobility, *The American Economic Review*, 47(3), 321–335.

Oliver, J.L.H., Garrigós, J.A. and Porta, J.I.D. 2008. External ties and the reduction of knowledge asymmetries among clusters within global value chains: the case of the ceramic tile district of Castellon, *European Planning Studies*, 16(4), 507–520.

Patto per lo Sviluppo del Distretto Vicentino della Concia, 2004, Confindustria Vicenza, unpublished document.

Porter, M.E. 1998. Clusters and the new economics of competition, *Harvard Business Review*, November–December.

Porter, M. 2000. Location, competition and economic development, *Economic Development Quarterly*, 14(1), 23–32.

Poster, 2005. Osservatorio del distretto vicentino della concia, report non pubblicato, Vicenza.

Sammarra, A. and Belussi, F. 2006. Evolution and relocation in fashion-led industrial districts: evidence from two case studies, *Entrepreneurship & Regional Development*, Special Issue on 'Industrial districts' relocation processes: evolutionary and policy issues', 18 November, pp. 543–562.

Saxenian, A. 1994. *Regional Advantage: Culture and competition in Silicon Valley and The Route 128*, Harvard University Press, Cambridge, MA.

Saxenian, A. 2000. Silicon Valley's new immigrant entrepreneurs, University of California Working paper n. 15.

Signori, F. 1980. *L'economia di Bassano dalle origini ad oggi*. AA. VV., *Storia di Bassano*, Stampa G. Rumor, Vicenza.

Sorenson, O. 2005. *Social networks and industrial geography*, in Cantner U., Dinopoulos.

Trebilcock, M. and Sudak, M. 2006. The political economy of emigration and immigration, *New York University Law Review*, 81(1), 234–292.

Unic, 2013, Il rapporto di sostenibilità del settore conciario italiano, Vicenza.

Welch, C., Piekkari, R., Plakoyinnaki, E. and Paavilainen-Mäntymäki, E. 2011. Theorising from case studies: towards a pluralist future for international business research, *Journal of International Business Studies*, 42(5), 740–772.

Yin, R. 1994. *Case Study Research: Design and methods*, 2nd edn, Sage Publishing, Beverly Hills, CA.

You, J. and Wilkinson F. 1994. Competition and cooperation: towards understanding industrial districts, *Review of Political Economy*, 6(3), 259–278.

Zaheer, S. 1995. Overcoming the liability of foreignness, *Academy Management Journal*, 38(2), 341–363.

Zampiva, F. 1997. *L'arte della concia: Ad Arzignano, nel Vicentino, nel Veneto e in Italia: dalle origini ai giorni nostri*. Egida.

Zeller, C. 2001. Clustering biotech: a recipe for success? Spatial patterns of growth of biotechnology in Munich, Rhineland and Hamburg, *Small Business Economics*, 17(1), 123–141.

Zucchella, A. 2006. Local cluster dynamics: trajectories of mature industrial districts between decline and multiple embeddedness, *Journal of Institutional Economics*, 2(1), 21–44.

6 Ethnic entrepreneurship in the Prato industrial district

An analysis of foundings and failures of Italian and Chinese firms*

Luciana Lazzeretti and Francesco Capone

6.1 Introduction

The recent economic crisis and the effects of globalization are two of the most important issues affecting the scientific debate on industrial agglomerations like geographical clusters and industrial districts (Humphrey and Schmitz, 2002; Nadvi and Halder, 2005; Rychen and Zimmermann, 2008).

In Italy some authors underline the need to rethink the industrial districts (IDs) in the wake of globalization (Rabellotti *et al.*, 2009; Accentuaro *et al.*, 2013) and the role played by medium-sized enterprises (Coltorti, 2013), but, above all, many wonder about the effects of the division of labour along the global value chain (Belussi and Sammara 2010; Chiarvesio *et al.*, 2010). These changes have affected the process of internationalization of the industrial districts, but in some cases they have also profoundly contributed to transforming their internal structure, as occurred in the emblematic case of the Marshallian ID of Prato (Becattini *et al.*, 2009) after the settlement of Chinese immigrants and entrepreneurs (Dei Ottati, 2009).

For some time now, the Prato ID has been characterised by the simultaneous presence of a multi-ethnic population of Italian and Chinese firms. The co-presence of these two communities of people and enterprises in the same territory ignited an intense debate on this local community, which involved scholars not only of local development but also of management and development economics, as well as journalists, sinologists and others, without necessarily reaching a coherent interpretation of the phenomenon (Johanson *et al.*, 2009).

Some contributions describe the evolution of the Prato ID, advancing a hypothesis about the presence of two separate districts with scarce relationships, in some cases also conjecturing a 'Chinese siege' (Pieraccini, 2008). Others, on the contrary, delineate the transformation of the textile ID into a new fashion district, partially integrated with Chinese firms (Ceccagno, 2003). In this context, even local institutions talk about a transformation from a (product-oriented) wool-textile ID towards a (market-oriented) textile fashion district (UIP, 2012). More recently, Dei Ottati (2013) discusses these contrasting perspectives and reminds us that the Prato economy has not seized all the opportunities provided by the settlement of Chinese immigrants, which might happen if the two communities develop more integrated relationships. Similarly, Pilotti *et al.* (2014), invoking the opportunity to rethink the policy of the district, hope for a re-emergence of districtual ecologies capable of transforming multiculturalism from a factor of conflict to a competitive one.

The phenomenon is complex and has become important also for public opinion because it represents a metaphor of the post-industrial decline of IDs due to the process of globalization (Gereffi and Memedovic, 2003; Belussi and Sedita, 2010). Prato becomes an interesting case study on the profound changes involving old Europe and the emerging countries, which are no longer in a development phase but are new players in the global economy.

The aim of this chapter is to contribute to this debate investigating the evolution of Chinese and Italian firms in Prato after the Second World War until today. Through a demographic analysis of firms' foundings, failures and density, we analyse the process of transformation that has occurred in the ID of Prato, with a specific focus on the past two decades, which have witnessed the settlement of Chinese immigrants and the emergence and development of 'fast fashion'. The work allows us to reconstruct the processes of internal transformation of the Prato ID up to its most recent changes and to discuss managerial implications of these changes.

Industrial demography is an approach that originates in organizational sciences (Carroll and Hannan, 1992; 2000) and has been applied to analyse the dynamics of industrial clustering and evolution of industries, IDs and clusters, also thanks to the contribution of organizational ecology (Staber, 2001; De Propris and Lazzeretti, 2009; among others). This approach explores the processes by which corporate populations change over time, including their organizational founding, growth, decline, structural transformation and mortality (Manigart, 1994). We focus on the effects of environmental constraints and on competition within and between populations to explain the processes of expansion and decline of populations of organizations, and thus propose design strategies (Aldrich *et al.*, 1984).

In management, there are an increasing number of contributions investigating foundings and failures of firms (in a particular population), which originate from the study of organizational ecology. Barnett (1997) affirms that the strongest organizations survive, and that it is important to investigate the dynamics of foundings and failures in an industry and the dynamics of competitive intensity. Low and Abrahamson (1997) states that entrepreneurship research has paid insufficient attention to the context in which new businesses are started, and it is therefore important to investigate the dynamics of foundings and failures in order to identify the factors that consistently lead to entrepreneurial success or failure. Manigart (1994) focuses on the sectorial and environmental forces that facilitate or inhibit the creation of venture capital companies in three European countries.

This approach focuses on firms' foundings and failures and reconstructs the demographic (and ecological) processes of a population. It has received relevant interest in both organization studies (Baum, 2003) and management sciences (Bogaert *et al.*, 2014). The obstacles in its application are mostly due to the difficulty of acquiring the *ad hoc* databases needed to reconstruct the entire history of organizations.

The chapter is structured as follows. The next section aims to contextualize the study of dynamics of industrial clustering, considering the settlement of foreign communities and the globalization process. The third section presents the research design, describing its objectives and data sources. The fourth section presents an historical summary of Chinese immigration to Prato. The fifth section presents the analysis of Italian and Chinese firms' foundings and failures. The chapter ends with a discussion of the transformation of the Prato ID.

6.2   Industrial districts between globalization and multiculturalism

The increasing presence of foreign firms in traditional industrial areas is related to the rapid process of globalization and to the worsening of the financial and economic crisis (Barberis, 2008). Some contributions have focused on the emergence of new Chinese entrepreneurs (Pietrobelli *et al.*, 2011), particularly within the manufacturing sectors localised in IDs (Lombardi *et al.*, 2015).

The presence of Chinese immigrants and firms in Prato has been at the centre of a wide debate. Besides representing one of the largest in Italy and Europe, the Prato Chinese community has drawn increasing interest also because of the relevance the ID of Prato has assumed in Italian studies of local development, after which it has asserted itself as an international case study (Becattini *et al.*, 2009).

An early stream of studies analysed the contribution of immigrants to IDs (Dei Ottati, 2009) and related entrepreneurial models (Guercini, 2001; Rabino *et al.*, 2009). In these investigations, foreign communities are considered as either a resource or a complex challenge. For instance, the recent debate on the difficulties of integration experienced by Chinese firms in Italy and Prato has echoed widely (Toccafondi, 2009).

More recently, research on multiculturalism has shifted the attention to ethnic entrepreneurship (Santini *et al.*, 2009; Zanni and Zucchella, 2009) and multicultural variety within local systems of production (Lazzeretti and Capone, 2014; Pilotti *et al.*, 2014) as well as to the socio-economic challenges faced by local and foreign communities (Johanson *et al.*, 2009). Meanwhile, the phenomenon of immigration has been increasingly linked to socio-demographic issues, such as regulation of migration flows and social cohesion (Bressan and Radini, 2009), offering new insights into the interplay of – global, national and local – scales in the complex dynamics between migrants and localities (Ceccagno, 2009).

In this context, the case of Prato has become an important point of observation over the decline of industrial clustering and the competitive relations between immigrants and local communities, especially regarding the challenges of economic and social integration (Baldassar *et al.*, 2015).

Against this background, the interpretation in the literature is not unanimous. For example, Ceccagno (2009) indicates an increasing integration between the two *filières*, estimating that in 2004 one third of the locally produced fabric was purchased by Chinese firms operating in 'fast fashion', while Bracci (2009) emphasizes the co-existence of two separate communities in the district with neither integration nor conflict.

Recently Dei Ottati (2013) indicates three main trends of study. A first strand considers the contributions that interpret the development of the Chinese immigrants in Prato as a functional adaptation of the local economy to the changes brought by globalization (Ceccagno, 2003; 2009). A second line refers to the writings in which such development is considered a threat to the local economy and society (Pieraccini, 2008). Finally, a third strand includes studies in which it is believed that the development of Chinese fast fashion has not, until now, favoured the adaptation of the Prato economy to globalization, but that this outcome could be achieved if the two populations of firms and people integrated with each other (Dei Ottati, 2013).

Whereas Saxenian's (2006) study of Silicon Valley has underlined the propelling power of the so-called New Argonauts in a leading high-tech cluster, the case of the Chinese firms in the Prato ID can be considered as an emblematic instance of the risks of globalization and of the dynamics of clustering and survival for low-tech foreign and local industries.

This issue also fits into the recent debate on cluster evolution and on the role of clusters' (and local networks') openness to multinational enterprises and foreign firms in renewing local knowledge pools (Hervás-Oliver and Albors-Garrigós, 2008; Hervás-Oliver and Boix-Domènech, 2013) and achieving superior performances (Eisingerich *et al.*, 2010).

The case study selected for the analysis is particularly representative also because, over the past two decades, the district has experienced relevant changes not only in its internal productive structure but also in its social texture, which has increasingly become multi-ethnic, similarly to the new clusters born out of the *diaspora effect* (Sonderegger and Täube, 2010).

The population of firms and people has recorded an increasing share of Chinese immigrants, whereas the pre-existing Italian, locally integrated *filière* has declined and been surpassed by the Chinese one, which is better integrated within global value chains and has a stronger specialization in clothing (ready-to-wear). These changes have generated an intense debate not only on the issue of the transformations and risks of globalization but also on the fundamental issue of district identity.

6.3   Research design and data sources

The present study investigates the transformation of the Prato ID and the evolution of the main Italian and Chinese firms, focusing in particular on the recent evolution from 1990 until 2011. This time period considers the whole life of the Chinese firms, as the first ones began to localize in Prato at the beginning of the 1990s (Dei Ottati, 2014).

The main data source to reconstruct the natality and mortality flows and the density of the two populations is the Economic-Administrative Registry (REA) collected by the Chamber of Commerce of Prato (CCIAA) and elaborated by its Research Office.

As regards the Chinese firms, it was possible to consult all the information on foundings and failures of foreign firms in the Province of Prato, together with other information related to the firm's localization, typology and NACE code of economic activity. This data source allows us to reconstruct the whole historical series of the Chinese firms because every firm must be recorded in this registry by law. The database on foreign firms includes more than 16,800 records, of which 11,400 (almost 70 per cent) regard Chinese firms. The database registers more than 11,000 foundings and 6,000 failures of Chinese firms.

Data on Italian firms (1946–1998) have been collected from the REA of the Chamber of Commerce of Prato and already elaborated in previous studies on the Prato ID (Lazzeretti and Storai, 1999; 2003). More recent information is drawn from surveys on the density, foundings and failures of firms in the province, carried out by the Prato CCIAA since 1995.

Regarding the territorial unit of analysis, the database refers only to the municipalities of the Province of Prato, so that the data on foreign firms are available only at provincial level. Although this is an administrative boundary, it should be noted that the labour local system of Prato used for the ISTAT's identification of IDs also comprises the seven municipalities of the province (Sforzi, 1997).

Finally, we decided to adopt the definition of a Chinese firm given by the CCIAA Research Office, i.e. a firm with at least an owner, manager or associate of Chinese nationality. It is therefore possible to consider also companies and not only individual firms.

6.4   Chinese entrepreneurs in the Prato industrial district: an historical summary

Over recent years, despite the recession at national and regional level, the number of foreign entrepreneurs in Tuscany has more than doubled, rising from 23,000 in 2000 to almost 49,000 in 2008, against a substantial stability in the number of Italian entrepreneurs. In the same period, the percentage of foreign entrepreneurs in the total number of businesses increased from 4 per cent to 8 per cent in Tuscany (IRPET, 2010). Given this background, Tuscany is confirmed as one of the country's regions with the highest rate of Italian as well as foreign entrepreneurship, localised mainly in IDs.

As for the nationality of the entrepreneurs, as already noted the Chinese are the predominant ethnic group and they are mainly localised in Prato.

The high Chinese entrepreneurial spirit is also related to the high percentage of Chinese residing in Tuscany (with a high 9.4 per cent), mostly concentrated in the districtual areas (Unioncamere, 2012). As pointed out in other contributions, this community shows a stronger propensity for entrepreneurship than other ethnic groups, and particularly for the Chinese group originated from Zhejiang and Fujian living in Prato (Johanson *et al.*, 2009). In fact, compared with the 10 per cent of Chinese residents making up the total of Tuscan foreign residents, the percentage of Chinese entrepreneurs almost doubles (18 per cent).

The Chinese community is often recognized as an 'ethnic entrepreneurial community' which has developed in indigenous local production systems through a system of closed relationships. In 2007, for example, 64 per cent of Chinese enterprises were located in Tuscan IDs (Dei Ottati, 2009). This phenomenon has continued to grow in recent years: recent data from Unioncamere (2012) report rank Prato in first place by far among the Italian provinces on the share of foreign companies (23 per cent).

Moreover, to understand the important evolution of this phenomenon, it should be noted that while in 1989 there were only thirty-eight Chinese residents in Prato, in 1991 they were already more than 1,000. At the end of 2006, there were over 10,000 Chinese, 78 per cent of who were born in China, while 18 per cent already belonged to the second generation (Ceccagno, 2003). In addition, 34 per cent of them were less than twenty years old, and 47 per cent were between the ages of twenty-one and forty. Only 17 per cent were over the age of forty (Johanson *et al.*, 2009). Analysing the percentage of self-employed immigrants, Prato ranks in first place again, with 14 per cent compared with the regional average of 8 per cent.

As already mentioned, Chinese companies began to develop in the early 1990s, when they started the activities of textile finishing and knitting (Toccafondi, 2009; Dei Ottati, 2014). At this stage they were mainly subcontractors of Italian companies and represented an opportunity for local businesses, because of both labour flexibility and lower subcontracting costs. With the recovery of production in the 1990s, knitting mills of Prato began to encounter more and more difficulties in finding Italian homeworkers and subcontractors willing to sew knitted garments. It was then that Chinese immigrants, already localized in Tuscany, and particularly in Campi Bisenzio, started to move to Prato (Dei Ottati, 2014).

This first development of Chinese immigrants in Prato satisfied local demand for jobs – at home and subcontracting in knitting, then gradually in clothing – that would otherwise have remained unsatisfied. In this period, companies operating in clothing grew at a fast pace and this provoked a first shift from the textile industry (mainly knitwear).[1] In practice, Chinese subcontracting textile enterprises amounted to less than 200 in 2011, and they worked mainly for final Chinese firms.

A very interesting aspect to note is that the Chinese firms, once settled in the ID in non-primary production (knitwear), promoted the development of a new mode of production, so-called fast fashion (Guercini, 2001), virtually absent in Prato before their arrival, and later on developed a whole new industry, clothing, which had been ignored by local entrepreneurs (Dei Ottati, 2014).

6.5   An analysis of foundings and failures in the Prato industrial district

6.5.1   *The evolution of the textile-clothing firms in Prato (1945–2011)*

The ID of Prato began to develop in the years after the Second World War from a 'double production circuit' based on large and small firms to mainly small and medium-sized enterprises (SMEs) (Becattini, 2001). Firms started to grow at the end of the 1940s (Figure 6.1). The canonical development in terms of long-period growth is ascribable to the period ending in 1975. With the crisis starting in the 1990s, the density of firms operating in the ID fell from the peak of almost 10,000 units in the mid-1980s to the 6,000 firms of 2011, although the effects were partly absorbed by the district, given the less intensive decrease in employment. The crisis of the ID of Prato was more acute in the last decade, also due to exogenous factors, such as the process of globalization, with the opening of the European market to China, the intensification of international competition from countries with lower labour costs (BRICs), the financial crisis and the dollar devaluation (Dei Ottati, 2014).

In the period 1995–2011, in the Province of Prato there was a significant decrease in the number of firms, from more than 7,000 to about 6,600, with a minimum of 6,000 in 2005.

This crisis is deeper, however, if we analyse the main sub-sectors within the macro-industry of textile-clothing. In fact, if we consider the main industry's statistical subdivision in the two economic activities of textile and clothing, we register different results. During the period, textile enterprises decreased from about 6,000 in 1995 to just fewer than 3,000 in 2011, with a drop of more than 50 per cent, while the clothing sector showed an inverse trend, passing from more than 1,000 enterprises at the beginning of the 1990s to about 4,000 in 2011, quadrupling in number.

In summary, while textile experiences a significant decline in its life cycle, clothing passes from the initial stage of birth to full development, and asserts itself as the principal activity at districtual level. Figure 6.2 shows the intersection of the density lines of the two populations' evolution in 2008, with the firms operating in clothing overtaking those operating in the textile industry. As well known, the development of the apparel industry is also due to the settlement and significant development of the Chinese community in Prato starting from the early 1990s.

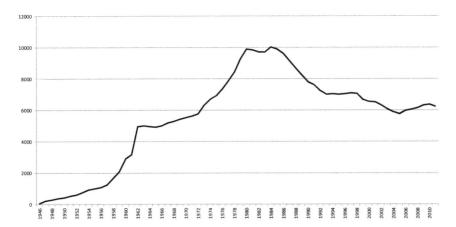

Figure 6.1 The evolution of textile-clothing firms in the Province of Prato, 1945–2011.
Source: Authors' elaboration on Prato CCIAA.

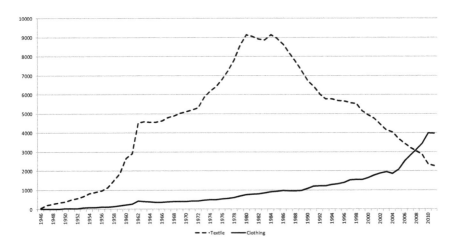

Figure 6.2 The evolution of textile firms and clothing firms in the Province of Prato, 1945–2011.
Source: Authors' elaboration on Prato CCIAA.

6.5.2 The evolution of Italian and Chinese firms (1990–2011)

Figure 6.3 presents the evolution of the two sub-sectors of textile and clothing by firms' nationality. As already mentioned, the two populations registered opposite trends: Italian firms started to steadily decrease in the 1990s, passing from more than 7,500 units to fewer than 3,000, while Chinese firms increased, with a remarkable peak right at the turn of the millennium, passing from about 1,000 units in 1999 to nearly 4,000 in 2011.

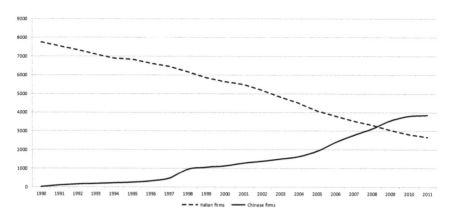

Figure 6.3 The evolution of Chinese and Italian firms in textile-clothing in the Province of Prato, 1990–2011.

Source: Authors' elaboration on Prato CCIAA.

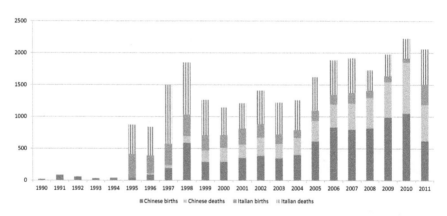

Figure 6.4 Foundings and failures of Chinese and Italian firms in textile-clothing in Prato, 1990–2011.

Source: Authors' elaboration on Prato CCIAA. Missing data for Italian firms before 1994.

Figure 6.4 presents the foundings and failures of Chinese and Italian firms in the Province of Prato. As expected, the natality rate of Chinese firms is larger than that of Italian firms and consequently the mortality rate of Italian firms is higher than that of Chinese firms. This is true only until 2008, when the mortality of Chinese firms exceeds that of Italian companies. In addition, through-out the period, although Chinese firms are clearly growing, their mortality is always relevant, which confirms a dynamism of Chinese enterprises, as they record high rates of both founding and failure. Other contributions confirmed the intense natality and mortality of Chinese population, in which many firms came into being, but also many others ceased their activities[2] (IRPET, 2010).

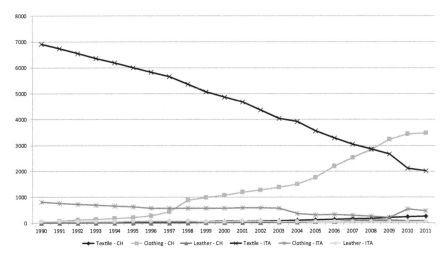

Figure 6.5 The evolution of Italian and Chinese firms in textile, clothing and leather in the Province of Prato, 1990–2011.

Source: Authors' elaboration on Prato CCIAA.

6.5.3 The evolution of the Chinese sub-sectors in the clothing industry

Figure 6.5 presents the evolution of Chinese and Italian firms subdivided by ATECO 2007 codes of economic activities (13 for textile, 14 for clothing and 15 for leather). The most important Italian population is the one operating in the textile industry, which recorded a significant decline from about 7,000 units at the beginning of the 1990s to almost 2,000 at the end of 2011. Italian firms operating in the clothing industry remained fairly stable over the period, except for a bend during the period 2004–2009.

The population of Chinese firms operating in the economic activity of clothing recorded instead its main growth for the period, passing from nearly 1,000 companies at the end of the 1990s to 3,500 units at the end of the period we are looking at.[3]

This background is also confirmed by the distribution of the Chinese firms in Prato by ATECO codes from 1990 to 2011, as registered in the REA. In fact, approximately 71.3 per cent of Chinese firms belong to clothing, while just 5.2 per cent belong to textiles. Leather is represented by about 2 per cent of firms, while those in trade of clothing are about 5 per cent, turning out to be the second most important statistical economic activity. If we consider all the activities of the enlarged *filière* of textile and clothing, Chinese companies record a percentage of more than 85 per cent (textile, clothing, leather and trade).

Figure 6.6 presents the evolution of Chinese sub-populations from the 1990s until 2011, exclusively in textile and clothing economic activities. Such evolution confirms the importance for Chinese enterprises of the clothing

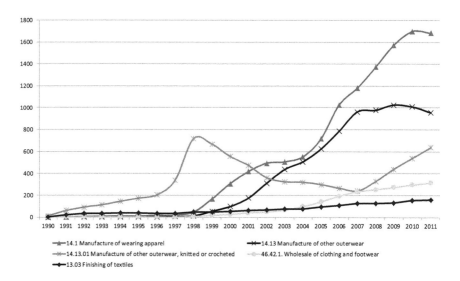

Figure 6.6 The evolution of Chinese firms by ATECO economic activity in the Province of Prato, 1990–2011.

Source: Authors' elaboration on Prato CCIAA.

industry, which basically is the most important sector, having almost 90 per cent of the Chinese enterprises active in 2011.

Figure 6.7 presents the evolution of different sub-populations by economic activity, with the exception of clothing, in order to investigate their evolution.

An important fact is the entrance of Chinese immigrants in the district's textile *filière* and, later on, the development of a Chinese clothing industry. Similarly important is to underline the development of Chinese enterprises in the import–export trade. In fact, in 2011 there were almost 400 importers and exporters who linked Prato Chinese firms to the Chinese global value chain, by benefiting from the low cost of raw materials imported from China (from the same ethnic community) and from the access to European distribution channels for finished products (Dei Ottati, 2014).

Chinese firms started their business in the 1990s mainly in clothing, specializing in the manufacturing of knitted and crocheted textile apparel, and particularly in the finishing of textiles. Over the years, the textile industry became incidental, and the activities related to clothing increased exponentially, coming to represent the main industry. This picture is only partially confirmed in the literature, due to the problem that the ATECO codes do not always identify the actual activity that a firm carries out. A final interesting issue regards the transition of Chinese enterprises from subcontractors in textiles to independent firms in clothing, a shift also highlighted in the literature; unfortunately, the data at our disposal do not allow us to show this aspect quantitatively.

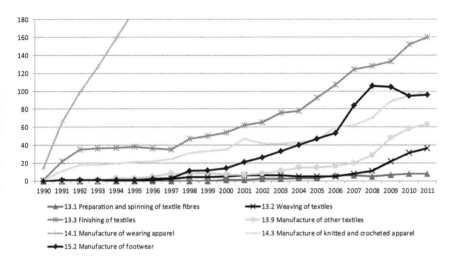

Figure 6.7 The evolution of Chinese firms by ATECO code (three digits).
Source: Authors' elaboration on Prato CCIAA.

Moreover, it is interesting to note that Chinese firms were subcontracted by Italian enterprises at the beginning of the 1990s and then collaborated with local entrepreneurs. In the shift towards the clothing activity, they began to work among them, creating an autonomous community and barriers with the Italian textile district to bring about the idea of a Chinese district separate from the Italian one (Santini *et al.*, 2009). In fact, even the collaboration with foreign firms importing textiles was often within the mother country and on a few occasions with local Italian companies (Guercini and Milanesi, 2015). There was indeed a significant growth of import–export businesses within the Chinese nationality that connected the Chinese local producers with the out-side. The main problems highlighted in the literature are whether it is possible and how to promote better integration between the two populations of firms (Dei Ottati, 2014; 2016).

It is interesting, then, to investigate whether the substitution effect between the Chinese and Italian firms also took place with regards to employment or whether the number of employees shrank to fewer than the population density and somewhat cushioned the crisis. As longitudinal data on employment from the 1990s are not available, we consulted the Census of Industry and Services in 1991, 2001 and 2011.

In 1991, the number of textile workers amounted to approximately 35,000 units, while the clothing industry employed around 3,000 workers. This was when Chinese companies began settling in Prato (Dei Ottati, 2009). In 2001, workers in the textile industry decreased to a little more than 32,000 units, with a reduction in the decade of about 8 per cent, while employees in the clothing industry amounted to almost 5,000, an increase of 66 per cent. This was the first effect of the crisis on the Italian firms combined with the first growth of Chinese enterprises. In 2011, the number of employees in the textile industry shrank to just over 16,000 units (a decline of 50 per cent), while workers in the textile industry increased to slightly more than 13,000 units, with a growth of 160 per cent in the decade.

From these figures it is clear that employment better absorbed the crisis than the firms' foundings and failures rates. The employment data show a slightly less dramatic situation than the real one.[4] In fact, clothing workers had not yet surpassed textile employees, although, with a little time lag, these data underscore the same criticalities raised in the study of mortality and birth rates.

6.6   Discussion and concluding remarks

To conclude, we summarize the main transformations that occurred in the Prato district from its founding to nowadays. In Table 6.1, the main phases of the ID are compared with the results of our demographic analyses. With respect to previous studies (Lazzeretti and Storai, 2003), this chapter has added a fourth phase in the Prato ID's evolution, in which Chinese firms at first active in the textile *filière* expanded in the clothing sector.

The first phase of the district's evolution is defined as metamorphosis and dates to the first years of the post-Second World War period. At that time, the structure of the productive system of Prato was based on two circuits centred on large integrated woollen mills and on the binomial '*impannatore*-subcontractors'. The second phase can be defined as canonical development and identifies a long period of growth leading to 1975, wherein development and consolidation of the ID model can be recognized. From a demographic point of view, the degree of external division of labour among district firms and the density of the existing populations increases. We also register the founding of new organizational populations (for instance, synthetic materials). In the 1980s, we record an important transformation in the district, which shifts from productive specialization to diversification and tertiarization. In particular, the district diversifies the activities related to the main area of production (textile), as regards not only manufacturing but also related services.

The third phase consists in a proper re-structuring, which begins in the mid-1980s and proceeds up to the 1990s, when there is an overall change in the organization of production among the firms located inside and outside the district. The purchase of some components and intermediary goods is now carried out outside the district together with the subcontracting of some activities. Demographically, this change denotes an increase in the population density of subcontractors specialized in the finishing phases of the productive cycle and a drop in the population density of subcontractors specializ ed in the first phases of the productive cycle.

We arrive then to the ID's recent developments. The fourth phase can be broadly defined as one of decline. The textile value chain records a growing

Table 6.1 The transformation of the Prato industrial district (1945–2011): focusing on the development of Chinese firms

Phases of Prato history		Industrial district	Demographic approach
1) 'The metamorphosis' (1945–1946 to 1953–1954)!		• From 'double production circuit' (i.e. large firms and small firms) to the ID	• Increase in the population density of *impannatori* and subcontractors specialized in the production of carded wool
2) 'The canonical development' – long period of growth (1954–1955 and 1974–1975)		• Development and consolidation of the ID model • Increase in the degree of external division of labour among district firms	• Increase in the density of existing populations • Founding of new organizational populations (e.g synthetic materials)
3) 'Prato transformation'	3a) Prato diversification (1975–1976 and 1993)	• Diversification of activities and functions within the ID • Development of service sectors related to textile production	• Fast growth of (both final and stage) firm populations specialized in the production of yarns, knitwear garments, new textile products and machinery for textile industry • Founding and fast growth of firm populations specialized in service sectors
	3b) Prato restructuring (1985–1990)	• ID organizational restructuring: a) change in the organization of production among firms located both inside and outside the district; b) purchase of components and intermediary goods outside the district; c) subcontracting of some activities outside the district	• Increase in the population density of subcontractors specialized in the finishing phases of productive cycle and drop in the population density of subcontractors specialized in the first phases of productive cycle • Increase in the population density of fabric traders and decline in the population density of yarn and weaving producers • Increase in the population density of *impannatori* and drop in the population density of subcontractors

(*continued*)

Table 6.1 The transformation of the Prato industrial district (1945–2011) (*continued*)

Phases of Prato history		Industrial district	Demographic approach
4) Decline of Italian textile ID (1990s–2011)		• Decline of Italian textile ID • Weakening of ID's social capital ties (in the Italian community) • Globalization, opening of the European market to China, intensification of international competition from countries with lower labour costs, financial crisis, etc. (external causes)	• Decrease of Italian textile firms • Entrance of Chinese firms operating in textile (knitting) from the 1990s
4a) Renewing or starting a new cycle?	Rise and affirmation of the clothing Chinese population (1990–2011)	• Rise and affirmation of the Chinese clothing *filière* • Increase of Chinese population • Emergence of a Chinese community with own rules and social capital ties • Social and business relationships with Chinese community in China • International relationships with global value chain	• Increase of population density in clothing • Increase of Chinese population density and decline in Italian population density • Increase of China import–export firms and development of the clothing *filière*

Source: Updated from Lazzeretti and Storai (1999; 2003).

crisis, whereas both the district's and the city's socio-economic structure transforms. The causes of the crisis can be referred both to endogenous and exogenous factors regarding the process of globalization, the opening of the European market to China, the intensification of international competition from countries with lower labour costs, and the current financial crisis (Dei Ottati, 2014). The social capital ties of the Italian community weaken, and likewise the district's resilience. The demographic processes are characterized by high mortality and low natality of Italian firms, causing a negative balance and an overall decline.

At the same time, a second opposite scenario emerges which can be considered as a renewing of the existing district or the start-up of a new and different one. In particular, a rise in and affirmation of the clothing Chinese population can be observed. After the initial Chinese settlement in the productive system of Prato, which dates back to the early 1990s and mostly concerns the sub-supplying phase in the Italian textile value chain, Chinese firms shift towards the final phases of the value chain, particularly in clothing. Afterwards, a new 'fast fashion' value chain asserts itself thanks to market, business and social relations with the homeland. The Chinese community roots itself locally and grows by building social capital based on idiosyncratic rules of conduct. Ties with the homeland are strengthened and a significant increase in the number of import–export Chinese firms occurs. Overall, the founding rates of Chinese clothing firms increase gradually up to configuring a second autonomous value chain. The clothing sector comes to clearly prevail over the textile sector at the level of local production systems, showing a counter-trend compared with the current decline.

What conclusions can be drawn from these observations?

The data gathered contribute to define different phases in the process of the district's transformation which are subject to manifold interpretations. Notwithstanding the different positions to be found in literature, a common element concerns the existence of a still active territory that shows an ability to transform; a territory that, despite a profound transformation, continues being dynamic.

Whether the identified transformations can be ascribed to a case of renewal of the existing district or the emergence of a new one still needs to be theoretically assessed. The true determinant is the lack of collaboration between the two productive *filières*, which is a fundamental element for setting up an industrial district. It is evident that the two populations operate in different value chains and distant market segments. For these and other reasons, the settlement of Chinese enterprises in the clothing industry was not followed by a reconversion of Italian firms, with just a few exceptions; this points out the need to develop more collaborations between the two populations and communities of people.

At the current stage, what can be concluded is that relevant transformations have concerned the very identity of the district form under exam as regards not only economic but also social aspects.

The main founding elements of the district form are still evolving, and probably, in the era of globalization, it is not sufficient to refer to a single place but to several, including virtual places. Moreover, the co-existence of two communities of people and firms – which are not necessarily integrated with each other but might be, and in different ways – should be investigated further, as well as the new division of work that tends to combine local and global value chains.

In the current scenario, the analysis of districtualization processes and of the district's physiology constitutes, in our opinion, a particularly useful interpretive key for an investigation of these transformations, which the analysis of the vital flows of firm populations proposed in this study has sought to exemplify.

Notes

* We express our gratitude to Dario Caserta, Chamber of Commerce of Prato, for data availability and to Gabi Dei Ottati and Simone Guercini for helpful comments on a previous version of this chapter. The responsibility of what is written lies solely with the authors.

1 For instance, knitwear is even surpassed by leather (in firms' number), which in Prato has always been residual.
2 These data are confirmed at national level, with foreign firms more fragile than the Italian ones, having a significantly higher mortality rate (17 per cent versus 7.8 per cent) (IRPET, 2010).
3 This evolution concerns the Prato ID only; in fact, if we consider the evolution of the employment at national level, textile responds better than clothing. From 1991 to 2011 the textile sector registers a decline of 23 per cent, while clothing (14) presents a decline of 29 per cent. In Prato, textile registers an 8 per cent decrease, while clothing a 66 per cent increase.
4 This is partly due to the average dimension of Chinese firms, which are smaller than Italian ones, and to the large number of their irregular employees.

References

Accetturo, A. *et al.* (2013) 'Il sistema industriale italiano tra globalizzazione e crisi', *Occasional Papers* 193, Banca d'Italia, Roma.
Aldrich, H.E., McKelvey, B. and Ulrich, D. (1984) 'Design strategy from the population perspective'. *Journal of Management*, 10(1): 68–86.
Baldassar, L., Johanson, G., McAuliffe, N. and Bressan, M. (eds) (2015) *Chinese Migration to Europe. Prato, Italy and Beyond.* London: Palgrave Macmillan.
Barberis, E. (2008) *Imprenditori immigrati. Tra inserimento sociale e partecipazione allo sviluppo.* Roma: Ediesse.
Barnett, W.P. (1997) 'The dynamics of competitive intensity'. *Administrative Science Quarterly*, 42(1): 128–160.
Baum, J.A.C. (2003) 'Organisational ecology', in Clegg, S.R., Hardy, C. and Nord, W.R. (eds) *Handbook of Organization Studies.* London: Sage.
Becattini, G. (2001) *The Caterpillar and the Butterfly. An exemplary case of development in the Italy of the Prato Industrial Districts.* Florence: Le Monnier.

Becattini, G., Bellandi, M. and De Propris, L. (2009) *Handbook of Industrial Districts*. London: Edward Elgar.

Belussi, F. and Sammarra, A. (2010) *Business Networks in Clusters and Industrial Districts: The governance of the global value chain*. Abingdon: Routledge.

Belussi, F. and Sedita, S.R. (2010) 'Moving immigrants into Western industrial districts', in Belussi, F. and Sammarra, A. (eds) *Business Networks in Clusters and Industrial Districts: The governance of the global value chain*. Abingdon: Routledge, pp. 136–145.

Bogaert, S., Boone, C., Negro, G. and Witteloostuijn, A. (2014) 'Organizational form emergence: a meta-analysis of the ecological theory of legitimation', *Journal of Management*, first published on 25 March 2014.

Bracci, F. (2009) 'Migranti cinesi e contesto locale: il distretto pratese e la transizione fredda', *Sviluppo locale*, 13(31): 91–111.

Bressan, M. and Radini, M. (2009) 'Diversity and segregation in Prato', in Johanson, G., Smyth, R. and French, R. (eds) *Living Outside the Walls: The Chinese in Prato*. Cambridge: Cambridge Scholars Publishing, pp. 130–148.

Carroll, G.R. and Hannan, M.T. (2000) *The Demography of Corporations and Industries*. Princeton University Press.

Ceccagno, A. (ed.) (2003) *Migranti a Prato: Il distretto tessile multietnico*, Milano: Franco Angeli.

Ceccagno, A. (2009) 'Chinese migrants as apparel manufacturers in an era of perishable global fashion: new fashion scenarios in Prato' in Johanson, G., Smyth, R. and French, R. (eds) *Living Outside the Walls: The Chinese in Prato*, Cambridge: Cambridge Scholars Publishing, pp. 42–74.

Chiarvesio, M., Di Maria, E. and Micelli, S. (2010) 'Global value chains and open networks: the case of Italian industrial districts', *European Planning Studies*, 18(3): 333–350.

Coltorti, F. (2013) 'Italian industry, decline or transformation? A framework', *European Planning Studies*, 21(12): 2037–2077.

De Propris, L. and Lazzeretti, L. (2009) 'Measuring the decline of a Marshallian industrial district: the Birmingham jewellery quarter', *Regional Studies*, 43(9): 1135–1154.

Dei Ottati, G. (2009) 'Italian industrial districts and the dual Chinese challenge', in Johanson, G., Smyth, R. and French, R. (eds) *Living Outside the Walls: The Chinese in Prato*, Cambridge: Cambridge Scholars Publishing, pp. 26–41.

Dei Ottati, G. (2013) 'Il ruolo dell'immigrazione cinese a prato: una rassegna della letteratura', in IRPET (ed.) *Prato: il ruolo economico della Comunità Cinese*, Firenze: IRPET, pp. 21–38.

Dei Ottati, G. (2014) 'A transnational fast fashion industrial district: an analysis of the Chinese businesses in Prato', *Cambridge Journal of Economics*, 38(5): 1247–1274.

Dei Ottati, G. (2016) 'Globalization, liberalization and finance in Italians industrial districts: some preliminary reflections', forthcoming in *Cambridge Journal of Economics*.

Eisingerich, A.B., Bell, S.J. and Tracey, P. (2010) 'The role of network strength, network openness, and environmental uncertainty', *Research Policy*, 39(2): 239–253.

Gereffi, G. and Memedovic, O. (2003) *The Global Apparel Value Chain: What prospects for upgrading by developing countries*. Vienna: UNIDO.

Guercini, S. (2001) 'Relation between branding and growth of the firm in new quick fashion formulas: analysis of an Italian case', *Journal of Fashion Marketing and Management*, 5(1): 69–79.

Guercini, S. and Milanesi, M. (2015) 'Liability of foreignness and liability of outsidership in the evolution of the immigrant Chinese entrepreneurship in Prato', presented in 'Liabilities of native and immigrant entrepreneurs in globalization. The case of Prato' Conference, 4 December 2015, Monash University Prato.

Hannan, M.T. and Carroll, G.R. (1992) *Dynamics of Organizational Populations: Density, legitimation and competition*. New York: Oxford University Press.

Hervás-Oliver, J.L. and Albors-Garrigós, J. (2008) 'Local knowledge domains and the role of MNE affiliates in bridging and complementing a cluster's knowledge' *Entrepreneurship and Regional Development*, 20(6): 581–598.

Hervás-Oliver, J.L. and Boix-Domènech, R. (2013) 'The economic geography of the meso-global spaces: integrating multinationals and clusters at the local–global level', *European Planning Studies*, 21(7): 1064–1080.

Humphrey, J. and Schmitz, H. (2002) 'How does insertion in global value chains affect upgrading in industrial clusters?', *Regional Studies*, 36(9): 1017–1027.

IRPET (2010) *L'imprenditoria straniera in Toscana*, Ebook 2/10. Regione Toscana.

Johanson, G., Smyth, R. and French, R. (eds) (2009) *Living Outside the Walls: The Chinese in Prato*, Cambridge: Cambridge Scholars Publishing.

Lazzeretti, L. and Capone, F. (2014) 'Multiculturalismo ed industrie creative. Il caso Toscano', in Pilotti, L., De Noni, I. and Ganzaroli, A. (2013) *Il cammino infinito. Imprenditorialità multiculturale tra varietà, innovazione e territorio*, Milano: Franco Angeli, pp. 161–187.

Lazzeretti, L. and Storai, D. (1999) *Il distretto come comunità di popolazioni organizzative. Il caso Prato*, IRIS: Prato.

Lazzeretti, L. and Storai, D. (2003) 'An ecology based interpretation of district "complexification": the Prato district evolution from 1946 to 1993', in Belussi, F., Gottardi, G. and Rullani, E. (eds) *The Net-Evolution of Local Systems. Knowledge creation, collective learning and variety of institutional arrangements*. Dordrecht: Kluwer, pp. 409–434.

Lombardi, S., Lorenzini, F., Sforzi, F. and Verrecchia, F. (2015) 'Chinese micro-entrepreneurship in Italy: a place-based explanatory analysis', in Baldassar, L. *et al.*, *Chinese Migration to Europe. The caso of Prato and Italy*. New York: Palgrave Macmillan.

Low, M.B. and Abrahamson, E. (1997) 'Movements, bandwagons, and clones: industry evolution and the entrepreneurial process', *Journal of Business Venturing*, 12(6): 435–457.

Manigart, S. (1994) 'The founding rate of venture capital firms in three European countries (1970–1990)', *Journal of Business Venturing*, 9(6): 525–541.

Nadvi, K. and Halder, G. (2005) 'Local clusters in global value chains: exploring dynamic linkages between Germany and Pakistan', *Entrepreneurship & Regional Development*, 17(5): 339–363.

Pieraccini, S. (2008) *L'assedio Cinese: il distretto parallelo del pronto moda di Prato*. Milano: Il Sole 24 Ore.

Pietrobelli, C., Rabellotti, R. and Sanfilippo, M. (2011) 'Chinese FDI strategy: the 'Marco Polo' effect', in *International Journal of Technological Learning, Innovation and Development*, 4(4): 277–291.

Pilotti, L., De Noni, I. and Ganzaroli, A. (eds) (2014) *Il cammino infinito. Imprenditorialità multiculturale tra varietà, innovazione e territorio*, Milano: Franco Angeli.

Rabellotti, R., Carabelli, A. and Hirsch, G. (2009) 'Italian industrial districts on the move: where are they going?', *European Planning Studies*, 17(1): 19–41.

Rabino, S., Santini, C. and Zanni, L. (2009) 'Chinese entrepreneurial model: an empirical investigation on Prato industrial district', in Vrontis, D. *et al.*, *Managerial and Entrepreneurial Developments in the Mediterranean Area*. Cyprus: EuroMed Press.

Rychen, F. and Zimmermann, J.B. (2008) 'Clusters in the global knowledge-based economy: knowledge gatekeepers and temporary proximity', *Regional Studies*, 42: 767–776.

Santini, C., Rabino, S. and Zanni, L. (2009) 'Chinese immigrants socio-economic enclave in an Italian industrial district: the case of Prato', *World Review of Entrepreneurship, Management and Sustainable Development*, 7(1): 30–51.

Saxenian, A. (2006) *The New Argonauts: Regional advantage in a global economy*. Cambridge, MA: Harvard University Press.

Sforzi, F. (1997) I sistemi locali in Italia. Rome: ISTAT.

Sonderegger, P. and Täube, F. (2010) 'Cluster life cycle and diaspora effects: evidence from the Indian IT cluster in Bangalore', *Journal of International Management*, 16: 383–397.

Staber, S. (2001) 'Spatial proximity and firm survival in a declining industrial district: the case of knitwear firms in Baden-Wuttemberg', *Regional Studies*, 35(4): 329–341.

Toccafondi, D. (2009) 'Prato's textile district and Chinese ethnic businesses', in Johanson, G. Smyth, R. and French, R. (eds) *Living Outside the Walls: The Chinese in Prato*, Cambridge: Cambridge Scholars Publishing, pp. 75–95.

UIP – Unione Industriale Pratese (2012) *Il Distretto Pratese*. Prato.

Unioncamere (2012) *Rapporto Unioncamere 2012. L'economia reale dal punto di osservazione delle camere di commercio*, Roma: Unioncamere.

Zanni, L. and Zucchella, A. (2009) 'I casi delle imprese nate globali e dell'imprenditoria etnica nei distretti industriali' in Pepe, C. and Zucchella, A. (eds) *L'internazionalizzazione delle imprese italiane*, Bologna: Il Mulino, pp. 175–209.

7 Cognitive inertia at bay

Global value chains and cluster openness favouring smart specialization in the Toy Valley cluster – Spain

Jose Luis Hervás-Oliver and Francisca Sempere Ripoll

7.1 Introduction

This chapter's objective consists of evidencing the necessity of connecting smart specialization with cluster openness and global value chains, in order to integrate fragmented frameworks for analysing a similar phenomenon: cluster evolution and renewal. When referring to cluster openness, this means the entrance of new knowledge, the renewal of technologies and actors, and the upgrading of the local environment and its competitiveness. Empirical evidence hitherto has shown positive effects from cluster openness in global value chains (e.g. Hervás-Oliver and Albors-Garrigós, 2008; Eisingerich *et al.*, 2010) which facilitate learning and contribute to avoiding cluster myopia. Nevertheless, cluster and industrial district literature has focused mainly on the strong tradition of local endogenous development, despite a clear shift in research agenda to understand non-cluster or external linkages within a globalization paradigm.

Describing cluster openness and global value chain, however, implies analysing a core player, usually less researched in the clusters and industrial district literatures: multinationals play a crucial role by connecting and coordinating those global value chains (GVCs) that connect different territories and transfer knowledge across different territories. Openness and GVCs, therefore, need to be tackled in conjunction with the understanding of MNEs which connect clusters (see more in Adams, 2011 or Harrison, 1994).

MNEs transfer knowledge throughout agglomerations through their own internal circuits between headquarters and subsidiaries (Hervás-Oliver and Boix-Domènech, 2013; Sedita *et al.*, 2013; Lorenzen and Mudambi, 2013; Tallman and Chacar, 2011; Harrison, 1994), thus facilitating inter-cluster connections. MNEs, however, are not the only way to insert cluster in GVCs, as other mechanisms (temporary clusters in trade fairs, labour mobility, subcontracting arrangements with other clusters and so forth) also accomplish that task. Cluster openness to those external sources of knowledge benefits local agglomerations, especially those local SMEs that adopt best practices and technologies proposed by those global players. When describing clusters and agglomerations alike, MNEs are basically those foreign ones. Despite this assumption, especially in IDs, there is evidence of small and local indigenous multinationals or homegrown ones that positively drag down local SMEs by orchestrating their local networks of knowledge and production, thus leading a process of knowledge transfer towards SMEs (e.g. Sedita *et al.*, 2013).

All in all, balancing local and global flows of knowledge that constitute learning processes becomes crucial in order to insert agglomerations in GVCs. This connectedness process, referred to as external linkages or global pipelines (see Hervás-Oliver and Boix-Domènech 2013 or Bathelt *et al.*, 2004), seeks to create bridges between organizations, industries, markets and technologies beyond local agglomerations, contributing to avoiding cognitive inertia and subsequent cluster decline by renewing networks and accessing non-local knowledge (e.g. Eisingerich *et al.*, 2010). As shown in the literature, a cluster lacking connection and openness to external knowledge, assumptions or paradigms may undermine its competitiveness, interrupting its renewal (e.g. Pouder and St John, 1996).

In this chapter we decipher that openness process, connecting it to GVCs and smart specialization, presenting an empirical real case in order to illustrate those intertwined phenomena. For this purpose, the Toy Valley cluster (Alicante, Spain) will be presented and analysed. In particular, its evolution and diversification process are scrutinized in order to disentangle those different components of cluster evolution and present measures to avoid cognitive inertia or lock-in by openness and insertion in GVCs. We ask in this chapter: how can clusters be renewed and decline stage be avoided?

The chapter is organized as follows: after this introduction, section 7.2 addresses the theory of cognitive inertia and the openness process. In section 7.3, the interaction between multinationals and clusters is discussed. Then, in section 7.4, the empirical evolution of the Toy Valley is analysed. Finally, in section 7.5, main conclusions are set out.

7.2 Understanding cluster evolution and openness

Cluster myopia or lock-in consists of a problem of over-embeddedness, caused by an over-exposure to mainly (or only) the absorption of local knowledge which can be, in the long term, counterproductive for clusters (Pouder and St John, 1996; Uzzi, 1997; Molina and Martínez, 2009), positive lock-in notwithstanding. Having said that, it seems that lock-in is not only due to over-embeddedness but also to low-quality or non-competitive local knowledge. This collective myopia (Maskell and Malmberg, 2007; Martin and Sunley, 2006) fosters cluster decline in the long term and prevents clusters and industrial districts from rejuvenation.

Following managerial literature, such as Rosenkopf and Nerkar (2001), it is assumed that searching beyond local spaces (geographic and technology ones) undermines firm lock-in. Similarly, in agglomeration literature, searching for non-cluster or external sources of knowledge has been extensively worked upon in the GVC approach but with little emphasis on the role of MNEs organizing and orchestrating those global value chains. Retaking previous debates in agglomeration literature, however, the role of multinationals was directly pointed out as a kind of solution to that lock-in, well in advance of the idea of global pipelines by Bathelt *et al.* (2004). Thus, Harrisson (1994) stated the key role of MNEs in preventing myopia in clusters, by complementing the local endogenous learning process with external knowledge. More recently, Eisingerich *et al.* (2010: 252) show how clusters and regions rich in local and dense networks and knowledge circulation perform better when there is cluster openness in order to facilitate inter-cluster connections, the entrance of new knowledge and new players, fostering also the renewal of local networks with new members entering the focal cluster. Along the same line of thought, Menzel and Fornhal (2010: 231) point out the necessity of introducing knowledge outside the thematic boundaries of the focal cluster in order to promote creative destruction. This process is well exemplified in Adams's (2011) study of Silicon Valley, showing its openness to new technologies, from electronics, semiconductors, computers and internet, among others, in part thanks to the multinationals implanted there and the subsequent renewal process triggered in the cluster. All in all, previous and recent literature, without using the GVC perspective, has emphasized the role of MNEs bridging and connecting clusters. Hence, the role of multinationals contributing to GVC and cluster openness needs to be unfolded for the sake of improving our understanding of mechanisms to avoid lock-in. Unfortunately, despite those recent attempts (e.g. Harrison, 1994), agglomeration literature has not deepened as regards MNEs and it is necessary to borrow knowledge from managerial perspectives, such as international business (IB) literature, whose key objective is to understand multinationals. Thus, in the following section we are going to connect agglomeration literature with that of MNEs.

7.3 Integrating MNEs and clusters: how does it work?

Clusters offer an excellent opportunity for a firm to conduct a fine-slice process of disaggregating activities, especially those which fit better into specific agglomerations (e.g. Tallman and Chacar, 2011, Hervás-Oliver and Boix-Domènech, 2013). Hence, MNEs should focus on finding specific geographic locations for collocating their specific activities: one-size-fits-all does not work, as only those activities fitting local resources will be improved in an internal and external (local) knowledge combination process. Therefore, MNEs should collocate only those activities that suit local resources. This idea is borrowed from the IB strand. Rugman *et al.* (2011), who point out that each subsidiary will display a different value chain depending on its integration-responsiveness to the local resources, connect the four FDI types available in a location (natural resources, market, efficiency and strategic assets – Dunning, 1993) to specific subsidiaries' activities and integration into the local agglomerations. In this way, each subsidiary has to configure specific value chains locally customized in order to take advantage from the focal territory (e.g. Mudambi and Venzin, 2010). This idea is consistent with MNEs 'resource-building' (Meyer *et al.*, 2011) by which internal and external resources and knowledge should be combined in order to achieve synergies and the best performance possible. The IB literature, however, has not especially referred to location as agglomerations but nations, focusing mainly on host nations, rather than in specific geographical spaces (MacCann and Mudambi, 2004), albeit with notable exceptions (e.g. Nachum and Keeble 2003a, b; Narula, 2014).

Focusing on specific agglomerations, rather than nations, Tallman and Chacar (2011) offer a consistent framework describing how MNEs collocate and absorb local knowledge by their integration in the local networks of practice, fitting their activities into the local available resources (Kogut and Zander, 1993; Birkinshaw and Hood, 2000), a phenomenon also described by Nachum and Keeble (2003b: 465) in the Soho cluster in Central London, stressing also the importance of embeddedness or interactions with local actors, as a main way to get access to local knowledge (Tallman and Chacar, 2011; Hervás-Oliver and Boix-Domènech, 2013). To sum up, the importance of integrating activities in local spheres in order to get access to the local tacit knowledge is pointed out. The agglomeration literature has not extensively researched MNEs, at least as much as that of IB has done, but the shortcomings of the IB strand is that nations or countries have usually been the unit of analysis connected to the construct location. The integration of both strands, however, constitutes a fruitful exercise to connect both strands and thus integrate fragmented frameworks and evidence that do not incorporate findings and thinking from different perspectives.

7.4 Empirical study

This empirical study was carried out during 2014 and early 2015, through twenty-four semi-structured interviews with relevant informants in the Toy Valley, including managers, former managers, officials, scholars and industry representatives. Interviews were designed to obtain evidence of the Toy Valley evolution on a longitudinal basis, showing an interesting case of smart specialization and openness to GVC that has rejuvenated the cluster and avoided lock-in.

Toy Valley evolution is mainly analysed from the perspective of (i) new knowledge and technology generation or adoption, mainly from foreign MNEs' entry, and (ii) formation of indigenous or homegrown multinationals that has also contributed to generating or adopting new technologies. In summary, the openness and diversification process experienced during the past forty years by the Toy Valley is presented, showing a particularly successful case of openness.

Toy Valley cluster is constituted by Ibi, Tibi, Onil, Castalla and Biar municipalities in the Alicante province, Spain. From its inception it was fully dedicated to toy manufacturing, using metals, wood and, later on, plastics and other electrical and mechanical mechanisms. At the present time, Toy Valley is a multi-industry cluster with many competencies and technologies built up and developed from those origins, serving a huge and diverse range of industries in those technologies (metallic products, plastics and other technologies) such as automobiles, machinery and equipment, electrical components, carbon fibre, advanced plastics, toys, plastic and cardboard containers (for food and beverages, pharmaceutics and other industries).

Historical antecedents date back to the turn of the twentieth century. In 1905 the Paya family initiated its activities in Ibi, producing in a rather rudimentary way metallic toys such as 'tinkers'. The Paya family and its business grew by incorporating products and models imitated from other countries, fostering the fermentation of an industry centred around metallic products, among which toys were prominent. From the Paya company many workers left and started up new spinoffs. Before the Spanish civil war (1936) four firms, all of them spinning off from Paya's family business, were central: Paya, Rico, Juguetes y Estuches and Claudio Reig. During the civil war those firms were forced to work for the Republican army producing rifles and weapons, absorbing new knowledge from the army that was subsequently used for civilian purposes. After the civil war, however, the industry, which was dependent on the internal market, became stuck, due to weak domestic demand and the level of poverty in Spain. The 1950s brought changes and exports of metallic products were allowed, a factor that, along with the boom of construction and demand in Spain, boosted the development of the industry, which began to flourish. In the 1960s there were around fifty factories in Ibi, all of them spinoffs from those four initial firms.

During the 1960s, and throughout the first Spanish construction boom, domestic demand grew and the industry took off, producing almost 80 per cent of Spanish toys and growing in political importance. During the 1960s, plastic injection technologies were adopted, renewing the stock of competences and entering into new segments and products, complementing and replacing wood and metallic components in most toys. This made possible a significant development of plastic injection capability that, subsequently, was transferred to other toy-related products and industries, facilitating an impressive process of diversification. During the 1960s an international trade fair, a technical institute for R&D and a vocational dual training system were implanted in the territory, led by pioneering firms. At that time the structure of production was concentrated on those big, initial firms which constituted and orchestrated a complex and interrelated network of suppliers, fostering gradually the division of labour, even though those big firms were mostly vertically integrated.

Before the 1970s, four main technologies were prominent in the Toy Valley: plastic toys, mechanical metallic toys, metallic tubes and auxiliary industries (packaging, logistics, services, all related to metallic and plastic toys). All these technologies were endogenously developed, albeit using Italian and German equipment and machinery. Besides, attendance at international trade fairs was also a way to tap into non-local knowledge and adopt many technologies and trends, increasing the level of exports to Europe. In the mid-1970s the two oil crises and low-cost foreign competition, mainly from China, undermined the cluster that had started off-shoring activities to China, in search of efficiency.[1] This initial internationalization triggered a process of multi-diversification in order to escape from specific low-cost segments, serving local industries in the region (vehicles, industrial products and other different consumer ones, such as containers for the food and beverage industry). Small family-business subcontractors, abandoned by their leading firms which had started off-shore activities, began to search for new segments and applications for their technologies. Industries receiving those technologies and competences were at that time (the late 1980s) construction, furniture, gardening, footwear, lighting, decoration, food and even graphic design. The diversification was accompanied by a more intensive process of vertical disintegration by which new activities (and spinoffs) were ignited by a fine-slice process of disaggregation of activities and processes by which new firms became specialized and fully dedicated to particular stages of the production process, products and parts of their value chains. For instance, most companies began to produce food containers by using similar plastic injection technologies: some focused on food and others on beverages or even containers for the pharmaceutical industry. Similarly, the packaging for toys was used in a diverse set of industries such as food, electrical components or construction. Plastics were also used in vehicles, batteries or even irrigation components. Even metallic tube technology was used in the production of metallic office chairs and furniture and other components for bikes, cars or construction. The renaissance of the cluster during the 1990s, in comparison with its previous decline, mainly due to external shocks, was triggered by openness, renewal of competences and technologies that were applied and diversified into different product categories and industries. From the 1990s the industry began growing, mainly by investing and serving in those industries, to the detriment of the traditional toy sector, even though toy production is still important in the territory. Since then, quality and design have been key ingredients in order to avoid low segments where Asian countries could be more efficient. Figure 7.1 shows the diversification of technologies and products depicting the transformation and diversification that occurred from the 1980s onward, depicting two basic periods: during the 1980s and the 2000s.

At the present time, Toy Valley is a leading industrial space for industrial and manufacturing process subcontracting, attracting foreign MNEs from a diverse range of industries, such as Smurfit Kappa (plastics and containers), Johnson Control (car components), Smooby (toys) and SGR Global (car components), or seed capital investors such as Vista Capital.

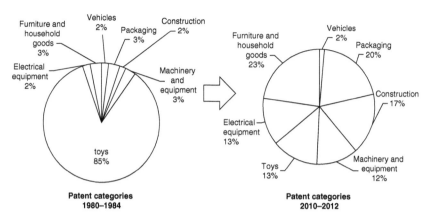

Figure 7.1 Evolution of patent distribution at the Toy Valley.
Source: Caja and Martí, 2014.

For example, Smurfit Kappa is one of the leading providers of paper-based packaging solutions in the world, with more than 43,000 employees in 33 countries and with revenue of €8.1 billion in 2014.[2] In 2007 Smurfit Kappa was a leader in the bag-in-box plastic-made container[3] for beverages sector, especially for soda, wine and others, with plants in France, Italy, Canada, Russia and Argentina. It acquired Plasticos Vicente, an Ibi-based plastic producer of containers for beverages, paying €33 million. The acquisition was made to improve efficiency in southern Europe while tapping into the cluster manufacturing advantages. Gradually, all manufacturing activities for bag-in-box were transferred to Ibi from Alessandria (Italy) and Epernay (France), along with product development and R&D investments for bag-in-box improvement. At the present time (2015), with around 110 employees, the Ibi plant was the most advanced, flexible and productive in the bag-in-box category, being the only one in the world developing and manufacturing the tap, which is the most sophisticated and value-added part of the product. Bag-in-box product has applications for wine, dairy products, fruit juices, liquid eggs, sauces, processed fruits, food preparation, water, edible oils, detergents, paints, laundry products, cosmetics and motor oils. The decision was made because of the excellent plastic technology available in the cluster, the auxiliary industries (logistics, equipment, plastic technicians, engineers, paper-based products and byproducts, among others), which combined with the cost efficiency in Spain (compared with Italy and France) made a really profitable investment. The acquisition of an existing business, instead of a startup (green field) option, was selected because the only way to tap into the cluster's social networks and informal relationships was to acquire an existing and really embedded business.[4] Due to the extensive subcontracting and orchestration of local subcontractors in networks, Toy Valley is becoming prominent for plastic-based and paper-based packaging solutions for multiple industries, with its excellent substrate of plastic and packaging technologies which started many decades before with the plastic toy manufacturing process. Johnson Control (car components) was a similar story, acquiring Plasticos Avenida, a local firm specialized in industrial plastics, that Johnson applied to the plastic part of car batteries; Smooby, a German giant in toys, did the same, acquiring a local factory specializing in small children's bikes, thanks to the excellent mechanical tube technology existing in the cluster, a technology that was easily applied to all different types of small children's vehicles. Furthermore, the same technology was applied to car components by SRG Global, a Guardian subsidiary from Detroit, which entered the local cluster in the same way to tap into that technology for car components. These acquisitions, combined with homegrown independent multinationals, and their leading role orchestrating local subcontractors, have made possible the rejuvenation of the cluster through its renewal of capabilities and technologies from a diverse set of locations and industries.

The entrance of foreign MNEs (mainly through the acquisition of existing local businesses) connected the cluster to GVCs, renewed the stock of competences and reinforced the local process of diversification. Besides, new MNEs subcontracted local SMEs, which received new knowledge, practices and processes that upgraded them all. The renewal and diversification of local companies, however, was also important for the cluster turnaround. Notably, it was an entrepreneurial and spontaneous bottom-up approach, with the regional government providing only that specific infrastructure to strengthen the cluster, creating a technology transfer office (TTO, AIJU), boosting the local trade fair or providing specific training and other activities (vocational training centres). Overall, private bottom-up initiatives were responsible for more than 70 per cent of the cluster success.

7.5 Conclusions

As observed, the empirical case depicts the interesting evolution and diversification in the Toy Valley, transforming from metallic toys to plastic toys, mechanical toys and a broad range of manufactured industrial products. This transformation was accomplished, in a bottom-up process, by combining old (metallic, mechanical, plastic, etc.) technologies with new ones and their recombination and application to different segments and industries, widening the portfolio of technologies, applications, product categories and customers. That process was leveraged by the entrance of foreign MNEs attracted by the available knowledge and efficiency, with distinctive technologies and applications. Besides, the openness process was also accomplished by the development of indigenous or homegrown (previously SMEs) MNEs and their reinforcing interaction with foreign MNEs. The insertion of the cluster in GVCs also permitted the continuous renewal of the stock of competences: openness and connection to GVCs, leveraged by the entrance of new actors (MNEs), has positively transformed the cluster into a complex, industrial-based, competitive hot spot, confirming previous studies in a diverse set of clusters that vindicated the benefits and necessity for cluster openness and insertion in GVCs (e.g. Hervás-Oliver and Boix-Domènech, 2013; Eisingerich *et al.*, 2010; Sedita *et al.*, 2013).

That insertion in GVCs and the combination of local and non-local sources of knowledge have built up and strengthened the cluster. This process, in recent years (from 2010 onwards), has also been reinforced by a back-shoring process. As Tate *et al.* (2014) or Kinkel (2012) have argued, the process of back-shoring to Europe, by which firms escape from growing Chinese salaries and costs and start to compete on quality and service, has brought new advantages for the local production systems, such as inventory and logistics cost reduction, improvement of flexibility for serving customers, facilitating the integration between R&D and manufacturing, IPR protection and better market perception by the 'Made in Europe' label, along with less exposure to financial and exchange rate risks. All in all, this case constitutes an example of smart specialization, combined with a diversification and back-shoring process in which MNEs, local clusters and GVCs are present. These topics will undoubtedly lead the cluster conversation in the coming years.

Acknowledgements

We thank the Spanish Ministry of Economy and Competitiveness for financially supporting this research (ECO2015-63645-R). We also thank Francisco Bernabeu, the AIJU team (Mr Aragones and Mr Ripoll), Smurfit Kappa (Pascual Martínez), Marcelino Huerta, Jaime Ferri (Famosa) and many other key informants.

Notes

1 See more at Ybarra and Santa María, 2008.
2 www.smurfitkappa.com/resources/documents/combined%20skg%20-%20final.pdf
3 www.smurfitkappa.com/vHome/com/Products/BaginBox/Pages/Default.aspx
4 From the interviews with Smurfit Kappa CEO in Ibi, Pascual Martínez.

References

Adams, S.B. (2011). Growing where you are planted: exogenous firms and the seeding of Silicon Valley. *Research Policy*, 40(3):368–379.
Anderson, P. and Tushman, M.L. (1990). Technological discontinuities and dominant designs: a cyclical model of technological change. *Administrative Science Quarterly*, 35(4):604–633.
Bathelt, H., Malmberg, A. and Maskell, P. (2004). Clusters and knowledge: local buzz, global pipelines and the process of knowledge creation. *Progress in Human Geography*, 28:31–56.

Birkinshaw, J. and Hood, N. (2000). Characteristics of foreign subsidiaries in industry clusters. *Journal of International Business Studies*, 31:141–154.

Caja, P. and Martí, J. (2014). La evolución de clusters en España: comparando los casos del juguete-plástico y la cerámica. *Economía industrial*, 391:151–162.

Crescenzi, R., Gagliardi, L. and Iammarino, S. (2015). Foreign multinationals and domestic innovation: intra-industry effects and firm heterogeneity. *Research Policy*, 44(3): 596–609.

Dunning, J.H. (1993). *Multinational Enterprises and the Global Economy*. Wokingham: Addison-Wesley.

Eisingerich, A., Bell, S.J. and Tracey, P. (2010). How can clusters sustain performance? The role of network strength, network openness, and environmental uncertainty. *Research Policy*, 39:239–253.

Harrison, B. (1994). *Lean and Mean: The Changing Landscape of Corporate Power in the Age of Flexibility*. New York: Basic Books.

Hervás-Oliver, J.L. and Albors-Garrigós, J. (2008). Local knowledge domains and the role of MNE affiliates in bridging and complementing a cluster's knowledge. *Entrepreneurship & Regional Development: An International Journal*, 20(6):581–598.

Hervás-Oliver, J.L. and Boix-Domènech, R. (2013). The economic geography of the meso-global spaces: integrating multinationals and clusters at the local–global level. *European Planning Studies*, 21(7):1064–1080.

Jensen, P.D. and Pedersen, T. (2011). The economic geography of offshoring: the fit between activities and local context. *Journal of Management Studies*, 48(2): 352–372.

Johanson, J. and Vahlne, E. (2009). The Uppsala internationalization process model revisited: from liability of foreignness to liability of outsidership. *Journal of International Business Studies*, 40(9):1411–1431.

Kinkel, S. (2012). Trends in production relocation and back-shoring activities: changing patterns in the course of the global economic crisis. *International Journal of Operations & Production Management*, 32(6):696–720.

Kogut, B. and Zander, U. (1993). Knowledge of the firm and the evolutionary theory of the multinational corporation. *Journal of International Business Studies*, 24(4):625–645.

Lorenzen, M. and Mudambi, R. (2013). Clusters, connectivity and catch-up: Bollywood and Bangalore in the global economy. *Journal of Economic Geography*, 13(3):501–534.

MacCann, P. and Mudambi, R. (2004). The location behavior of the multinational enterprise: some analytical issues. *Growth and Change*, 35(4):491–524.

Martin, R. and Sunley, P. (2006). Path dependence and regional economic evolution. *Journal of Economic Geography*, 6(4):395–437.

Maskell, P. and Malmberg, A. (2007). Myopia, knowledge development and cluster evolution. *Journal of Economic Geography*, 7(5):603–608.

Menzel, M. and Fornahl, D. (2010). Cluster life cycles – dimensions and rationales of cluster evolution. *Industrial and Corporate Change*, 19(1):205–238.

Meyer, K.E., Mudambi, R. and Narula, R. (2011). Multinational enterprises and local contexts: the opportunities and challenges of multiple embeddedness. *Journal of Management Studies*, 48(2):235–252.

Molina, F.X. and Martínez, M.T. (2009). Does homogeneity exist within industrial districts? A social capital-based approach. *Papers in Regional Science*, 88(1):209–229.

Mudambi, R. and Venzin, M. (2010). The strategic nexus of offshoring and outsourcing decisions. *Journal of Management Studies*, 47(8):1510–1533.

Nachum, L. and Keeble, D. (2003a). Neo-Marshallian clusters and global networks: the linkages of media firms in Central London. *Long Range Planning*, 36(5):459–480.

Nachum, L. and Keeble, D. (2003b). MNE linkages and localised clusters: foreign and indigenous firms in the media cluster of Central London. *Journal of International Management*, 9(2):171–192.

Narula, R. (2014). Exploring the paradox of competence-creating subsidiaries: balancing bandwidth and dispersion in MNEs. *Long Range Planning*, 47(1–2): 4–15.

Pouder, R. and St John, C.H. (1996). Hot spots and blind spots: geographical clusters of firms and innovation, *Academy of Management Review*, 21(4):1192–1225.

Rosenkopf, L. and Nerkar, A. (2001) Beyond local search: boundary-spanning, exploration, and impact in the optical disk industry. *Strategic Management Journal*, 22(4):287–306.

Rugman, A., Verbeke, A. and Yuan, W. (2011). Re-conceptualizing Bartlett and Ghoshal's classification of national subsidiary roles in the multinational enterprise. *Journal of Management Studies*, 48(2):253–277.

Sedita, R., Caloffi, A. and Belussi, F. (2013). Heterogeneity of MNEs entry modes in industrial clusters: an evolutionary approach based on the cluster life cycle model. 35th DRUID Celebration Conference 2013, Barcelona, Spain, 17(19) June.

Solvell, O. and Zander, I. (1998). International diffusion of knowledge: isolating mechanisms and the role of the MNE. In *The Dynamic Firm: The Role of Technology, Strategy, Organization, and Regions*, Oxford: Oxford University Press.

Sorenson, O., Rivkin, J.W. and Fleming, L. (2006). Complexity, networks, and knowledge flow. *Research Policy*, 35(7):994–1017.

Tallman, S. and Chacar, A. (2011). Communities, alliances, networks and knowledge in multinational firms: a micro-analytic framework. *Journal of International Management*, 17(3):201–210.

Tate, W.L., Ellramb, L.M., Tobias Schoenherrc, T. and Petersen, V. (2014). Global competitive conditions driving the manufacturing location decision. *Business Horizons*, 57(3):381–390.

Tushman, M.L. and Anderson, P. (1986). Technological discontinuities and organizational environments. *Administrative Science Quarterly*, 31(3):439–465.

Uzzi, B. (1997). Social structure and competition in interfirm networks: the paradox of embeddedness. *Administrative Science Quarterly*, 42(1):35–67.

Ybarra, J.A. and Santa Maria, M.J. (2008). El distrito del juguete de la Foia de Castalla y su evolución. 'Los distrititos industriales'. *Colección Mediterráneo económico*, 13.

Ybarra, J.A., Giner, J.M., Golf, E. and Santa María, M.J. (2000). Innovación y desarrollo local en el sector del juguete: El sistema productivo local de Ibi, in Alonso, J.L. and Méndez, R. (eds) *Innovación, Pequeña Empresa y Desarrollo Local en España*, Cívitas, Madrid, pp. 211–229.

8 Collaboration and competition inside an industrial district

A social capital approach

Edoardo Mollona and Manuela Presutti

8.1 Introduction

Recently, industrial districts have been affected by increasing internationalisation and delocalisation of production (Crestanello and Tattara, 2010; Chiarvesio *et al.*, 2010; Sammarra and Biggiero, 2008). More specifically, in the 1990s many 'made in Italy' districts in the clothing, leather and footwear industries began to produce abroad and to develop an export strategy in many foreign markets (Mariotti and Piscitello, 2001). This process caused a transformation of districts' traditional industrial structures along with a territorial fragmentation of the previous, local value chain (Porter, 2000; Lazerson and Lorenzoni, 1999; McCann and Folta, 2009; Belussi *et al.*, 2008). Moreover, one focus of the interest has been the development of foreign investments by small firms and multinational companies inside the most important Italian districts (Gorg and Greenaway, 2004; Driffield, 2006; Cooke *et al.*, 2004). Foreign investments inside industry agglomerations stimulated empirical work addressing the effect that such investments may produce on districts (Cooke *et al.*, 2004). Specifically, in the industrial district literature, significant investments by foreign actors seem to have an impact on districts' internal structures, particularly in terms of inter-organisational relationships among incumbent small and medium-sized firms (Scott-Kennel, 2007; Waxell and Malmberg, 2007).

How the localisation of foreign actors in an existing industrial district triggers dynamics of integration and competition among co-located business actors is a pressing and open question (Keeble *et al.*, 1998; Andersson *et al.*, 2004; Romanelli and Khessina, 2005; Bellandi, 2006; Presutti *et al.*, 2011, 2013).

In this chapter, we used longitudinal data on an Italian district in the textile industry to discuss this research question. In particular, the study explores the pattern of fragmentation of production and the changes in actors' internal rules inside a textile industrial district localised in central Italy – Val Vibrata – after the 'internal invasion' of foreign business players at different stages of the value chain. Methodologically, this chapter is original because it is a longitudinal study of the entire population of local and foreign actors inside the district since its initial development. In addition, using modelling and computer simulation, we developed theory to explain interaction and competitive dynamics among sub-populations of incumbent and foreign firms in an industrial district. We present a number of testable hypotheses to underpin a theory of interaction behaviour among sub-populations in industrial districts.

8.2   Theoretical framework

Since the 1960s, many countries' business systems have been characterised by the development of an industrial model based on a significant concentration of small and medium firms specialising in various types of traditional production. In this context, industrial districts have been considered increasingly important in explaining small firms' competitiveness on both the national and the international level, and in strengthening the international expansion of the production system (Saxenian, 1994; Rallet and Torre, 2000; Andersson, 2004; Beccattini *et al.*, 2003).

Within the district literature (Enright, 2000; Porter, 2000; Belussi *et al.*, 2008), it is generally accepted that 'district embeddedness' allows a firm to take advantage of several externalities, which have a positive impact on competitiveness and international presence. Such externalities include firms' access to specialised labour forces, specialised technological and administrative services, or marketing complementarities (Tallman and Chacar, 2011; Porter, 2000). This, in turn, tends to increase the entrepreneurial ability of co-located firms to manage information flows and to speed up knowledge and innovation spillovers (Piscitello and Sgobbi 2004; Chetty and Holm, 2000). The efficiency and flexibility that characterise the organisational pattern of an industrial district reinforce its international expansion, particularly in terms of export activity and de-localisation of production (McCann and Folta, 2008; Klepper and Malerba, 2010). Local strong networks among co-located firms help firms to expose themselves to new international opportunities, obtain foreign knowledge, learn from international experience (Belussi and Sammarra, 2010; Belussi and Sedita, 2012; Odorici and Presutti, 2013; Iammarino and McCann, 2013) and benefit from the synergic effect of pooled resources within international markets (Al-Laham and Soutirias, 2008; Huggins and Johnston, 2010). The contribution of co-located firms to the internationalisation process has increased rapidly during the past twenty years in various countries, but it has reached a significant level in Italy because nearly two-thirds of Italian exports come from districts (Belussi *et al.*, 2003; Crestanello and Tattara, 2010; Lazerson and Lorenzoni, 1999). In particular, the textile sector, which is concentrated inside well-known local industrial districts, is a traditional manufacturing sector in which Italy has a comparative advantage (both at the national and international levels) in terms of superior performance (Arikan and Schilling, 2011; Mariotti and Piscitello, 2001).

Another observable tendency, which is correlated to the globalisation process of industrial districts, is an increased number of competitive foreign business operators that decide to localise inside those districts (Driffield and Munday, 2000; Gorg and Greenaway, 2004; Driffield, 2006; Cooke *et al.*, 2004). The presence of consolidated skills and profitable knowledge inside a specific area is a key factor for explaining the decision of foreign firms to localise within an industrial district (Driffield and Hughes, 2003; Cooke *et al.*, 2004; Li *et al.*, 2013). At the same time, many empirical studies envisage a positive relationship between the presence of foreign MNCs in a country and its endogenous development (Hilbert and Voicu, 2010: Blomstrom *et al.*, 2000; Baldwin *et al.*, 2005; Scott-Kemel, 2007).

In this vein, studies have identified a number of positive externalities that industrial districts may exploit to attract foreign firms (Porter, 2000). An industrial district may represent a facilitating environment that reinforces collective learning processes (Chiarvesio *et al.*, 2004) and a number of authors have concluded that the significant presence of similar industrial activities in a region attracts foreign business actors, which will benefit from local economies such as access to resources, technological capabilities and knowledge spillovers. Thus, the advantages of local linkages can be exploited within international markets, especially when 'local networks' are embedded into global supply and marketing circuits (Markusen, 2003; Gereffi *et al.*, 2005; Bell *et al.*, 2009).

This increasingly significant development of foreign investments within industrial districts has generated much interest among scholars over the past two decades, and much of their research is based on existing industry agglomeration – that is, the attraction of foreign investments to leading districts and the effect of foreign investments on existing districts (Phelps, 2008; Phelps *et al.*, 2003; Majocchi and Presutti, 2009). In particular, studies of inward foreign investments have predominantly focused on the contribution that foreign investors can make to districts and their effect on districts' structure and dynamics (Gorg and Greenaway, 2004; Driffield, 2006). It seems that the presence of foreign actors within a district creates significant bridges to foreign markets for that district's firms in terms of added strategic skills, services and competitive dynamics. In particular, investments by foreign actors within an industrial district create new sources of spillovers, reducing the danger of lock-ins and encouraging local firms to seek new external growth paths (Sammarra and Biggiero, 2008; Tallman and Chacar, 2011; Camisón and Villar-Lopez, 2012). The idea that immigrant workers can change the social and working norms in firms located in industrial districts, paving the way to a new form of internationalisation, was first considered in Belussi and Sedita (2010) and labelled as 'reverse relocation'. Finally, empirical evidence suggests that when several foreign investments are located inside a district, the likelihood of systematic and fruitful external contacts by local firms tends to grow by exploiting both horizontal (i.e. intra-industry) and vertical (i.e. customer/supplier relations) spillovers (Amann *et al.*, 2014; Driffield and Hughes, 2010).

However, in addition to the positive contribution that foreign inward investments can make to a district, the literature highlights negative effects (Helpman *et al.*, 2004; Frost, 2001; Markusen, 2003). Specifically, foreign investors can create a competition or market-stealing effect whereby they are able to capture a significant portion of local firms' market share. In turn, this results in a loss of productivity for domestic firms, but that is offset by spillover gains from foreign to local firms (Nicolini, 2001; Phelps *et al.*, 2003; White, 2004; Aharonson *et al.*, 2007). Thus, the development of inward foreign investments within an industrial district gives rise to a potential conflict between the local system network and newly entered foreign business players, due to the economic and socio-cultural integration of the foreign actors into the consolidated local business systems (Crestanello and Tattara, 2010; Chiarvesio *et al.*, 2010).

In other words, the question is whether foreign business actors create or exploit value when they localise within an industrial district (McCann and Folta, 2011; Andersson *et al.*, 2004). The impact of localisation is clearly ambiguous and difficult to judge (Malerba and Nelson, 2011) because industrial districts, particularly in traditional sectors such as textiles, are also experiencing dramatic changes. There does not seem to be a dominant tendency; rather, idiosyncratic patterns are observable. Empirically, it seems that when foreign actors are deeply embedded into a local system and have intense profitable relationships with local actors, they contribute to the district's growth, and local firms benefit from their presence (White, 2004; Aharonson *et al.*, 2007). However, when foreign actors unilaterally appropriate local knowledge and expertise (Greenaway *et al.*, 2004; Young *et al.*, 1994; Enright, 2000; Phelps *et al.*, 2003; White, 2004) or increase the 'competition' effect (Aitken and Harrison, 1999), they cause the district to decline and disintegrate.

In summary, although the de-localisation of activity and the export process by firms within industrial districts have been shown to strongly influence the dynamics of the evolution of industrial districts, much less empirical work has focused on the analysis of foreign inward investments within a district and the specific consequences of those investments for the dynamics of competition among co-located business actors within an industrial district (Rugman and Verbeke, 2003; Exposito-Langa *et al.*, 2011).

This theme is delicate. The globalisation process requires a new perspective on the district model, and local firms face a dilemma. On the one hand, an incentive exists to activate economic relationships with newly located foreign firms, particularly when the latter offer competitive prices for productive factors of low differentiation. On the other hand, incumbent producers of intermediate goods confronted by a decreasing demand from incumbent clients may be induced to sell their goods to newly located foreign firms. The activation of these economic relationships, however, may result in undesired long-term consequences. Although productive industrial processes require a tight relationship among the producers that are vertically distributed along a value chain, activation of commercial relationships may imply the reciprocal transfer of skills and know-how between different stages of the chain (Becchetti and Rossi, 2000). Because a geographical district's competitiveness depends on the productive processes and the competences that are distributed across the boundaries of numerous small firms, which come to share the same destiny, the weaknesses of firms located at a particular stage of a district's value chain may endanger the entire district's survival (Wennberg and Lindqvist, 2010; Capo-Vicedo *et al.*, 2008).

Consequently, capturing the unfolding dynamics of interactions among populations of firms located in different geographical districts is difficult because intra-district relationships are intertwined with inter-district competitive and commercial relationships. In addition, the diversity of industrial districts and the heterogeneity of foreign actors still pose significant barriers to a systematic investigation of longitudinal districts' dynamics and to the generalisation of findings (Bellandi, 2006).

8.3   The empirical context: the Val Vibrata district

We use longitudinal secondary data to investigate a geographical district of micro and small textile-industry firms localised in the Val Vibrata district in the Abruzzo Region, approximately 14 km from Teramo province. This district has been already studied following different perspective of analysis (i.e. Sammarra, 2010).

Over time, the firms located in this context created a homogenous agglomeration, which today represents a significant example of an Italian textile district. This industrial district sprang up after 1960. The period of greatest expansion was the 1970s, with the number of local employees increasing from 10,000 in 1960 to 15,000 in 1975, and with total co-localised firms growing from 900 to 1,100 during the same period (Figure 8.1). Labour was divided among local firms in this phase, which witnessed the establishment of a district characterised by a production system that was stimulated by the outsourcing of large firms located elsewhere. The outsourcing strategy implemented by large, well-known companies in the clothing industry had a visible effect on the growth of the Val Vibrata district.

To satisfy flexibility needs due to instability produced by the 1973 oil shock, many larger producers in the sector, particularly those concentrated in northern Italy, focused their efforts on design and marketing and developed strong outsourcing processes. With the aim of reducing costs, these firms began to formalise a significant number of contracts with a few medium-sized firms (e.g. Wampum and Casucci) that were located in the Val Vibrata area.

Consequently, the number of subcontracting firms specialising in different stages of production grew. These firms were highly specialised at various stages of the production cycle and held close relationships with nearby firms. The organisation of local production, based on a shared division of labour, offered the possibility of achieving very high levels of flexibility and efficiency (Minardi and Di Federico, 2012).

The population of firms in the industrial district was articulated in final firms (i.e. branded and non-branded final producers) and suppliers specialised in labour-intensive subcontracts (e.g. textile-cutting firms for yarns and

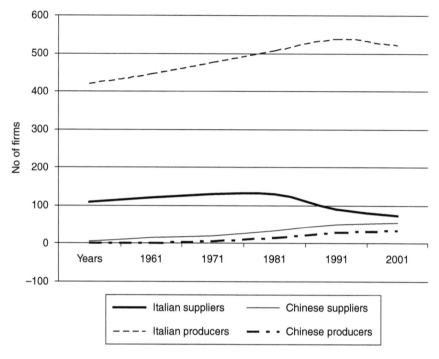

Figure 8.1 Observed demographic dynamics in the Val Vibrata district.

woven fabrics, knitwear firms and wrapping firms). On average, the final firms were medium size and the subcontractor firms were small. During this period, the industrial district had Marshallian features. Production was fractured into myriad small and medium-size firms with a shared division of labour among actors (Keeble *et al.*, 1998). Consequently, the relationships between these actors were characterised by high levels of social capital: significant exchanges of knowledge, informality in business activity management and high levels of reciprocal trust that differentiated this business local network of relationships in respect to other territorial contexts.

This situation of internal equilibrium changed during the 1990s due to rapid localisation within the district of many small, foreign, specialised suppliers devoted to labour-intensive phases of subcontracting (Mollona and Presutti, 2006; 2010).

Strong competition emerged between local and foreign suppliers in the same restricted area. With respect to local system development, the spread of small foreign actors had contradictory implications. On the one hand, it ensured a further competitive supply of labour in textile manufacturing, which became a profitable factor reinforcing the productive capacity, the supply of competencies and the bargaining power of local final producers.

Moreover, the presence of these new, competitive players allowed total sales to increase (Corazziari, 1992). In contrast, during this decade local firms were subject to extensive downsizing: there was a sharp fall in the number of firms and in employment, and local industry lost importance compared with other manufacturing activities in the Abruzzo region. Local subcontracting firms lost approximately 2,000 employees from 1990 to 1998. During the same period, jobs at the local final firms decreased from 8,000 to 6,700. Job loss was significant to both the final local producers and the specialised wrapping-industry firms.

However, until the beginning of the 2000s, the process of substituting foreign players for local traditional actors was common at the level of small subcontracting firms but not at the level of the final producers. This resulted in different rates of firm failures at different stages of the value chain.

During this period, new relationships between local final producers and foreign subcontracting firms emerged. Rather than on cognitive identification and trust, these relationships were built upon reciprocal interests and opportunism, without a real knowledge exchange.

The history of the Val Vibrata district is only one of the variety of possible outcomes. We suspect that different histories might have described unfolding dynamics of integration between incumbent and foreign producers, and a variety of possible district structures might have emerged from the interaction between the sub-populations of local and foreign producers.

8.4 Methodology

Given the heterogeneity of industrial clusters, which still pose significant barriers to systematically investigating longitudinal clusters' dynamics and to generalising findings (Staber 1998; Staber and Morrison 2000), we decided that formal modelling was an appropriate strategy to capture stylised traits of the complex interaction between two geographical clusters.

To rigorously produce testable hypotheses, while retaining the richness of details typical of field studies, field research, formal modelling and computer simulation were integrated. The formal model was built by formalising a number of assumptions. The assumptions used as inputs were either hypotheses collected from theoretical literature or conceptual categories, and relationships among categories, as observed in a typical field study.

To enhance the internal validity of this study's theoretical framework, the relationships among variables were formalised and the formalisation was calibrated on the observations collected in the field. Afterwards, the implications of the formalization were explored through computer simulation. In this way, we generated a new set of hypotheses. In particular, we modelled cluster dynamics using a system of differential equations. Since we model competition among a population of firms sharing key features, we use the theoretical framework of the competing species model (Boyce and Diprima, 1997), which we borrow from biology.

As for the selection of the empirical context, the Val Vibrata cluster had key desirable features. First, the cluster underwent a dramatic change following the birth of a population of foreign entrepreneurs. Second, the longitudinal data were available reporting demographic dynamics of Italian and foreign firms. Third, contacts with a number of local actors were available that allowed interviews to be conducted to collect empirical data on prices and products. The availability of data was a key factor in our research strategy in order to test and calibrate the model.

8.5   The model

The situation analysed in Val Vibrata can be generalised to address the competition among different co-located value chains, each articulated in sub-populations of suppliers and producers.

There are four factors that may intervene to mould interaction dynamics and to decide the district's fate.

The first is the size of the population of newly located firms. We are interested in investigating whether the number of newcomer firms at each stage of a district value chain plays a role in deciding the unfolding interaction dynamics. The relevance of size is related both to the legitimacy effect and to the possibility of sharing knowledge and competencies among small, culturally close foreign firms. Conversely, size may constrain population growth as the resources in a specific competitive niche reach the limits of its carrying capacity.

The second factor is the elasticity of substitution between incumbents' and newcomers' products at each stage of the value chain, that is, the extent to which a sub-population is threatened by the settlement of a newcomer sub-population at its stage of the district's value chain.

The third factor is the competitive advantage that a sub-population of firms may have on others that are located at the same stage of the district's value chain. Competitive advantage depends on the effectiveness of business strategy. For example, a sub-population of firms may have a competitive advantage when offering a differentiated product to a market segment ready to pay a premium price or when building cost leadership in a price-sensitive market segment.

The last factor is the role of the sub-population's rate of growth, that is, how rapidly the number of firms in a sub-population of newly located firms grows.

To analyse how these four factors mould interaction dynamics among sub-populations, we built a stylised model that provides an ideal type of district. To formalise the model, we started from an existing work on modelling species interaction. In particular, we used the competing species model (Boyce and Diprima, 1997).

We assume a closed environment, where two different species live – for example, two species of fish in a pond. Of course, rather than a pond, we assume we are dealing with a geographical area where two clusters compete against each other. We assume the species do not predate each other, but they compete on the same resource for survival. In our example of fish in the pond, the survival resource would be the limited amount of food present in the pond. If we have just one of the species in our environment, the equation that rules the dynamic evolution of the system is as follows:

$$\frac{dx}{dt} = x(e_1 - s_1 \cdot x)$$

where $x = x(t)$ is the variable counting the number of specimens of the species at a given time t, e_1 is the growth rate and s_1 is the inhibition of the population on its same growth, while $\frac{e_1}{s_1}$ gives the level of saturation, given the specific carrying capacity of an environment. These are positive constants, whose values can be determined by an empirical observation of the system. In fact, it is very reasonable that, even if just one species of fish is present in a pond, after a while the number of fish will stop growing, reaching an equilibrium, based on the amount of the resources (food) present in the environment (the pond).

When both species are present, each species will interfere and reduce the growth rate of the other. The simplest system of equations describing this phenomenon is the following:

$$\begin{cases} \dfrac{dx}{dt} = x(e_1 - s_1 x - a_1 y) \\ \dfrac{dy}{dt} = y(e_2 - s_2 y - a_2 x) \end{cases}$$

where the constants a_1 and a_2 measure the interference of one species on the other and can be determined again by an empirical observation of our system.

The competing species model was created to account for the competition among two species. We enlarged the model to account for a more complex interaction dynamics (Fioresi and Mollona, 2010).

The diagram in Figure 8.2 sketches the relationships among four populations. We have two populations of suppliers, x_1 and x_2, which supply populations of producers of finished goods y_1 and y_2. The four populations are located in the same district. Populations x_1 and y_1 are 'incumbent' producers and populations x_2 and y_2 are 'newly located' firms. In the case of Val Vibrata, the latter are Chinese. We assume that both x_1 and x_2 can sell to y_1 and y_2. Therefore, the two suppliers (x_1 and x_2) compete for a scarce resource – that is, the total number of 'producers of finished goods' $y_1 + y_2$. Similarly, the populations of 'producers of finished goods', $y_1 + y_2$, compete to reach the greatest number of buyers, which represent the potential market u of consumers.

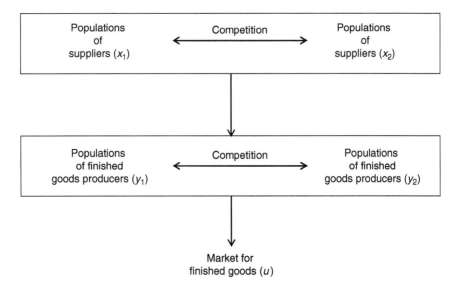

Figure 8.2 Generalized model of interaction in the Val Vibrata district.

We investigate the long-term survival dynamics that arise as the result of two classes of processes: horizontal competitive dynamic between suppliers and vertical commercial relationships that connect suppliers and finished goods producers (Figure 8.2).

The growth rate of the four populations x_1, x_2, y_1 and y_2 is modelled analogously to the competing species model using four differential equations:

$$\begin{cases} \dfrac{dx_1}{dt} = \dfrac{g_1 x_1 (y_1 + y_2 - c_{21} x_2 - x_1)}{y_1 + y_2} \\[2ex] \dfrac{dx_2}{dt} = \dfrac{g_2 x_2 (y_1 + y_2 - c_{12} x_1 - x_2)}{y_1 + y_2} \\[2ex] \dfrac{dy_1}{dt} = \dfrac{\tilde{g}_1 y_1 (u - \tilde{c}_{21} y_2 - y_1)}{u} \\[2ex] \dfrac{dy_2}{dt} = \dfrac{\tilde{g}_2 y_2 (u - \tilde{c}_{12} y_1 - y_2)}{u} \end{cases}$$

where g_1, g_2, $\tilde{g}_1$, $\tilde{g}_2$ are positive constants representing the growth rate of each population x_1, x_2, y_1 and y_2; c_{12}, c_{21}, $\tilde{c}_{12}$, $\tilde{c}_{21}$ are positive constants which represent the competition rate. The populations' rates of growth positively depend on the stock of existing firms. This reflects a legitimacy hypothesis: the larger the stock of foreign firms, the more legitimated they will be and the easier it will be for a foreigner to build their business. The competition rate c in a typical competing species model incorporates two elements that contribute to explain sub-populations' competitive aggressiveness. To describe the two elements, we borrow the concepts of preference overlap and preference asymmetry from Adner's (2002) work on substitution dynamics among competing technologies. The first element is the extent to which preferences in the market niche of two sub-populations overlap. For example, when c_{12} and c_{21} are equal to zero, the rate of substitution among products of the two sub-populations is zero and the supplies of the two sub-populations target independent market niches. However, when both c_{12} and c_{21} are equal to 1, the market niches of the two sub-populations compose a single larger market for both of the sub-populations. Thus, a second element is crucial to capture competitive dynamics that refer to the case in which $c_{12} \neq c_{21}$ and $c_{21} > 0; c_{12} > 0$. In this case, one sub-population has a competitive advantage over the other and the overlap of preferences unveils a preference asymmetry.

8.6 Simulation experiments

Our analysis proceeds in two steps. First, we test the computer simulation by exploring how our model reproduces the empirically observed phenomenon. Second, we use simulations to connect a theoretical structure to a variety of behaviours that are possibly emerging and often are unexpected.

8.6.1 Testing the model

After working with our formal model, we investigated whether the behaviour reported in Figure 8.1 is somehow similar to any behaviours produced by our formal model. We thus performed a number of simulation experiments to see whether, once plausibly calibrated, the formal model could generate a behaviour that shared any characteristics with the real-time series.[1]

We assigned to the four populations and to the final market the values that they had in 1961. We collected information about average product prices. We learned that the price of intermediate goods sold by a foreign supplier is an average of three times cheaper than when that product is sold by incumbent suppliers. In addition, very low brand recognition and product differentiation protects local intermediate products. The situation is slightly different with respect to producers of finished goods; the price difference is similar, but the local finished good is more recognisable and thus maintains a competitive advantage over the foreign product.

Armed with this information, we calibrated our simulation model, setting the values of parameters to represent the competitive advantages of foreign and local firm populations. We assumed foreign suppliers to be three times more competitive than Italian suppliers and foreign producers of finished goods to be twice as competitive as their Italian competitors. In the case of finished goods producers, we balanced out the price disadvantage of Italian producers with local finished goods' brand recognition. We ran the model and

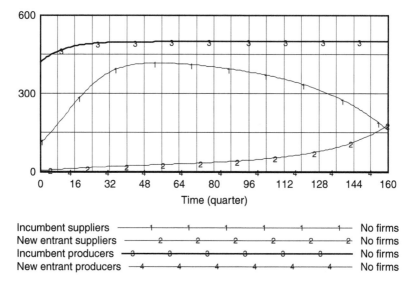

Figure 8.3 History-convergent simulation run.

we stopped the simulation after 160 time steps, each representing a quarter (together corresponding to 40 years), which is the time span of the phenomenon empirically observed and reported in Figure 8.1.

In Figure 8.3, we report a typical simulation behaviour. The reported simulation suggests that the observed empirical behaviour may be an example of a class of behaviour produced by our causal structure. The pattern matching between the simulated and the empirically observed behaviours suggests that the causal mechanisms described in our formal model may provide hints to articulate theoretical hypotheses that explain the observed phenomena.

8.7   Discussion of results

Table 8.1 portrays the set of simulation experiments performed to investigate the effects of sub-population size, preference overlap and preference asymmetry on competition dynamics. Graphs in figures 8.4 and 8.5 report simulation runs. In Table 8.1, we report the specific parameter values used to generate runs in figures 8.4 and 8.5. We started calibrating the initial sizes of populations as in the real case observed in Val Vibrata, with incumbent sub-populations larger than foreign ones. In this scenario, we ran a sensitivity analysis varying both preference overlap and preference asymmetry between zero and two. More specifically, we structured our analysis in two experiments. In the first experiment, we assumed a preference asymmetry in favour of incumbent sub-populations ($c_{12} > c_{21}; \tilde{c}_{12} > \tilde{c}_{21}$). In the second experiment,

Table 8.1 Parameter calibration varies in the range 0–2

Preference asymmetry	Size♣ of new sub-populations < Size♣ of incumbent sub-populations		Size♣ of new sub-populations = Size♥ of incumbent sub-populations	
	High PO $c_{12}c_{21} > 1$ $\tilde{c}_{12}\tilde{c}_{21} > 1$	Low PO $c_{12}c_{21} < 1$ $\tilde{c}_{12}\tilde{c}_{21} < 1$	High PO $c_{12}c_{21} > 1$ $\tilde{c}_{12}\tilde{c}_{21} > 1$	Low PO $c_{12}c_{21} < 1$ $\tilde{c}_{12}\tilde{c}_{21} < 1$
$c_{12} > c_{21}$	$c_{12} = 2; c_{21} = 1.5$	$c_{12} = 0.8; c_{21} = 0.5$	$c_{12} = 2; c_{21} = 1.5$	$c_{12} = 0.8; c_{21} = 0.5$
$\tilde{c}_{12} > \tilde{c}_{21}$	$\tilde{c}_{12} = 2; \tilde{c}_{21} = 1.5$	$\tilde{c}_{12} = 0.8; \tilde{c}_{21} = 0.5$	$\tilde{c}_{12} = 2; \tilde{c}_{21} = 1.5$	$\tilde{c}_{12} = 0.8; \tilde{c}_{21} = 0.5$
$c_{12} < c_{21}$	$c_{12} = 1.5; c_{21} = 2$	$c_{12} = 0.5; c_{21} = 0.8$	$c_{12} = 1.5; c_{21} = 2$	$c_{12} = 0.5; c_{21} = 0.8$
$\tilde{c}_{12} < \tilde{c}_{21}$	$\tilde{c}_{12} = 1.5; \tilde{c}_{21} = 2$	$\tilde{c}_{12} = 0.5; \tilde{c}_{21} = 0.8$	$\tilde{c}_{12} = 1.5; \tilde{c}_{21} = 2$	$\tilde{c}_{12} = 0.5; \tilde{c}_{21} = 0.8$
$c_{12} > c_{21}$	$c_{12} = 2; c_{21} = 1.5$	$c_{12} = 0.8; c_{21} = 0.5$	$c_{12} = 2; c_{21} = 1.5$	$c_{12} = 0.8; c_{21} = 0.5$
$\tilde{c}_{12} < \tilde{c}_{21}$	$\tilde{c}_{12} = 1.5; \tilde{c}_{21} = 2$	$\tilde{c}_{12} = 0.5; \tilde{c}_{21} = 0.8$	$\tilde{c}_{12} = 1.5; \tilde{c}_{21} = 2$	$\tilde{c}_{12} = 0.5; \tilde{c}_{21} = 0.8$
$c_{12} < c_{21}$	$c_{12} = 1.5; c_{21} = 2$	$c_{12} = 0.5; c_{21} = 0.8$	$c_{12} = 1.5; c_{21} = 2$	$c_{12} = 0.5; c_{21} = 0.8$
$\tilde{c}_{12} > \tilde{c}_{21}$	$\tilde{c}_{12} = 2; \tilde{c}_{21} = 1.5$	$\tilde{c}_{12} = 0.8; \tilde{c}_{21} = 0.5$	$\tilde{c}_{12} = 2; \tilde{c}_{21} = 1.5$	$\tilde{c}_{12} = 0.8; \tilde{c}_{21} = 0.5$

♣ Initial calibration of all sub-populations is that of real empirical observations.
♥ Initial calibration of all sub-populations is experimental and set to 100.
PO = preference overlap.

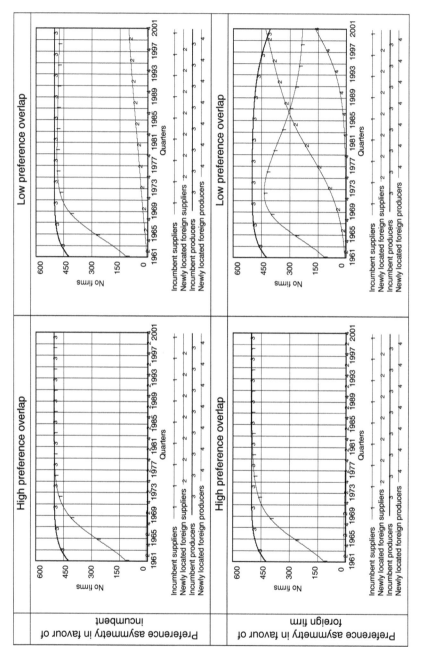

Figure 8.4 Experiments with artificial data (smaller-size foreign sub-populations).

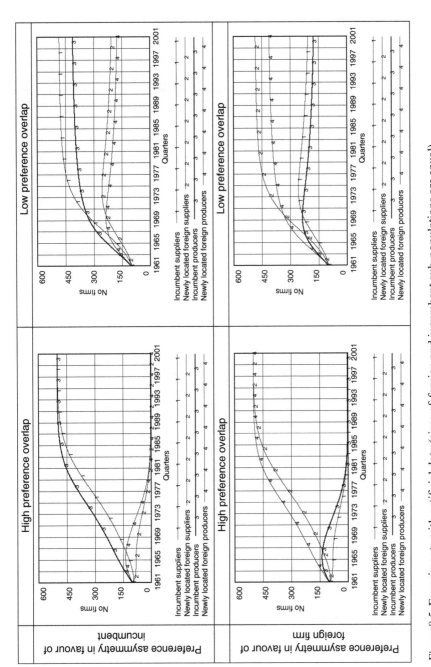

Figure 8.5 Experiments with artificial data (sizes of foreign and incumbent sub-populations are equal).

we assumed a preference asymmetry in favour of foreign sub-populations ($c_{12} < c_{21}; \tilde{c}_{12} < \tilde{c}_{21}$). Finally, we repeated the four experiments assuming that the sizes of the populations are equal at each stage of the supply chain.

A first insight concerns population size. Comparing results in figures 8.4 and 8.5, as expected, the size of the foreign population is important. When sizes of incumbent and foreign sub-populations are equal, foreign sub-populations fail, surviving only in the case with high preference overlap and preference asymmetry in favour of incumbent sub-populations.

> Hypothesis 1: The larger the relative size of foreign sub-populations, the higher the likelihood that foreign sub-populations will survive and take over.

Incumbent populations' size supports legitimacy and network externalities, thereby protecting districts from competition. This clashes with the empirical observation that small sub-populations of foreign firms grow until they reach a critical mass that overtakes incumbent competitors. The problem is that it is often hard to assess the real size of newly located populations. For example, the evidence of powerful populations of entrepreneurs of Chinese origins is easily explained by the pre-existence of a sizeable community of Chinese workers. The size of that community supports legitimacy and network externalities of incoming foreign populations. In this respect, our analysis of the role of the size of competing sub-populations highlights the role played by pre-existing local communities that provide an anchor to incoming foreign firms.

> Hypothesis 2: The larger the relative size of local communities that have cultural or family connections with incoming foreign sub-populations, the higher the likelihood that the foreign sub-populations will survive and take over.

As shown by our experiments, however, sub-populations' sizes interact with preference asymmetry to explain emerging patterns within a district. This suggests that:

> Hypothesis 3: When the relative size of incumbent and foreign sub-populations is similar, preference asymmetry determines the survival performances of foreign sub-populations.

In addition, simulation experiments reveal that size is a protective agent for incumbent sub-populations only when preference overlap is high. In this case, the mass of incumbent sub-populations can directly attack foreign sub-populations. Interestingly, in the lower-left quadrant of Figure 8.4, we observe that despite the fact that newly located sub-populations are more competitive (i.e. the preference asymmetry is in their favour), they fail to survive because their competitive advantage is offset by the network externalities that incumbents enjoy. Yet when preference overlap is low, foreign sub-populations have the opportunity to survive in a protected niche. As shown in the upper right-hand corner of Figure 8.4, even with size and preference asymmetry in favour of incumbent sub-populations, the sub-population of foreign suppliers, which is more sizeable than the foreign sub-population of producers, is able to survive by escaping direct confrontation with incumbent sub-populations (line 2). To highlight the role of preference overlap, in the lower part of Figure 8.4 we report two simulations in which preference asymmetry favours foreign sub-populations. In the simulations, we note that the preference asymmetry is not a sufficient condition for population survival. Assuming that the size of the foreign sub-populations is initially small, preference asymmetry plays a role only when preference overlap is low.

Hypothesis 4: The success of foreign sub-populations' entry is negatively correlated with the preference overlap at the time of entry.

Comparing figures 8.4 and 8.5, we notice that when the initial sizes of sub-populations are equal, preference overlap loses explanatory power and preference asymmetry explains patterns of districts' emerging structure.

Another important issue is how relationships among the four sub-populations are interconnected by non-obvious interconnections. As an example, let us examine the case in which two new sub-populations, one of suppliers and one of producers, both of which are smaller than the relative incumbent sub-populations, attempt to locate in a district. Let us assume that the new sub-populations have high preference overlap within incumbent competitors and have preference asymmetry in their favour.

The results are reported in the lower right-hand graph of Figure 8.4. As shown, the incumbent sub-population of suppliers is the first to suffer competition from the newly located sub-population of suppliers. This is expected because we assumed that the incumbent sub-population is less competitive than the incoming one. The sub-population of incumbent producers, who are equally less competitive than the newly located sub-population of incumbent producers, takes longer to suffer from competition because its size is larger than that of sub-population 4 (newly arrived producers). However, what is interesting to note is the unfolding dynamics. Sub-population 2 (newly arrived suppliers) grows exponentially until 1980, at which point its growth rate begins to decrease, and it then becomes stable asymptotically. However, why must the market saturate if the sub-population of newly located producers is growing (population 4)? The problem is that the market is composed of both incumbent and newly arrived producers. The population of incumbent producers begins to erode in 1980, and the loss of incumbent clients is only partially counterbalanced by the increase in the sub-population of newly arrived producers (line 4). This simulation clarifies an important dynamic. Because the newly located sub-population of producers is initially very small, the sub-population of newly located suppliers could not grow had not it exploited the market provided by the larger population of incumbent producers. This suggests that new, incoming sub-populations of suppliers leverage large incumbent sub-populations of producers to grow.

> Hypothesis 5: The success of entry by foreign sub-populations of suppliers is positively correlated to the size of incumbent producers (see Figure 8.5).

8.8   Conclusions

Our findings have relevant implications for managers and entrepreneurs who are interested in the dynamics of industrial districts and for local authorities that plan the growth of industrial districts. First, the indicated role of population size emphasises the need for coordination among incumbent producers. Size is an important protective agent when it translates in externalities and legitimisation. From this perspective, building shared intellectual and physical infrastructures strengthens an industrial district's defensive walls. Conversely, because externalities also relate to the economisation of coordination costs due to shared logics and entrenched cultural habits, when assessing the strength of barriers to entry into a district, the concept of size must be interpreted in a subtle way.

For example, by considering a cultural community as a pre-existing anchor for immigrants' entrepreneurial activities, it is possible to explain why populations of firms owned by foreign entrepreneurs rapidly reach a considerable size after having been established in a specific territory. In this respect, our work provides another angle to interpret the recent evolution of Italian industrial districts, such as the textile district of Prato, now well known for its growing sub-populations, Chinese-entrepreneur-owned firms, which are overtaking pre-existing Italian firms. In this district, the recent growth in Chinese entrepreneurship is grounded on the large community of Chinese workers that moved to the area decades ago and who have been employed by Italian firms. The accumulation of competencies by immigrant workers, along with the failure to integrate into the local cultural and social milieu, created the basis for the recently observed substitution trend. These considerations remind economists and organisational theorists of the importance of including the perspectives of sociologists and anthropologists to provide managers and local administrators with useful insights.

Second, the concept of preference overlap that emerges from our study emphasises the lack of an appropriate analysis of market segmentation and of the elasticity of substitution among products by small entrepreneurs located in industrial districts. Too often the gains produced by reducing logistic and coordination costs have shielded incumbent entrepreneurs located within industrial districts. Protected by such an environment, rather than exploiting coordination to research and develop new products, entrepreneurs have exploited cost advantages. Conversely, districts that survived the pressures of passive internationalisation are those that have proved able to segment their markets and to move towards higher-quality niches.

Finally, the concept of preference asymmetry stresses the need for rigorous strategic analysis. As shown in the simulation experiments, in the presence of preference overlap, the issue shifts to the question of how to preserve competitive advantage. In this respect, our work forces us to face a very simple fact. Assuming preference overlap, preference asymmetry is the decisive factor governing the fate of a district that is threatened by incoming sub-populations. This means that if incoming sub-populations exploit cost leadership strategies, incumbent sub-populations have to choose: either they try to further decrease their costs or they reduce their preference overlap by moving to another market niche.

In conclusion, we encourage more explicit attention to the local and foreign co-located actors as the unit of analysis when the efficiency and effectiveness of foreign investment development inside a district are discussed. This means that the internal relationships among different sub-populations of different nationalities are elements that will play a critical role in analysing the future development of an industrial district in which a significant investment of foreign actors has been developed over time. In evaluating the evolution of industrial districts, future research needs to consider not only their size but also their integration in terms of social capital (Lin *et al.*, 2001; Pirolo and Presutti, 2010).

In addition, our work emphasises the role of local policies to support the internal development of a district confronted by an invasion of foreign business actors. First, it calls for a deep sociological and anthropological analysis of the composition of the tissue that comprises an industrial district; those districts' social capital and its role in influencing the dynamics of local relationships must be deeply investigated. Second, it highlights the need to move from a passive exploitation of the gain from co-location to an active design and exploitation of social institutions that include, rather than fear, immigrant workers.

Some limitations of our study must be discussed to pinpoint opportunities for further research. First, our results cannot be generalised because of the specific features of our empirical setting. For that reason, a promising line of future research would be to test our results in other industries or local contexts. Moreover, the effects of FDI on an industrial district can be very different from our empirical findings when populations of different nationality are considered since Chinese people seem to be characterised by specific internal and external characteristics making the FDI process more similar to an immigrant entrepreneurship process. Future longitudinal research could broaden these results with an in-depth longitudinal analysis of other populations of different nationality than Chinese people, with a deeper focus on the performance effects and consequences.

Note

1 The values reported in 1961 are as follows: $x_1 = 110; x_2 = 5; y_1 = 420; y_2 = 0$.

References

Adner, R. (2002). When are technologies disruptive? A demand-based view of the emergence of competition, *Strategic Management Journal*, 23(8): 667–688.

Aharonson, B.S., Baum, J.A.C. and Feldman, M.P. (2007). Desperately seeking spillovers? Increasing returns, industrial organization and the location of new entrants in geographic and technological space, *Industrial and Corporate Change*, 16(1): 89–130.

Aitken, B.J. and Harrison, A.E. (1999). Do domestic firms benefit from direct foreign investment? Evidence from Venezuela, *American Economic Review*, 89(3): 605–618.

Alcacer, J. and Chung, W. (2007). Location strategies and knowledge spillovers, *Management Science*, 53(5): 760–776.

Al-Laham, A. and Souitaris, V. (2008). Network embeddedness and new-venture internationalization: analyzing international linkages in the German biotech industry, *Journal of Business Venturing*, 23(5): 567–586.

Amann, B., Jaussaud, J. and Schaaper, J. (2014). Districts and regional management structures by Western MNCs in Asia: overcoming the distance challenge, *Management International Review*, 54(6): 879–906.

Andersson, S. (2004). Internationalization in different industrial contexts, *Journal of Business Venturing*, 19(6): 851–875.

Andersson, T., Serger, S.S., Sorvik, J. and Hansson, W.E. (2004) *The Districts Policies*, Malmo: Whitebook.

Arikan, A.T. and Schilling, M.A. (2011). Structure and governance in industrial districts: implications for competitive advantage, *Journal of Management Studies*, 48(4): 772–803.

Baldwin, R.E., Braconier, H. and Forslid, R. (2005). Multinationals, endogenous growth, and technological spillovers: theory and evidence, *Review of International Economics*, 13(5): 945–963.

Becchetti, L. and Rossi, S.P.S. (2000). The positive effect of industrial district on the export performance of Italian firms, *Review of Industrial Organization*, 16(1): 53–68.

Bell, S.J., Tracey, P. and Heide, J.B. (2009). The organization of regional districts, *Academy of Management Review*, 34(4): 623–642.

Bellandi, M. (2006). A perspective on districts, localities, and specific public goods. In Pitelis, C., Sudgen, R. and Wilson, J.R. (eds) *Districts and Globalization. The Development of Urban and Regional Economies*, Cheltenham: Edward Elgar.

Belussi, F., Gottardi, G. and Rullani, E. (eds) (2003). *The Technological Evolution of Industrial Districts*, Boston, MA: Kluwer.

Belussi, F. and Sammarra, A. (eds) (2010). *Business Networks in Clusters and Industrial Districts*, London: Routledge.

Belussi, F., Sammarra, A. and Sedita, S. (2008). Managing long distance and localised learning in the Emilia Romagna life science district, *European Planning Studies*, 16(5): 665–692.

Belussi, F. and Sedita, S.R. (2010). The evolution of the district model: 'reverse relocation' and the case of the leather-tanning district of Arzignano, *European Review of Industrial Economics and Policy* (ERIEP), 1, online since 28 April 2010, http://testrevel.unice.fr/eriep/index.html?id=3067

Belussi, F. and Sedita, S.R. (2012). Industrial districts as open learning systems: combining emergent and deliberate knowledge structures, *Regional Studies*, 46(2): 165–184.

Belussi, F., Sedita, S.R. and Pilotti, L. (2008). Learning at the boundaries for industrial districts between exploitation of local resources and exploration of global knowledge flows. In Leoncini, R. and Montresor, S. (eds) *Dynamic Capabilities between Firm Organization and Local Systems of Production*, London: Routledge.

Blomström, M., Kokko, A. and Zejan, M. (2000). *Foreign Direct Investment. Firm and Host Country Strategies*, London: Macmillan.

Boyce, W.E. and Diprima, R.C. (1997). *Elementary Differential Equations and Boundary Value Problems*, New York: John Wiley.

Camisón, C. and Villar-Lopez, A. (2012). On how firms located in an industrial district profit from knowledge spillovers: adoption of an organic structure and innovation capabilities, *British Journal of Management*, 23(3): 361–382.

Capó-Vicedo, J., Expósito-Langa, M. and Molina-Morales, F.X. (2008). Improving SME competitiveness reinforcing interorganizational networks in industrial districts, *International Entrepreneurship and Management Journal*, 4(2): 147–169.

Chetty, S. and Holm, B.D. (2000). Internationalisation of small to medium–sized manufacturing firms: a network approach, *International Business Review*, 9(1): 77–93.

Chiarvesio, M., Di Maria, E. and Micelli, S. (2004). From local networks of SMEs to virtual districts? Evidence from recent trends In Italy, *Research Policy*, 33(10): 1509–1528.

Chiarvesio, M., Di Maria, E. and Micelli, S. (2010). Global value chain and open networks: the case of Italian industrial districts, *European Planning Studies*, 18(3): 333–350.

Cooke, P., Heidenreich, M. and Braczyk, H. (2004). *Regional Innovation Systems*, London: Routledge.

Corazziari, G. (1992). Lo sviluppo industrial della Val Vibrata, in Istituto Alcide Cervi, *Contributi per una storia d'Abruzzo contemporanea*, Franco Angeli, Milano, 219–245.

Crestanello, P. and Tattara, G. (2010). Industrial districts and the governance of the global value chain: the Romania-Veneto network in footwear and clothing, *Regional Studies*, 45(2): 187–203.

Driffield, N. (2006). On the search for spillovers from foreign direct investment (FDI) with spatial dependence, *Regional Studies*, 40(1): 107–119.

Driffield, N. and Hughes, D. (2003). Foreign and domestic investment: regional development or crowding out? *Regional Studies*, 37(3): 277–288.

Driffield, N.L. and Munday, M.C. (2000). Industrial performance, agglomeration, and foreign manufacturing investment in the UK, *Journal of International Business Studies*, 31(1): 21–37.

Enright, M.J. (2000). Regional districts and multinational enterprises: independence, dependence or interdependence? *International Studies of Management and Organization*, 30(2): 114–138.

Expósito-Langa, M., Molina-Morales, F.X. and Capó-Vicedo, J. (2011). New product development and absorptive capacity in industrial districts: a multidimensional approach, *Regional Studies*, 45(3): 319–331.

Fioresi, R. and Mollona, E. (2010). Devices for theory development: why use computer simulation if mathematical analysis is available? in Mollona, E. (ed.) *Computational Analysis of Firms' Strategy and Organizations*, New York: Routledge.

Frost, T.S. (2001). The geography sources of foreign subsidiaries' innovation, *Strategic Management Journal*, 22(2): 101–123.

Gereffi, G., Humphrey, J. and Sturgeon, T. (2005). The governance of global value chains, *Review of International Political Economy*, 12(1): 78–104.

Gordon, I. and McCann, P. (2005). Innovation, agglomeration and regional development, *Journal of Economic Geography*, 5(5): 523–543.

Gorg, H. and Greenaway, D. (2004). Much ado about nothing? Do domestic firms really benefit from foreign direct investment? *World Bank Research Observer*, 19(2): 171–197.

Greenaway, D., Sousa, N. and Wakelin, K. (2004). Do domestic firms learn to export from multinationals, *European Journal of Political Economy*, 20(4): 1027–1043.

Helpman, E., Melitz, M.J. and Yeaple, S.R. (2004). Export versus FDI with heterogeneous firms, *American Economic Review*, 94(1): 300–316.

Hilbert, C.A. and Voicu, I. (2010). Agglomeration economies and the location of foreign direct investment: empirical evidence from Romania, *Regional Studies*, 44(3): 355–371.

Huggins, R. and Johnston, A. (2010). Knowledge flow and inter-firm networks: the influence of network resources, spatial proximity and firm size, *Entrepreneurship & Regional Development*, 22(5): 457–484.

Iammarino, S. and McCann, P. (2013). *Multinationals and Economic Geography: Location, Technology and Innovation*, Cheltenham: Edward Elgar Publishing.

Keeble, D., Lawson, C., Smith, H.L. and Wilkinson, F. (1998). Internationalisation processes, networking and local embeddedness in technology-intensive small firms, *Small Business Economics*, 11(4): 327–342.

Klepper, S. and Malerba, F. (2010). Demand, innovation and industrial dynamics: an introduction, *Industrial and Corporate Change*, 19(5): 1515–1520.

Lazerson, M.H. and Lorenzoni, G. (1999). The firms that feed industrial districts: a return to the Italian source, *Industrial Corporate and Change*, 8(2): 235–266.

Li, W., Veliyath R. and Tan, J. (2013). Network characteristics and firm performance: an examination of the relationships in the context of a district, *Journal of Small Business Management*, 51(1): 15–22.

Lin, N., Cook, K. and Burt, R. (2001). *Social Capital*, New York: Walter de Gruyter.

Majocchi, A. and Presutti, M. (2009). Industrial districts, entrepreneurial culture and the social, environment: the effects on FDI distribution, *International Business Review*, 18(1): 76–88.

Maksell, P. (2001) Towards a knowledge-based theory of the geographical district, *Industrial and Corporate Change*, 10(4): 921–943.

Malerba, F. and Nelson, R. (2011). Learning and catching up in different sectoral systems: evidence from six industries, *Industrial and Corporate Change*, 20(6): 1645–1675.

Mariotti, S. and Piscitello, L. (2001). Localized capabilities and internationalization of manufacturing activities by SMEs, *Entrepreneurship and Regional Development*, 13(1): 65–80.

Markusen, A. (2003). Fuzzy concepts, scanty evidence, policy distance: the case for rigour and policy relevance in critical regional studies, *Regional Studies*, 37(6–7): 701–717.

McCann, B.T. and Folta, T.B. (2008). Location matters: where we have been and where we might go in agglomeration research, *Journal of Management*, 34(3): 532–565.

McCann, B.T. and Folta, T.B. (2009). Demand- and supply-side agglomerations: distinguishing between fundamentally different manifestations of geographic concentration, *Journal of Management Studies*, 46(3): 362–392.

McCann, B.T. and Folta, T.B. (2011) Performance differentials within geographic clusters, *Journal of Business Venturing*, 26(1): 104–123.

Minardi, E. and Di Federico, R. (2012). *La frontiera come spazio di intelligenza, creatività ed innovazione. Il caso Vibrata_Tronto.* Homeless Book, Collana Best Practices.

Mollona, E. and Presutti, M. (2006). A population ecology approach to capture dynamics of cluster evolution: using computer simulation to guide empirical research. 24 International Conference System Dynamics Society, Conference Proceedings.

Mollona, E. and Presutti, M. (2010). Da sistemi chiusi a contesti aperti: simulazione di scenari e analisi empirica sui distretti italiani in una logica di capitale sociale, in Boari, C. (ed.) *Dinamiche evolutive nei cluster geografici di imprese*, Bologna: Il Mulino, pp. 59–73.

Nicolini, R. (2001). Size and performance of local districts of firms, *Small Business Economics*, 17(3): 185–195.

Odorici, V. and Presutti, M. (2013). The entrepreneurial experience and strategic orientation of high-tech born global start-ups: an analysis of novice and habitual entrepreneurs, *Journal of International Entrepreneurship*, 11(3): 268–291.

Phelps, N.A. (2008). District or capture? Manufacturing foreign direct investment, external economies and agglomeration, *Regional Studies*, 42(4): 457–473.

Phelps, N.A., Mackinnon, D., Stone, I. and Braidford, P. (2003). Embedding the multinationals? Institutions and the development of overseas manufacturing affiliates in Wales and North East England, *Regional Studies*, 37(1): 27–40.

Pirolo, L. and Presutti, M. (2010). The impact of social capital on the start-up's performance growth, *Journal of Small Business Management*, 48(2): 197–227.

Piscitello, L. and Sgobbi, F. (2004). Globalisation, e-business and SMEs: evidence from the Italian district of Prato, *Small Business Economics*, 22(5): 333–347.

Porter, M.E. (2000). Location, competition, and economic development: local districts in a global economy, *Economic Development Quarterly*, 14(1): 15–34.

Presutti, M., Boari, C. and Majocchi, A. (2011). The importance of proximity for the start-ups' knowledge acquisition and exploitation, *Journal of Small Business Management*, 49(3): 361–389.

Presutti M., Boari, C. and Majocchi, A. (2013). Inter-organizational geographical proximity and local start-ups' knowledge acquisition: a contingency approach, *Entrepreneurship & Regional Development: An International Journal*, 25(5–6): 446–467.

Rallet, A. and Torre, A. (2000). Is geographical proximity necessary in the innovation networks in the era of global economy? *Geojournal*, 49(4): 373–380.

Romanelli, E. and Khessina, O.M. (2005). Regional industrial identity: district configurations and economic development, *Organization Science*, 16(4): 344–358.

Rugman, A.M. and Vebeke, A. (2003). Multinational enterprises and districts: an organizing framework, *Management International Review*, 43: 151–169.

Sammarra A. (2010). A 'low road' to competitiveness in the global apparel industry: the case of the Vibrata Valley, in Belussi, F. and Sammarra, A. (eds) *Business Networks in Clusters and Industrial Districts*, London and New York: Routledge, pp. 114–135.

Sammarra, A. and Biggiero, L. (2008). Heterogeneity and specificity of inter-firm knowledge flows in innovation networks, *Journal of Management Studies*, 45(4): 800–829.

Saxenian, A. (1994). *Regional Advantage: Culture and Competition in Silicon Valley and Route 128*, Cambridge, MA: Harvard University Press.

Scott-Kennel, J. (2007). Foreign direct investment and local linkages: An empirical investigation, *Management International Review*, 47(1): 51–77.

Staber, U. (1998). Inter-firm co-operation and competition in industrial districts, *Organization Studies*, 19(4): 701–724.

Staber, U. and Morrison, C. (2000). The empirical foundations of industrial district theory, in Wolfe, D. and Holbrook, A. (eds) *Innovation, Institutions and Territory: Regional Innovation Systems in Canada*, Montreal: McGill-Queen's University.

Tallman, S. and Chacar, A.S. (2011). Knowledge accumulation and dissemination in MNEs: a practice-based framework, *Journal of Management Studies*, 48(4): 278–304.

Waxell, A. and Malmberg, A. (2007). What is global and what is local in knowledge-generating interaction? The case of the biotech district in Uppsala, Sweden, *Entrepreneurship and Regional Development*, 19: 137–159.

Wennberg, K. and Lindqvist, G. (2010). The effect of districts on the survival and performance of new firms, *Small Business Economics*, 34(3): 221–241.

White, M.C. (2004). Inward investment, firm embeddedness and place. An assessment of Ireland's multinational software sector, *European Urban and Regional Studies*, 11(3): 243–260.

Young, S., Hood, N. and Peters, E. (1994). Multinational enterprises and regional economic development, *Regional Studies*, 28(7): 657–677.

Zaheer, S. (1995). Overcoming the liability of foreignness, *Academy of Management Journal*, 38(2): 341–363.

9 Cluster life cycles and path dependency

An exploratory assessment of cluster evolution in the Basque Country

Aitziber Elola, Jesús M. Valdaliso, Susana Franco and Santiago M. López

9.1 Introduction

There is growing agreement in evolutionary economic geography on the necessity for historical perspectives, to fully understand both the origins and the evolution of clusters (Boschma and Fornahl, 2011; Menzel and Fornahl, 2010; Ter Wal and Boschma, 2011). This chapter aims to contribute to this research line. We draw on in-depth case studies on six Basque industrial clusters – papermaking, maritime industries, machine tools, energy, electronics and ICTs, and aeronautics – to identify the driving forces behind the origins and evolution of the selected clusters. This analysis allows both scholars and policy makers to understand the basis for past and current competitive advantages of clusters and to evaluate whether such advantages may be sustainable in the future. From a broader and more ambitious point of view, and given the link between clusters' performance and regional competitiveness, it also attempts to introduce the role of history into the analysis of regional policy (see Aranguren *et al.*, 2012; Boschma, 2004; Martin, 2010; 2011; Martin and Sunley, 2006; Navarro *et al.*, 2014; Valdaliso, 2013).

The case of the Basque Country proves to be particularly appropriate for this exercise. It was an old industrial region, specialised in heavy industries (iron and steel, shipbuilding, mechanical engineering), which faced a severe economic crisis and industrial restructuring in the 1980s. Following Michael E. Porter's advice, in the early 1990s the regional government pioneered within the EU a competitiveness policy based on clusters, with proven and recognised results (Ketels, 2004; Navarro *et al.*, 2014; OECD, 2011; Porter *et al.*, 2013)[1]. The Basque Country, like other old industrial regions of Europe, managed to avoid lock-in situations, renewing its industrial base by upgrading some of its mature clusters and by promoting new high-technology ones (Aranguren *et al.*, 2012; Trippl and Tödtling, 2008).

The next section of the chapter reviews the literature on cluster evolution. Then, 9.3 presents the sample of clusters selected along with its main figures in 2012 and the methodology employed. Section 9.4 is devoted to the presentation of the main empirical findings relating to the triggering factors of cluster origins and evolution in the Basque Country. Finally, we offer some initial conclusions and raise some implications of this research.

9.2   Theoretical background

9.2.1   *Life cycles and path dependence in cluster evolution*

Although clusters have acquired 'something akin to hegemonic status' (Martin and Sunley, 2011), both among scholars and policy makers, much of the existing literature still focuses on understanding the existence and functioning of contemporary successful clusters, rather than on their evolution and change over time (Bergman, 2008; Menzel and Fornahl, 2010). The recent development of an evolutionary paradigm in economic geography has stressed the necessity of dynamic and historical perspectives to fully understand issues such as cluster or even regional economic evolution (Boschma and Fornahl, 2011; Boschma and Martin, 2007; Martin, 2010; Martin and Sunley, 2006; Ter Wal and Boschma, 2011).

The first works that dealt with cluster evolution stressed that cluster competitive advantages were not permanent and that factors that accounted for cluster emergence might become later factors of cluster decline (or the other way around) (Brenner and Mühlig, 2013; Bresnahan *et al.*, 2001; Feldman *et al.*, 2005; Martin and Sunley, 2006; Porter, 1990). Two theoretical models have been proposed to study cluster evolution, one based on a traditional life cycle approach, industry or cluster-based (Bergman, 2008; Menzel and Fornahl, 2010), and another based on an adaptive life cycle model (Martin and Sunley, 2011). Although cluster life cycles tend to co-evolve with the life cycle of the dominant industry, the stylised life cycle model does not capture the full complexity of cluster evolution. Clusters do not necessarily follow the life cycles of their dominant industries and their evolution may be driven by local factors such as factor endowments, entrepreneurship and firms' capabilities, institutions and/or social capital, among others (Belussi and Sedita, 2009; Elola *et al.*, 2012; Menzel and Fornahl, 2010; Valdaliso *et al.*, 2016).

So far, only a few empirical studies on this issue have explicitly followed a life cycle model, either single case studies on specific clusters (Shin and Hassink, 2011; Staber and Sautter, 2011; Van Klink and De Langen, 2001) or more ambitious meta-studies based on larger samples of clusters (Belussi and Sedita, 2009; Brenner and Mühlig, 2013; Elola *et al.*, 2012; Valdaliso *et al.*, 2016). Regardless of the theoretical framework employed or the empirical approach, all of them reckon that clusters are driven by path-dependent forces that may have both negative and positive effects on cluster evolution and can be used to explain why change goes in a particular direction (Henning *et al.*, 2012; Lagerholm and Malmberg, 2009; Martin, 2010; Martin and Sunley, 2006). Belussi and Sedita (2009) have coined the term 'multiple path dependency' to stress the broad scope of evolutionary trajectories adopted by the industrial districts studied.

9.2.2 Driving factors of cluster emergence and evolution: a typology

In order to identify the driving factors of cluster emergence and evolution, this chapter slightly adjusts the framework developed by Elola *et al.* (2012), building on existing literature (Belussi and Sedita, 2009; Brenner and Mühlig, 2013; Lorenzen, 2005; Menzel and Fornahl, 2010). The framework distinguished between local and global factors in the emergence and evolution of clusters (see Table 9.1).

Among the local factors that may trigger the emergence of a cluster we distinguish a category of historical legacies, which refers to tradition and historical preconditions; another category related to regional factor endowment such as natural resources, qualified labour and infrastructure; and some triggering factors, including local demand, local and national policies, and anchor firms and local entrepreneurship (for further discussion see Belussi and Sedita, 2009; Brenner and Mühlig, 2013; Elola *et al.*, 2012).

Regarding cluster evolution, which encapsulates development, maturity and decline, along with three out of the four aforementioned factors, we distinguish two further local factors. The first one is related to the cluster prior trajectory, which usually substitutes that of tradition and historical

Table 9.1 Driving factors of clusters' life cycles

	Life cycle stages	
	Cluster emergence	*Cluster evolution*
Local factors	Tradition and historical preconditions	Development of factors specific to the cluster
	Factor endowment	Factor endowment
	Anchor firms and entrepreneurship	Anchor firms and entrepreneurship
	Local demand	Local (sophisticated) demand
	Local and national policies	Local and national policies
		Strategic capabilities and dynamic capabilities
Global factors	Entry of MNCs*, foreign investment and entrepreneurship	Entry of MNCs*, foreign investment and entrepreneurship
	Inflow of external knowledge and technology	Inflow of external knowledge and technology
	International demand growth ('windows of opportunity')	International demand growth ('windows of opportunity')
	Global competition	Global competition

Note: * MNCs: multinational corporations.
Source: Authors' elaboration.

preconditions in cluster origins. Under the development of factors specific to the cluster, we consider highly specialised human capital, technological and educational infrastructures, or the development of social capital, among others. The second factor deals with the strategic capabilities developed by clustered firms: strategic capabilities in the strict sense, that we classify under two different competitive strategies – cost leadership, and diversification and/or differentiation strategies (see Belussi and Sedita, 2009 for further discussion); and dynamic capabilities (see Zollo and Winter, 2002), and particularly, absorptive capacity at firm and cluster level (see Giuliani, 2005; Zahra and George, 2002). The role of local demand now is also considered in terms of not only volume and trends but of sophistication as well (see Elola *et al.*, 2012; Malerba *et al.*, 2006). Notice that these local factors tend to exhibit a strong place and path dependence, hence conditioning the scope of cluster trajectory in the future (see Martin, 2010; Martin and Sunley, 2006; 2011).

We consider the same categories of global factors in both the emergence and the evolutionary stages. However, their importance and the type of influence they exert are not necessarily the same during the different stages of a cluster's life cycle. First, we assume that factors such as the entry of foreign firms and entrepreneurs, with capital, technology and/or knowledge, may play an important role in both phases. Additionally, we take into account the role of international demand growth and the extent of global competition, which is regarded as one of the most difficult challenges for industrial districts and clusters nowadays (Belussi and Sedita, 2009).

9.3   Methodology

The empirical base of this chapter draws from in-depth case studies on six industrial clusters particularly representative of the industrial trajectory of the Basque Country in the nineteenth and twentieth centuries: papermaking, maritime industries, machine tools, energy, electronics and ICTs, and aeronautics. The former three belong to industries of the first industrial revolution that go back to the nineteenth century and even earlier: the late eighteenth century in the case of papermaking, the sixteenth century for machine tools, when a fire arms industry appeared, or the twelfth century for shipbuilding. The energy cluster dates back to the beginning of the twentieth century, linked to the spread of electricity in the region, and comprises not only the activities of production and distribution of energy but the manufacturing of energy equipment as well. The last two clusters correspond to young industries that emerged in the second half of the twentieth century. In the electronics and ICTs cluster, the first firms appeared in the 1940s and 1950s; in the case of aeronautics, they were created in the 1980s, growing out of an already existent manufacturing industry of automobile components and parts, engines, and of a few engineering companies. Therefore, we have three 'mature' clusters that have followed the entire life cycle of creation, development and maturity, and another three 'younger' clusters that have gone from the emergence to the development phase. Regarding the former ones, maritime industries and machine tools have been able to escape from lock-in and decline, transforming and renewing themselves. In the papermaking cluster, pulp and paper producers managed to maintain their competitive position based on scale economies and cost efficiency, while equipment manufacturers followed a combined strategy of product differentiation, innovation and internationalisation. Despite this, the papermaking cluster is still declining. The energy cluster has also recently experienced a phase of change linked to the diffusion of renewable energies (see Table 9.2).

The current size of the clusters studied is quite heterogeneous. In 2012, the clusters of energy, electronics and ICTs, and maritime industries comprised about 300 firms each, while those of aeronautics, machine tools and papermaking were quite a lot smaller. In terms of employees and turnover in facilities located in the Basque Country, the biggest cluster was that of energy; electronics and ICTs ranked second; then came maritime industries and machine tools; and the smallest ones were the aeronautics and papermaking clusters (see Table 9.3). Three clusters – aeronautics, machine tools, and electronics and ICT – show relatively high ratios of R&D expenditures over turnover, while that of energy has the highest absolute figure. Overall, firms of these six clusters represented about 78 per cent of the firms and about 54 per cent of the employment of the whole population of firms in the clusters regarded as strategic by the Basque government, and about 26 per cent of the industrial employment of the region in 2011 (building sector excluded).[2]

For each cluster, a historical (longitudinal) in-depth case study, based on different sources of information, was conducted first.[3] Second, we established the life cycle of every cluster according mainly to the evolution of firms and employment figures, along with other qualitative factors related to the industry life cycle and the competitive trajectory of the most representative firms (see Table 9.2). Then, drawing on our aforementioned classification of driving factors, we identified the most important triggering factors in each cluster life cycle stage. After that, a qualitative meta-study approach was employed, akin to that conducted by Van der Linde (2003) for world clusters and by Belussi and Sedita (2009) for Italian industrial districts, in order to pool the results from these case studies. This chapter's sample is smaller but has a distinctive advantage: it is based on uniform case studies, conducted by the same team and with a standardised methodology, which avoids the problems of inconsistency related to the employment of too many methodologically dispersed studies. Table 9.4 summarises the results and highlights the more important driving factors in our sample. However, it has to be reckoned that this approach allows for descriptive statistics and associations rather than for causal relationships (Van der Linde, 2003).

Table 9.2 Basque clusters' life cycles

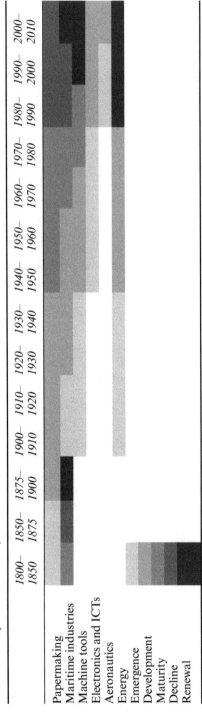

	1800– 1850	1850– 1875	1875– 1900	1900– 1910	1910– 1920	1920– 1930	1930– 1940	1940– 1950	1950– 1960	1960– 1970	1970– 1980	1980– 1990	1990– 2000	2000– 2010
Papermaking														
Maritime industries														
Machine tools														
Electronics and ICTs														
Aeronautics														
Energy														
Emergence														
Development														
Maturity														
Decline														
Renewal														

Source: Authors' elaboration, based on number of firms and employees.

Table 9.3 Main figures of the Basque clusters in 2012

	Firms	Employment	Turnover	Exports	R&D expenditures	Exports/Turnover	R&D/Turnover
Aeronautics	60	4,142	771	694	195	90.0%	25.3%
Electronics and ICT	289	11,900	2,950	1,210	122	41.0%	4.1%
Maritime industries	350	6,430	985	837	n.a.	85.0%	n.a.
Papermaking*	20	1,650	614	302	n.a.	49.2%	n.a.
Energy	350	23,336	15,943	n.a.	253	c.36%	1.6%
Machine tools	108	5,762	1,107	846	46	76.4%	4.2%

Source: SPRI, *Observatorio de Coyuntura Industrial 2013-I*; and ACE, *Panorama del Clúster de Energía del País Vasco 2011*. Data on turnover, exports and R&D expenditures, in million €.

Note: * Figures refer to 2010 and to the firms affiliated to the cluster association, which represents about 50 per cent of the whole cluster.

9.4   Discussion of empirical findings

Clusters' birth and evolution seem to be determined by multiple factors, rather than by a single one. Contrary to what Belussi and Sedita (2009) did for their sample of Italian industrial districts, we argue that a qualitative analysis does not allow the establishment of a single factor that accounts for the origin of each cluster.

9.4.1   Cluster emergence

In the case of Basque clusters, a combination of local and global factors accounted for their origins (see Table 9.4). Among the local factors, demand, entrepreneurship and anchor firm, factor conditions, tradition and historical preconditions, plus local policies, played a key role, while the entry of multinational corporations (MNCs) or foreign entrepreneurs and/or the inflow of external knowledge and technology appear as the most important global factors. Our findings on the significance of local demand and factor conditions for the origins of clusters broadly agree with those of Van der Linde (2003) for a large sample of world clusters, although his classification does strictly follow Porter's diamond vectors.

Local demand played a key role in all the cases studied: it came from a playing cards manufacturer in the papermaking cluster at the end of the eighteenth century, and from the 1840s onwards, from the final demand associated with the regional economic development; from the Basque merchant shipping and fishing fleets, the first and the second largest fleets of Spain at the beginning of the twentieth century, respectively, in the maritime cluster; from the large demand for energy of the Basque industry, in the case of the energy cluster; from multiple well-developed industrial sectors in the machine tool and electronics clusters, in the first third of the twentieth century and in the 1940s and 1950s, respectively, and in the latter, from the electrical sector as well; and from both national (CASA) and foreign demand (Embraer, McDonnell-Douglas) in the aeronautics cluster in the 1980s and 1990s.

With regard to factor conditions, except for availability of water for the papermaking industry, both as raw material and as power source, the rest were linked to the previous industrial trajectory of the region that provided a qualified labour force, local entrepreneurship and technical expertise from related sectors in the maritime, machine tools, electronics, energy and aeronautics clusters, a hydraulic and transport infrastructure in the papermaking and maritime cluster, respectively, and a local banking sector that invested heavily in the new electrical companies. The existence of local entrepreneurship, frequently from related sectors and industries, played a more important role than a single anchor firm. This was due, again, to the long historical tradition of the Basque Country in many industrial activities. Local entrepreneurs created a pool of founding firms that played a driving role in the subsequent stages of cluster development, setting up a technological trajectory, shaping the cluster borders,

Table 9.4 Strength of the driving factors for each phase of the cluster life cycle

	Nature of the driving factor	Origins						Development						Maturity						Decline and/or renewal					
		P	Mar	M-T	Ele	Aer	Ene	P	Mar	M-T	Ele	Aer	Ene	P	Mar	M-T	Ele	Aer	Ene	P	Mar	M-T	Ele	Aer	Ene
Local factors	Tradition and historical preconditions	X	X	X			X	X					X			X									X
	Factor endowment	X	X	X	X	X	X	X	X	X	X					X						X			X
	Anchor firms and entrepreneurship	X	X	X	X	X	X	X	X	X	X	X	X	X							X				X
	Local/national demand	X	X	X	X		X	X	X	X	X		X	X	X					X					X
	Local/national policies	X	X	X	X			X	X	X	X			X	X	X				X	X				X
	Development of factors specific to the cluster							X	X	X	X	X	X	X	X	X				X	X				X
	Strategic capabilities							X	X	X	X	X	X	X	X	X				X	X	X			X
Global factors	Entry of MNCs, foreign investment and entrepreneurship	X	X		X	X	X						X							X					X

(continued)

Table 9.4 Strength of the driving factors for each phase of the cluster life cycle (*continued*)

Nature of the driving factor	Origins						Development						Maturity						Decline and/or renewal					
	P	Mar	M-T	Ele	Aer	Ene	P	Mar	M-T	Ele	Aer	Ene	P	Mar	M-T	Ele	Aer	Ene	P	Mar	M-T	Ele	Aer	Ene
Inflow of external knowledge and technology	X	X		X			X	X	X	X		X			X						X			X
International demand growth					X				X	X	X		X	X	X				X	X	X			X
Global competition					X						X		X	X	X				X	X	X			X

Source: Authors' elaboration. Marked with X appear the driving factors for each phase of the cluster life cycle. In grey, cluster life cycles stages that do not apply for the indicated clusters.

promoting new firm creation by spin-off processes, and/or creating new institutions and organisations for the cluster's benefit (cf. Feldman, 2001; Feldman *et al.*, 2005): the first papermaking firms of the Tolosa region in the 1840s to 1870s; the two large shipyards of Euskalduna (1900) and La Naval (1909) in the maritime cluster; firms such as Sacia (1910) and Ciarán, Estarta & Ecenarro (1913) in the machine tool cluster; Hidroeléctrica Ibérica (1901) and Saltos del Duero (1918) in the energy cluster; a group of firms in the electronics sector in the 1940s and 1950s (Arteche, JEMA, Ikusi, Fagor Electrónica, GEPCE); and the triangle of firms SENER-Gamesa-ITP in the aeronautics cluster.

Local and national policies also played a triggering role, but their nature was very different depending on the time they were employed, as were their implications for long-term cluster development. Tariffs were the most widely used policy instrument for industry promotion in the clusters of papermaking, maritime industries, machine tools, electrical equipment and electronics in the nineteenth and the first half of the twentieth centuries. While their positive impact in the emergence of these clusters is clearly acknowledged, its long-term maintenance contributed to isolate them and to erode the competitive capabilities of their firms. After Spain's entry into the European Economic Community in 1986, the Basque industry had to face a new scenario of cut-throat global competition to which firms were not always able to respond successfully. On the contrary, policies devoted to promote (technological learning, R&D activities, internationalisation), rather than to protect, played a very positive role in the machine tools, electronics, energy and aeronautics clusters from the 1980s, and in the maritime one from the 2000s. The aeronautic cluster, in particular, is a clear case of a picking-winners strategy of the Basque government in the 1990s aimed at promoting industrial diversification into high-tech sectors.

Local factors provided the necessary conditions, but they were not enough. In a relatively backward country such as Spain, the inflow of external knowledge and technology was also needed. It originally came from France, in the case of the first craft papermaking mills of the late eighteenth and early nineteenth centuries; from Britain in the shipbuilding industry in the late nineteenth century; or from international leaders as in the machine tools, electronics and aeronautics clusters. The electric energy cluster drew initially on foreign sources of knowledge transferred by patents and local engineers, but very soon the first movers (Ibérica and Duero, eventually merged in Iberduero) developed their own capabilities in the field of hydroelectricity. In some cases, the direct involvement of MNCs in local firms[4] made the transference of external knowledge and technology easier in those early stages. Thus, our sample points to a combination of local and global factors as an essential prerequisite for cluster formation.

9.4.2 Cluster evolution

In the evolution of clusters, along with local entrepreneurship and demand, more sophisticated in the electronics, aeronautics, machine tool and energy cluster, or less sophisticated in papermaking and shipbuilding, other local factors played a triggering role: the development of cluster-specific factors and the strategic capabilities developed by the clustered firms. Among the former, the most common ones that appear during this stage are specialised educational and training centres,[5] public research organisations (PROs),[6] and related and supporting industries.[7] The last one is particularly important as it enhances and diversifies the regional knowledge base, thus making it easier to escape from possible situations of lock-in (Martin, 2010; Martin and Sunley, 2006). In the case of the energy cluster, from the 1980s it attracted companies from other mature and/or declining clusters. A significant example is Guascor, a maritime diesel engines manufacturer, which geared its products towards renewable energies. The same went for the aeronautics cluster, which in the 1990s attracted firms from sectors in crisis (special steels, metal parts and components).

Local political institutions ('Diputaciones' –provincial councils – and municipalities) played an important role in this process as they supported the creation of several specialist training and educational centres for the papermaking, machine tools, maritime and electronics clusters, among others (Aranguren *et al.*, 2012; Belussi and Sedita, 2009). Industry and cluster associations – institutions for collaboration – were key agents in social capital formation, fostering inter-firm cooperation in several fields, and coordinating interaction between firms, universities and PROs and policy makers, in a way similar to that of trade associations for some Italian industrial districts (Carbonara, 2002; Valdaliso *et al.*, 2011). Three out of the six cluster associations – AFM (machine tools), GAIA (electronics and ICTs) and FORO MARITIMO VASCO (maritime industries) – were formerly industry associations created in 1946, 1983 and 1993, respectively, that transformed into cluster associations in the 1990s.

Firms' strategic capabilities were developed around two broad strategies: cost leadership and scale economies, and product upgrading and differentiation and diversification (scope economies). The former involved more specialisation and entailed a higher probability of driving the cluster to a lock-in situation in its maturity stage, as was the case with the papermaking and maritime industries' clusters. The companies of both clusters faced a new situation of fierce global competition from lower-cost producers from the mid-1970s onwards, to which they were not able to react. Interestingly enough, only the small and medium shipyards that in the development and maturity stages followed a strategy of product differentiation and scope economies were able to survive the great shipping crisis of the 1970s and 1980s, and to drive the cluster as a whole to a new stage of renewal in the 2000s, as also happened in other European shipbuilding clusters (see, for example, Karlssen, 2005). Firms of the machine tool cluster, on the contrary, from the beginning followed a strategy of product differentiation and diversification, and during the maturity stage strengthened substantially their R&D and innovative capabilities, which in turn renewed substantially the knowledge base and competitive advantage of the cluster as a whole. In the energy sector, Iberduero (later Iberdrola) and Petronor, thanks to their market power, became large firms with enough resources and capabilities to invest in R&D and go international when the market opportunities appeared. With regard to the younger clusters, more R&D and knowledge intensive, the clustered firms developed a solid base of resources and capabilities allocating high sums to R&D activities, following a strategy of technological innovation, product upgrading and differentiation (and sometimes even diversification), and creating larger business groups. This different strategy may also be explained by the fact that the two clusters appeared and developed in an economy much more open to foreign competition (from the 1970s onwards) than those of the other four.

Accordingly, almost since their origins firms of these young clusters had to build up absorptive capacities, augmented and developed by the internationalisation process that speeded up in the 1990s. In the two older clusters, the firms that developed an absorptive capacity were precisely those more dependent and/or linked to the international market and to the external sources of knowledge: the manufacturers of equipment goods for the papermaking firms and shipyards, and the small and medium shipyards. With regard to the machine tool cluster, from the 1960s the regular presence of firms at international fairs, the creation of an international trade fair in Bilbao (BIEMH) and the integration of AFM into CECIMO (European Association of Machine Tool Industries) channelled foreign sources of knowledge to the cluster and contributed to the development of absorptive capacities, further enhanced thereafter by increasing participation in joint R&D international programmes and technological platforms.

In relation to the global factors, whereas the inflow of external knowledge and technology and the entry of MNCs were the two most important in the origin and development stages, global competition and international demand growth played an increasingly prominent role from the 1990s, no matter the phase involved, something that Belussi and Sedita (2009) also stressed for the Italian industrial districts. Basque firms' responses to global competition differed greatly across clusters: in the energy cluster Iberdrola's international expansion allowed demand pull for companies like Gamesa, and both became well-known global players in renewable energies at the beginning of the twenty-first century (Elola *et al.*, 2013); in the machine tools, electronics and ICTs, and aeronautics clusters, the companies strengthened their R&D and innovative capabilities and focused on global sophisticated customers and markets. They went international too, setting up commercial and manufacturing (even R&D) facilities abroad, and building up large and powerful business groups in the former two (Valdaliso *et al.*, 2011; 2016), as also happened in the Italian industrial districts (Cainelli, 2008; Carbonara, 2002), and moving upwards in global value chains in the latter (Elola *et al.*, 2013). In the papermaking and maritime industries, only a small segment of the clustered firms was able to survive and grow: the aforementioned small and medium shipyards and, in both clusters, the manufacturers of equipment goods. In both clusters, these companies from the related and supporting industries started to develop their own products and solutions in the 1960s and 1970s to serve the local and national markets, and transformed into world-class manufacturers in the 1980s and 1990s.

9.5   Conclusions

The chapter aims to analyse the factors that account for the emergence and evolution of six industrial clusters of the Basque Country in the nineteenth and twentieth centuries. Drawing on in-depth case studies, it employs a meta-study approach to select the factors responsible for the emergence, development, maturity and, if that is the case, decline and/or renewal of clusters. The chapter shows how different clusters evolved over time and how their evolutionary patterns were determined not only by the life cycle of their dominant industry but by a mix of local and global factors too.

Cluster origins are explained by a mix of local and global factors, although the former predominate. Among the local factors, demand, factor conditions and entrepreneurship, plus historical preconditions, play a triggering role, while entry of MNCs and/or inflow of external knowledge and technology appear as the most important global factors. The cluster development stage is mainly driven by local entrepreneurship and firms' strategic capabilities, and by the existence of path-dependent mechanisms, thus, development of factors specific to the cluster. Two other important factors were increasing demand, either local and/or international, and the inflow of external knowledge and technology. As clusters evolved from development to maturity, it seems that former local factors no longer provided sources of competitive advantages to the firms and to the cluster as a whole, and that both the firms and the cluster had to 'reinvent' themselves to differentiate in a global market more and more important. At this stage, the strategic capabilities at the firm and cluster level to build up new competitive advantages, to quickly react to the changes (dynamic capabilities) and to setting-up of global pipelines to other clusters and firms (absorptive capacities) seemed to be crucial to escape from lock-in situations and to drive the cluster to a renewal phase.

As Belussi and Sedita (2009) already pointed out for the case of the Italian districts, our analysis shows that the existence of a life cycle does not imply a straightforward growth path. Basque clusters followed a multiple evolutionary pattern in their development. In this sense, they could fit easily within the concept of complex adaptative systems proposed by Martin and Sunley (2011). The heterogeneity of evolutionary patterns was, in some cases, due to different initial conditions. However, despite similar initial conditions and/ or resource endowments and opportunities for development, we can observe heterogeneous evolutionary patterns. Clusters reacted differently to the same external shocks, such as international demand, technological change and global competition, and evolved differently according to their learning capabilities (Belussi and Sedita, 2009; Martin and Sunley, 2011). Thus, cluster evolution cannot be accommodated only within the straight jacket of its dominant industry life cycle, but also depends on the local mechanisms of learning and introduction of technological innovation that work at firm, cluster and regional level. In the two more mature clusters of our sample that followed an entire life cycle, the firms that were able to escape from the 'tyranny' of the industry life cycle were those smaller and less specialised, more flexible and innovative than the larger ones. Another factor that seemed to play a strong de-locking role was the existence of absorptive capacities (Giuliani, 2005; Ter Wal and Boschma, 2011). In this regard, the external openness of the firms to global competition and the building up of global pipelines to foreign sources of knowledge avoided the dangers of an excessive specialisation, insulation or myopia (Bathelt *et al.*, 2004; Maskell and Malmberg, 2007; Porter, 1998).

To sum up, the results of this study add new insights to the present literature on evolutionary economic geography. On the one hand, it contributes to the literature on cluster life cycles, indicating some factors responsible for both the origin and the volution of clusters. On the other, it offers additional empirical evidence, coming from a region with a long trajectory of industrial development, for the multiple path dependency argument and/or for the existence of several possible evolutionary trajectories (Belussi and Sedita, 2009; Martin, 2011; Martin and Sunley, 2011).

Finally, our study also presents some important implications for policy makers. At least in the case of the Basque Country, cluster policies have been designed to be applied equally in all clusters that have been considered as strategic by the Basque government, without taking into consideration the phase they are at. However, as different factors are behind the emergence and evolution of clusters, government policies affecting the trajectory of clusters should be adapted to the different stages of such cycles, developing stage-specific measures to create environments that are more targeted in order to contribute to the emergence of new clusters, prevent existing clusters from decline, and/or transform declining clusters into new clusters.

Acknowledgements

This work was supported by the Spanish Ministry of Science and Innovation (MICINN) under grant HAR2009-09264; the Spanish Ministry of Economy (MINECO) under grant HAR2012-30948; and SPRI-Basque Government, under the project "Competitiveness Observatory".

Notes

1 For further details on the origins and evolution of Basque cluster policy see, for example, Aranguren (2010).
2 The other clusters the Basque government considers to be strategic are: home appliances, automotive, port of Bilbao, environmental, and audiovisual clusters. For further details on the Basque cluster policy and selection of priority clusters, see, for example, Aranguren (2010).

3 For further details on individual cases, see López *et al.*, 2008; 2012; Valdaliso *et al.*, 2008; 2010.
4 Palmer in Astilleros del Nervión in 1889; Vickers, Armstrong and Brown in La Naval since its creation in 1909 in the maritime industries cluster; General Electric and AEG in the 1920s in the electronics and ICT cluster; or Rolls-Royce in ITP in the 1980s in the aeronautics cluster.
5 Centres of technical education for the papermaking, maritime, machine tools and electronics clusters.
6 Research associations, technological centres and universities, particularly important in the machine tool and electronics clusters since the 1980s.
7 Manufacturers of equipment and machinery for the papermaking and shipbuilding industries; engineering firms for the shipbuilding, electronics, energy and aeronautics clusters; electrical and industrial companies for the electronics and energy clusters; metal and fire arms industries for the machine tools cluster.

References

Aranguren, M.J. (2010). Cluster policy in the Basque Country: learning experiences and challenges, *Revista EAN*, 68: 86–99.
Aranguren, M.J., Magro, E., Navarro, M. and Valdaliso, J.M. (eds) (2012). *Estrategias para la Construcción de Ventajas Competitivas Regionales: el Caso del País Vasco*, Madrid, Marcial Pons.
Bathelt, H., Malmberg, A. and Maskell, P. (2004). Clusters and knowledge: local buzz, global pipelines and the process of knowledge creation, *Progress in Human Geography*, 28 (1): 31–56.
Belussi, R. and Sedita, C. (2009). Life cycle vs. multiple path dependency in industrial districts, *European Planning Studies*, 17 (4): 505–528.
Bergman, E.M. (2008). Cluster life-cycles: an emerging synthesis, in Karlsson, C. (ed.) *Handbook of Research on Cluster Theory*, Cheltenham, Edward Elgar.
Boschma, R.A. (2004). Competitiveness of regions from an evolutionary perspective, *Regional Studies*, 38 (9): 1001–1014.
Boschma, R. and Fornahl, D. (2011). Cluster evolution and a roadmap for future research, *Regional Studies*, 45 (10): 1295–1298.
Boschma, R. and Martin, R. (2007). Editorial: constructing and evolutionary economic geography, *Journal of Economic Geography*, 7 (5): 537–548.
Brenner, T. and Mühlig, A. (2013). Factors and mechanisms causing the emergence of local industrial clusters: a summary of 159 cases, *Regional Studies*, 47 (4): 480–507.
Bresnahan, T., Gambardella, A. and Saxenian, A. (2001). 'Old Economy' inputs for 'New Economy' outcomes: cluster formation in the new Silicon Valleys, *Industrial and Corporate Change*, 10 (4): 835–860.
Cainelli, G. (2008). Industrial districts: theoretical and empirical insights, in Karlsson, C. (ed.) *Handbook of Research on Cluster Theory*, Cheltenham, Edward Elgar.
Carbonara, N. (2002). New models of inter-firm networks within industrial districts, *Entrepreneurship and Regional Development*, 14 (3): 229–246.
Elola, A., Parrilli, M.D. and Rabellotti, R. (2013). The resilience of clusters in the context of increasing globalization: the Basque wind energy value chain, *European Planning Studies*, 21 (7): 989–1006.
Elola, A., Valdaliso, J.M., Aranguren, M.J. and López, S.M. (2012). Cluster life cycles, path dependency and regional economic development: insights from a meta study on Basque clusters, *European Planning Studies*, 20 (2): 257–279.

Elola, A., Valdaliso, J.M. and López, S.M. (2013). The competitive position of the Basque aerospace cluster in global value chains: a historical analysis, *European Planning Studies*, 21 (7): 1029–1045.

Feldman, M.P. (2001). The entrepreneurial event revisited: firm formation in a regional context, *Industrial and Corporate Change*, 10 (4): 861–891.

Feldman M.P., Francis, J. and Bercovitz, J. (2005). Creating a cluster while building a firm: entrepreneurs and the formation of industrial clusters, *Regional Studies*, 39 (1): 129–141.

Giuliani, E. (2005). Cluster absorptive capacity: why do some clusters forge ahead and others lag behind? *European Urban and Regional Studies*, 12 (3): 269–288.

Henning M., Stam, E. and Wenting, R. (2012). Path dependence research in regional economic development: cacophony or knowledge accumulation? *Regional Studies*, 47 (8): 1348–1362.

Karlssen, A. (2005). The dynamics of regional specialization and cluster formation: dividing trajectories of maritime industries in two Norwegian regions, *Entrepreneurship and Regional Development*, 17 (5): 313–338.

Ketels, C. (2004). European clusters, in *Structural Change in Europe 3 – Innovative City and Business Regions*, Boston, MA, Harvard Business School.

Lagerholm, M. and Malmberg, A. (2009). Path dependence in economic geography, in Magnusson, L. and Otosson, J. (eds) *The Evolution of Path Dependence*, Cheltenham, Edward Elgar.

López, S.M., Elola, A., Valdaliso, J.M. and Aranguren, M.J. (2008). *Los Orígenes Históricos del Clúster de la Electrónica, la Informática y las Telecomunicaciones del País Vasco y su Legado para el Presente*, Donostia-San Sebastián, Orkestra and Eusko Ikaskuntza.

López, S., Elola, A., Valdaliso, J.M. and Aranguren, M. J. (2012). *El Cluster de la Industria Aeronáutica y Espacial del País Vasco: Orígenes, Evolución y Trayectoria Competitiva*, Donostia-San Sebastián, Orkestra and Eusko Ikaskuntza.

Lorenzen, M. (2005). Why do clusters change?, *European Urban and Regional Studies*, 12 (3): 203–208.

Malerba, F., Nelson, R.R., Orsenigo, L. and Winter, S.G. (2006). Demand, innovation, and the dynamics of market structure: the role of experimental users and diverse preferences, *Journal of Evolutionary Economics*, 16 (1–2): 3–23.

Martin, R. (2010). Rethinking regional path dependence: beyond lock-in to evolution, *Economic Geography*, 86 (1): 1–27.

Martin, R. (2011). Regional economies as path-dependent systems: some issues and implications, in Cooke, P. (ed.) *Handbook of Regional Innovation and Growth*, Cheltenham, Edward Elgar.

Martin, R. and Sunley, P. (2006). Path dependence and regional economic evolution, *Journal of Economic Geography*, 6 (4): 395–437.

Martin, R. and Sunley, P. (2011). Conceptualizing cluster evolution: beyond the life cycle model? *Regional Studies*, 45 (10): 1299–1318.

Maskell, P. and Malmberg, A. (2007). Myopia, knowledge development and cluster evolution, *Journal of Economic Geography*, 7 (5): 603–618.

Menzel, M.P. and Fornahl, D. (2010). Cluster life cycles – dimensions and rationales of cluster evolution, *Industrial and Corporate Change*, 19 (1): 205–238.

Navarro, M., Valdaliso, J.M., Aranguren, M.J. and Magro, E. (2014). A holistic approach to regional strategies: the case of the Basque Country, *Science and Public Policy*, 41 (4): 532–547.

OECD (2011). *OECD Reviews of Regional Innovation: Basque Country, Spain*, Paris, OECD.

Porter, M.E. (1990). *The Competitive Advantage of Nations*, London, Macmillan.

Porter, M.E. (1998). *On Competition*, Boston, MA, Harvard Business Review.

Porter, M.E., Ketels, C. and Valdaliso, J.M. (2013). *The Basque Country: Strategy for Economic Development*, Boston, MA, Harvard Business School Case.

Shin, D.H. and Hassink, R. (2011). Cluster life cycles: the case of the shipbuilding industry cluster in South Korea, *Regional Studies*, 45 (10): 1387–1402.

Staber, U. and Sautter, B. (2011). Who we are and do we need to change? Cluster identity and life cycle, *Regional Studies*, 45 (10): 1349–1361.

Ter Wal, A. and Boschma, R. (2011). Co-evolution of firms, industries and networks in space, *Regional Studies*, 45 (7): 1–15.

Trippl, M. and Tödtling, F. (2008). Cluster renewal in old industrial regions – continuity or radical change? in Karlsson, C. (ed.) *Handbook of Research on Cluster Theory*, Cheltenham, Edward Elgar.

Valdaliso, J.M. (2013). Las estrategias de desarrollo económico del País Vasco. Una perspectiva histórica, *Ekonomiaz*, 83 (2): 146–173.

Valdaliso, J.M., Aranguren, M.J., Elola, A. and López, S. (2008). *Los Orígenes Históricos del Clúster del Papel en el País Vasco y su Legado para el Presente*, Donostia-San Sebastián, Orkestra and Eusko Ikaskuntza.

Valdaliso, J.M., Elola, A., Aranguren, M.J. and López, S. (2010). *Los Orígenes Históricos del Clúster de la Industria Marítima en el País Vasco y su Legado para el Presente*, Donostia-San Sebastián, Orkestra and Eusko Ikaskuntza.

Valdaliso, J.M., Elola, A., Aranguren, M.J. and López, S. (2011). Social capital, internationalization and absorptive capacity: the electronics and ICT cluster of the Basque Country, *Entrepreneurship and Regional Development*, 23 (9–10): 707–733.

Valdaliso, J.M., Elola, A. and Franco S. (2016). Do clusters follow the industry life cycle? Diversity of cluster evolution in old industrial regions, *Competitiveness Review*, 26 (1): 66–86.

Van Der Linde, C. (2003). The demography of clusters – findings from the cluster meta-study, in Bröcker, J., Dohse, D. and Soltwedell, R. (eds) *Innovation, Clusters and Interregional Competition*, Berlin, Springer.

Van Klink, A. and De Langen, P. (2001). Cycles in industrial clusters: the case of the shipbuilding industry in the northern Netherlands, *Tijdschrift Voor Economische en Sociale Geografie*, 17 (2): 281–301.

Zahra, S.A. and George, G. (2002). Absorptive capacity: a review, reconceptualisation and extension, *Academy of Management Review*, 27 (2): 185–203.

Zollo, M. and Winter, S.G. (2002). Deliberate learning and the evolution of dynamic capabilities, *Organization Science*, 13 (3): 339–335.

10 Driving factors of cluster evolution

A multi-scalar comparative perspective

*Franz Tödtling, Tanja Sinozic and
Alexander Auer*

10.1 Introduction

Clusters have been a prominent topic in regional development research for the past two decades. They are defined as geographically concentrated and interconnected firms and institutions in a specific field (Porter 2008). Studies have investigated cluster competitiveness, networks of innovation and knowledge relations (Braunerhelm and Feldman 2006, Karlsson 2008, Asheim *et al.* 2011, Tödtling *et al.* 2013). More recently their long-term development has been explored with life cycle and evolutionary models (Bergman 2008, Belussi and Sedita 2009, Menzel and Fornahl 2010). However, knowledge gaps remain as to driving forces and factors for cluster change and the relevance of different spatial scales. Dominant approaches have stressed supply and demand, related industries and networks, among others. Such factors tended to be analysed from a static perspective, and the geographical focus was placed on the respective locality or region, or on an overly schematic local–global perspective (Bathelt *et al.* 2004). We suggest that driving factors of cluster evolution are the result of interdependencies at several spatial scales, and that these patterns change over time from early to later stages of cluster evolution (Martin and Sunley 2006, Bergman 2008, Menzel and Fornahl 2010) depending on the industry and knowledge base (Asheim *et al.* 2011). Based on cluster life cycle and evolutionary theories, we investigate to what extent factors for cluster evolution change in their importance over time, and how they shift between geographical scales throughout cluster evolution. By 'scales' we refer to geographical levels such as regional, national, European and global representing different institutional contexts. This chapter investigates and compares the environmental technology cluster of Upper Austria (ET) to the new media cluster of Vienna (NM) in this regard. The cases were selected because of their different knowledge bases (predominantly synthetic and symbolic knowledge bases, respectively) and regional settings.

10.2   Conceptual approaches to the evolution of clusters and driving factors

This section deals with approaches to cluster development and identifies factors relevant for their emergence, growth and evolution. One of the most popular approaches to the development and competitiveness of clusters was provided by Michael Porter (2008). Porter focused on the factors that help to explain why firms in clusters are more competitive than those in non-clustered locations, or why some clusters perform better than others. Factors referred to in the Diamond model are factor conditions such as the quality of inputs, for instance qualified labour, R&D, risk capital, demand conditions (sophisticated customers), related firms and support organisations, and the context for firm strategy and rivalry. Although there is a role for policy in cluster upgrading and for cooperation among actors, the emphasis is placed on the propelling force of competition among cluster firms. Porter's approach is illustrative for framing the competitiveness position and key development factors of clusters, but lacks a systematic dynamic view of cluster emergence, growth and transformation.

Maskell and Kebir (2006) in their search for a better cluster theory have applied a more dynamic perspective and have reviewed different approaches, such as (Marshallian) local spill-over approaches, competitiveness concepts (based on Porter) and territorial approaches (innovative milieu) in this regard. They have analysed the logic and key arguments of these approaches for different phases such as the coming into existence, the extension and the potential exhaustion of clusters.

Menzel and Fornahl (2010) and Bergman (2008) have provided a more systematic perspective for cluster change using a cluster life cycle approach (CLC). Clusters are considered to move through stages (emergence, growth, sustaining, decline, rejuvenation) that show differences in local technologies, learning and innovation capabilities of firms. Key elements are actors, networks and institutions inside or outside the cluster, industry and region. Among the actors are firms, support and policy organisations. Networks are defined by the density and quality of interactions, whereas institutions include the regulatory setting, and formal and informal rules shaping actor behaviour. Driving factors vary by stage, and factors relevant in cluster emergence differ from those in the growth and maturity stages. The emergence stage is characterised by start-ups, spin-offs, technologically diverse companies, and a need for finance and a supportive science and skills base. In the second stage firm growth is dominant, and there are an increasing number of new and specialised firms in the cluster. But also a shake-out of companies occurs, with knowledge becoming more homogeneous, leading towards a dominant design. There is a growing density of companies and institutions, and the cluster offers possibilities for intensified customer–supplier relations and innovation networks. The stage of sustainment is characterised by relatively stable state and dense networks. Too rigid networks and knowledge relationships may result in 'lock-in' (Hassink 2007), however. The cluster then lags behind other clusters in the same sector. Under certain conditions clusters might transform and renew themselves as their companies integrate and apply new knowledge and technologies (Trippl and Tödtling 2008).

The evolutionary economic geography approach (EEG) also helps us to understand the development of clusters in particular regions. Industries begin from and follow certain paths rooted in pre-existing industrial and institutional regional structures (Martin and Sunley 2006). At the centre are evolutionary processes of firm variation and creation related to existing industrial trajectories. Frenken and Boschma (2007) suggest that industries emerge and grow where their knowledge base relates to other existing local sectors. Competences can be transferred from old to new sectors, for example through the branching of firms, spin-offs and mobility of entrepreneurs or other qualified labour. Factors shaping cluster evolution are pre-existing sectoral and firm structures, technological competencies, and institutional settings including rules, habits and routines leading to specific development paths. These may, for example, be changed through external shocks such as radical new technologies or global market shifts. In this context, Belussi and Sedita (2009) in a meta-study of twelve industrial districts have shown that triggering factors and driving actors for cluster evolution differ strongly between early and late stages and that clusters can take multiple paths depending on initial conditions among others.

Furthermore, the knowledge base approach helps us to understand how specific types of industries innovate, based on the kind of knowledge they use predominantly and where they draw their knowledge from (Asheim *et al.* 2011, Tödtling *et al.* 2013). Knowledge and innovation are regarded as key for cluster performance and development, whereby knowledge bases and innovation processes are seen to differ between sectors (SAS: synthetic, analytic and symbolic knowledge base). Sectors based on analytical knowledge rely more on scientific knowledge, frequently of a codified nature, interacting with universities and research organisations. Sectors based on synthetic knowledge (such as environmental technologies) recombine more often existing knowledge, using both codified and tacit forms thereof, and interact more with other firms from the value chain. Sectors based on symbolic knowledge (such as new media) also use symbols and artefacts in their innovation process, drawing on both local and global sources and networks. Factors shaping cluster evolution from this perspective are, thus, sector-specific knowledge bases, multi-scalar knowledge networks, and conditions for innovation within the region and beyond.

10.2.1   *Which geographical scale of driving factors?*

The 'scale' dimension of driving factors for cluster evolution has often remained implicit and used in an unclear or flexible way in the presented approaches. Porter, for example, refers to clusters as localised phenomena that benefit from various advantages of colocation, including local advantages regarding factor inputs, sophisticated demand, supporting industries, and knowledge flows and innovation. However, this and related approaches are unclear on the geographical scale of business environments and what 'local' actually means. In this cluster literature, relevant spatial levels reach from local labour markets and metropolitan areas to regions, provinces and states depending on the cluster dimension. However, not only the spatial scales remain unclear; a dynamic perspective also is often lacking in this regard.

As regards the spatial scale of cluster interactions, the knowledge base approach has been useful. Moodysson *et al.* (2008), for example, emphasise local–global patterns of knowledge interactions in industrial clusters along the lines of 'local buzz and global pipelines' (Bathelt *et al.* 2004). It has been pointed out that different knowledge bases (SAS) have particular geographies of knowledge relationships. Companies reliant upon an analytical knowledge base predominantly exchange codified knowledge and are more globally oriented (see also Belussi *et al.*, 2010 for the life science industry in Emilia Romagna), whereas companies relying on symbolic and synthetic knowledge bases more often use and exchange local tacit knowledge. For the synthetic knowledge base (relevant for engineering, machinery and auto- motives, for example) we find contradictory views: Moodysson *et al.* (2008) as well as Gertler and Wolfe (2006) identify a strong role for local learning and informal (tacit) knowledge exchange with local suppliers and clients, whereas Tödtling *et al.* (2012) find that knowledge exchange in such sectors often takes place within the value chain at national and international spa- tial scales. Several empirical studies have used the knowledge base approach in a multi-scalar and comparative perspective for analysing knowledge rela- tions in different types of clusters (for example, the 'Constructing Regional Advantage' project: Asheim *et al.* 2011, Tödtling *et al.* 2013). This research has shown firms' knowledge sources to be distributed at several spatial scales, including regional, national, European and global, and these patterns shaped by the respective knowledge base as well as regional contexts. Despite these important insights regarding the scales of cluster interactions there is a lack of studies investigating changes of interaction spaces in the course of cluster evolution, which is the focus of the present study.

Based on these considerations we argue that geographies of driving factors for cluster evolution can reach from local to global scales and that they will shift in their relevance from early to late stages. Often they are not rooted in particular predefined levels or territories, but along a continuum from local to global interactions, such as relations to markets, suppliers and clients, or knowledge and innovation networks of firms (Bunnell and Coe 2001). However, predefined territorial levels *do* matter, since the institutional and the policy dimension is tied to territories such as regions (provinces), coun- tries (national states) and the European Union. In the empirical section below we therefore use these territorial levels to analyse the spatial dimension and respective shifts of driving factors for cluster evolution.

From these conceptual approaches and the literature review we derive the following observations for a framework of cluster evolution and driving factors:

- Cluster development can be understood as an evolutionary process characterised by start-ups, firm-growth, and the growth of employment and sales in a local cluster. 'Evolutionary' in this context implies that cluster emergence and growth are related to pre-existing industrial structures and institutional settings (Frenken and Boschma 2007) and that clusters evolve along paths that may show growth but also stagnation, decline or rejuvenation in certain phases (Martin and Sunley 2006).

- Driving factors are expected to change in their importance during cluster evolution, as emphasised by the cluster life cycle model and evolutionary approaches (Bergman 2008, Belussi and Sedita 2009, Menzel and Fornahl 2010). In the emergence phase companies rely partly on knowledge from related industries or from research organisations for developing new business models and products, and they use their personal and social networks in order to overcome problems and barriers for start-up processes and company development. The region is an important interaction space during this phase, since start-ups and spin-offs are often geographically close to originating sectors, firms and organisations (Frenken and Boschma 2007).

- During the growth phase Porter's diamond model (2008) seems to gain more relevance, as the conditions for acquiring key inputs such as qualified labour (risk) capital and necessary infrastructure, the access to markets and sophisticated customers, and the availability of related firms and services become more important. For some of these factors such as local infrastructure, a qualified workforce and tacit knowledge exchange, the region is important; for others, such as markets, related firms (suppliers, clients) and formal innovation relationships, higher spatial scales (national, European and global) matter more. Although there is a tendency for the cluster space and driving factors to expand towards higher spatial scales as the cluster grows, this movement is not of a general nature. The cluster co-depends upon the region for qualified workforce and skills, and for the exchange of tacit knowledge and informal networking. For these latter aspects, sectorial and institutional contexts matter.

- The importance and spatial scale of factors and their changes differ between types of industries and knowledge bases (Asheim *et al.* 2011). Whereas firms in industries with a synthetic knowledge base such as environmental technologies are expected to rely upon suppliers, clients and service firms as knowledge sources for innovation at various spatial scales, companies in 'symbolic industries' such as new media are expected to rely more on local skills, qualifications and informal networks in their activities and innovations. However, due to their reliance on modern ICTs and the internet, global virtual communities and relationships matter to an increasing extent.

10.3   Empirical setting

This section focuses on factors that have supported the emergence and development of the investigated clusters. It is based on a review of literature and of documents, as well as on ten qualitative interviews with industry and policy experts in these two fields.

10.3.1   *Environmental technologies in Upper Austria*

Environmental technologies can be traced back to the early 1970s when pollution problems from basic industries spurred the creation of end-of-pipe products for their abatement (OECD 1999; Weber 2005). In the 1980s and 1990s the use of information technologies (IT) allowed environmental technology industries to shift towards more integrated and process-oriented clean technologies and products. In the 2000s, an integration of diverse technology areas such as IT, biotechnology, nanotechnology and materials science into process-based environmental technologies could be observed, aiming at resource and energy efficiency and pollution reduction within the production process itself. These have been called 'sustainable' technologies (Weber 2005). These processes were reflected in a convergence of environmental and high-tech industries, and the emergence of 'cleantech' clusters, notably in Germany and the US (Cooke 2008).

The origins of Upper Austrian environmental technology firms are predominantly in materials, engineering, machineries and instruments sectors. Some of these firms, based on their technical competencies, have diversified into environmental technologies. Relying predominantly on a synthetic knowledge base, firms have integrated environmental solutions into their product range to gain competitive advantages (De Marchi 2012). The strongest areas in Upper Austria are renewable energy, energy efficiency, water and waste. Similar to the Ruhrgebiet in Germany (Hilbert *et al.* 2004), emergence and growth were triggered by pollution problems caused by manufacturing industries in the 1960s and 1970s. Contamination of air, water and soil by heavy industries prompted local activism for its reduction and control. Societal protests pushed the local industry towards the reduction of emissions and wastewater. Regulations and policies for pollution control in manufacturing were further factors gaining momentum during this period (Pirgmaier 2011). Such regulations were implemented at national and EU levels, setting incentives for searching new solutions to reduce pollution. Existing technological capabilities, supplying firms and sophisticated local buyers (such as steel and engineering firms and public demand) were thus essential factors for the emergence and growth of these new products and technology areas. In addition, two cluster initiatives and policy organisations were set up to support companies in this field since the 2000s (Tödtling *et al.* 2014).

10.3.2 Creative industries and new media in Vienna

New media is part of the wider group of creative industries that have been studied internationally for at least two decades, not least because of their increasing role for growth and competitiveness in advanced economies (see, for example, Lazzeretti 2012; for Austria, ZEW, 2008; for Vienna, Ratzenböck *et al.* 2004). As regards the definition of this industry we follow Lazzeretti *et al.* (2008) differentiating between 'traditional creative industries' (for example, printing and reproduction of recorded media, motion picture, video, television, architectural and engineering activities, creative arts, entertainment and museums) and 'non-traditional creative industries' (such as software and computer services, scientific research and development, advertising and market research), the latter including new media products and services (Sinozic and Tödtling 2014).

Creative industries including new media tend to develop and sell products and services by organising in temporary projects that cross organisational boundaries and include freelancers from different communities (Grabher 2001: 354, Lorenzen and Frederiksen 2008). Uncertain markets and demand make more stable structures expensive and risky. Skills (human capital), work relationships (social capital) and trust built up in latent networks are of key importance for participating in such projects (Sedita 2008, Bettiol and Belussi 2011, 2013). Projects are oriented towards client needs, and these influence the work organisation and interactions among creative firms. An important driver of networks is technological diversity. For example, in advertising, client needs may not refer only to advertising but also to marketing and communication strategies. Projects tend to be based upon social relations, and over time create and interrelate with communities of practice and latent networks in the region and beyond (Sydow and Staber 2002, Bettiol and Belussi 2011, 2013).

New media are a relatively small segment of Vienna's broader creative industries. These have a long tradition, as Resch (2008) has demonstrated using Austrian national census statistics from 1910, 1951 and 2001. In 1910, the creative industries in Vienna (composed at the time of traditional creative industries, such as architecture, audio-visuals, arts, print and publishing, music, museums and libraries) employed around 200,500 people. Between 1910 and 1951 Vienna lost its imperial role and political position in Europe, causing a decline in sectors such as graphics, fashion, design, museums and libraries. During the same period, driven by new technology and growing demand, the audio-visuals and music sectors grew. In the period from 1951 to 2001 some creative sectors went through dramatic growth phases (especially architecture, museums, libraries, advertising, and audio-visuals), whereas graphics, fashion, design, print, publishing and music declined. In this period the global ICT industry emerged, starting off new media. Between 2000 and 2010, the NM cluster in Vienna (including film and video, advertising, software applications, gaming and computer services) grew by approximately 40 per cent, the most dramatic growth of all creative industries during that last period. These sectors have become a major focus of government support in Vienna in the recent period.

10.4   Factors underlying cluster evolution

10.4.1   Methodology

Driving factors and their change as well as the importance and shift of spatial scales have been evaluated in several steps. The emergence, evolution and growth of the two clusters were explored using available documents, materials and a number of qualitative interviews with experts and policy actors (section 10.3 above). Then, based on semi-standardised interviews with firms, we analysed factors for companies to locate and stay in the region, and multi-scale factors for company and cluster development in different points in time (section 10.4).

This section thus compares cluster evolution for the two industries and regions and investigates relevant factor from the perspective of surveyed firms. Empirically it is based on fifty-five semi-standardised company interviews and other sources. An interview guideline was designed based on the conceptual framework of the CLC project[1] and a combination of theoretical and statistical sampling was used to select the firms. In the ET cluster in Upper Austria, a sample of 30 companies was drawn from the populations of the two cluster initiatives in the region in this field, the eco-energy cluster (164 firms and organisations as members) and the environmental technology cluster (136). It was more difficult to statistically define the NM sector because it is changing rapidly and NACE codes are not always up to date. We therefore relied on previous studies on this topic, such as Lazzeretti *et al.* (2008), and included the following NACE categories: advertising (7311), film and video production (5911), selected ICTs (7311; 6209), publishing (1812). Based on these criteria, the NM cluster in Vienna had a total of 480 firms in 2013, from which we interviewed 25. Firm interviews were carried out face to face with general managers, and lasted between one and three hours.

10.4.2   Characteristics of sample firms

Comparing the two samples in terms of company age and size, cluster stage and markets, we find some differences that also matter for the spatial rootedness of the two clusters. As regards the age of firms, we find that both sectors are rather young, with most of the interviewed companies starting after 1990, but the ET firms in Upper Austria have older roots. This is reflected in the cluster stages where we find for the ET cluster a dominance of the growth phase, but also about one third of companies that indicated being in the sustainment phase. For the NM cluster in Vienna we could observe a segmented structure. On the one hand, a high share of firms is in the growth phase. On the other hand, there is an even higher share that indicated being in the transformation phase. This pattern might be explained by the high speed of technological and/or organisational change and relatively short product life cycles in this sector. As regards size, we find that companies in the ET sample are larger, with 37 per cent of them having more than fifty employees (Tödtling *et al.* 2014). The fact that we find also many micro-firms in the ET cluster indicates a vital start-up process. The NM firms are mainly micro and small firms. This is due to the low capital intensities and lower entry barriers in this sector in comparison with environmental technologies. In addition, NM firms often work in project-based networks, so small size is not necessarily a disadvantage for doing business. For the spatial scale of markets, NM firms in Vienna are more oriented to the regional market (one third of the sales), whereas ET firms in Upper Austria address relatively more the Austrian market (46 per cent of sales). The global market outside Europe is still relatively unimportant for both sectors, although it is of increasing relevance for the ET sector.

10.4.3   *Factors relevant for locating and for staying in the region*

Since we were interested in factors for cluster development from an evolutionary perspective we investigated factors both for locating and for staying in the region, asking companies about their respective importance by using a five-point Likert scale. Figure 10.1 shows that the location of companies in the region is dominated by personal factors in both clusters. This is basically in line with other studies on firm establishment that have shown similar results (Sternberg 2007, Tödtling *et al.* 2009). Also, regional demand and the existence of other firms in the cluster as potential business partners were considered relevant for the location phase by firms in both cases. Demand was even more relevant for ET firms, showing a strong regional market focus in the initial years. For new media, in addition, skills and qualifications are highly important for locating in Vienna. Unsurprisingly, NM firms rely more on human capital and skills than on physical capital or material inputs than other sectors. Supporting policies and regulations (these were fewer then) and the role of universities and research were considered as relatively unimportant. In the foundation stage, companies focused on core activities, such as production. Innovation factors were considered as less relevant.

Factors for staying in the region were evaluated generally as more important in both clusters compared with the factors for location. This indicates that firms have become more embedded in their region as regards the recruitment of skilled and qualified labour, links to universities, supporting policies and reliance on social norms. The exception is 'demand' that relies less on the region but on markets at higher spatial scales. In both clusters the strongest increase in importance for staying can be observed for skills and

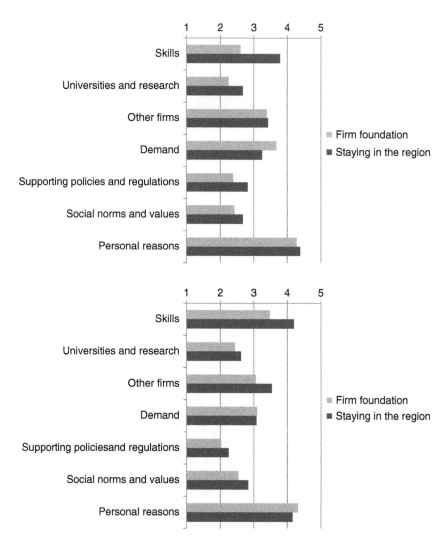

Figure 10.1 Factors relevant for locating and for staying in the region.
Note: (1 = low importance, 5 = high importance).

qualifications in comparison with the factors for location. This finding might be due to a growing sophistication of production and business processes, such as the increasing role of marketing, management, innovation and R&D. This is reflected in a higher relevance of universities and research, and supporting policies and regulations. In particular, for new media 'other firms' along the value chain have grown in importance, such as suppliers and clients, indicating a process of cluster formation.

10.4.4 Multi-scale factors for company and cluster development

In addition to the factors for locating and staying in the region, the survey focused on factors regarded as important for the further development of the companies and the cluster. The questions focused on the spatial scales (regional, national and international) and respective shifts of these factors. We studied them both for the past (3–5 years ago) and at present, using a five-point Likert scale. As regards factors relevant for the development of companies (figures 10.2 and 10.3), 'skills' (such as qualified personnel) were

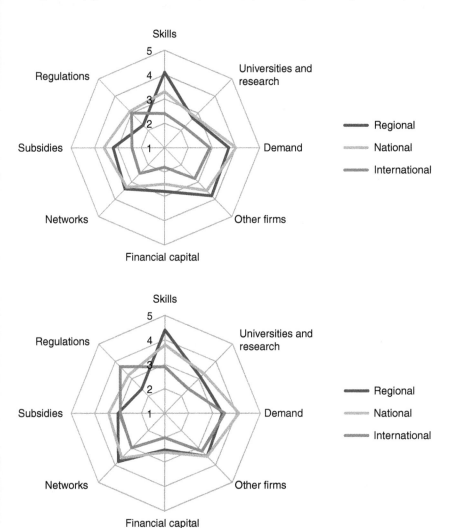

Figure 10.2 Factors relevant for company development in environmental technologies in Upper Austria (n = 30).

Note: a) Factors previously relevant; b) Factors presently relevant.

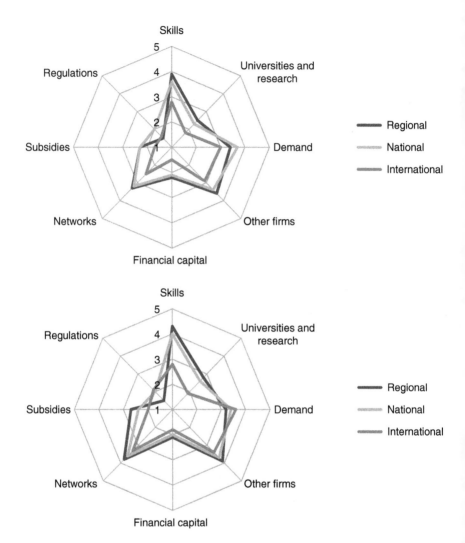

Figure 10.3 Factors relevant for company development in new media in Vienna (n = 25).

Note: a) Factors previously relevant; b) Factors presently relevant.

most important for both cases and both points in time. As to be expected, these skills are highly localised. Firms rely on the respective regional labour market and recruit qualified labour also from the Austrian labour market. NM firms in Vienna in addition draw talent from abroad.

Further factors rated as important for the development of the companies include other firms from the cluster indicating a supportive role of suppliers and services in the region and in Austria. Related firms from the region are more important for the NM cluster than for the ET cluster. This finding might be due to frequent exchange of services and knowledge with other cluster firms in Vienna that we have observed. In the time perspective we see for NM in Vienna a higher importance of other firms at present than in the past, and for both sectors, a higher importance of other firms in the region and in Austria. For firms in both sectors, geographical proximity to potential business partners is supportive for their development. For NM firms this has become even more important over time.

We can observe a similar pattern for the factor 'networks' (i.e. more durable relations with other firms and organisations) where a high importance is given to proximate links (regional, national) that increase in importance over time. Obviously, it takes time to build up such relationships and trust and we see rather more than less embedding into the region and the country in the course of cluster evolution. In addition, links to international partners have become more important over time, indicating an extension towards multiscalar networks in particular in NM, but also in the ET cluster.

The factor 'demand' seems to be more important for ET firms than for NM companies. ET firms are strongly oriented to the national market, although we see also a certain role of the regional and a shift to the international markets. This is in line with findings from our earlier study based on the broader data set that also showed clear shift towards international markets for Upper Austria ET firms (Tödtling *et al.* 2014). Also in the case of NM, demand has shifted from the national to the international scale.

Subsidies are more relevant for firms in the ET sector where previously regional and national ones have played a role and presently all three levels are relevant. This is due to the relatively high priority this sector receives within regional, national and EU promotion schemes. Regulations and directives were reported as having no relevance for the NM sector (both at company and cluster level). They clearly had a higher and increasing importance for the ET sector (both for the firms and the cluster) and they were more important at the international and then the national level.

10.5 Conclusions

The aim of this chapter was to investigate to what extent driving factors for cluster evolution are different in their spatial scales and rootedness between industries and how these patterns change over time in the course of cluster evolution. For this purpose the environmental technologies cluster in Upper Austria and the new media cluster in Vienna were compared. Driving factors for cluster evolution were investigated mainly from a firm perspective by interviewing two samples of companies in the two sectors and regions on their evaluation of the relevance, spatial scale and shifts of importance in driving factors.

We found that the two clusters clearly differ in this respect. Whereas companies in the ET cluster in Upper Austria are more dependent on public demand as well as on the regulatory setting and subsidies at the Austrian level, the NM cluster of Vienna relies more on the demand from other businesses located in the region and in Austria. Other key factors for company and cluster development in new media are qualifications and skills available in regional and Austrian labour markets, the possibility to interact with other cluster firms in Vienna and in Austria, and to engage in respective networks. Partly, the spatial pattern of driving factors is related to differences in the knowledge base and innovation process as we have shown in other research. ET firms in Upper Austria rely more often on knowledge from universities, colleges and transfer agencies, leading to a strong rootedness in the regional and national innovation systems (Tödtling *et al.* 2014). NM firms in Vienna, meanwhile, mainly interact with other cluster firms in a local–global pattern (Sinozic and Tödtling 2014). Due to the importance of temporary projects (Grabher 2001) these companies rely both on personal interactions in the region and the country, and on internet-based communities at a global level.

The second interest of this chapter was to what extent factors relevant for company and cluster evolution change over time, as the CLC concept and evolutionary approaches suggest. Indeed, such shifts are partly similar and partly different in the two clusters. In both cases we find a strong role of personal factors and social relationships within the region in the initial years of company foundation. Also, in both clusters demand from the region and the country, as well as qualifications and skills on the labour market, matter most in the early stages. This is basically in line with studies on company location that usually stress the role of personal factors as well as with the view that Marshallian labour market externalities matter in this phase. Different from other cluster studies, relationships to other firms in the region (supporting firms and services) as well as networks do not seem to be of highest importance initially, but become more relevant later on.

In recent years, companies have reached beyond the region and the country in several dimensions. For companies in both clusters, international (often European) markets and clients get more relevance, as well as relationships to other firms from the sector and along the value chain. Networks of knowledge sourcing and innovation become extended in geographical space and include, increasingly, European and global partners. However, despite much talk on 'globalisation' in the literature, we do not find a replacement or hollowing out of the region or the country as interaction spaces since these territories both keep their importance in various respects. Instead, we observe a shift towards multi-scalar factors and interactions. There are two marked differences between the two clusters in this process of spatial extension. For ET firms in Upper Austria we observe that international (mainly European) regulations have become a key factor recently, whereas for NM firms in Vienna it is demand on an international scale as well as networks that matter strongly in recent years.

Overall, our findings reject on the one hand the Porterian view, that cluster competitiveness and growth are mainly based on local and regional factors.

We find that clusters to some extent always depend also on national and international factors, although the regional setting indeed matters more in the early stages. On the other hand, our findings also reject a globalisation argument that suggests that industries and clusters predominantly depend on global markets and technologies, accompanied by an erosion of local, regional and national business environments as interaction spaces. Also the view that industries move towards a schematic local–global paradigm where firms and clusters are rooted socially and informally in their region, and compete, trade and collaborate mainly at a global scale, does not seem supported by our data. From our study it appears that, indeed, international factors *do* matter to an increasing extent, but 'international' in our cases is more often 'European' than truly global, and both regional and national business environments keep their relevance regarding specific factors for company and cluster development. What we observe is a shift towards multi-scalar factors of cluster evolution that depend on type of industry and knowledge base in their more specific configuration.

Acknowledgements

This work was supported by the European Science Foundation 'Cluster Life Cycles Project' and by the Austrian Science Fund (FWF) (Grant number I 582-G11), and coordinated by Professor Robert Hassink, University of Kiel. We gratefully acknowledge the support of our project partners in the research on which this chapter is based.

Note

1 The framework and interview guidelines were developed within a cooperative European research project ('Cluster Life Cycles') supported by the European Science Foundation and the Austrian Science Fund (FWF, see Acknowledgements).

References

Asheim, B.T., Moodysson, J. and Tödtling, F. (2011) Constructing regional advantage: towards state-of-the-art regional innovation system policies in Europe? *European Planning Studies*, 19 (7), 1133–1139.

Bathelt, H., Malmberg, A. and Maskell, P. (2004) Clusters and knowledge: local buzz, global pipelines and the process of knowledge creation, *Progress in Human Geography*, 28 (1), 31–56.

Belussi, F., Sammarra, A. and Sedita, S.R. (2010) Learning at the boundaries in an 'open regional innovation system': a focus on firms' innovation strategies in the Emilia Romagna life science industry, *Research Policy*, 39 (6), 710–721.

Belussi, F. and Sedita, S.R. (2009) Life cycle vs. multiple path dependency in industrial districts, *European Planning Studies*, 17 (4), 505–528.

Bergman, E.M. (2008) Cluster life-cycles: an emerging synthesis, in Karlsson, C. (ed.) *Handbook of Research in Cluster Theory*, Cheltenham: Edward Elgar, pp. 114–132.

Bettiol, M. and Sedita, S.R. (2011) The role of community of practice in developing creative industry projects, *International Journal of Project Management*, 29 (4), 468–479.

Bettiol, M. and Sedita, S.R. (2013) Design at work. The interwoven effect of territorial embeddedness, social ties and business networks, in Lazzeretti L. (ed.) *Creative Industries and Innovation in Europe. Concepts, Measures and Comparative Case Studies*, New York: Routledge, pp. 266–285.

Braunerhjelm, P. and Feldman, M. (eds) (2006) *Cluster Genesis: Technology-Based Industrial Development*, Oxford: Oxford University Press.

Bunnell, T. and Coe, N. (2001) Spaces and scales of innovation, *Progress in Human Geography*, 25 (4), 569–589.

Cooke, P. (2008) Regional innovation systems, clean technology & Jacobian cluster-platform policies, *Regional Science Policy and Practice*, 1 (1), 23.

Cooke, P. (2012) Transversality and transition: green innovation and new path creation, *European Planning Studies*, 20 (5), 817–834.

De Marchi, V. (2012) Environmental innovation and R&D cooperation: empirical evidence from Spanish manufacturing firms, *Research Policy*, 41 (3), 614–623.

Frenken, K. and Boschma, R. (2007) A theoretical framework for evolutionary economic geography: industrial dynamics and urban growth as a branching process, *Journal of Economic Geography*, 7 (5), 635–649.

Gertler, M.S. and Wolfe, D.A. (2006) Spaces of knowledge flows: clusters in a global context, in Asheim, B.T., Cooke, P. and Martin, R. (eds) *Clusters and Regional Development – Critical reflection and explorations*, UK and Canada: Regional Studies Association, Routledge.

Grabher, G. (2001) Ecologies of creativity: the Village, the Group, and the heterarchic organisation of the British advertising industry, *Environment and Planning A*, 33 (2), 351–374.

Hassink, R. (2007) The strength of weak lock-ins: the renewal of the Westmünsterland textile industry, *Environment and Planning A*, 39 (5), 1147–1165.

Karlsson, C. (ed.) (2008) *Handbook of Research on Cluster Theory*, Cheltenham: Edward Elgar.

Lazzeretti, L. (2012) *Creative Industries and Innovation in Europe: Concepts, Measures and Comparative Case Studies*, London, New York: Routledge.

Lazzeretti, L., Boix, R. and Capone, F. (2008) Do creative industries cluster? Mapping creative local production systems in Italy and Spain, *Industry and Innovation*, 15 (5), 549–567.

Lorenzen, M. and Frederiksen, L. (2008) Why do cultural industries cluster? Localisation, urbanization, products and projects, in Cooke, P. and Lazzeretti, L. (eds) *Creative Cities, Cultural Clusters and Local Economic Development*, Cheltenham: Edward Elgar, pp. 55–179.

Martin, R. and Sunley, P. (2006) Path dependence and regional economic evolution, *Journal of Economic Geography*, 64 (4), 395–437.

Maskell, P. and Kebir, L. (2006) What qualifies as a cluster theory? In Asheim, B., Cooke, P. and Martin, R. (eds) *Clusters and Regional Development: Critical reflections and explorations*, London, New York: Routledge, pp. 30–49.

Menzel, M.-P. and Fornahl, D. (2010) Cluster life cycles – dimensions and rationales of cluster evolution, *Industrial and Corporate Change*, 19 (1), 205–238.

Moodysson, J., Coenen, L. and Asheim, B.T. (2008) Explaining spatial patterns of innovation: analytical and synthetic modes of knowledge creation in the Medicon Valley life-science cluster, *Environment and Planning A*, 40 (5), 1040–1056.

OECD (1999) *The Environmental Goods and Services Industry. Manual for Data Collection and Analyses*, Paris and Brussels: OECD and Eurostat.

Pirgmaier, E. (2011) Eco-Innovation Observatory. EIO Country Brief 2010. Austria. April.

Porter, M. (2008) *On Competition*, Cambridge, MA: Harvard Business Press (updated and expanded edition).

Ratzenböck, V., Demel, V., Harauer, R., Landsteiner, G., Falk, R., Leo, H. and Schwarz, G. (2004) *Endbericht: Untersuchung des Ökonomischen Potenzials der 'Creative Industries'*, Wien: Stadt Wien.

Resch, A. (2008), Anmerkungen zur langfristigen Entwicklung der 'Creative Industries' in Wien, in Mayerhofer, P., Peltz, P. and, A. Resch *'Creative Industries' in Wien: Dynamik, Arbeitsplaetze, Akteure*, Vienna and Berlin: LIT Verlag.

Sedita, S.R. (2008) Interpersonal and interorganizational networks in the performing arts: the case of project-based organizations in the live music industry, *Industry and Innovation*, 15 (5), 493–511.

Sinozic, T. and Tödtling, F. (2014) Adaptation and change in creative clusters: findings from Vienna's new media sector, *European Planning Studies*, 23 (10), 1975–1992.

Sternberg, R. (2007) Entrepreneurship, proximity and regional innovation systems, *Tijdschrift voor Economische en Sociale Geografie*, 98, 652–666.

Sydow, J. and Staber, U. (2002) The institutional embeddedness of project networks: the case of content production in German television, *Regional Studies*, 36 (3), 215–227.

Tödtling, F., Asheim, B. and Boschma, R. (2013) Knowledge sourcing, innovation and constructing advantage in regions of Europe, *European Urban and Regional Studies*, 20 (2), 161–169.

Tödtling, F., Grillitsch, M. and Höglinger, C. (2012) Knowledge sourcing and innovation in Austrian ICT companies – how does geography matter? *Industry and Innovation*, 19 (4), 327–348.

Tödtling, F., Höglinger, C., Sinozic, T. and Auer, A. (2014) Factors for the emergence and growth of environmental technology industries in Upper Austria, *Mitteilungen der Österreichischen Geographischen Gesellschaft*, 15 (6), 115–140.

Trippl, M. and Tödtling, F. (2008) Cluster renewal in old industrial regions: continuity or radical change? in Karlsson, C. (ed.) *Handbook of Research on Clusters*, Cheltenham: Edward Elgar, pp. 203–218.

Weber, K.M. (2005) Environmental technologies. Background Paper for the European Commission's High Level Group on 'Key Technologies'.

ZEW Zentrum für Europäische Wirtschaftsforschung (2008) Beitrag der Creative Industries zum Innovationssystem am Beispiel Österreichs, Project Report, Mannheim.

11 On the emergence and evolution of clusters

The role of agency and external factors in the Galician turbot industry

Gonzalo Rodríguez-Rodríguez, Andrea Morrison and Rodrigo Troncoso-Ojeda

11.1 Introduction

In recent years the literature on clusters has paid increasing attention to dynamics and two prominent approaches have emerged: the cluster life cycles (CLC) and regional path dependence (RPD). Both approaches adopt an historical perspective to study the socio-economic landscape. In this chapter, we build on an analytical cross-fertilization framework between the CLC and RPD approaches. Our main argument is that cluster dynamics is based on the interplay between external and internal factors[1] and that entrepreneurs play a key role in articulating the pre-existent local capabilities and institutions. In doing so, we are able to address some unresolved issues in the literature, namely the role of human agency in the emergence and evolution of industrial clusters (Trippl *et al.*, 2015; Martin, 2011; Garud and Karnøe, 2001), the role of external factors in shaping the evolution of clusters (Martin and Sunley, 2011; Santner and Fornahl, 2014), how transition between different stages of cluster development occurs and which factors are more prominent (Brenner and Schlump, 2011).

We explore these issues by analysing the turbot aquaculture cluster of Galicia (north-west of Spain), which employs around 500 people directly in the farming companies, which in 2012 billed €61.6 million (García-Negro *et al.*, 2014) and includes a wide institutional infrastructure made up of university departments, research and training centres and specific policy makers distributed along the marine provinces of the region. Semi-structured interviews were conducted in Galicia during 2010–2014 and involved former R&D departments' directors, former managers, CEOs, owners, leading academics and entrepreneurs. In addition, we conducted archival research looking at industry and firms reports, official statistics, local newspapers and industry magazines.

This chapter is structured as follows. Section 11.2 presents the theoretical framework. Sections 11.3 and 11.4 present the findings on the emergence and evolution of the cluster respectively. Section 11.5 discusses the evidence. In section 11.6 we conclude.

11.2 Theoretical background

The pattern of uneven regional development exhibits both continuity and change, and a key concern is to explain why some regions and clusters are more resilient than others, and more in general how clusters emerge and evolve over time (Simmie and Martin, 2010; Boschma, 2015). This challenging question has been addressed by two prominent approaches – i.e. the CLC and RPD, which provide a framework to investigate regional patterns of industry development in a historical perspective. In our study, we use a theoretical cross-fertilization between these approaches. We believe that both approaches could shed light on the interplay among internal–external factors and mechanisms behind a cluster trajectory as well as its co-existence with other local industries within a regional context.

11.2.1 The CLC and RPD approaches

The CLC approach adopts a dynamic view to investigate social phenomena, where the time is irreversible, and it aims at identifying the mechanisms and factors behind cluster evolution (Van Klink and De Langen, 2001; Bergman, 2008; Menzel and Fornahl, 2010; Martin and Sunley, 2011; Ter Wal and Boschma, 2011). The CLC looks at the emergence and evolution along different stages, where each stage has a set of particular characteristics.

The central idea is that a cluster trajectory evolves across different stages over time, such as emergence, growth, maturity, decline or re-inventing (Isaksen, 2011). Brenner and Schlump (2011) have observed that the transition phase across stages is a remarkably slow process. In this vein, Knop and Olko (2011) suggest that transitions occur via different crises where issues such as agency of entrepreneurs, trust, capital social, organizational structure, identity and governance are key factors. It should be noted that stages are not predetermined, as clusters can evolve in different ways (Martin and Sunley, 2011), as shown by a rich empirical evidence (see Shin and Hassink, 2011; Saxenian, 1994; Belussi and Sedita, 2009).

Within the evolutionary CLC literature, Menzel and Fornahl (2010) outlined a model where knowledge variety drives the dynamic of clusters. Internal knowledge variety depends on the absorptive capacity of firms and is associated with their spatial and cognitive proximity as well as the relatedness of different sources of knowledge (Santner and Fornahl, 2014). Nevertheless, the heterogeneity in the cluster holds a controversy, called 'cluster paradox': cluster specialization leads to higher technological synergies between the firms while similarity bears the risk of lock-in (Menzel and Fornahl, 2010). This model also suggests that a cluster can shift its dynamics along three main mechanisms: adaptation, renewal and transformation.

However, these shifts depend on both internal factors (e.g. demand conditions, entrepreneurship) and external factors (e.g. FDI, technology) and are shaped by human agency. Instead, CLC models have paid most attention to the endogenous processes within a single cluster. Clusters are highly open systems, subject to constant competition from other clusters in the same industry and to other 'exchanges' with their 'external environment' (Martin and Sunley, 2011). Entrepreneurs in clusters actively engage with the local environment (Trippl *et al.*, 2015), adapt to new situations, risks or opportunities using location-specific assets (e.g. local social networks), and build and augment local institutions (Feldman *et al.*, 2005).

We complement the CLC approach, incorporating the RPD approach to explore the external factors and the exogenous dynamic of cluster evolution. A key concern in the RPD approach is to understand, 'how do technological, industrial and regional paths come into being?' (Martin and Sunley, 2006: 424). This latter question is related on the one hand to the creation of new technological, industrial and regional paths, and on the other hand to who contributes to it. A central stage is given to entrepreneurs, who have the 'capacity to reflect and act' as well as 'shape paths in real time, by setting processes in motion that actively shape emerging social practices and artefacts' (Garud and Karnøe, 2001: 2).

In our case study we follow this latter intuition to investigate the role of entrepreneurs in the early stages of the formation of the industry in Galicia. In particular we draw on the path dependence model of Martin (2010), which spells out the main phases of cluster evolution:

- Pre-formation phase: driven by the pre-existing local economic and technological structures, knowledge and competences.
- Path creation phase: purposive experimentation and competition among agents leads to the emergence of a new local path.
- Path development phase: local increasing returns and network externalities reinforce the path.
- Stability or evolution: the new path can follow the canonical path dependence process. In Martin's words this is a 'path as movement to state', with reinforcement of selected technologies and increasing rigidification of associated structures, networks and knowledge of firms. The alternative is a process of endogenous change and evolution, where there is an enabling environment for the creation and emergence of new technologies and industries. It is identified as the 'path as dynamic process', where the conversion, layering and recombinant effects lead to incremental, path-dependent evolution and renewal of a local industry or technology.

11.3   Path dependence and the local context: the pre-conditions for the emergence of the turbot farming industry

At the beginning of the 1970s several locations in the UK, France, Spain and a bit later Norway were in the race for developing turbot farming. The industry eventually developed in the region of Galicia. In what follows we examine the local technological, institutional and economic pre-conditions for the industry formation, which will help to understand the *why* of path creation.

11.3.1 *Techno-scientific and market pre-conditions*

To begin with, it is worth mentioning that aquaculture strongly relies on scientific research. Indeed, during the early days of the industry, in the 1960s and 1970s, most prominent research was conducted by public institutions, as the MAFF[2] and the WFA[3] (now the SFIA) in the UK, and the CNEXO[4] (now the IFREMER) in France (Person-Le Ruyet *et al.*, 1991). Norway lagged behind, though had a strong background in technology and business development of salmon aquaculture. As far as Galicia was concerned, despite three research centres[5] dedicated to fishing, on top of the laboratories of the University of Santiago de Compostela (USC), the science and technology system was still incipient (Labarta, 1985) and no specific research was conducted on turbot farming.

The UK was pioneering also in the process of commercial exploitation of scientific results. An important factor was the creation of applied research facilities by the WFA, which combined both scientific research and demonstration. As soon as 1966, a plant using heated waters from the Hunterston nuclear power station was established at Largs, in Ayrshire, in an attempt to accelerate growth rates (Nash, 2011).

The endowment of natural capital was another critical factor. Turbot growth is highly dependent on environmental conditions, mainly the average annual temperature of the water, which should be around 14–19°C (Person-Le Ruyet *et al.*, 1991). The production in northern European countries is limited to sea sites where warm water is available or can be generated using technologies such as recirculation systems (Imsland, 2010). In southern European countries, though there is no such limitation (Cacabelos, 2006), easy access to high-quality water (essential to avoid both diseases and high energy cost) and sufficient shelter is more problematic (Adoff, 2014). Finally, demand conditions were similar across countries, turbot being a prime fish in all these markets (MAFF, 1977; Person-Le Ruyet *et al.*, 1991).

In the end, several regions were well endowed with generic conditions for developing the industry.

11.3.2 *Industry dynamics*

Once the basic technology was developed in the UK and France, scientific knowledge became available to firms, which began farming turbot. A pioneer was Golden Sea Produce (GSP), which in 1973 established a joint venture with WFA at the Hunterston hatchery for the production of both salmon and turbot (Nash, 2011; Mace, 2012). The facility was divided into two sections, one devoted to production and one focused on R&D (WFA, 1975), which allowed GSP to easily and quickly access critical scientific discoveries. However, by the mid-1980s, the Hunterston plant specialized in salmon and turbot production was transferred to Galicia (Mace, 2012).

In Spain, as early as 1973 Tinamenor SA was founded in Cantabria by a professional biologist. Two years later Finisterre Mar SA was established in

Merexo (Galicia), which was closely linked to eels and crustaceans fishing and marketing. These firms were focused on the hatchery of oysters and clams, but they also tried with turbot, sea bream and sea bass. Both Tinamenor and Finisterre Mar drew on French technicians to launch their facilities. However, they both failed, mainly because they could not tackle the specific technological challenges of turbot farming and they also had to face the lack of demand for fry (Fernandez, 2008).

In 1980, Shearwater Fish Farming (initially established by British Oxygen and later sold out to Kraft) founded Ferme Marine de Douhet (FMD) in the Oleron Island, on the Atlantic coast of France. Alan Jones, one of the outstanding researchers at Hunterston, was commissioned by Shearwater to run the plant (Caillaud, 1989). Therefore, FMD was able to rely on both British and French turbot farming technology. It originally started as a farm and hatchery rearing turbot. Then, in 1983, it gradually shifted to the exclusive production of fry of sea bream, sea bass and turbot, and in the mid-1980s it gave up turbot and focused on the production of sea bass only, which was technically and economically more viable (Dosdat *et al.*, 2001). This process led to strong specialization in the French industry, which nowadays produces a small amount of about 500 tonnes of turbot, although France Turbot is the largest fry producer in Europe.

In Norway, from 1983 Tinfos grew turbot in heated sea water from the thermal plant in Kvinesdal. In 1987 Norway was the leading country in the world regarding fry production of turbot and in 1990 it reached a peak in fry production of about 615,000 units (Imsland, 2010). After that, competition from other countries, especially Spain, led to a decline until this market disappeared. At the beginning of the new century only one fry producer remained and the Tinfos plant (run by SSF since 1992) was the only turbot farm in the country, with annual production of 250 tonnes. The inability to develop a turbot industry in spite of the possibilities of developing onshore factories using heat waters was defined by Imsland (2010) as a missed opportunity.

Of the above national experiences, none led to the emergence of a successful industry. Most firms focused on i) the fry market, and ii) the improvement of the fry technology, before moving forward to the final market. However, latecomers, in particular the Galician firms, deviated from this path and focused directly on growing and marketing the turbot rather than on upstream activities (i.e. fry production). In so doing they were able to leapfrog the incumbents. The evolution of the Galician industry is discussed in the next section.

11.4   The evolution of the turbot industry in Galicia

For convenience we have divided the emergence and evolution of the turbot industry in Galicia into four stages.

11.4.1 Entrepreneurial discovery

The first stage (1978–1985) covers the initial trials of Sergio Devesa, the founder of the first successful turbot company in Galicia, Insuiña, until the take-off of the industry.

By 1977 Devesa, a student of biology at USC, was already convinced that he would work in aquaculture. In the beginning he focused on trout farming, but due to the price crisis, he turned his attention to turbot. It was in 1972 that he first came across an article by Alan Jones, who carried out pioneering research on larvae rearing methods at the WFA facility in Hunterston (MAFF, 1977). Devesa decided to visit the UK in order to check in situ the viability of the farming method. Back in Galicia, he started his own trials, with the support of a local businessman, Angel López Soto, who was active in the fishing sector. The trials began in 1978 and lasted for fifteen months, using fry from both GSP and those collected from wild turbots in Galicia. After a serious pathological problem, the trials were abruptly terminated. López Soto decided to give up, but Devesa remained convinced of the huge potential of the industry, so he started looking for new partners. He faced both lack of investors and distrust, so decided to write a scientific report based on the data obtained from the trials, which was eventually submitted to the *Galician Shellfish Plan* (later CIMA). Before publication, the report had already attracted the attention of Alfredo Fernández, one of the extension officers of the plan. Fernández, who was well connected with the local business community, managed to find financial partners for Devesa's project. The first block of Insuiña SL was set up.

In 1981, the three partners of Insuiña got the support of CIMA to carry out new trials, which were successful. In 1983 Insuiña was founded and in 1985 the first 40 tonnes of farmed turbot came to the market (Devesa, 1995). The firm was to become a major player in the creation and development of the turbot cluster in Galicia.

11.4.2 Take-off and shake-out

The second phase, from 1986 to 1992, covers the take-off to the cluster's first crisis. For about two years from 1983, Insuiña was the only firm in the market, reaching high visibility. Its success attracted many new firms to the market, which tried to imitate the Insuiña model. In 1990 there were already sixteen firms operating in Galicia (Rodríguez and Fernández, 2004). A noticeable feature was that several of those new firms were propelled by Insuiña itself, which provided them with technical assistance and training. Though paradoxical, Insuiña had good reasons to follow such a strategy: on the one hand, the assistance was a good source of funding, which was desperately needed at that time; on the other hand, and perhaps more importantly, Fernández sincerely believed that building a strong cluster of small fishing cooperatives represented a successful model of rural development (as in the

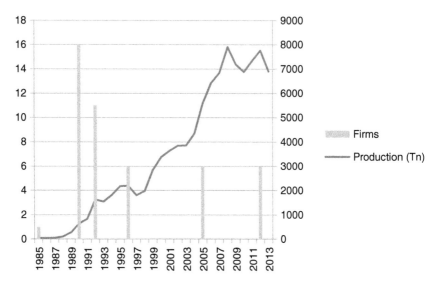

Figure 11.1 Number of aquaculture firms and production of turbot fish (tonnes).
Source: Fao, Fishstat, 2015 and various sources.

case of the Norwegian aquaculture, or COREN[6] in Galicia) and a necessary
basis to face broader market challenges. Actually, several of those firms
had a small production capacity (between 15 and 50 tonnes) and in some
cases the human resources lacked the appropriate qualifications (Santos and
Fernández, 1990).[7] The phase of fast growth came to an abrupt end with the
price crisis of 1991/1992. The cash shortfall forced companies to lower prices,
which led to a price war and a huge rise in production. In 1992 the number of
firms fell to eleven and in 1996 there were only six. Closures and take-overs
were due also to i) the small size, ii) insufficient mastery of the technology
and high production costs, and iii) lack of external commercial networks and
inability to market the additional production.

11.4.3   *FDI-led growth*

The third phase (1993–2004) is characterized by the arrival of FDI and
the race for the hatchery. Foreign investment came to the Galician turbot
aquaculture in 1985, when Norsk Hydro created PRODEMAR, but it was
after the crisis that FDI became a key pillar of the cluster. As previously
stated, many firms were facing financial problems in the 1990s – some of
them closed, while others were taken over by foreign companies, with the
Norwegian firms being the most active. Øye Havbruk took over Marfish and
Granja Atlántica de Couso in 1993, through its Spanish subsidiary Neptuno
Atlántico SA. Meanwhile, SSF acquired PRODEMAR in 1993 from another

Norwegian firm, Norsk Hydro, Aquazul SA in 1996, and Neptuno Atlántico in 1999, and two others in the next decade, becoming the biggest producer. All things considered, FDI did not play a role during the emergence phase, though it did become a key factor in the development phase, making up for the lack of financing.

If SSF grew via acquisitions, Insuiña (with the support of the Spanish multinational Pescanova) grew mainly via the establishment of new plants. The race for size launched the race for the hatchery. The dependence on external providers of fry suddenly became a major weakness in a far more competitive and concentrated market than it was at the infancy of the industry. Therefore, Spanish firms in this period set up new plants for hatchery before reaching full autonomy from foreign providers.

The latter represents the maturity of the industry in the technological field, since the hatchery was the only part of production process largely missing in the Galician cluster. On the institutional side, this maturity materialized in the creation of the 'cluster of the Galician aquaculture' and, linked to it, the set-up of the CETGA (Technological Centre of the Galician Aquaculture) in 2001. The latter provided important technical support to small firms and achieved relevant research outcomes, jointly with the USC.

The appearance of the CETGA almost two decades after the first firm illustrates how local institutions are often a consequence of the development and success of the industry and not the other way round (Boschma, 2007).

11.4.4 Maturity

During the fourth phase (2005 to date), local public authorities shaped the evolution of the cluster. 2005 marked a turning point as the regional government did not authorize any new plants or even extension of already existing sites. In this period, firms solved the main technological challenges and tried to increase efficiency and scale up their facilities. Some companies established new plants in other countries (for example, SSF went to Iceland and France, Insuiña to Portugal). Others, like Aquacria, optimized the available space inside existing plants. Finally, some firms diversified into related species (for example, SSF with sea sole and Aquacría with Dover sole).

11.5 Discussion: the drivers of the emergence and evolution of the Galician turbot cluster

11.5.1 Entrepreneurship

The key driver behind the emergence of the industry in Galicia centred around the role of a bunch of entrepreneurs in combination with some local conditions, most notably the presence of a strong local demand for turbot. Indeed, the target of these firms, such as Insuiña, was not the national or the international market but the local one. Historically, Galicia is characterized by high and diverse fish consumption and the Galician coast has plenty of restaurants ranging from popular to high end, where turbot is easy to sell in small amounts and at relatively high prices. In the end, entry barriers were low for entrepreneurs (personal interviews, Estévez, 28 March 2014 and Devesa, 8 April 2014). Bigger firms such as GSP or FMD were probably looking for more regular and structured demand based on their experience in salmon production, which included both high-end restaurants and, from the 1980s, national and international supermarkets (Asche and Bjorndal, 2011).

Second, while firms such as GSP, FMD and Finisterre Mar, among others, were working with several species, Insuiña was the only one exclusively focused on turbot, which gave it an advantage. Indeed, Insuiña, instead of solving technological problems in the upstream stages of the production process, skipped this bottleneck and focused on production to serve final consumers. In so doing it reached the market first and gained a solid advantage over its competitors. This strategy shows how agency matters – Devesa not only acted as an entrepreneur who took a risk, but more importantly he understood that in order to circumvent bottlenecks, he should break down the typical sequential model of development in aquaculture (i.e. from fry to turbot farming).

Interestingly, the technology developed in Hunterston came to Galicia by two routes. The first was Insuiña's adaptation, the second was the direct transfer from Hunterston through direct investment in Galicia. In 1983, Norsk Hydro bought out GSP and decided to move the turbot farming to Galicia. In 1985, jointly with the Bank of Bilbao, it founded PRODEMAR and in 1987 it started production, though several firms were already in the sector. Therefore, technology without entrepreneurship was not enough to trigger path creation.

In our vision the presence of local entrepreneurs makes the difference in the constitution of the local system of innovation in aquaculture. Foreign firms had strong links with their national systems of innovation (in the UK or Norway), as was the case with PRODEMAR, and therefore they probably would have relied more on those relationships than on new ones established with local institutions. In this sense it was the local firms that first opened their doors to regional researchers. In fact, when SSF (which took over PRODEMAR in 1993) took part in the CETGA, it was partially due to political pressure, as it was confident that with its capacity and its links with the Nordic countries' system of innovation, it could face technological challenges. Nevertheless, the presence of local interest in this sector attracted the political intervention to stimulate innovation.

11.5.2   *Techno-economic conditions*

Once the industry emerged, with the establishment of Insuiña, many entrepreneurs were attracted by the growing business opportunities. After the initial rapid growth followed an abrupt shake-out. The selection process was mainly driven by financial and technological factors (APROMAR *et al.*,

2007). The orientation to a demand composed by numerous small clients near the farming sites triggered a path led by small-scale firms. Market saturation in the early 1990s forced firms to shift to national and international markets, which required regular supply. It was necessary to scale up the installations, which needed large investments at a time when firms were nearly insolvent, as they lacked cash due to the crisis and had to repay the loans to the banks that had funded the start-up phase (personal interview, Estévez, 28 March 2014). When banks cut funding as a strategy to minimize losses, this provoked the financial asphyxia of the turbot farms. The lack of any alternative financial actor, either public or private, such as venture capital, clearly affected the evolution of the cluster.

Firms that could not expand production went into bankruptcy (e.g. Ricoymar), while those with potential were acquired by foreign companies (e.g. Granja Atlántica de Couso and Marfish bought out by Neptuno Atlántico (Oye Havbruk) or Aquazul taken over by SSF). Those foreign firms had the financial resources and they knew the business.

The second selection factor was technology. Two examples can illustrate this process. When the Spanish multinational Pescanova bought out Insuiña in 1986, the main reason was its knowledge related to turbot farming (personal interview, Devesa, 8 April 2014). In fact, Pescanova had tried to farm turbots in cages, with no success. Similarly, Oye Havbruk's decision to invest in Galicia (through Neptuno Atlántico) was accelerated when it managed to attract Devesa to its staff after he left Insuiña because of disagreements with management.

In the long term, two types of firms survived in the cluster: small firms focused on market niches and a small group of large companies with their own hatchery: SSF, Insuiña, Acuidoro-Alrogal (recently taken over by SSF) and Aquacria. In the end, the biggest firms were those that combined economy of scale in production with specialized R&D.

11.5.3 *Institutional factors*

Local institutions appeared when the industry already existed, so they were not relevant for the emergence of turbot farming in Galicia, but this does not mean that the local institutional context does not matter at all in the whole process of path creation.

Prior to the emergence of the industry, no specialized resources were present in the region, but once the industry had emerged, a specialized infrastructure appeared, which resembled a proper local innovation system. It has been argued that new paths emerge where related knowledge is present already (Boschma, 2007). Our case study, along with others (see, for instance, Fornahl *et al.*, 2012), shows that this also happens when local knowledge is missing but some actors are able to adapt generic knowledge for specific purposes. For example, Devesa's use of water tanks of a shellfish purifier as a sort of laboratory for running his first trials of turbot farming illustrates this idea.

Therefore, the organizations that provided a proper technological infrastructure appeared after the industry had survived to the launching phase. For instance, as regards public research, once the farms were already operating and growing at a rapid pace, some research teams at the biology department of USC saw the opportunity to involve themselves in a promising field and decided to focus on turbot-related research (personal interview, Rey, 29 March 2010). One of those teams was to develop two key vaccines in 1989 and 2000 (Fernández, 2013).

Similarly, the CETGA was established in 2001 when the industry was reaching maturity. Nevertheless, it gave an important contribution to increasing industry competitiveness. For example, it patented the vaccine against *Philasterides dicentrarchi*, from which all the Galician farms benefited. Other tools developed by the CETGA included the design of vaccination programmes against the furunculosis or the creation of epidemiologic maps that have been useful for small companies. That relationship between the industry and the scientific and technological infrastructure may be defined as co-evolutive. The general dynamic is driven by research–industry interaction.

11.6   Conclusion

In this chapter we have shown how agency and external factors (i.e. knowledge and foreign investment) are important drivers in the emergence and evolution of a cluster. We used a case study approach to unveil micro dynamics, which are usually averaged out by quantitative studies. This approach has proved to be useful in providing a great deal of detail concerning the mechanisms and actors that participate in the different stages of a cluser life cycle. In particular we have shown how a new industry emerges and prospers in a technologically lagging region, as was the case with Galicia in the beginning. Several regions were competing for the development of the industry, each of them with different endowments of natural, technological and market factors. In the beginning every region had some chances to enter the industry. The reasons for the emergence in Galicia had to do with specific internal factors: the availability of resources from related sectors, the small scale, the fragmented demand in the area and the entrepreneurial spirit.

Therefore, although some factors remain quite inapprehensible, such as the appearance of the Devesa's 'entrepreneurial spirit', our work shows that it is necessary that entrepreneurs' features match with the territorial endowment, and how they are able to deploy local and non-local resources via conflicting and non-linear processes. In this sense, the adaptive cycle through which resources are aggregated and transformed, allowing for new opportunities for innovation (Gunderson and Holling, 2002), seems to relate more to spiral processes of panarchy than to stochastic phenomena, although this statement needs further research.

Neither local public organisations nor foreign investment were relevant for the emergence of the new industry, though they become necessary for its development. In fact, the same factors that enabled the emergence of the industry (e.g. low entry barrier and local demand for turbot) at later stages constrained its further development and triggered the shake-out.

One last point concerns the role of the local public research organisations. They appeared when the industry had developed fully; nevertheless, it can be argued that i) they played an important role in its survival, and ii) without them, small firms would not have been able to access relevant knowledge and technical assistance.

Acknowledgements

We would like to thank for their comments and suggestions Dirk Fornahl, Koen Frenken and Björn Asheim, and participants on the PhD course on Economic Geography (Utrecht University), at the Geography of Innovation Conference 2014 at Utrecht University, and at the Regional Innovation Policies Conference 2014 at the University of Stavanger. Andrea Morrison acknowledges the financial support from NWO (the Netherlands Organisation for Scientific Research), Innovational Research Incentives Scheme/Vidi project number 452-11-013.

Notes

1 We refer to factors that are internal and external to the cluster.
2 Ministry of Agriculture Fisheries and Food, Fisheries laboratory, Lowestoft, Suffolk, England.
3 White Fish Authority, now SFIA (Sea Fish Authority). Marine Farming Unit, Ardtoe, Acharache, Argyll, Scotland.
4 Centre National pour l'Exploitation des Oceans. Centre de Brest, France, IFREMER: Institut Français pour l'Exploitation de la Mer.
5 The Spanish Institute of Oceanography (IEO), the Fisheries Research Institute of Vigo (IIM-CSIC) and the Experimental Center of Vilaxoan (CIMA).
6 COREN is the most successful cooperative model in Galicia.
7 It is fair to say that some firms were able to hire high-level technicians thanks to a Spanish government training programme called 'Training Plan for Advanced Technicians in Aquaculture' (1984–1987).

References

Adoff, G. (2014). *A Guide to Marine Aquaculture*. Leezen: AQUAFIMA, viewed 11 August 2015, http://www.aquafima.eu/export/sites/aquafima/documents/WP4/Guide-to-marine-aquaculture.pdf
APROMAR, Vela-Vallejos, S. and Ojeda González-Posa, J. (2007). *Acuicultura: La Revolución Azul*, Madrid, FOESA.
Asche, F. and Bjorndal, T. (2011). *The Economics of Salmon Aquaculture*, Chichester, Wiley-Blackwell.
Belussi, F. and Sedita, S.R. (2009). Life cycle vs. multiple path dependency in industrial districts, *European Planning Studies*, 17 (4): 505–528.
Bergman, E.M. (2008). Cluster life-cycles: an emerging synthesis. In: Karlsson, C. (ed.) *Handbook of Research on Cluster Theory*, Cheltenham, Edward Elgar, pp. 114–132.

Boschma, R. (2007). Path creation, path dependence and regional development. In: Simmie, J. and Carpenter, J. (eds) *Path Dependence and the Evolution of City Regional Development, Working Paper Series No. 197*, Oxford, Oxford Brookes University, pp. 40–55.

Boschma, R. (2015). Towards an evolutionary perspective on regional resilience, *Regional Studies*, 49 (5): 733–751.

Brenner, T. and Schlump, C. (2011). Policy measures and their effects in the different phases of the cluster life cycle, *Regional Studies*, 45 (10): 1363–1386.

Cacabelos, J. (2006). El cultivo de rodaballo en Galicia. In *VIII Foro dos Recursos Mariños e da Acuicultura das Rías Galegas – 2005*, O Grove (Pontevedra), pp. 57–61.

Caillaud, L.F. (1989). Ile d'Oléron: La Plus Grande Écolserie de France, *L'actualite*, 9: 31.

Devesa, S. (1995). El Cultivo de Rodaballo (Scophthalmus Maximus L.). In: *Acuicultura Mariña en Galicia, 2as Xornadas de Medio Mariñoe Acuicultura, Novembro-92/ Febrero-93*, Sada (A Coruña), Edicións do Castro, pp. 95–112.

Dosdat, A., Chatain, B. and La Pomélie (de), C. (2001). Development and achievements of marine juvenile production. In: Coimbra, J. (ed.) *Modern Aquaculture in the Coastal Zone: Lessons and Opportunities*, Porto, IOS Press, pp. 70–82.

Feldman, M., Francis, J. and Bercovitz, J. (2005). Creating a cluster while building a firm: entrepreneurs and the formation of industrial clusters, *Regional Studies*, 39 (1): 129–141.

Fernández, A.I. (2008). Cultivar Ríos y Mares: La Acuicultura Española en el Siglo XX, *Areas: Revista Internacional de Ciencias Sociales*, 27: 81–92.

Fernández, J. (2013). Aquaculture in Galicia: a review of the past 25 years and prospects for the next 25, *Trébol*, 66 (3): 4–17.

Fornahl, D., Hassink, R., Klaerding, C., Mossig, I. and Schröder, H. (2012). From the old path of shipbuilding onto the new path of offshore wind energy? The case of Northern Germany, *European Planning Studies*, 20 (5): 835–855.

García-Negro, M.C., Rodríguez-Rodríguez, G., Sálamo-Otero, P. and Martínez-Ballesteros, V.H. (2014). Input-output tables for the Galician fish and preserved sector 2011, Xunta de Galicia, A Coruña.

Garud, R. and Karnøe, P. (2001). Path creation as a process of mindful deviation. In: Garud, R. and Karnøe, P. (eds) *Path Dependence and Creation*, London, Lawrence Erlbaum Associates, pp. 1–38.

Gunderson, L. and Holling, C.S. (2002). *Panarchy: Understanding Transformations in Human and Natural Systems*, Washington, DC, Island.

Imsland, A.K. (2010). The flatfishes (order: Pleuronectiformes). In: Le François, N.R., Jobling, M., Carter, C., Blier, P. and Arianne, S. (eds) *Finfish Aquaculture Diversification*, Oxfordshire, CABI, pp. 450–496.

Isaksen, A. (2011). Cluster evolution. In: Cooke, P., Asheim, B., Boschma, R., Martin, R., Schwartz, D. and Tödtling, F. (eds) *Handbook of Regional Innovation and Growth*, Cheltenham, Edward Elgar, pp. 293–302.

Knop, L. and Olko, S. (2011). Crises in the cluster life-cycle. In Dermol, V., Trunk Širca, N., Dakovic, G. and Lindav, U. (eds) *Management Knowledge and Learning – International Conference 2011*, Celje, Econpapers, pp. 355–364.

Labarta, U. (1985). La Investigación del Mar en Galicia, *Revista de Estudios Agro-Sociales*, 34 (132): 209–232.

Mace, G. (2012). Personal interview, *Fish Farmers*, special edition, pp. 14–15.

MAFF (1977). *Fish Cultivation Research*, Lowestoft, Laboratory Leaflet-MAFF, No. 35.

On the emergence and evolution of clusters 189

Martin, R. (2010). Roepke Lecture in Economic Geography: Rethinking regional path dependence: beyond lock-in to evolution, *Economic Geography* (86) (1): 1–27.

Martin, R. (2011). Regional economies as path dependent systems: some issues and implications. In: Cooke, P., Asheim, B., Boschma, R., Martin, R., Schwartz, D. and Tödtling, F. (eds) *Handbook of Regional Innovation and Growth*, Cheltenham, Edward Elgar, pp. 198–210.

Martin, R. and Sunley, P. (2006). Path dependence and regional economic evolution, *Journal of Economic Geography*, 6 (4): 395–437.

Martin, R. and Sunley, P. (2011). Conceptualizing cluster evolution: beyond the life cycle model?, *Regional Studies*, 45 (10): 1299–1318.

Menzel, M.-P. and Fornahl, D. (2010). Cluster life cycles – dimensions and rationales of cluster evolution, *Industrial and Corporate Change*, 19 (1): 205–238.

Nash, C. (2011). *The History of Aquaculture*, Ames, IA, Wiley-Blackwell.

Person-Le Ruyet, J., Baudin-Laurencin, F., Devauchelle, N., Metailler, R., Nicolas, J.-L., Robin, J. and Guillaume, J. (1991). Culture of turbot (Scophthalmus Maximus). In: McVey, J.P. (ed.) *Handbook of Mariculture, Vol. 2, Finfish Aquaculture*, Boston, MA, CRC Press, pp. 21–41.

Rodríguez, J.L. and Fernández, J. (2004). Evolución del Cultivo de Rodaballo, *Skretting Informa*, 8: 3–5.

Santner, D. and Fornahl, D. (2014). *From Here, From There, and From Beyond: Endogenous and Exogenous Factors Triggering Change Along the Cluster Life Cycle in a Multi-Scalar Environment*, University of Marburg Working Papers on Innovation and Space No. 02.14, viewed 11 August 2015, ftp://137.248.191.199/RePEc/pum/wpaper/wp0214.pdf

Santos, S. and Fernández, A. (1990). Entrevista con Alfredo Fernández Prieto, Presidente do Consello Recto da Cooperativa Galega de Criadores de Rodaballo, S. Coop. Ltda., *Cooperativismo e Economía Social*, 1 (2): 37–46.

Saxenian, A. (1994). *Regional Advantage: Culture and Competition in Silicon Valley and Route 128*, Cambridge, MA, Harvard University Press.

Shin, D.-H. and Hassink, R. (2011). Cluster life cycles: the case of the shipbuilding industry cluster in South Korea, *Regional Studies*, 45 (10): 1387–1402.

Simmie, J. and Martin, R. (2010). The economic resilience of regions: towards an evolutionary approach, *Cambridge Journal of Regions, Economy and Society*, 3 (1): 27–43.

Ter Wal, A. and Boschma, R. (2011). Co-evolution of firms, industries and networks in space, *Regional Studies*, 45 (7): 919–933.

Trippl, M., Grillitsch, M., Isaksen, A. and Sinozic, T. (2015). Perspectives on cluster evolution: critical review and future research issues, *European Planning Studies*, 23 (10): 2028–2044.

Van Klink, A. and De Langen, P. (2001). Cycles in industrial clusters: the case of the shipbuilding industry in the Northern Netherlands, *Tijdschrift Voor Economische En Sociale Geografie*, 92 (4): 449–463.

WFA (1975). *Preliminary Report on Dover Sole Rearing at the Hatchery on the WFA Site at Hunterston (Jan 74 – Feb 75)*, Edinburgh, WFA, T.R. No. 122.

12 Cluster decline and political lock-ins

Robert Hassink

12.1 Introduction

Over the years clusters (defined by Porter, 2000: 16) as 'a geographically proximate group of interconnected companies and associated institutions in a particular field, linked by commonalities and complementarities') have become the target for policy makers and a key concept in supporting innovativeness and competitiveness initiated at several spatial levels (supranational, national, regional) (see, for instance, Porter, 2000; Asheim *et al.*, 2006). Martin and Sunley (2003), however, are very critical about the ambiguities and identification problems surrounding the cluster concept. An important criticism of clusters concerns the fact that the literature strongly focuses on how clusters function, whereas their evolutionary development – i.e. how clusters actually become clusters, how and why they decline, and how they shift into new fields – is disregarded (Lorenzen, 2005; Staber, 2010). Examples of declining clusters illustrate that the economic advantages that stem from cluster dynamics are not permanent. In fact, the decline of clusters seems to be caused by factors that were advantages in the past (Martin and Sunley, 2006). The concept of political lock-ins in particular is promising, explaining the decline of mature production clusters. Political lock-ins, which will be described in Section 12.3, were introduced by Grabher (1993) in his studies on the Ruhr area in Germany. They can be considered as thick institutional tissues aiming at preserving existing industrial structures and therefore unnecessarily slowing down industrial restructuring and indirectly hampering the development of indigenous potential and creativity. The main aim of this chapter[1] is to define research gaps and derived from that research questions concerning political lock-ins (Section 12.4). Before that, in Section 12.2, lock-ins will be framed in broader discussions about cluster life cycles and cluster evolution, and there will be a review of literature on cluster decline and political lock-ins in Section 12.3.

12.2 Cluster life cycles and cluster evolution

Many cluster advocates assume that geographical concentration of industrial activities positively affects competitiveness. This correlation is not watertight, however. According to Saxenian (1994: 161) 'spatial clustering alone does not create mutually beneficial interdependencies. An industrial system may be geographically agglomerated and yet have limited capacity for adaption. This is overwhelmingly a function of organizational structure, not of technology or firm size'. Therefore, many scholars stress that clustering may also be responsible for the loss of national or regional competitive advantage (Grabher, 1993; Hassink, 1997). Geographically concentrated clusters can become insular, inward-looking systems, as many clusters in old industrial areas, both resource-based monostructural areas, dominated by, for instance, steel, coal-mining and shipbuilding industry, and clusters specialised in consumer goods (textiles, for instance) (Schamp, 2000), have shown us (Hassink and Shin, 2005; Hudson, 1994).

A reaction to this criticism is the emerging literature on cluster life cycles, with clear links to key evolutionary notes such as path dependence, lock-ins and path creation (Menzel and Fornahl, 2007, 2010; Fornahl *et al.*, 2015; Hervás-Oliver and Albors-Garrigós, 2014). It considers the stage of the cluster in its life cycle and recommends adapting policies to the position of the cluster in its life cycle. By doing this the cluster is put in an evolutionary perspective. The life cycle of clusters goes from emerging to mature and declining stages, albeit not in a deterministic way (see also Lorenzen, 2005; Enright, 2003). Menzel and Fornahl (2007: 3) highlight the difference between industrial and cluster life cycle and its consequences for local peculiarities and hence fine-tuned policies: 'Comparisons of clustered and non-clustered companies during the industry life cycle highlight additional differences: clustered companies outperform non-clustered companies at the beginning of the life cycle and have a worse performance at its end ... This shows that the cluster life cycle is more than just a local representation of the industry life cycle and is prone to local peculiarities.' In a next step Menzel and Fornahl (2007: 35–36) describe the different stages and the particular policy consequences of these stages in development. Clusters can display long-term growth if they retain their knowledge diversity (Saxenian, 1994) and benefit from related variety to other industries. There are also examples of clusters renewing themselves and entering new growth phases (Trippl and Tödtling, 2008). Clusters are therefore able to enter new life cycles in other industries and leave a maturing industry if they manage to go through processes of renewal and transformation. This recently emerging literature on cluster life cycles and cluster evolution is part of a broader paradigm of evolutionary economic geography, in which, among others, Boschma and Martin (2010) have tried to bring together economic geography and the evolutionary school of technological change.

12.3 Political lock-ins as an explanation for cluster decline

What, then, are the reasons for the decline of some regional production clusters? Grabher (1993: 256) gives a first broad explanation for the problem, as he states: 'The initial strengths of the industrial districts of the past – their industrial atmosphere, highly developed and specialized infrastructure, the close inter-firm linkages, and strong political support by regional institutions – turned into heavy obstacles to innovation. Regional development became "locked in" by the very socioeconomic conditions that once made these regions "stand out against the rest". In other words, they fell into the trap of "rigid specialization".' There are also more specific failure mechanisms of regional clusters. Some regional production clusters might decline through competition from other clusters (cutlery of Sheffield, for instance, was overtaken by Solingen, whereas Solingen is challenged by the 'Japanese Solingen', Seki) (Enright, 1995). Most authors, however, point to the decrease in competition and domestic rivalry through ossification that might occur in regional production clusters (Enright, 1995). If cooperation in regional production clusters is going too far and coordination is allowed to insulate firms from competitive pressures, incentives can become skewed, and the localised industry can lose its vitality (Enright, 1995). Overall, however, many of the studies on clusters in old industrial areas point in one way or another at the evolutionary terms path dependence and lock-ins, be it functional, cognitive or political lock-ins, or a combination of the three forms of lock-ins, as the main internal barriers to industrial restructuring. In a broad sense, 'a path-dependent process or system is one whose outcome evolves as a consequence of the process's or system's own history' (Martin and Sunley, 2006: 399) and 'lock-in is this notion that most fully captures the idea that the combination of historical contingency and the emergence of self-reinforcing effects, steers a technology, industry or regional economy along one "path" rather than another' (Martin, 2010: 3; for a recent, new application of the lock-in concept in community resilience and land degradation, see Wilson *et al.*, 2015). However, the line between successful and open cluster and old industrialised, insular, inward-looking clusters can be very thin (Grabher, 1993; Maskell and Malmberg, 1999). As milieus tend to change more slowly than industries, a sclerotic milieu can remain in a cluster even after the industrial structure to which it belonged has already disappeared. Maskell and Malmberg (1999) distinguish 'good' from 'bad' agglomerations by pointing at their ability to 'un-learn', which necessitates the removal of formerly significant institutions which act as a hindrance to further development. The potentially fast and sudden development of lock-ins and the thinness of the line between 'good' and 'bad' industrial agglomerations (Hassink, 1997; Saxenian, 1994) show the importance of studying and understanding this phenomenon in economic geography.

A regional lock-in refers to a set of interrelated, functional, cognitive and political lock-ins that manifests itself at the regional level (Grabher, 1993), but is influenced and affected by both intra-regional and extra-regional factors (Hassink, 2010). In a way regional lock-ins explain why we can find in some mature industry clusters adjustment, 'which refers to an extension of established trends, resulting in stagnation or gradual decline', or a lack of renewal, which would involve 'a significant change of the existing trajectory of development, enabling the cluster to sustain its prosperity' (Chapman *et al.*, 2004: 383). In the case of adjustment, firms tend to focus on cost reduction and copying, whereas in the case of renewal, the focus will be on innovation and diversification. If institutional resistance to restructuring is strong in mature industrial clusters suffering from de-industrialisation (strong cognitive and political lock-ins), there is a significant tendency for conserving existing structures or for modernising existing production facilities (adjustment). If institutional resistance to restructuring is weak, there might be more room for setting up new industries, partly emerging out of the existing industries (renewal), although this is no deterministic relationship, as also in a situation of weak resistance there might be no evolution of new industries.

As stated above, regional lock-ins consist of a combination of functional, cognitive and political lock-ins. Functional lock-ins refer to close relationships between firms which may eliminate the need for firms to develop certain functional specialities, such as marketing, that are carried out through personal relationships within clusters. Geographically impacted information may prevent firms from reacting quickly and effectively to stimulus from outside the cluster. Cognitive lock-ins can be regarded as a common world-view that might confuse secular trends with cyclical downturns. Closely related to the decreasing competition and dynamism is the possibility of a political lock-in that might come up in a production cluster (Morgan and Nauwelaers, 1999; Rösch, 2000; Hassink, 2010). Political lock-ins are thick institutional tissues aiming at preserving existing traditional industrial structures and therefore unnecessarily slowing down industrial restructuring and indirectly hampering the development of indigenous potential and creativity. Institutional tissues consist both of organisations ('formal structures with an explicit purpose'), such as political administrations at all spatial levels, trade unions, large enterprises and business support agencies, and 'things that pattern behavior' such as norms, rules and laws (Edquist, 1997: 26). With regard to the latter part, there seems to be, therefore, a strong relationship between cognitive lock-ins and political lock-ins. Such a particular and thick institutional tissue together with the firms and workers can form a so-called self-sustaining coalition (Grabher, 1993; Hudson, 1994). In such a situation, large companies do not want to give up sites for the attraction of inward investment, as they are afraid to lose qualified employees to competitors. Local authorities do not see the point in attracting inward investment or promoting restructuring in another way, as large tax incomes are paid by traditional industries. In some regional production clusters the spirit of the Schumpeterian entrepreneur might dwindle due to increasing industrial concentration and the domination of large companies. The self-sustaining coalition also lobbies for sectoral interventions often at a national or supranational level, which hamper the restructuring process more than they support it, as they remove the incentives to take initiatives for entrepreneurs and thus paralyse competition and tranquillise large industries (Hamm and Wienert, 1989). Morgan and Nauwelaers (1999) stress that in these kinds of networks, status is privileged over knowledge, power over learning and the past over the present. Closely related to the concept of political lock-ins are non-productive political networks launched by Fürst and Schubert (1998) and traditional elites 'that desperately try to hang on to rapidly eroding positions of power' (Swyngedouw, 2000: 552).

Several authors suggest that mono-structural regional economies with a high degree of specialisation, in particular, are most prone to regional lock-ins (Schamp, 2000: 136; Hamm and Wienert, 1989; Grabher, 1993; Martin and Sunley, 2006). Going one step further, it is suggested that regional lock-ins are relatively strong in spatial concentrations of capital-intensive industries, such as the steel, coal-mining and shipbuilding industries, which are spatially more concentrated than labour-intensive traditional industries, such as textiles, and which are often characterised by high entry and exit barriers, above-average company size, oligopolistic market structure, influential trade unions, and high degrees of state involvement at national and supranational level leading to stronger protests and resistance in case of politically influenced plant closures (Hudson and Sadler, 2004: 291; Schamp, 2000; Hamm and Wienert, 1989). It is also stressed that regional lock-ins are embedded in varying national and supranational institutional contexts (Martin and Sunley, 2006; Schamp, 2000: 145; Hudson and Sadler, 2004). At the national level, for instance, in a federal political system local and regional actors are expected to be more strongly involved in lock-ins than in more centralised political systems.

In order to analyse the strengths of political lock-ins in regions, the following indicators should be used (see also Rösch, 2000):

- subsidies given to traditional industries;
- number of lobby organisations for traditional industries and the strength of their voice in policy making;
- long-term stability of institutional set-up and tasks carried out by institutions;
- weak linkages between regional institutions and institutions outside the region and/or outside the institutions' realms of interest;
- weak support for both foreign direct investment and business start-ups in new industries (institutionally, financially and concerning availability of industrial estates);
- weak participation in newly formed institutional networks;
- a high level of conformity and authority in clubs, associations and institutions.

Methodically, research on political lock-ins in clusters in old industrial areas builds upon a thorough analysis of the industries in a region, their development over time and their socio-economic environment. Information on lock-ins affecting the industries in case areas is gathered through in-depth interviews with local, regional, national and supranational policy makers, trade unions, industry associations, business support agencies and the main enterprises in the region and some of their suppliers. Conducting these interviews about the negative sides of networking is not easy, however, since they might touch upon the intimacy of insiders (Fürst and Schubert, 1998).

After Grabher (1993) coined lock-ins in a regional economic context with his study on the mature industrial steel and coal-mining cluster of the Ruhr area, the concept has been taken up to explain the decline of clusters in a large variety of industries and regions. Braczyk *et al.* (1996), for instance, pointed at potential lock-ins in some industrial clusters in Baden-Württemberg, Germany, whereas Isaksen (2003) used the concept to investigate off-shore engineering clusters in Norway, and Hassink (1999) used it to do research on the defence industry. In a recent paper, Coenen *et al.* (2015) investigated the forest industry cluster in the Örnsköldsvik-Umeå area in northern Sweden and the role of technology policy in breaking out of lock-ins. Mossig and Schieber (2014) compared the evolution of two packaging machinery clusters located in the German regions of Schwäbisch-Hall and Mittelhessen and concluded that in contrast to the former cluster, the Mittelhessen cluster declined due to negative functional and cognitive lock-ins. Underthun *et al.* (2014) researched the mature industrial cluster of Grenland in Norway and found out how political and other forms of lock-ins co-evolved with renewal and adjustment into a complex regional restructuring process. Greco and Di Fabbio (2014) identified a strong institutional and political lock-in in their study of the case of the steel industry cluster of Taranto, Italy, hindering its restructuring. In a research project, Evenhuis (2015) compared mature industry clusters in Saarland, Germany, and the North East of England from an evolutionary perspective and showed how regional lock-ins are affected by national institutional frameworks. Morgan (2012) used the political lock-in concept, analysing the history of the coal-mining cluster in a regional economic context. Recently, the lock-in concept has also been used by Hu (2014, 2015) to study adaptability processes of coal-mining clusters in China. For other studies on the role of lock-ins in mature industrial clusters, see, for instance, Schamp, 2005; Chapman, 2005; Hudson, 2005, Tödtling and Trippl, 2004; Trippl and Otto, 2009; and Hodson, 2008.

Moreover, Hassink (2010) conducted a long-term comparative research project on the role of regional lock-ins in shipbuilding clusters and textile industry clusters in Germany and South Korea. He observed interesting differences between the investigated clusters concerning the pace and extent of restructuring processes in these mature industrial clusters. He also concluded that each individual case study can be explained only by a unique set of impact factors. Mono-structure does not necessarily lead to regional lock-ins, as the case of Westmünsterland shows us (see also Hassink, 2007). Also the industrial structure does not explain the differences in lock-ins in all cases, as can be seen in South Korea, where a lock-in-prone industry such as shipbuilding does not show regionally induced lock-in tendencies, whereas the regionally induced lock-in unexpectedly emerged in the textile region in Daegu (see also Cho and Hassink, 2009). Regionalism and national political factors which led to clientelism play a role here. To understand, therefore, why the intensity of lock-ins differs between regional settings, contingent path dependence and context-specific factors need to be taken into account for each individual case. These results fit well in the current institutional, relational and evolutionary paradigms of economic geography, which all stress the role of path dependence and contingency (Martin and Sunley, 2006, Hassink *et al.*, 2014). They also confirm the main argument expressed by Martin and Sunley (2006: 414), namely that 'we need to understand regional "lock-in" as a multiscaled process, and one which also has a high degree of place-dependence, rather than as a universal principle that applies everywhere and anywhere and that is inexorable in its emergence and consequences'. In order to forecast where lock-ins could block regional renewal in the future, it is thus of utmost importance to go beyond the narrow spatial focus on the local and regional, from which many studies of old industrial areas have been suffering. For studying regional lock-ins in mature industrial clusters, one has to take into account the institutional context at all spatial levels, i.e. local, regional, national and supranational.

The concept of political lock-ins has interesting yet unexplored relationships with four older theories in social and economic sciences. First, the concept bears strong similarities with Olson's (1982) arguments on the negative impact of institutional sclerosis on economic development at the national level. According to Wößmann (2001), Olson's concept of institutional sclerosis can be well applied at the regional level. At both levels the emergence of interest groups can stimulate rent-seeking behaviour of actors. Not only can institutional rigidities hinder economic restructuring at both levels, in a worst-case scenario these rigid institutions at the regional and national levels mutually reinforce each other. Second, the concept of sunk costs (costs that are irrevocably committed to a particular use and therefore are not recoverable in case of exit), which stems from industrial organisation studies, explains why particular regional industrial structures do not change. Sunk costs are strongly related with the emergence of oligopolies, as they operate as an entry barrier for new firms and as an exit barrier for old firms. Although Melachroinos and Spence (2001) have introduced the concept into economic geography, they focus heavily on the corporate level and neglect to some extent the impact of sunk costs on the regional institutional context. Sunk costs, however, seem to affect to a large extent a whole range of decision makers in the mature clusters of old industrial areas. Not only may corporate managers continue to fund failing projects in a desperate attempt to turn them profitable, but also political decision makers will be inclined to keep alive old plants that have received funding from them in the past, rather than admit to the electorate that they have been subsidising ailing enterprises. Sharp and Salter (1997) show that the cultural context, such as the collectivism in East Asia versus individualism in North American, strongly affects the willingness of managers to commit themselves to failing projects. Third, there are interesting links between Hirschman's (1970) theory of exit, voice and loyalty and the concept of political lock-ins. Hirschman (1970) discusses exit, voice and loyalty options in terms of consumers who feel that the products of a particular company are degenerating. Although his theory is stated in terms of businesses and the market, he also briefly discusses a further possible application to the dissatisfaction of interest group members with a group. Hirschman's theory states that if a customer is dissatisfied with a particular product, they have the choice of either complaining to the firm (voice) or simply taking their custom elsewhere (exit). Crucially, the voice and exit options interact with each other, and also with a further option, loyalty. Relevant to a decision is the issue of whether there is any available alternative. In a situation where there is no sufficiently similar alternative, as might be the case in many clusters in old industrial areas, actors might opt for voice and a political lock-in might emerge. Fourth, social capital can be linked to the political lock-in concept (OECD, 2001). Low stocks of them can impede learning; high stocks, meanwhile, can lead to path dependence and lock-ins (OECD, 2001).

12.4 Cluster decline and regional lock-ins: research gaps and research questions

Of all modern theories in economic geography, concepts in the paradigm of evolutionary economic geography can be regarded as promising to understand the negative consequences of path-dependent development and the importance of regions' capabilities to adjust their institutional endowments ('un-learning') (Maskell and Malmberg, 1999; Schamp, 2000). Of the three lock-ins (functional, cognitive and political), political lock-ins, in particular, seem to be the most crucial concept in order to understand the negative sides of clustering, as in mature industrial clusters it is often political decision makers who eventually decide about subsidies or plant closures (McGillivray, 2004).

However, despite a recently growing literature on lock-ins explaining mature industrial cluster decline, there are still a number of research gaps and related research questions that need to be tackled in future research.

First, little research has been done on whether geographical concentration of an industry affects an industry's incentives to lobby (McGillivray, 2004). Potentially political lock-ins might be stronger in regions with a strong concentration of the industry. So the following research question can be posed:

Research question 1: What is the relationship between the geographical concentration of an industry and the tendency towards political lock-ins?

Second, little research has been done on the relationship between political-administrative systems, on the one hand, and the strength or weakness of political lock-ins, on the other hand (McGillivray, 2004). In federal political systems, regional actors have more leeway both to lobby the central government for subsidies and to devise their own industry policies than in centralised political systems (Evenhuis, 2015). Moreover, in proportional representation systems, regardless of regional voting strongholds, all large parties care about the fate of workers in traditional industrial clusters, particularly if the districts are large (such as the *Länder* in Germany). In contrast, in majoritarian political systems, central governments are prepared to lose vote share in opposition strongholds or in their safe districts. The research question derived from this gap is:

Research question 2: Are political lock-ins stronger in regions in federal political systems with a proportional representation system?

Third, more research could be done on the effects of supranational political organisations, such as the European Commission, on the strength or weakness of political lock-ins. Actors involved in lock-ins are increasingly situated at several spatial levels (from local to supranational) and are co-operating with each other in an interactive way (Schamp, 2000). The following research question can be derived from this issue:

Research question 3: Do supranational political organisations increasingly affect the strength or weakness of political lock-ins?

Fourth, not enough systematic, comparative research has been done on the relationships between industry characteristics and political lock-ins. The latter might be stronger in regions with industries that are characterised by large firms, mainly male labour and a strong role of labour unions than in regions with industries dominated by small and medium-sized enterprises, female labour and a weak role of the labour unions. Sturgeon *et al.* (2008: 312) hinted at this issue in their paper on automotive clusters: 'The willingness of governments to prop up or otherwise protect local automotive firms is comparable to industries such as agriculture, energy, steel, utilities, military equipment and commercial aircraft.' Moreover, some industries might be more prone to the issue of sunk costs (costs that are irrevocably committed to a particular use and therefore are not recoverable in case of exit), which could also be more explored in relation to regional lock-ins (Melachroinos and Spence, 2001). The related research question would be:

Research question 4: To what extent do the characteristics of an industry affect the strength of political lock-ins?

Fifth, more research needs to be done on social capital and political lock-ins. Political lock-ins are potentially weak in low-trust, family-oriented societies with relatively little social capital, whereas they might be strong in high-trust, group-oriented societies with high stocks of social capital (Fukuyama, 1995). Safford (2009) made an interesting contribution in this respect explaining how different configurations of social capital in two similarly structured mature industrial clusters in the US affected the restructuring processes. The research question could be:

Research question 5: Are political lock-ins stronger in clusters with high stocks of social capital and trust?

Finally, more work should be done on new regional policy concepts and their effects on the emergence of lock-ins. Recently, for instance, the smart specialisation strategy has been discussed by Boschma (2014) in relation to potential problems with vested interests and political lock-ins, but no empirical research has been done yet on this topic. A research question derived from this gap could be:

Research question 6: What are the effects of new regional policy concepts, such as smart specialisation, on political lock-ins?

This agenda should lead to research that generates a better understanding of what affects the strengths and weaknesses of political lock-ins affecting mature industrial cluster decline. This in turn helps us to better understand both how the negative sides of geographical clustering of economic activities work and what distinguishes positive from negative lock-ins. More knowledge of these matters helps economic geographers both to develop the evolutionary economic geography paradigm and to become better advisers of regional policy makers at the same time.

Note

1 This chapter draws from Hassink (2010) and Hassink and Shin (2005).

References

Asheim, A., Cooke, P. and Martin, R. (eds) (2006) *Clusters and Regional Development; Critical Reflections and Explorations.* London, New York: Routledge.

Boschma, R. (2014) Constructing regional advantage and smart specialisation: comparison of two European policy concepts. *Scienze Regionali* 13, 51–68.

Boschma, R. and Martin, R. (eds) (2010) *The Handbook of Evolutionary Economic Geography.* Cheltenham: Edward Elgar.

Braczyk, H.-J., Schienstock, G. and Steffensen, B. (1996) Die Regionalökonomie Baden-Württembergs – Ursachen und Grenzen des Erfolgs. In: Braczyk, H.-J. and Schienstock, G. (eds) *Kurswechsel in der Industrie: Lean Production in Baden-Württemberg.* Stuttgart, Berlin, Köln: Kohlhammer, 24–51.

Chapman, K. (2005) From 'growth centre' to 'cluster': restructuring, regional development, and the Teesside chemical industry. *Environment and Planning A* 37, 597–615.

Chapman, K., Mackinnon, D. and Cumbers, A. (2004) Adjustment or renewal in regional clusters? A study of diversification amongst SMEs in the Aberdeen oil complex. *Transactions of the Institute of British Geographers* 29, 382–396.

Cho, M.-R. and Hassink, R. (2009) The limits to locking-out through restructuring: the textile industry in Daegu, South Korea. *Regional Studies* 42, 1183–1198.

Coenen, L., Moodysson, J. and Martin, H. (2015) Path renewal in old industrial regions: possibilities and limitations for regional innovation policy. *Regional Studies* 49, 850–865.

Edquist, C. (1997) Systems of innovation approaches – their emergence and characteristics. In: Edquist, C. (ed.) *Systems of Innovation: Technologies, Institutions and Organizations*. London, Washington, DC: Pinter, pp. 1–35.

Enright, M.J. (1995) Regional clusters and economic development: a research agenda. Harvard Business School Working Paper, Boston, MA.

Enright, M.J. (2003) Regional clusters: what we know and what we should know. In: Bröcker, J., Dohse, D. and Soltwedel, R. (eds) *Innovation Clusters and Interregional Competition*. Berlin: Springer, pp. 99–129.

Evenhuis, E. (2015) *The Political Economy of Adaptation and Resilience in Old Industrial Regions: A Comparative Study of South Saarland and Teesside*. Unpublished PhD Thesis, Newcastle University.

Fornahl, D., Hassink, R. and Menzel, M.P. (2015) Broadening our knowledge on cluster evolution. *European Planning Studies* 23, 1921–1931.

Fukuyama, F. (1995) *Trust: The Social Virtues and the Creation of Prosperity*. London: Hamish Hamilton.

Fürst, D. and Schubert, H. (1998) Regionale Akteursnetzwerke; Zur Rolle von Netzwerken in regionalen Umstrukturierungsprozessen. *Raumforschung und Raumordnung* 56, 352–361.

Grabher, G. (1993) The weakness of strong ties; the lock-in of regional development in the Ruhr area. In: Grabher, G. (ed.) *The Embedded Firm; On the Socioeconomics of Industrial Networks*. London, New York: Routledge, pp. 255–277.

Greco, L. and Di Fabbio, M. (2014) Path-dependence and change in an old industrial area: the case of Taranto, Italy. *Cambridge Journal of Regions, Economy and Society* 7, 413–431.

Hamm, R. and Wienert, H. (1989) *Strukturelle Anpassung altindustrieller Regionen im internationalen Vergleich*. Essen: Rheinisch-Westfälisches Institut für Wirtschaftsforschung.

Hassink, R. (1997) What distinguishes 'good' from 'bad' industrial agglomerations? *Erdkunde* 51, 2–11.

Hassink, R. (1999) Der Strukturwandel der Rüstungsindustrie und seine Bedeutung für die Wirtschaftsgeographie. *Zeitschrift für Wirtschaftsgeographie* 43, 76–89.

Hassink, R. (2007) The strength of weak lock-ins: the renewal of the Westmünsterland textile industry. *Environment and Planning A* 39, 1147–1165.

Hassink, R. (2010) Locked in decline? On the role of regional lock-ins in old industrial areas. In: Boschma, R. and Martin, R. (eds) *Handbook of Evolutionary Economic Geography*. Cheltenham: Edward Elgar, pp. 450–468.

Hassink, R., Klaerding, C. and Marques, P. (2014) Advancing evolutionary economic geography by engaged pluralism. *Regional Studies* 48, 1295–1307.

Hassink, R. and Shin, D.-H. (2005) Guest editorial: the restructuring of old industrial areas in Europe and Asia. *Environment and Planning A* 37, 571–580.

Hervás-Oliver, J.L. and Albors-Garrigós, J. (2014) Are technology gatekeepers renewing clusters? Understanding gatekeepers and their dynamics across cluster life cycles. *Entrepreneurship & Regional Development* 26, 431–452.

Hirschman, A.O. (1970) *Exit, Voice, and Loyalty; Responses to Decline in Firms, Organizations, and States*. Cambridge, MA.: Harvard University Press.

Hodson, M. (2008) Old industrial regions, technology, and innovation: tensions of obduracy and transformation. *Environment and Planning A* 40, 1057–1075.

Hu, X. (2014) State-led path creation in China's rustbelt: the case of Fuxin. *Regional Studies, Regional Science* 1, 294–300.

Hu, X. (2015) *Exploring Differentiated Economic Adaptation and Adaptability of Old Industrial Areas in Transitional China.* Kiel: Christian-Albrechts-Universität Kiel (doctoral dissertation).

Hudson, R. (1994) Institutional change, cultural transformation, and economic regeneration: myths and realities from Europe's old industrial areas. In: Amin, A. and Thrift, N. (eds) *Globalization, Institutions, and Regional Development in Europe.* Oxford: Oxford University Press, pp. 196–216.

Hudson, R. (2005) Rethinking change in old industrial regions: reflecting on the experiences of North East England. *Environment and Planning A* 37, 581–596.

Hudson, R. and Sadler, D. (2004) Contesting works closures in Western Europe's old industrial regions: defending place or betraying class? In: Barnes, T.J., Peck, J., Sheppard, E. and Tickell, A. (eds) *Reading Economic Geography.* Malden, Oxford, Carlton: Blackwell Publishing, pp. 290–303.

Isaksen, A. (2003) 'Lock-in' of regional clusters: the case of offshore engineering in the Oslo region. In: Fornahl, D. and T. Brenner (eds) *Cooperation, Networks and Institutions in Regional Innovation Systems.* Cheltenham: Edward Elgar, pp. 247–273.

Lorenzen, M. (2005) Why do clusters change? *European Urban and Regional Studies* 3, 203–208.

Martin, R. (2010) Roepke lecture in economic geography-rethinking regional path dependence: Beyond lock-in to evolution. *Economic Geography* 86, 1–27.

Martin, R. and Sunley, P. (2003) Deconstructing clusters: chaotic concept or policy panacea? *Journal of Economic Geography* 3, 5–35.

Martin, R. and Sunley, P. (2006) Path dependence and regional economic evolution. *Journal of Economic Geography* 6, 395–437.

Maskell, P. and Malmberg, A. (1999) Localised learning and industrial competitiveness. *Cambridge Journal of Economics* 23, 167–185.

McGillivray, F. (2004) *Privileging Industry: The Comparative Politics of Trade and Industrial Policy.* New Jersey: Princeton University Press.

Melachroinos, K.A. and Spence, N. (2001) Conceptualising sunk costs in economic geography: cost recovery and the fluctuating value of fixed capital. *Progress in Human Geography* 25, 347–364.

Menzel, M.-P. and Fornahl, D. (2007) *Cluster Life Cycles – Dimensions and Rationales of Cluster Development.* Jena: Jena Economic Research Papers 2007–076.

Menzel, M.-P. and Fornahl, D. (2010) Cluster life cycles – dimensions and rationales of cluster evolution. *Industrial and Corporate Change* 19, 205–238.

Morgan, K. (2012) Path dependence and the state: the politics of novelty in old industrial regions. In: Cooke, P. (ed.) *Re-framing Regional Development: Evolution, Innovation and Transition, Regions and Cities.* London: Routledge, pp. 318–340.

Morgan, K. and Nauwelaers, C. (1999) A regional perspective on innovation: from theory to strategy. In: Morgan, K. and Nauwelaers, C. (eds) *Regional Innovation Strategies; The Challenge for Less-Favoured Regions.* London: The Stationery Office and Regional Studies Association, 1–18.

Mossig, I. and Schieber, L. (2014) Driving forces of cluster evolution – growth and lock-in of two German packaging machinery clusters. *European Urban and Regional Studies.*

OECD (2001) *Cities and Regions in the New Learning Economy.* Paris: OECD.

Olson, M. (1982) *The Rise and Decline of Nations; Economic Growth, Stagflation, and Social Rigidities.* New Haven and London: Yale University Press.

Porter, M.E. (2000) Location, competition, and economic development: local clusters in a global economy. *Economic Development Quarterly* 14, 15–34.

Rösch, A. (2000) Kreative Milieus als Faktoren der Regionalentwicklung. *Raumforschung und Raumordnung* 58, 161–172.

Safford, S. (2009) *Why the Garden Club Couldn't Save Youngstown: The Transformation of the Rust Belt*. Cambridge, MA.: Harvard University Press.

Saxenian, A. (1994) *Regional Advantage: Culture and Competition in Silicon Valley and Route 128*. Cambridge, MA and London: Harvard University Press.

Schamp, E.W. (2000) *Vernetzte Produktion: Industriegeographie aus institutioneller Perspektive*. Darmstadt: Wissenschaftliche Buchgesellschaft.

Schamp, E.W. (2005) Decline of the district, renewal of firms: an evolutionary approach to footwear production in the Pirmasens area, Germany. *Environment and Planning A* 37, 617–634.

Sharp, D.J. and Salter, S.B. (1997) Project escalation and sunk costs: a test of the international generalizability of agency and prospect. *Journal of International Business Studies* 28, 101–121.

Staber, U. (2010) Clusters from an evolutionary perspective. In: Boschma, R. and Martin, R. (eds) *Handbook of Evolutionary Economic Geography*. Cheltenham: Edward Elgar, pp. 221–238.

Sturgeon, T., Van Biesebroeck, J. and Gereffi, G. (2008) Value chains, networks and clusters: reframing the global automotive industry. *Journal of Economic Geography* 8, 297–321.

Swyngedouw, E. (2000) Elite power, global forces, and the political economy of 'glocal' development. In: Clark, G.L., Feldman, M.P. and Gertler, M.S. (eds) *The Oxford Handbook of Economic Geography*. New York: Oxford University Press, pp. 541–558.

Tödtling, F. and Trippl, M. (2004) Like phoenix from the ashes? The renewal of clusters in old industrial regions. *Urban Studies* 41, 1159–1179.

Trippl, M. and Otto, A. (2009) How to turn the fate of old industrial areas: a comparison of cluster-based renewal processes in Styria and the Saarland. *Environment and Planning A* 41, 1217–1233.

Trippl, M. and Tödtling, F. (2008) Cluster renewal in old industrial regions – continuity or radical change? In: Karlsson, C. (ed.) *Handbook of Research on Cluster Theory*. Cheltenham: Edward Elgar, pp. 203–218.

Underthun, A., Hildrum, J.M., Svare, H., Finsrud, H.D. and Vareide, K. (2014) The restructuring of the old industrial region of Grenland in Norway: between lock-in, adjustment, and renewal. *Norsk Geografisk Tidsskrift* 68, 121–132.

Wilson, G., Quaranta, G., Kelly, C. and Salvia, R. (2015) Community resilience, land degradation and endogenous lock-in effects: evidence from the Alento region, Campania, Italy. *Journal of Environmental Planning and Management*.

Wößmann, L. (2001) Der Aufstieg und Niedergang von Regionen: Die dynamische Markttheorie von Heuß in räumlicher Sicht. *Jahrbuch für Regionalwissenschaft* 21, 65–89.

13 The evolutionary dynamics of creative clusters

How can they best be captured?

Flávio Nunes and Patrícia Romeiro

13.1 Introduction

Traditionally, the agglomeration of creative activities occurred spontaneously, emerging from the interstices of planning practices. However, in the last decade, the scenario has changed considerably. The creative activities' agenda has shifted towards political and economic development strategies, through their contribution to employment and income, and its positive influence on innovation and R&D strategies. Likewise, creative clusters are increasingly being organised and purposely built as part of broader strategic visions of urban and regional development.

There is a large volume of literature on creative clusters. However, there is a lack of empirical studies on the life cycle of organised creative clusters, even if the literature often points out that political interventions that are appropriate in the early stages of cluster development do not fit the later stages. Thus, if in emerging clusters it is essential to encourage collaboration and support information flows, for mature or declining clusters, it is essential to encourage openness and innovation to prevent local and regional lock-in.

Nevertheless, existing empirical studies often analyse the performance and dynamics of clusters using quantitative methodologies. Understanding the different elements of clusters and their respective performance is an important step in identifying where clusters might be strong or weak, and where subsequent intervention may be appropriate, and this must involve quantitative methodologies as well as qualitative analysis.

This chapter explores the drivers that influence the life cycle of creative clusters and how they can be best captured by empirical studies. The study of the creative cluster in the Porto City region, and specifically those dynamics related to entertainment and educational software, is a starting point to this analysis. This area has been the focus of recent policy efforts by regional and national policy makers, aimed at creating a creative cluster based on the potential of its endogenous resources and emergent dynamics.

13.2 Clusters' life cycle: organic *versus* organised clusters

While there is growing recognition that the analysis of cluster dynamics can be captured only if we consider their dynamics through time (Audretsch and

Feldman, 1996; Pouder and St John, 1996; Swann *et al.*, 1998; Maggioni, 2002; Brenner, 2004; Iammarino and McCann, 2006; Menzel and Fornahl, 2010; Ter Wal and Boschma, 2011), some authors have wondered about the conceptual frame most suitable to analyse the development of clusters.

In the study of the development trends of organic clusters, initiated at the end of the 1990s, the approach most accepted and recognised was the metaphor of the 'cluster life cycle' (for example, Brenner, 2004; Menzel and Fornahl, 2010; Ter Wal and Boschma, 2011), an expression adapted from the theory of the life cycle of industrial products. The advantage of this theory is its simplicity, as it combines in a single expression the idea of a succession of critical stages that tends to be present in the development process of clusters, and highlights the cognitive dimension (particularly the heterogeneity of knowledge and skills within the cluster context) and the network dimension (the position of companies within and outside the cluster) (Boschma and Fornahl, 2011).

However, the 'life cycle' is not the only paradigm explaining the evolutionary trend of clusters. For example, Iammarino and McCann (2006) would rather state that clusters may show different relationships between their agents over time and that they are infinite, although not predetermined. Braunherjelm and Feldman (2006), meanwhile, claim that there is an unending variety of development trends of a cluster, and it is not possible to limit it to a single predefined design. More recently, Martin and Sunley (2011) have also criticised the theory of the cluster life cycle, believing there is no automatic transition mechanism between the four evolutionary stages that this theory considers. So, the theory of the cluster's 'life cycle' has been criticised mostly because of its fatalism or determinism in the way the development trend of a cluster manifests itself (emergence → growth → maturity → decline). According to Lefebvre (2012), the fact that this theory is unpredictable may be due to either exogenous factors, such as the limitations from the external context of the cluster that may affect it, or endogenous factors, such as the impact of an agent's change of performance in a cluster that may affect the way the latter generally evolves.

In the field of cluster trends, attention has been directed particularly at how these clusters emerge, develop and decline over time, which can be termed as 'organic clusters', as opposed to 'organised clusters' (those that arise from initiatives to deliberately motivate cluster dynamics in some sectors of activity), the development dynamics of which have attracted less attention, even despite the significant increase of these political initiatives over the last two decades and on a global scale.

The specificity of 'organised clusters' requires a different approach to the cluster development issue. Solvell *et al.* (2003) were among the first authors to draw attention to this specificity, soon suggesting the layout of a specific life cycle for the clusters arising from public initiatives aiming to organise a given sector of activity in a region. Thus, these incorporate a different stage, termed 'antecedence', which precedes the first stage of the life cycle of an organic cluster, the emergence stage, which, in the case of these clusters, is preferably called 'formation'. Another difference is the omission of a stage of 'decline', assuming that the organisation that manages the operation of the cluster will be able to strengthen it permanently so that it continues to grow.

Knop and Olko (2011) have also focused attention on the development of organised clusters. Their contribution is relevant because, just as Martin and Sunley (2011) did for organic clusters, they also criticise in organised clusters any automatism and determinism in the succession of stages, regardless of their number and designation, defending that the theory of the life cycle of organised clusters must be able to predict the existence of multiple alternative scenarios in the development trends of a cluster. Another important contribution from these authors was the systematisation of the policies underlying the different stages into which a cluster is organised throughout its development trend.

According to these authors, the clustering process is marked by crises that occur throughout five main stages, which, as they see it, determine the development of an organised cluster. A suitable political action is associated to each of these stages to overcome each of these crises.

I   'Identification stage' – at this stage, the scope for cooperation is identified within a group of agents from a certain region operating in a certain sector of activity. At this moment, policies must aim to identify partners with cluster cooperation potential, and to plan the conditions to favour logics of mutual cooperation.

II   'Initiative stage' – at this stage, options are taken to benefit certain forms of cooperation, resulting in problems related to different expectations, shown in the sceptical attitudes of certain agents. This process generates an initiative crisis, the resolution of which needs policies on the development of the cluster by means of its specialisation, through measures to establish the principles of cooperation that may strengthen the competitive advantage of the cluster (economies of scale, complementarity of competences ...) and the promotion of its innovation (ideas for new technologies, products ...).

III Innovative development stage – at this stage, the attempt to have the different agents working on a common goal generates a 'crisis of confidence' based on the fear that the involvement of agents will be different and the use made of these agents will be different from the benefits generated by joint cooperation. To solve this crisis, policies must be implemented to develop social capital within the cluster, through measures aimed at working on shared values particularly meaningful for the members of the cluster, and the launching of innovative joint projects, so that agents in the cluster can be emotionally involved in the cooperation processes.

IV   Maturity stage – at this stage, the growth of the agents' confidence in the cluster originates the need for new activities and competences, thus generating a 'crisis of structure' associated with the need for more initiatives and competences required for the ongoing coordination of cooperation activities. To solve this crisis, policies must be implemented to develop the cluster's governance, mostly benefiting the facilitation of innovation processes, in order to ensure the maintenance of sustainable competitive advantages for the cluster, even if these rely on the reorientation of the cluster's strategy.

V   Transformation stage – at this stage, the agents begin to show their dissatisfaction with the lack of new ideas, partners and concepts, and so a 'crisis of identity' emerges, discouraging cooperation. To solve this crisis, policies must be implemented to promote openness to innovation, favouring new ideas as a way to starting new relationship networks and organisational structures, which, in turn, may generate new clusters, the agents of which perpetuate simultaneous cooperation and competition with the agents of the original cluster.

Thus, the model of Knop and Olko (2011) incorporates alternative futures in the life of a cluster, playing down the traditional hegemonic and deterministic vision of its development process (emergence – growth – maturity – decline) as far as it argues that the decline of an organised cluster can occur earlier than expected, following each of the four crises that identify and demand policies adapted to the different stages of a cluster's development. However, assuming that a cluster can overcome these crises, which policies must be pursued to ensure the continuity of a cluster over time, preventing its decline?

Schretlen *et al.* (2011) contribute to this challenge by examining clusters in which knowledge is their main production factor (intensive knowledge clusters). These authors have suggested the continuous survival of such clusters on a dependence of a cyclic management process that, provided with suitable policies, may guide the performance of the entity responsible for the organisation and coordination of those clusters. Therefore, they have developed a model that addresses this management process as a cyclic, continuous activity, structured around six stages that can be articulated in a less linear and more interactive way.

According to this model, a management cycle process seeking to guarantee the competitive maintenance of a cluster should be based on a limited system of performance indicators to evaluate and monitor the development of an organised cluster. These indicators must be selected so as to allow the evaluation of the achievement of the various goals that govern a cluster's activity:

• To follow the realisation of strategic goals (long term), evaluation indicators are selected to enable the assessment of improvements in the visibility and reputation of the cluster, in the attraction of external investment, in the breakthrough of the cluster enterprising environment, among other areas of analysis.

- To follow the realisation of specific goals (medium term), the evaluation indicators may include the volume of the attracted venture capital, the number of new businesses created, the number of spin-offs, created jobs, among other things.
- To follow the realisation of operational goals (more immediate and short term), the evaluation indicators may include the number of networking initiatives (seminars, workshops …), the number of cooperation projects showing joint actions between the agents of the cluster, the number of entries (press releases, media participation, mailing lists) in communication platforms to disclose news of the cluster or to divulge information between the agents of the cluster, the number of training courses or its participants, among other things.

The advantage of this model of the cluster management cycle is the fact that in an extremely unpredictable environment (financial instability, political changes, amendments of laws, rapid technological changes, intense external competition and so forth) this model ensures that the policies devised along the development of a cluster are adaptive policies, capable of responding to the countless challenges to be faced and difficult to predict. Ultimately, they are capable of permanently circumventing the much feared stage of a cluster's decline.

13.3 Creative clusters' particularities

There are not many studies that show the development of clusters from a systemic perspective; most focus on partial aspects of their dynamics (e.g. growth of employments, exports evolution, R&D investment) or use only one type of information source (e.g. statistics). In fact, the tendency at the moment is to have analyses focused on the performance of clusters, capturing their outcomes but not the drivers of their positive development or crises.

In academic studies, different variables and indicators are associated with the clusters' growth: industrial concentration, market access, especially the global market, measured through the increase of exports, the demand for the cluster's products/services, company turnover, the contribution for regional GDP, employment rates (Porter, 1990). Nevertheless, some recent studies have called our attention to the influence of soft factors on the dynamics of clusters (e.g. social capital, reliability) (Knop and Olko, 2011). Authors such as Andersson *et al.* (2004) identified the 'actor type' and 'collaboration' as dimensions that allow us to describe the clusters' life cycle stages. Menzel and Fornahl (2010) take it a step further and associate the clusters' life cycle with several dimensions, direct and systemic, taking into consideration quantitative and qualitative variables (e.g. number of firms, total employment, organisational conditions, knowledge, competencies, networks and network condition, such as the value chain, and synergies). However, in practice, these qualitative aspects that are enhanced in literature as being relevant to the development of clusters are not consistently considered and analysed.

Soft factors are particularly relevant in the development of the creative industries. Lately, this has been emphasised by extensive scientific literature, which has contributed to the deepening of the knowledge about creative clusters' particularities. It is known that this economic sector has specific characteristics:

- It is largely formed by micro companies and independent creative people (UNCTAD, 2009).
- Project work is an important component for the majority of creative activities, requiring strong collaboration among its sub-sectors during a limited period of time (Chapain and Comunian, 2010).
- Territory ('local, creative atmosphere') is highly influential in the creative process (Cox, 1997; Grabher, 2002; Scott, 2000, 2001; Gu, 2014).
- Informal networks are greatly relevant in the creation/production of creative products/services (e.g. in the exchange of information and knowledge, complementarity of competences) and worker recruitment (Oakley, 2006).
- The sector is mostly composed of small organisations or even independent producers/creative people, reflecting the awareness that individual work, and work at a small scale, is more protected from the replication of processes/products, which favours the production of original contents and suits the emerging of new business opportunities (Chapain and Comunian, 2010).
- The market of creative products/services is subject to quick changes, particularly in the technological area, and competitiveness is highly associated with innovation capability (UNCTAD, 2009).
- For creative activities the importance of reputation and the image of clusters and territories in which they are competing are relevant (Chapain and Comunian, 2010).

The analysis of these characteristics allows us to question the effectiveness of statistics as the only source for learning about the dynamics of creative clusters. In fact, statistics do not easily capture information related to freelance workers and micro companies, to intersectorial exchange of knowledge and among independent workers, and to the local creative atmosphere. Moreover, national statistics on the creative economy are poor; despite recent efforts (and advances) in the disaggregation level of economic activities, statistics do not yet allow the individualisation of some of the creative activities.

Yet creative activities have some particular features leading us into thinking that the quantitative analysis of creative clusters' dynamics requires some adaptations in terms of the interpretation of the variables that are often used in the analyses of other clusters. If the generated wealth and employment are recurrent variables in this type of studies, denoting the positive development and global growth of the cluster or companies forming it, for many creative people/creative companies business growth is not a goal (Lange *et al.*, 2008) and artistic value often has priority over economic value (Chapain and Comunian, 2010).

13.4 Clusters' life cycle: combining qualitative and quantitative approaches

Nowadays it is pertinent the development of new approaches to the clusters' life cycles that combine quantitative and qualitative variables; variables related to the objective dimension of the cluster and variables of a relative nature; variables related to incomes and outcomes, and direct and systemic variables. This combination is the only way to obtain a global understanding of the cluster's dynamics. Focusing our attention on the major drivers of creative cluster dynamics, we propose three fundamental components for analysis: companies and other organisations, networks, and cooperation and market (Figure 13.1).

13.4.1 Companies and other organisations

According to Porter's definition (1990), companies are one of the essential elements of a cluster, but other types of institutions (e.g. universities and research centres, financial institutions, sectorial organisations) form the institutional frame that will support that cluster. In this way, a positive development of the cluster would correspond to an increase in the number of companies and other support organisations representing the sector, as argued in other studies related to the life cycle approach.

We consider that the development and maturity stages of the creative clusters would correspond to an increase in the complementarity of agents (e.g. in terms of knowledge, products/services). Besides the companies directly related with the sector in question, the cluster would integrate the university, R&D centres, financial institutions, among others, ideally following the logics of the 'related variety' (Boschma and Fornahl, 2005) and the maximisation of the benefits of co-localisation of agents acting along the entire value chain.

It is also relevant that companies and external organisations recognise the cluster, its location and activities, so the external legitimisation is a relevant dimension for the analysis of the cluster's development (Table 13.1).

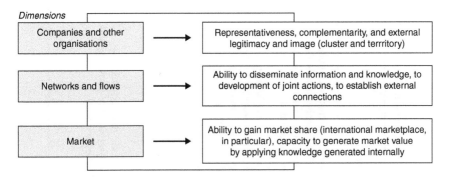

Figure 13.1 Components for the analysis of creative clusters' life cycle.

Table 13.1 Life cycle of creative clusters: 'companies and other organisations' dimension

Variables	Creative clusters' life cycle stage		
	Emerging clusters	Developing clusters	Mature clusters
Proportion of cluster companies and other organisations in the context of the economic sector where it's included	Not very significant	Significant	Very significant
Proportion of employment generated intra-cluster in the context of the economic sector where it's included	Not very significant	Significant	Significant
Agents' complementarity (e.g. abilities, products/services)	Large/reputed companies and other organisations directly related with the cluster's activity sector	Large and small companies and other organisations directly related with the cluster's activity sector	Great diversity and heterogeneity of companies and other organisations (e.g. companies, university, R&D centres, financial institutions), in a logics of 'related variety' and complementarity along the value chain
Cluster external legitimisation and the projection of its image and established territory	Weak legitimisation and perception of the cluster's activities and territory in which it is established	Moderate legitimisation, vague recognition of the cluster and vague association of the territory to the sector in question	Strong legitimisation, recognition of the cluster as a reference entity within the sector and strong territorial association to the economic sector in question

13.4.2 Networks and flows

Scientific literature emphasises the fact that the possible development of privileged relations between companies and other organisations is one of the most important advantages associated with clusters (Menzel and Fornahl, 2010; Porter, 1990, 2003). Indeed, more than the simple co-localisation of companies, the cooperation between agents makes it possible to revitalise synergies and, with it, bring benefits.

In this context, the ability to disseminate information and knowledge in real time is crucial to promote stronger relations between cluster agents. These relations may refer to either the trade of products/services or cooperation, involving mutual reliance and technological proximity (Menzel and Fornahl, 2010). The analysis of agreements (formal and informal) signed between creative cluster agents is needed to understand the level and characteristics of horizontal and vertical cooperation, as well as the dynamics associated with the development of governance processes.

In this context, the stages of development and maturity of the cluster would correspond to increased knowledge and trust among agents and to the development of more organic and direct cooperation relationships (with less mediation by other agents). We also believe that the increase in the strength of intra-cluster relationships would bring, in these stages, greater involvement of companies/organisations of creative clusters in larger networks and external projects, relevant to their competitiveness (Table 13.2).

13.4.3 Market

The ability to enter the market is frequently considered an important advantage in the formation of clusters (Maggioni and Riggi, 2008). Accepting this idea, we believe that this dimension is relevant to analyse the development of a cluster over time, and propose the regional and national market share and the market scale in which the cluster operates as evaluating indicators. The development and maturity stages of the cluster would correspond not only to the increase in market share in the activity sector in which the cluster operates but also to the greater ability of the cluster to operate in the global market.

Furthermore, in the creative clusters the development and maturity stages would still correspond to a greater ability to create value within the market through the innovative application of the intra-cluster generated knowledge, in particular through patents or intellectual propriety (Table 13.3).

This analytical framework implies a certain association between these three components – companies and other organisations, networks and flows, market – and it also assumes there is not a single path for the development of creative clusters. Considering that each cluster combines these dimensions in different ways, the approach we suggest allows us to compare the relative position of clusters, but mostly to analyse the existence of distinct trends.

Table 13.2 Life cycle of creative clusters: 'networks and flows' dimension

Variables	Creative clusters' life cycle stage		
	Emerging clusters	*Developing clusters*	*Mature clusters*
Volume of projects, companies and innovative products/services developed/created together by cluster agents (formally or informally)	Not very significant	Significant	Very significant
Wealth internally generated through the trading of products/ services among cluster agents	Not very significant	Significant	Very significant
Internal flows of information and knowledge in the cluster: **> Density** **> Quality**	> Weak > Mechanic	> Moderate > Mechanic and organic	> Dense > Organic
Intra-cluster collaboration: **1# Type; 2# Mechanisms; 3# Strategies; 4# Mediation**	1# Transactional relations; 2# Market share; 3# Communication; 4# Cooperation with mediation by the organisation operating the cluster/large company	1# Transactional and coordination relations; 2# Market share and subcontracting; 3# Communication, reliance, commitment; 4# Cooperation with and without mediation by the organisation operating the cluster/large company	1# Transactional, coordinating and synchronised relations; 2# Market share and subcontracting, information and knowledge share, R&D; 3# Communication, reliance, commitment, coordination and resolution of conflicts; 4# Prevalence of cooperation relations without mediation
Involvement of companies / organisations of the cluster in networks and external projects	Weak	Moderate	Strong

Table 13.3 Life cycle of creative clusters: 'market' dimension

Variables	Creative clusters' life cycle stage		
	Emerging clusters	Developing clusters	Mature clusters
Regional and national market share within the activity sector in which the cluster operates	Not very significant	Significant	Very significant
Market scale in which the cluster operates	Local	Local and national	Local, national and international
Patents/intellectual property generated by the companies/ organisations from the application of the knowledge generated intra-cluster	Not very significant	Significant	Very significant

13.5   The case of the educational and entertainment software cluster in the Porto City region

With the purpose of evaluating the behaviour of the development trend of creative clusters in the north of Portugal, this study aims to discuss the results obtained through a methodology founded on a qualitative approach, based on a content analysis of the information gathered in interviews with some of the most representative agents related to the creation and development of the entertainment and educational software in the Porto City region (companies, universities, research centres, vocational centres and industry associations). We chose this cluster because there is a regional policy that invests in its development, as it consists in one of the four predominant goals of the Agency for the Development of Creative Industries (ADDICT).

The information collected was systematised around the three components highlighted in the previous section as being the most relevant for the analysis of the development of creative clusters.

13.5.1   Businesses and other organisations of the entertainment and educational software cluster

In the case of the Porto City region, the development of this cluster has benefited from the presence of universities and polytechnics in the region, where research teams of great international reputation have been established to work on highly specialised technological development (for example, in the area of computer graphics specialised in facial animation). These research centres are articulated with teaching projects which progressively tend to combine strong technological development with a much needed creative dimension (in terms of contents such as educational, historical, artistic, sensorial, etc.) so that users can become immersed in the virtual reality of the applications of these software programs.

In terms of the specialised training required by these activities, to which the academy in the region (university and polytechnic education) has been trying to respond within a logics of diversification by exploring new areas of interest (such as the video game industry, now seen as an economic activity able to create jobs and not just as an entertainment activity), we also highlight the presence of training companies in the region, with new training offers in the game design area. These professional trainings have sought to integrate the technological and creative components, and some of these training projects are integrated in international networks (just as in the academy), thus attracting knowledge developed abroad, essential for the stimulation of innovation dynamics in the region associated with these activities.

Side by side with the regional dynamics of higher education institutions, research centres and training companies, the dynamics of the business fabric associated with this cluster can be found locally. On the one hand, the region has successful companies developing and marketing complex video games abroad that have already attracted the interest of large multinationals of the sector, which have bought and are marketing these games in the global market. On the other hand, the region also has smaller successful companies developing and marketing games for mobile platforms or to be integrated in websites, or that have even proven themselves in the development of solutions to be integrated in products led and developed abroad. Moreover, there are also small companies with an acknowledged value in the development of educational software (in some cases sold to international markets), benefiting from relevant agents in the region with a vast tradition of producing their own educational contents.

A constraint to the development of this cluster in the region is the difficulty of capturing funding. The risk capital is reduced to support the development of these products (many entrepreneurs resort to regular credit lines), mostly because financial institutions find it difficult to support a business area they ignore and in which they fail to evaluate the success potential of its production. The absence of risk capital largely limits activities that may need years before they make their first profit (the development of this software is slow and time consuming). This fact hinders entrepreneurship (through start-ups or spin-offs), because setting up a new business entails various costs which mount up from the moment the business is created.

Still considering the organisations related to the development of this activity, it is also important to mention that the most relevant association in the country that promotes the sector is located in the Porto City region (Portuguese Society of Videogames), alongside ADDICT, which, as already mentioned, has elected entertainment and educational software as one of the four priority sub-sectors to promote the region.

13.5.2 Networks and flows of the entertainment and educational software cluster

The research teams of the region's universities and polytechnic institutions operating in this field of expertise are integrated in international R&D networks, in many cases managing to attract to the region considerable international funding for technology development projects that the industry incorporates only later (for example, applications for entertainment software with therapeutic purposes for autistic people). This dynamics has contributed to the region's visibility and international projection in the development of these activities, which, in turn, has been acknowledged by the public administration. In this respect, it should be mentioned that recently public resources have supported in this territory the creation of IPCA Digital Games Lab, which is a pioneer project in Portugal for the creation of an R&D centre specifically intended for digital games. This research centre benefits from a cooperation protocol signed with Microsoft and its main purpose is the joint development of a series of initiatives seeking to encourage education and research into the development of digital games.

In activities such as these, whose innovation is based on the knowledge and creativity of its human resources, it is a cause for concern that external research centres tend to absorb the most qualified and skilled human resources, thus proving that the region is capable of providing the expert training of technical resources. In a global employment market, this transference may, in time, have positive effects for the region, either in the sense that it favours the integration of the region's agents into international networks of cooperation or because these human resources may later on return to the region, bringing more knowledge and connections. However, these transfers mean that the difficulty in training work teams is one of the main problems for companies in this cluster in the region, because they are still not able to compete with the work conditions these professionals obtain abroad.

In the north-west of Portugal, a territory marked by contexts of strong economic specialisation in activities of little added value and labour-intensive work, the investment in activities such as educational and entertainment software is considered a priority. And it is a priority because not only does it contribute to gradually redefine the development trends of the region into more profitable, highly technological and more knowledgeable activities, but also because the high added value of this software contributes to promoting other economic activities relevant for the region, including the sector of creative industries (for example, music, design or audio visuals). So, flows exist between these and other activities, thus potentially strengthening the competitiveness of the region's business fabric.

13.5.3 The market of the entertainment and educational software cluster

The entertainment and educational software cluster represents activities with a leading role in the context of knowledge economy, gathering highly technological companies, which, in the context of the current economic stagnation/slow-down, have asserted themselves for their ability to create jobs and wealth. The growth trend of this cluster is likely to continue because it benefits from the development of the education, health (therapeutic) and advertising (advert games) sectors, but also because it operates in a growing market with a strong potential to attract new audiences (the entertainment software user is still predominantly male).

The entertainment software is, therefore, a cluster with strong potential and is expanding rapidly around the world, especially at a time when the expansion of the online market enables new companies to enter the global market, in addition to the opportunities created by the new mobile distribution platforms of these telematic applications (such as iPads or mobile phones). In other words, new players tend to join this cluster, and there have been attempts to find alternative ways to enter the international market of software edition and distribution mostly dominated by a small number of large companies.

The Porto City region has been exploring the potential of this market. The region has companies responsible for creating the first Portuguese video games that have been bought by large multinationals (Nintendo and Sony), which stresses the regional momentum of this activity that can already perform in a very competitive global market. It is also important to highlight other companies, smaller but equally integrated in international networks, which are increasingly recognised as creators of parcel components for video games, and whose development process is led by foreign multinationals.

13.6   Conclusion

There is growing recognition that the dynamics of clusters have distinct characteristics when analysed over time. Among the numerous concepts, the approach of life cycle has been preponderant in this study. However, this type of analysis still entails a significant number of challenges. In most cases, these studies focus on partial aspects of cluster dynamics (e.g. cluster growth, R&D investment) or resort to a single source of information (e.g. statistics), and there are few studies that enable the understanding of the development of clusters from a systemic perspective. Moreover, some studies identify some dimensions that enable the identification of the clusters' life cycle stages but fail to present the qualitative characteristics associated with each stage.

This chapter reviews the main theoretical models and methodologies used in empirical studies to explain the development of clusters over time. Based on this information, we question the effectiveness of the methodology most frequently used when applied to the study of the creative clusters. Even when we take most clusters into consideration, an analysis focused on statistics does not allow the understanding of the factors that limit the dynamics and change or the associated processes of clusters. This type of study is clearly inefficient when much of how the sector is organised cannot be captured by statistics.

By posing the question 'which dimensions and variables better enable the analysis of the temporal dynamics of creative clusters?', we propose an approach that integrates the three components we believe are relevant for the analysis of creative cluster development – companies and other organisations, networks and flows, and market. These dimensions combine different types of variables – quantitative and qualitative; related to the objective dimension of the cluster and of a relative nature; related to incomes and outcomes; as well as variables to allow direct and systemic analysis.

Through the empirical study of educational and entertainment software in the Porto City region the existing difficulties in the most often used approach in clusters dynamics studies was debated, as well as the feasibility of the approach proposed by the authors. The regional business fabric associated with the development of entertainment and educational software in the north-west of Portugal is still incipient, but it has grown substantially in recent years. Although this is an emerging business in the region, the strong investment in its quality has been internationally acclaimed and has attracted the interest of large multinationals for regional production. In this region, it is clear that there is an ongoing process of creating a community of agents associated with the production of entertainment and educational software, marked by the establishment of networks and partnerships characterised by a good cooperation environment between its main agents. Nevertheless, the integration of its chain of value in the territory is still weak. In fact, although it is recognised that the region has good local resources, international personal networks often motivate them to work with agents external to the region (sometimes very distant), with which there is already a highly valued work tradition and climate of confidence. These networks of relations and international cooperation projects are very relevant for the promotion of this cluster in the region, although the challenge is to integrate other regional agents in these projects. Therefore, cooperation practices among regional agents can potentially be developed.

Assuming that there is no single formula for clusters to develop, and that each cluster differently combines the identified three components, one of the added values of the approach proposed in this chapter is the fact that it allows us to compare the relative position of creative clusters, but mostly to analyse their existing distinct trends.

Acknowledgements

This work is funded by the European Regional Development Fund through Operational Programme Factors of Competitiveness – COMPETE 2020, Programa Operacional Competitividade e Internacionalização (POCI) – and by national funds through FCT – Foundation for Science and Technology under the project POCI-01-0145-FEDER-006891 (Refª FCT: UID/GEO/04084/2013).

References

Andersson, T. *et al.* (2004). *The Cluster Policies Whitebook.* Malmö: IKED – International Organisation for Knowledge Economy and Enterprise Development.

Audretsch, D. and Feldman P. (1996). Innovative clusters and the industry life cycle. *Review of Industrial Organization*, 11(2), 253–273.

Boschma, R. and Fornahl, D. (2005). Proximity and innovation: a critical assessment, *Regional Studies*, 39(1), 61–74.

Boschma, R. and Fornahl, D. (2011). Cluster evolution and a roadmap for future research. *Regional Studies*, 45(1), 1295–1298.

Braunerhjelm, P. and Feldmann, M. (eds) (2006). *Cluster Genesis.* Oxford: Oxford University Press.

Brenner, T. (2004). *Local Industry Cluster: Existence, Emergence and Evolution.* London and New York: Routledge.

Chapain, C. and Comunian, R. (2010). Enabling and inhibiting the creative economy: the role of the local and regional dimensions in England. *Regional Studies*, 44(6), 717–734.

Cox, K. (ed.) (1997). *Spaces of Globalization: Reasserting the Power of the Local.* New York: The Guilford Press.

Grabher, G. (2002). Cool projects, boring institutions: temporary collaboration in social context, *Regional Studies*, 36 (3), 205–214.

Gu, X. (2014). Cultural industries and creative clusters in Shanghai, *City, Culture and Society*, 5, 123–130.

Immarino, S. and McCann, P. (2006). The structure and evolution of industrial clusters: transactions, technology and knowledge spillovers, *Research Policy*, 5, 1018–1036.

Knop, L. and Olko, S. (2011). Crises in the cluster life-cycle. In *Management Knowledge and Learning International Conference 2011.* http://issbs.si/press/ISBN/978-961-92486-3-8/papers/ML11-39.pdf..

Lange, B. *et al.* (2008). Berlin's creative industries: governing creativity? *Industry and Innovation*, 15(5), 531–548.

Lefebvre, P. (2012). Organised clusters evolutions: from cluster life-cycle approaches to the action trajectories approach. Paper presented at the *7th International Seminar on Regional Innovation Policies, Cluster Life-Cycle Sessions*, Porto (Portugal), 11–12 October 2012, 41p.

Maggioni, M. (2002). *Clustering Dynamics and the Location of High-Tech-Firms.* Heidelberg/New York: Physica-Verlag.

Maggioni, M. and Riggi, M. (2008). High-tech firms and the dynamics of innovative industrial clusters. In Karlsson C. (ed.) *Handbook of Research on Clusters: Theories, Policies and Case Studies.* Cheltenham: Edward Elgar.

Martin, R. and Sunley, P. (2011). Conceptualizing cluster evolution: beyond the life cycle model? *Regional Studies*, 45(10), 1299–1318.

Menzel, M. and Fornahl, D. (2010). Cluster life cycles – dimensions and rationales of cluster evolution. *Industrial and Corporate Change*, 19(1), 205–238.

Oakley, K. (2006). Include us out – economic development and social policy in the creative industries, *Cultural Trends*, 15(4), 255–273.

Porter, M. (1990). The competitive advantage of nations, *Harvard Business Review*, March–April, 73–93.

Porter, M. (2003). The economic performance of regions, *Regional Studies*, 37(6 and 7), 549–578.

Pouder, R. and St John, C. (1996). Hot spots and blind spots: geographical clusters of firms and innovation, *Academy of Management Review*, 21(4), 1192–1225.

Schretlen, J., Dervojeda, K., Jansen, W. and Schaffmeister, B. (2011). *Uncovering Excellence in Cluster Management*. Amsterdam: PricewaterhouseCoopers.

Scott, A. (2000). *The Cultural Economy of Cities*. London: Sage.

Scott, A. (2001). Capitalism, cities and the production of symbolic forms, *Transactions of the Institute of British Geographers*, 26(1), 1–23.

Sölvell, Ö., Lindqvist, G. and Ketels, C.H. (2003). *The Cluster Initiative Greenbook*. Stockholm: Ivory Tower AB.

Swann, G., Prevezer, M. and Stout, D. (eds) (1998). *The Dynamics of Industrial Clustering: International Comparisons in Computing and Biotechnology*. Oxford: Oxford University Press.

Ter Wal, A. and Boschma, R. (2011). Co-evolution of firms, industries and networks in space, *Regional Studies*, 45(7), 919–933.

UNCTAD (2009). *Creative Economy Report 2008: The Challenge of Assessing the Creative Economy towards Informed Policy-making*. Geneva: United Nations Conference on Trade and Development.

14 Understanding the dynamics of cluster competitive advantage

Empirical evidence using a capability-based perspective

Jose Luis Hervás-Oliver

14.1 Introduction

Despite works on the innovation capacity of clusters throughout different life cycle stages and their potential cognitive inertia due to over-embeddedness (Pouder and St John, 1996), which insulates cluster firms from external information beyond the cluster (Uzzi, 1997), an important issue that remains unclear is the mechanism by which clusters evolve and create a system of capabilities that drives their competitive advantage. Following Tallman *et al.* (2004), based on Matusik and Hill's (1998) idea of component versus architectural knowledge,[1] we use the following definitions: component knowledge refers to specific and individual abilities and knowledge, while architectural knowledge refers to the use of these component competencies and their effective integration into complex systems of organizational routines or capabilities. In order to understand component knowledge in clusters, it is also worthwhile to recognize that a cluster is an environment in which there are frequent and multiple relationships (Brusco, 1982). Specifically, and drawing on Tallman *et al.* (2004) and their elaboration on component and architectural knowledge on clusters, scholars have not yet disentangled the different types of component knowledge created from differing technological changes, that is, sustaining versus radical discontinuities (in the sense of Christensen, 1997) and the distinct impacts on the cluster combinative capability or architectural knowledge system. Assuming that in clusters inter-firm interaction is the relevant construct (e.g. Powell *et al.*, 1996; Brusco, 1982; Becattini, 1990; Saxenian, 1994), distinguishing those discontinuities and their subsequent types of knowledge created through firms' interaction may permit us to extend our knowledge on cluster-level systems of capabilities that drive competitive advantage. Our framework serves to enrich agglomeration[2] and cluster literature.

Differing types of technological change discontinuities (sustaining versus radical) trigger the formation of component knowledge that creates a system of interconnected capabilities underpinning cluster-level competitive advantage. This study elaborates on cluster dynamic systems of capabilities using managerial capability-based perspectives, and thus addressing dynamic cluster capabilities with the purpose of building up a framework through which to understand the mechanisms of cluster evolution and competitive advantage. Extensions of the capability-based approach from the firm to the territory or cluster level in the economic geography literature (e.g. Foss, 1996; Lawson, 1999; Lawson and Lorenz, 1999) have argued that territories can develop higher order capabilities (Foss, 1996). However, these works have been limited to using a competence or capability lens to simply conceptually describe clusters (a) without using a formal and dynamic approach drawn from the dynamic capabilities perspective and (b) without connecting the concept of cluster capability to that of cluster evolution. This is the purpose of this chapter.

14.2   A capability-based view to framework cluster capabilities

At the firm level, dynamic capabilities (DC) have been defined as 'the capacity to renew competencies so as to achieve congruence with the changing business environment' by 'adapting, integrating, and reconfiguring internal and external organizational skills, resources, and functional competencies' (Teece *et al.*, 1997: 515). Dynamic capabilities are embedded in the firm during its evolution and are utilized to reconfigure the firm's capabilities by dropping redundant or obsolete resources or recombining old resources in new ways (Simon and Hitt, 2003). DC are path dependent (Dierickx and Cool, 1989) as they are formed by past decisions. DC integrate and coordinate an organization's capabilities, reshaping an existing 'complex system' formed by interconnected assets, through the incorporation of new resources and the deletion of decaying ones, thereby maintaining or creating new competitive advantage.

Cluster dynamic capabilities (CDCs) are defined in our work as the capabilities to renew and adapt the cluster resources and capabilities, orchestrating changes in cluster stocks of resources by channelling new component knowledge, modifying and reconfiguring existing capabilities, and replacing the ones that become redundant. These CDCs are similar to the architectural knowledge pointed out by Pinch *et al.* (2003: 378) as that knowledge embedded in the whole system that serves as a framework to establish the relationships among members, setting the 'rules of the game', and is developed through evolutionary processes based on members' interactions over time, fostering absorptive capacity for facilitating the dissemination and circulation of component knowledge and preventing knowledge flows among clusters.

At the cluster level, the notion of architectural knowledge is similar to other ideas, such as collective knowledge (Spender, 1994), 'dynamic capabilities' (Teece *et al.*, 1997), 'combinative capabilities' (Kogut and Zander, 1992), or 'organizational architecture' (Nelson, 1991). As Tallman *et al.* (2004) pointed out, architectural knowledge refers to the cluster as a whole. It is tacit in nature, path-dependent, and is embedded and non-transferable. As such, it is a similar concept to that of resources and capabilities (cf. Tallman *et al.*, 2004: 264) when applied to the cluster as a complete system. Architectural knowledge is the language through which component knowledge is effectively integrated and which allows the exchange and mobility of tacit component knowledge within communities, without the need to codify and decode such component knowledge (Tallman and Chacar, 2011). Component knowledge is easily transferable within the cluster because the architectural knowledge enables quick interpretation. The component knowledge is spread through daily interactions and exchange of ideas, including, especially, tacit knowledge.

The new component knowledge locally generated or adopted[3] might combine with existing knowledge or/and substitute for other knowledge, shaping the architectural system by adding new routines or transforming the entire system. CDCs establish a common set of norms and understandings that facilitates innovation within the cluster, in so far as they decipher, decode, interpret and facilitate the rapid dissemination and absorption of component knowledge in an idiosyncratic way that is possible only in that focus cluster. The set of capabilities forming the system or architectural knowledge articulates that generation and circulation and allows the regeneration or deletion of the existing capabilities from the circulation of new component knowledge. CDCs facilitate the renewal of the cluster capabilities and, subsequently, the cluster evolves through a process of capability accumulation and/or deletion. CDCs permit the management of new knowledge, integrating, coordinating and reshaping the existing complex system of local and external interactions in which the capabilities are rooted. These CDCs are embedded in the cluster and are path dependent, allowing the elimination of obsolete capabilities, the recombination of existing ones in new ways and the creation of new capabilities. CDCs integrate and coordinate a cluster's capabilities, reshaping the existing 'complex system' formed by interconnected assets, through incorporating new capabilities, deleting decaying ones and thus maintaining, or creating, competitive advantage.[4]

14.3   Technological discontinuities and the dynamics of cluster capability

Capability formation and accumulation in clusters is located at the levels of firms and networks, where new component knowledge is shaped and reshaped in the context of local, and also local–global, interactions. Component knowledge, however, can present diverse typologies and differing consequences for the cluster architecture and its evolution. When derived from engagement in sustaining innovations (in the sense of Dosi, 1988 and Christiansen, 1997) it exploits the potential of established designs and often reinforces the dominance of established firms (Tushman and Anderson, 1986; Nelson and Winter, 1982). In contrast, component knowledge associated with the introduction of a radical or disruptive innovation relies on different engineering and scientific principles, and often opens up whole new markets and potential applications (Ettlie *et al.*, 1984), which create great difficulties for established firms (Tushman and Anderson, 1986). Radical (or disruptive) innovation establishes a new dominant design and new knowledge components are linked together in a new architecture. Thus, it can be expected that radical or disruptive innovations will affect a cluster's capabilities, reconfiguring an established system, creating new social interactions and new linkages with existing and new knowledge components. In particular, a radical innovation usually destroys[5] the existing capabilities of incumbents ('competence destroying', Tushman and Anderson, 1986). Yet sustaining innovations will be mainly based on alterations of knowledge components which usually will not alter the system, or the cluster's capabilities, due to the fact that incremental innovations reinforce the competitive positions of established firms since they build on their core competences ('competence enhancing', Tushman and Anderson, 1986).

Component knowledge based on sustaining innovations, usually rooted in strong and dense local ties within technology-related areas, provokes an adjustment of existing capabilities. This competence- or capability-enhancing process maintains the same cluster resources and contributes to simply expanding a cluster's central stages. This knowledge creation constitutes only an improvement of existing technological trajectories rather than the creation of new ones and therefore existent capabilities will be adjusted or improved, forming competence-enhancing capabilities throughout the same dominant design, in the sense of Tushman and Anderson (1986) and Anderson and Tushman (1990). That combination of sustaining innovations in strong local networks, together with technology-related knowledge, will only result in an adjustment of existing capabilities, that is, a production of competence-enhancing discontinuities. In this case the architectural knowledge remains the same, adjusting existing capabilities without renewing them. The result is the expansion of the central stages of the cluster life cycle. Both forms of capability formation can occur in the different cluster life cycles (CLC) stages, but the performance consequences will be different: while competence-enhancing technical change should expand the CLC central stages, competence-destroying ones will renew the cluster, creating new growth stages and rejuvenation. In addition, a combination of the two forms of component knowledge could also occur, producing hybrid forms throughout the spectrum of possibilities.

Radical (or disruptive) innovation might result from the generation of novel information and might be associated with exploratory learning (in the sense of March, 1991). This new knowledge will be combined with existing knowledge and will even result in the substitution of existing technologies (producing new technological trajectories), forming competence-destroying capabilities in the sense of Tushman and Anderson (1986) and Anderson and Tushman (1990). Component knowledge based on disruptive innovations is based on technology-distant knowledge related to new capabilities. These new capabilities are combined with existing ones, resulting in the destruction of redundant capabilities and the reshaping of the cluster stock of capabilities, thus renewing the CLC and creating a new period of growth. A cluster's ability to configure radical component knowledge (first its networks produce it) needs special conditions. That radical component knowledge requires going beyond a local knowledge search and reconfiguring its existing knowledge with that acquired from non-local domains is a function of its absorptive capacity (Cohen and Levinthal, 1990) or its 'combinative capability' (Kogut and Zander, 1992). This involves a capability to access new knowledge lying outside the boundaries (organizational and technological) of the cluster and to integrate the new knowledge with existing knowledge. Thus, the process of exploration for new knowledge can be carried out by spanning both organizational (cluster) and technological (embedded) boundaries.

To sum up, it is expected that the growth and renewal (rejuvenation of capabilities) stage will be shaped by the formation of a competence-destroying capability. This capability is created by combining new technology-distant exploratory and radical knowledge, resulting in radical innovations. This will drive the renewal of cluster capabilities, deleting redundant capabilities and providing new ones, and changing the architectural knowledge or CDCs.

As Ennen and Richter (2010) suggest, competitive advantage not only results from developing resources but also from the capability to integrate them in a unique way. Thus, for example, establishing 'entire systems of mutually reinforcing design elements' enhances performance, and due to the complexity achieved, imitation is prevented (e.g. Rivkin, 2000). Therefore, firms able to develop resources and capabilities which form rare, valuable and inimitable repositories of knowledge are thereby able to foster innovation and generate above-normal incomes, prevent imitation from competitors and so sustain a competitive advantage (e.g. Barney, 1991; Peteraf, 1993). A cluster system of capabilities is based on the idea of synergies or systems of mutually reinforcing elements, that is, complementarities underpinning cluster competitive advantage. As mentioned above, cluster dynamic capabilities integrate and coordinate cluster capabilities, reshaping an existing 'complex system' formed by interconnected assets or component knowledge, through the incorporation of new knowledge and the deletion of decaying knowledge, thereby maintaining or creating competitive advantage based on complementarities. Milgrom and Roberts (1995: 81) refer to that reinforcing system as 'complements', a relationship among groups of activities, stating that 'if the levels of any subset of activities are increased, then the marginal return to all of the remaining activities rises'. Similarly, Ichniowski et al. (1997) state that complementarity among practices implies that the magnitude of the performance effect of the entire system is larger than the sum of the marginal effects of adopting each practice individually. Activities that are mutually complementary need to be adopted together. If not, then the lack of coordination or integration may diminish returns. At the cluster level that coordination of capabilities is also required.

14.4 An example of the application of the dynamics of the cluster capability framework

14.4.1 The Castellon cluster in Spain

The Castellon ceramics cluster is a meta-cluster (Hervás-Oliver and Albors-Garrigós, 2007) that includes all the activities of the ceramics value chain (including clay processing, ceramic tile production, frits and glaze decoration based on high-tech chemistry, and ceramic equipment production) as well as various public world-class R&D organizations such as the Institute of Ceramic Technology (ITC-ALICER, hereafter), educational centres such as the Jaume I Universitat, and multiple supportive private trade associations (including Ascer, Anffecc and Asebec). According to the trade association ASCER, the cluster, the first European producer, provided around 14,300 direct jobs in 2013 and there are around 300 firms in related ceramic industries.[6] Within the cluster the decoration capability based on advanced chemistry (frits and glazing) is the key resource (Meyer-Stamer *et al.*, 2004; Hervás-Oliver and Albors-Garrigós, 2007). The Castellon frits and glazing sub-industry is the world leader, with twenty-six firms exporting around 66 per cent of their total production valued at €1.2 billion and employing around 3,470 workers in 2014.[7] It has extensive off-shore operations in other clusters, including in Sassuolo (Italy), Brazil, Indonesia, Mexico, India and China, among others (see Hervás-Oliver and Boix-Domènech, 2013). Inter-organizational interaction is a crucial part of the cluster's 'innovation engine' (Meyer-Stamer *et al.*, 2004) based on the interactions and their complementarities.

14.4.2 Cluster evolution and the formation of capabilities

We summarize and synthesize longitudinal data covering the past sixty years of the Castellon cluster in Spain from Albors (2010), Hervás-Oliver and Albors-Garrigós (2014), Hervás-Oliver and Boix-Domènech (2013) and Hervás-Oliver *et al.* (2016), extending their analysis by collecting and combining complementary secondary data analysis from ASCER[8] and interviews with their team.

As remarked in those works, the Castellon cluster goes back to the eighteenth century with the establishment of the Royal Fabric of Ceramics (Real Fábrica de Cerámica), but it achieved a critical mass and a sense of industrial identity only in the 1960s. The late 1950s and the 1960s witnessed industrial takeoff and the transition from the traditional Arab kiln method to a mechanized kiln using fuel (kerosene). It is documented that in those days, new entrepreneurial startups, diversifying from other industries, were established, boosting the numbers of existing incumbents, which also adapted their technologies. In the late 1960s there were officially 59 ceramic producers; this rose to 200 in 2003 and 154 in 2012.[9]

The ceramic equipment manufacturing subsector of the Italian tile district of Sassuolo originated in the 1960s and was responsible for the technological advances in the world industry (Russo, 2000; Albors, 2002). After 1967, the twice-fired production and decoration process using a tunnel kiln method, using Italian (Sassuolo cluster) technology, was taken up in the Castellon cluster. This technological advantage was first adopted by leading technological gatekeepers in Castellon, working hand in hand with Sassuolo MNEs established in Castellon. This strong collaboration allowed the transference of Italian knowledge to the Castellon production process and different clays and products.[10]

In the late 1970s (1979/1980 for floor tiles) the transition to the single-fired process began in Castellon, using Italian kilns and Castellon decoration technology, ending in the late 1980s. This radical change dramatically impacted all the production processes, shortening them from twenty-four hours to forty-five minutes, and reshaped the chemical decoration process. Its adoption was started by the leading Castellon technological gatekeepers (TGs) working hand in hand with local glazing (chemical) firms and Italian equipment manufacturers. The adoption of the single-fired process triggered important collective actions in Castellon, such as the installation of a gas pipeline for the entire cluster, the creation of ASCER (the ceramics trade association) and the location of the Institute of Technological Ceramics (ITC, previously located in Valencia University) in the heart of the Castellon cluster. As regards technology, the single-fired process changed the way tiles were decorated and also required a change from a dry grinding clay to a wet grinding process. This new Castellon technology was quickly adopted by the Italian cluster (and was the first time knowledge transferred from Castellon to Sassuolo, rather than vice versa).

The single-fired production and the endogenous generation of porous new single-fired-based decoration fostered the development of local Castellon frits and glazing firms (specialized in decoration), which started an outbound FDI process in the late 1980s and which since the mid-1990s have been part of a leading world-class industry in the field of ceramic tiles, and presently are the world leaders.[11] The Castellon cluster leapfrogged and began to specialize in decoration technology, developing the best knowledge from the interaction between the different agents of the system. Indeed, inter-organizational interaction is a crucial part of the cluster's 'innovation engine' (Meyer-Stamer *et al.*, 2004; Hervás-Oliver and Albors-Garrigós, 2007). The true strength of the Castellon cluster lies in its systemic behaviour of interactions organized around the frits and glaze (decoration) innovators with the local ceramics producers and the ITC. These local interactions are also supported and complemented by interactions with Sassuolo equipment producers localized in the Castellon cluster.

From the early 1970s, in the twice-fired production process, classic tile ceramic decoration was based on the use of plain screens, using serigraphy. Initially, screens were made of silk but today they are made of polyester because of its higher resolution. Serigraphy was used indistinctively in both the twice- and the single-fired with some adjustments and modifications. In 1994, the TGs introduced a substantial innovation and a clear improvement over the rotary screen silicon cylinder canvas: Rotocolor technology. This technology decorates patterns onto ceramic tiles by means of engraved silicon cylinders which produce high-definition images. The Rotocolor process, after 1994, was developed by two leading firms: Porcelanosa in the Castellon cluster and the Ricchetti group in Sassuolo (Russo, 2000). After four years of trial and error, Porcelanosa, a leading TG in Castellon, ordered 400 Rotocolor machines, announcing in 1998 that the new system was highly productive and competitive.

During the 2000s, when the Rotocolor technology for tile decoration was becoming fully established, a local Spanish computer entrepreneur engineer, with extensive experience in the ceramic tiles industry, along with a chemist working in a leading glaze and pigment multinational firm (FERRO) and a former worker from Porcelanosa, began exploring new possibilities for decorating ceramic tiles based on digital technologies. They founded the new firm Kerajet with the purpose of fulfilling the development of a digital decoration process based on IT in order to abandon a mechanical process with plenty of drawbacks. In 1999, Kerajet developed a first prototype technology based on inkjet printing, with the aim of digitalizing the decoration process. Based on a design consisting of multiple inkjet head systems, control hardware, software design transmission and inkjet handling subsystems, Kerajet presented its first industrial prototype at the CEVISAMA exhibition in 2000, and also registered two PCT patent applications related to ink and technology. In no time at all, a cooking craft process (Russo, 2004) was replaced by a digitized process (Albors, 2010). FERRO, a leading TG, allied with Kerajet to develop the new inks for the new technology. It was the first time that the Castellon cluster led the development of a cutting-edge technology without relying on Sassuolo knowledge. Instead, Kerajet made use of knowledge external to the industry, particularly from the Cambridge printing cluster in the UK. Kerajet research cooperation was carried out with two inkjet print-head manufacturers, one from the Cambridge printing cluster (a company called XAAR) and another from Japan (called SEIKO).

14.4.3 Summarizing findings

Traditionally, the Castellon cluster was originally absorbing new Italian cluster-generated knowledge via interactions orchestrated by both local Spain-based TGs and leading Italy-based TGs in the ceramics equipment manufacturing sector with branches in Castellon. The Castellon cluster managed to absorb and adapt the knowledge generated through interaction build-up of its cluster dynamic capabilities based on decoration. Later on, an effective orchestration of endogenous component knowledge creation among the glazing firms' and local ceramic producers' interactions, together with the effects of the interaction of these firms with Italian equipment suppliers and

Table 14.1 Summary of the main technological shifts in the cluster

Technological change	Discontinuities	Cluster capability	Evolution: renewal (rejuvenation) or extension of central CLC
Twice-fired (production)	Competence-destroying	Deletion of tunnel kiln technology. Vertical disintegration between first and second steps in twice-fired	Rejuvenation, new actors and TGs. External linkages with Italian (Sassuolo cluster) and German firms, producers of kilns and other ceramic equipment
Single-fired (production)	Competence-destroying	Deletion of twice-fired. Development of new decoration technologies (porous decoration). Vertical disintegration in decorations capabilities (prominence of frits and glazing firms)	Rejuvenation, new actors and TGs. Strengthening linkages with Italy (Sassuolo cluster)
Rotocolor (decoration)	Competence-enhancing	New decoration system (deleting serigraphy) based on single-fired production technology	Extension of central CLCs. Same actors and TGs
Digital inkjet (decoration)	Competence-destroying	Deletion of Rotocolor, transition from mechanical to digital decoration on single-fired production technology. Vertical disintegration for head printers, colour design management, graphics and nano-technology.	Rejuvenation. New actors and TGs. External linkages (global value chains). Strengthening linkages with Silicon Valley and Cambridge cluster

Source: Author's own, based on Albors (2010); Hervás-Oliver and Boix-Doménech (2013); Hervás-Oliver and Albors-Garrigós (2014) and Hervás-Oliver et al. (2016), plus ASCER team interviews (during summer 2014).

local ceramic producers, expanded the cluster's capabilities and subsequent (new) growth stages were embarked upon.

There are clear-cut differing effects on cluster evolution according to whether development is based on technological discontinuities associated with sustaining innovation or, rather, on disrupted 'turns' due to radical knowledge creation. The former is related to the adjustment of existing capabilities and to the expansion of a cluster's central stages. This is what happened in the case of the Rotocolor decoration development. The architectural knowledge in Castellon related to decoration absorbed the new knowledge and adjusted the entire system, deleting the serigraphy technology and adjusting in the system the new Rotocolor one. In contrast, radical competence-destroying learning renewed the cluster's stock of capabilities, making existing knowledge redundant, and reshaped the complex set of resources or architectural knowledge, effectively driving the rejuvenation of the cluster and contributing to its renewal. The development of the digital inkjet decoration capability and the single-fired process are good examples of how the cluster was renewed thanks to disruptive technological change. In all, each type of knowledge, with its particular impact on a cluster's capabilities, determined a different shift in a cluster's capabilities. See Table 14.1 for a summary of this section.

14.5   Conclusions

This chapter has elaborated on the managerial capability-based framework to describe the evolution of a cluster, through the formation of frits capabilities, constructing an appropriate capabilities-based conceptual framework through which to understand the evolutionary process of clusters. As such, this study has extended both conceptually and empirically the application of micro-level theories to the cluster level.

Through this approach, it is theorized how differing types of new component knowledge created at the firm or network level are diffused and orchestrated through the filter of the higher-order cluster dynamic capabilities. This results in the modifying and reshaping of the cluster stock of capabilities, or architectural knowledge, which, subsequently, leads to a particular type of evolution through life cycle stages. This advance in the understanding of an organization's dynamic routines or capabilities applied to the cluster construct has constituted a novel approach of cross-fertilization of perspectives which can help to understand cluster capabilities and competitive advantage evolution, providing scholars with a new integrated conceptual framework. In all, new knowledge based on sustaining knowledge facilitates the adjustment of existing capabilities, provoking the enlargement of the central stages of a cluster's life cycle, and the sustenance of existing architectural knowledge. In contrast, the creation or adoption of disruptive knowledge leads to the creation of new capabilities, the deletion of redundant ones, and change in a cluster's architectural knowledge, in the process rejuvenating and renewing the cluster with the creation of new growth stages.

To sum up, and following previous Tallman *et al.* (2004) and Menzel and Fornahl (2010) frameworks, our integration presents the following propositions:

- Proposition 1: Cluster-level dynamic capabilities are the filter and set of mostly tacit assumptions and knowledge that facilitate the generation, absorption and diffusion of discontinuities, forming a coordinated system of interconnected capabilities responsible for the generation of complementarities that explains competitive advantage throughout clusters.
- Proposition 2: Sustaining discontinuities can enlarge a cluster's central stages through the adaptation and renewal of existing capabilities (creation, adoption or deletion) from new knowledge.
- Proposition 3: Radical discontinuities can foster cluster rejuvenation through the transformation and reshaping of the entire cluster system of capabilities.

Our results also provide insights for regional policy makers. The identification of cluster core capabilities, their mechanisms and formation, along with the recognition that not all activities can be properly developed in a cluster, but those forming part of the core capabilities, is necessary in order to provide timely and precise policy making adapted to each particular stage and type of knowledge by reinforcing or abandoning specific capabilities.

Acknowledgements

This research is in debt with the Spanish Ministry of Economy and Competitiveness for financially supporting this research (ECO2015-63645-R). We also thank José Albors, Carlos Camahort, María José Soriano, Carlos Cabrera, Michael Toumi, Kerajet, Ferro, Mr. Baigorri (Anffecc) and many other informants.

Notes

1 Based on Henderson and Clark (1990), Cohen and Levinthal (1990) and Henderson and Cockburn (1994).
2 We refer to Marshall (1890) externalities due to concentration of firms in the same (or related Porter, 1998) industries.
3 Knowledge transfer and adoption between clusters occurs, mainly, through organizational pipelines orchestrated by MNE subsidiaries (Jenkins and Tallman, 2010; Tallman and Chacar, 2011; Hervás-Oliver and Boix-Domènech, 2013).
4 Similarly, from the EG perspective, there is also a description of a collective learning process (Camagni, 2002) and the building up of flexible networks (Saxenian, 1994) forming relational assets through which cluster capabilities are improved and assembled, and externalities or local-regional assets shaped (Becattini, 1990; Maillat, 1989).
5 Incumbents can also disrupt, see Ahuja and Lampert, 2001 and Ansari and Krop, 2013.

6 www.ascer.es/homeinstitucional/sectorDatos.aspx?lang=en-GB (accessed September, 2015).
7 www.anffecc.com/es/cifras-del-sector (accessed September, 2015).
8 www.ascer.es/homeinstitucional/sectorDatos.aspx?lang=en-GB.
9 www.ascer.es/homeinstitucional/sectorDatos.aspx?lang=en-GB.
10 Castellon mainly developed red body tiles while Italian firms were more focused on white body ones, due to differences in raw materials.
11 www.anffecc.com/es/cifras-del-sector.

References

Agrawal, A.K. and Cockbrun, I. (2003). The anchor tenant hypothesis: exploring the role of large, local, R&D-intensive firms in regional innovation systems, *International Journal of Industrial Organization*, 21, 1227–1253.

Ahuja, G. and Lampert, C.M. (2001). Entrepreneurship in the large corporation: a longitudinal study of how established firms create breakthrough inventions, *Strategic Management Journal*, June–July Special Issue 22, 521–543.

Albors, J.G. (2002). Networking and technology transfer in the Spanish ceramic tiles cluster: its role in the sector, *Competitiveness Journal of Technology Transfer*, 27 (3), 263–273.

Albors, J. (2010). Kerajet, In Hidalgo, A. (ed.) *Sectores De Nueva Economia, Eoi, Fundación Eoi, Ministerio De Industria*. Madrid, pp. 185–196.

Albors-Garrigós, J. and Hervás-Oliver, J.L. (2012). Radical innovation and technology diffusion in traditional clusters: how high-tech industries reinvented a traditional clusters, In Bas, T.G. and Zhao, J. (eds) *Comparing High Technology Firms in Developed and Developing Countries: Cluster Growth Initiatives*, Hershey, PA: Igi Global, pp. 99–110.

Anderson, P. and Tushman, M.L. (1990). Technological discontinuities and dominant designs: a cyclical models of technological change, *Administrative Science Quarterly*, 35 (4), 604–633.

Ansari, S.S. and Krop, P. (2013). Corrigendum to 'incumbent performance in the face of a radical innovation: towards a framework for incumbent challenger dynamics', *Research Policy*, 2 (42), 577.

Barney, J. (1991). Firm resources and sustained competitive advantage, *Journal of Management*, 17 (1), 99–120.

Becattini, G. (1990). The Marshallian district as a socio-economic notion, in Pyke, F., Becattini, G. and Sengenberger, W. (eds) *Industrial Districts and Inter-firm Co-operation in Italy*, Geneva: OMT.

Brusco, S. (1982). The Emilian model: productive decentralisation and social integration, *Cambridge Journal of Economics*, 6 (2), 167–184.

Camagni, R. (2002). On the concept of territorial competitiveness: sound or misleading? *Urban Studies*, 13, 2395–2412.

Christensen, C.M. (1997). *The Innovator's Dilemma: The Revolutionary Book that Will Change the Way You Do Business*, London: Collins Business Essentials.

Cohen, W. and Levinthal, D. (1990). Absorptive capacity: a new perspective on learning and innovation, *Administrative Science Quarterly*, 35 (1), 128–152.

Dierickx, I. and Cool, K. (1989). Asset stock accumulation and sustainability of competitive advantage, *Management Science*, 35 (12), 1504–1511.

Dosi, G. (1988). Sources, procedures, and microeconomic effects of innovation, *Journal of Economic Literature*, 26 (3), 1120–1171.

Ennen, E. and Richter, A. (2010). The whole is more than the sum of its parts or is it? A review of the empirical literature on complementarities in organizations, *Journal of Management*, 36 (1), 207–233.

Ettlie, I.F., Bridges, W.P. and O'Keefe, R. (1984). Organization strategy and structural differences for radical versus incremental innovation, *Management Science*, 30 (6), 682–695.

Foss, N.J. (1996). Higher-order industrial capabilities and competitive advantage: some analytical suggestions, *Journal of Industry Studies*, 3, 1–20.

Henderson, R. and Cockburn, I. (1994). Measuring competence? Exploring firm effects in pharmaceutical research, *Strategic Management Journal*, Winter Special Issue 15, 63–84.

Henderson, R.M.Y. and Clark, K.B. (1990). Architectural innovation – the reconfiguration of existing product technologies and the failure of established firms, *Administrative Science Quarterly*, 35, 1, 9–30.

Hervás-Oliver, J. and Boix-Domènech, R. (2013). The economic geography of the meso-global spaces: integrating multinationals and clusters at the local–global level, *European Planning Studies*, 21 (7), 1064–1080.

Hervás-Oliver, J.L. and Albors-Garrigós, J. (2007). Do the cluster's resources and capabilities matter? An application of resource-based view in clusters, *Entrepreneurship & Regional Development*, 17 (2), 113–136.

Hervás-Oliver, J.L. and Albors-Garrigós, J. (2014). Are technology gatekeepers renewing clusters? Understanding gatekeepers and their dynamics across cluster life cycles, *Entrepreneurship & Regional Development*, 26 (5–6), 431–452.

Hervás-Oliver, J.L., Lleo, M. and Cervello, R. (2016). Entrepreneurship and new ventures' learning mechanisms in clusters: knowledge legacy from parents or agglomeration effects? The case of the Castellon cluster in Spain: 1727–2010, *Research Policy*, forthcoming.

Ichniowski, C., Shaw, K. and Prennushi, G. (1997). The effects of human resource practices on manufacturing performance: a study of steel finishing lines, *American Economic Review*, 87 (3), 291–313.

Jenkins, M. and Tallman, S. (2010). The shifting geography of competitive advantage: clusters, networks and firms, *Journal of Economic Geography*, 10 (4), 599–618.

Kogut, B. and Zander, U. (1992). Knowledge of the firm, combinative capabilities, and the replication of technology, *Organization Science*, 3 (3), 383–397.

Lawson, C. (1999). Towards a competence theory of the region, *Cambridge Journal of Economics*, 23, 151–166.

Lawson, C. and Lorenz, E. (1999). Collective learning, tacit knowledge and regional innovative capacity, *Regional Studies*, 33 (4), 303–317.

Maillat, D. (1989). *SMES, Innovation and Territorial Development*, Arco, Italy: European Summer Institute of the Regional Science Association.

March, J.G. (1991). Exploration and exploitation in organizational learning, *Organization Science*, Special Issue: Organizational Learning: Papers In Honour Of (And By) James G. March, 2 (1), 71–87.

Marshall, A. (1920). *Principles of Economics*, London: Macmillan.

Matusik, S.F. and Hill, C.W. (1998). The utilization of contingent work, knowledge creation, and competitive advantage, *Academy of Management Review*, 23 (4), 680–697.

Menzel, M. and Fornahl, D. (2010). Cluster life cycles – dimensions and rationales of cluster evolution, *Industrial and Corporate Change*, 19 (1), 205–238.

Meyer-Stamer, J., Maggi, C. and Seibel, S. (2004). Upgrading the tile industry of Italy, Spain, and Brazil: insights from cluster and value chain analysis, in Schmitz, H. (ed.) *Local Enterprises in the Global Economy*, Cheltenham: Edward Elgar, pp. 174–199.

Milgrom, P. and Roberts, J. (1995). Complementarities and fit strategy, structure, and organizational change in manufacturing. *Journal of Accounting and Economics*, 19 (2), 179–208.

Nelson, R. (1991). Why do firms differ and how does it matter? *Strategic Management Journal*, 12 (1), 61–74.

Nelson, R. and Winter, S. (1982). *An Evolutionary Theory of Economic Change*, Cambridge, MA: The Belknap Press of Harvard University Press.

Peteraf, M. (1993). The cornerstones of competitive advantage: a resource-based view, *Strategic Management Journal*, 14 (3), 179–191.

Pinch, S., Henry, N., Jenkins, M. and Tallman, S. (2003). From 'industrial districts' to 'knowledge clusters': a model of knowledge dissemination and competitive advantage in industrial agglomerations, *Journal of Economic Geography*, 3 (4), 373–388.

Porter, M.E. (1998). Cluster and the new economics of competition, *Harvard Business Review*, 76 (6), 77–90.

Pouder, R. and St John, C.H. (1996). Hot spots and blind spots: geographical clusters of firms and innovation, *The Academy of Management Review* 21 (4), 1192–1225.

Powell, W.W., Koput, K.W. and Smith-Doerr, L. (1996). Interorganizational collaboration and the locus of innovation: networks of learning in biotechnology, *Administrative Science Quarterly*, 41 (1), 116–145.

Rivkin, J.W. (2000). Imitation of complex strategies, *Management Science*, 46 (6), 824–844.

Russo, M. (2000). Innovation dynamics and industrial dynamics in a local production system. Changes in the agents space in tile decoration: from silk screen to laser engraved silicon cylinders. Working paper 295, Dipartimento Di Economia Politica, Universita Di Modena E Reggio Emilia. Modena.

Russo, M. (2004). The ceramic industrial district facing the challenge from China. Working paper for the Research Project, Distretti Industriali Come Sistemi Complessi.Universita Di Modena, Italy.

Saxenian, A. (1994). Regional networks: industrial adaptation in Silicon Valley and route 128, published online.

Simon, D.G. and Hitt, M.A. (2003). Managing resources: linking unique resources, management, and wealth creation in family firms, *Entrepreneurship Theory and Practice*, 27, 339–358.

Spender, J. (1994). Knowing, managing, and learning, *Management Learning*, 25 (3), 387–412.

Tallman, S. and Chacar, A.S. (2011). Knowledge accumulation and dissemination in MNEs: a practice-based framework, *Journal of Management Studies*, 48 (2), 278–304.

Tallman, S., Jenkins, H., Henry, J. and Pinch, S. (2004). Knowledge, clusters, and competitive advantage, *Academy of Management Review*, 29, 258–271.

Teece, D., Pisano, G. and Shuen, A. (1997). Dynamic capabilities and strategic management, *Strategic Management Journal*, 18, 509–533.

Tushman, M. and Anderson, P. (1986). Technological discontinuities and organizational environments, *Administrative Science Quarterly*, 31, 439–465.

Uzzi, B. (1997). Social structure and competition in interfirm networks: the paradox of embeddedness, *Administrative Science Quarterly*, 35–67.

15 Organizational configurations in footwear industrial districts
Fit, performance and localization

*Gloria Parra Requena, Maria Jose Ruiz Ortega,
Pedro Manuel García Villaverde and
Raquel Rubio Fernández*

15.1 Introduction

The economic literature has traditionally recognized advantages in the territorial agglomeration of firms (Marshall, 1890). From industrial district (ID) literature (Becattini, 1990), in the last decades several studies have shown companies belonging to an ID obtain greater levels of performance to those which, while belonging to the same industry, are located outside (Molina and Martínez, 2003; Ruiz-Ortega *et al.*, 2013; Wang *et al.*, 2014). Recently, other approaches, such as the cluster life cycle theory (Menzel and Fornahl, 2010) and the adaptive cycles perspective (Martin and Sunley, 2011), have contributed to understanding the cluster's evolution. These approaches have been of great interest in understanding the characteristics and the development of the clusters/districts. However, as different authors highlight (Belussi and Sedita, 2009; Hervás-Oliver and Albors-Garrigós, 2014), they have not addressed the heterogeneity of firms in IDs with respect to strategic behaviour, nor have they tried to explain what different roles companies adopt to interact and compete in the IDs, this being a crucial issue for a correct interpretation of the operation of the clusters. We consider that the configurational approach (Miller, 1996) provides an adequate explanation to this heterogeneity in the strategic behaviour of firms in the IDs and we propose to determine the organizational configurations (OCs) that are present in the IDs and the performance differences that there are between them.

We focus this study from the configurational approach because it allows us to interpret the heterogeneity of strategic behaviour of firms in terms of distinctive configurations of dimensions related to a context and a period of time (Meyer *et al.*, 1993). Thus, we expect that among companies belonging to an ID there will emerge a certain number of OCs in which relational and competitive factors are aligned (Short *et al.*, 2008). From this approach, the firms' performance arises from internal consistency between those factors and their consistency with the ID to which they belong (Bantel, 1998; García-Villaverde and Ruiz-Ortega, 2007). Despite the interest of the configurational approach to gain insight into how those companies belonging to IDs relate and compete, there are no studies that address empirically the existence and efficiency of OCs in the context of the IDs (Camisón and Molina, 1998).

In this study our main aim is to identify the OCs located in IDs and to explain their differences in performance according to the internal coherence and adaptation to the environment. Complementarily, we intend to explore the presence and the role of the OCs in different IDs according to their features.

The empirical study was carried out with a sample of 165 companies located in the IDs of the footwear industry in Spain. This industry is mature and traditional, and most of the companies are located in a number of industrial districts whose origins and evolutionary processes are different, which are specialized in certain product segments and markets, and maintain a business structure and different institutional support (Belso-Martínez and Molina-Morales, 2011). We differentiate the footwear companies located in the districts of Almansa, Arnedo, Illueca, Elche, Elda, Valverde and Villena. Companies located in the rest of the districts were included in another group, given its reduced presence in the sample.

This study contributes to connect the configurational approach with the ID literature, which has been scarcely addressed previously (Camison and Molina, 1998). It contributes to a better understanding about the competitive and relational heterogeneity in regional agglomerations.

In order to identify OCs we have developed a conglomerates analysis, by means of an inductive approach. Once several configurations were identified, we performed a comparison of their performance, detecting significant differences on the basis of competitive positioning and internal coherence. We finished the study by exploring the presence of configurations in each district, depending on their characteristics and their evolutionary pattern.

15.2   Theory

15.2.1   *Industrial districts: dynamism and competitive heterogeneity*

IDs are defined as local production systems consisting of a set of small and medium-sized enterprises integrated in a network of relationships, located in a geographical area and with a degree of specialization in one or more phases of the production process (Carbonara *et al.*, 2002). The ID's influence on the competitive ability of the firms from which it is comprised has been evidenced by various studies (Grando and Balvedere, 2006). They demonstrated the existence of positive externalities in the IDs that allow their companies to get excellent operating results without the resources of big companies. These advantages of location are based on economies of specialization, labour market economies and knowledge spillovers (Krugman, 1991). Bresci and Lissoni (2001: 1000) provide a critical posture about localized knowledge spillover based in three issues: (1) knowledge externalities are mediated by economic mechanisms; (2) knowledge spillovers are well-regulated knowledge flows between institutions and firms or among firms, which are managed with deliberate appropriation purposes; and (3) a large amount of knowledge flowing in this way has much more to do with enhancing the innovation appropriation strategies of focal companies rather than their innovation opportunities.

The literature on IDs has traditionally defended the homogeneity of their companies (Becattini, 1990). However, numerous empirical studies have demonstrated the heterogeneity of their behaviour and performance (Molina and Martínez, 2003; Ruiz-Ortega *et al.*, 2013). This diversity has increased in the last decades, since IDs face an increasingly more complex, dynamic and competitive environment, and not all the companies in the district adapt to this kind of environment in the same way, or take advantage similarly of the benefits of belonging to the ID.

Menzel and Fornahl (2010) analysed how the firms in and out of the cluster modify its strategic behaviour, develop their skills and generate relationships with organizations both internal and external to the cluster along its life cycle. Martin and Sunley (2011) define the cluster as a complex adaptive system, whose evolution is conditioned by environmental factors. Both approaches are linked to the current development that dominates IDs, which is determined by a changing environment that requires rapid adaptation, where opportunities are exploited and generate defence mechanisms against future threats and changes. These approaches include the change of the physiognomy of the IDs (Belussi and Sedita, 2012). However, they do not address the heterogeneity among the companies of the IDs that can be derived from those changes (Chiaversio *et al.*, 2010). We consider that in this context of IDs' evolution a growing heterogeneity of resources and capabilities, strategic behaviours and performance between firms belonging to the IDs will emerge (Hervás-Oliver and Albors-Garrigós, 2009; Molina-Morales and Martínez-Fernández, 2009).

15.2.2   *Organizational configurations in industrial districts*

The configurational approach of strategy allows us to analyse the set of distinctive dimensions that when related to a specific context gives as a result a certain strategic behaviour (Miller, 1996). In the firms we find the grouping of certain variables of strategy, structure and process which form configurations, whose coherence generates greater business performance. Therefore, in a large group of companies we can find a small number of configurations in which certain factors are aligned (Meyer *et al.*, 1993). From the configurational approach, the performance will depend on the congruence between a set of factors, both organizational and strategic, and certain contextual variables (Wiklund and Shepherd, 2005).

We conducted an inductive analysis. Thus, we expect to identify a taxonomy that defines the main organizational settings that interact in IDs. We highlight two key variables that affect the way they interact and compete in IDs – social capital and pioneer orientation (PO).

Social capital is 'the sum of the actual and potential resources embedded within, available through, and derived from the network of relationships possessed by an individual or social unit' (Nahapiet and Ghoshal, 1998: 243). We focus on the cognitive dimension of social capital, poorly analysed in the literature, whose interaction with the strategy can significantly affect the results of the companies in the IDs (Krause *et al.*, 2007). Cognitive proximity (CP) can be associated with the similarity in the way that actors perceive, interpret, understand and evaluate the world (Wuyts *et al.*, 2005). Thus, firms in IDs can immerse themselves in a given local culture (Dei Ottati, 1994) and share a set of values, ideas and a homogeneous language (Becattini, 1990), developing codes, values and common practices. This common understanding improves firms' interpretation of knowledge.

PO is defined as the proactive orientation of an organization to be the first entrant, with a new product or a new market so far not exploited by the competition (Covin *et al.*, 2000). From developing a PO firms can obtain important first-mover advantages, although certain disadvantages can also be generated (Garret *et al.*, 2009; Zachary *et al.*, 2015). The PO performance is affected by the conditions of the environment – specifically in IDs there is a set of relationships and mechanisms that can influence the effectiveness of this orientation. The physical proximity to consumers in IDs provides firms with relevant information about preferences and habits of consumption, detecting changes and the emergence of new needs. This information, which can be easily interpreted when there is CP, increases the expectations of firms located in the IDs to obtain the advantages of early entry into the market against companies external to the district (Robinson and Min, 2002).

Despite the importance and interactions among the CP and the PO, there are very few studies that analyse both variables simultaneously (García-Villaverde *et al.*, 2010), especially in the context of the IDs (Camisón and Molina, 1998). We highlight the relevance of these factors in the field of IDs, where the geographical proximity and cooperation–competition relationships have implications in the development of different OCs and their performance. To deepen the analysis of the consistency of the OCs we include three strategic dimensions – innovation differentiation, marketing differentiation and low costs – and three organizational dimensions – managerial, marketing and technological capabilities. Using this approach, we try to identify which are the main OCs that coexist in IDs, which are those that get better performance, and their presence in the different IDs according to their evolution and characteristics.

15.3 Methods

To carry out the empirical study we utilize a population of 1,086 companies located in the IDs of the footwear industry in Spain. This sector is characterized by its tradition, maturity, highly competitive environment and export vocation. These features justify the configurational approach of our study in the area of the IDs, where both CP, whose development requires an extended period of time, and orientation pioneer, linked with the constant search for new products and markets, are especially important. After sending out the questionnaire we obtained a sample of 165 companies, which represents a response rate of 15.19 per cent, obtaining a sampling error of 6.99 for a confidence level of 95 per cent and the most unfavourable situation of p=q=0, 5. To check the representativeness of the sample, we performed an ANOVA analysis with size and age, not finding significant differences between the sample and the population. In addition, we analysed the 'non-response bias' and we did not obtain significant difference between the analysed variables.

15.3.1   Variables and measurement instruments

Cognitive proximity. Shared goals and shared culture are two main aspects of cognitive proximity. To measure the shared goals construct we used an adapted scale of six items validated in studies of Tsai and Ghoshal (1998) and Yli-Renko *et al.* (2001), linked to share ambition, vision, collective goals, objectives, strategy and needs with firm contacts. Shared culture is the set of institutionalized norms and rules that guides an appropriate behaviour on the network. In order to measure this variable we used a two-item scale based on Simonin (1999) linked to business practices – the business practices and operational mechanisms of your contacts are very similar to yours – and management style – the corporate culture and management style of your contacts are very similar to yours.

Pioneer orientation. This variable has been measured as a continuum that extends from the pioneer to the late follower (Shepherd and Shanley, 1998) by means of an adapted three-item scale (Zahra, 1996) – this company is usually among the first to introduce new products to the market, this company is this industry's leader in developing innovative ideas and is well known for introducing breakthrough products and ideas. With this measurement, we can obtain a variable that reflects the propensity of the company towards the development of a pioneering orientation. This scale has allowed us to use a variable that reflects the greater or lower tendency to be first mover to introduce breakthrough products and ideas into a new product-market arena. This scale reflects the firm's level of leadership in the product market, market timing and distinctiveness. We have used a seven point Likert scale which, though it supports a bias, derived from a subjective valuation of entry timing in the market.

Firm capabilities. To explore these variables we have measured three core competencies of the company – managerial, marketing and technological – measured through scales adapted from Spanos and Lioukas (2001) in terms of a firm's strength relative to competition. Managerial capabilities are linked to organizational and management process. The construct includes seven items linked to firm climate, efficiency in the organizational structure, mechanisms of efficient coordination, knowledge and skills of employees, managerial competence, strategic planning and the ability to attract creative employees. Marketing capabilities refer to the output-based competences. This scale comprises four items linked to the advantages in relationships with clients, the customer 'installed base', control and access to distribution channels and market knowledge. Technological capabilities refer to the necessary technical and technological abilities needed to transform inputs into products. The construct includes three items linked to technological capabilities and equipment, the economies of scale and technical experience and the efficient and effective manufacturing department.

Competitive strategies. The analysis of business strategies has been developed by means of the Spanos and Lioukas (2001) scales, relating to innovation differentiation – four items – marketing differentiation – four items – and cost leadership – three items. This seven-point Likert scale gathers information about the extent of use of specific tactics through which the firm develops specific competitive strategies that provide the fundamental basis for achieving competitive advantages (Porter, 1980). In this study we included this classification because of its suitability for gathering the selected strategic typology, which has been widely tested.

Size and age. We have also included the variables size, in terms of number of employees, and age, measured as the number of years since the firm's creation.

General performance. According to Gupta and Govindarajan (1984), the measures of a firm's performance are established by a subjective index, obtained by the valuation of the company manager of the degree of importance and satisfaction with five items, using a seven-point Likert-type scale. These five items, along with the item that measures the performance in a broad sense, are profitability over investment, net margin of benefits, market share, growth of sales and general performance. We have calculated the correlations between the measures of performance included in the study and objective measures obtained from the SABI database, growth of sales and returns over investment. We used a sub-sample of eighty-five firms and found that the correlations were positive and significant. Therefore, we have verified the reliability of our measures of performance.

15.3.2 Techniques

To analyse the OCs we performed a cluster analysis using the analytical software Statistical Package for the Social Sciences (SPSS). The different units of analysis are classified on the basis of their peculiarities, detecting and describing subgroups of homogeneous variables based on the values observed in a seemingly heterogeneous group. Subsequently, we compared the means of the variables at a general level through the Fisher's F test and between pairs of groups using the Scheffé test for factors that define configurations, age, size and performance.

15.4 Results

15.4.1 Evolution and characteristics of the districts

The sectorial structure of the Spanish footwear industry has a long tradition, boasting companies exceeding 100 years in age. The origin of

IDs that are part of our study date mostly from the nineteenth century, since with industrialization the proliferation of industrial investments began, although we also found locations where footwear is an ancient craft. These districts have the support of various institutions that provide business competitiveness. Regardless of the evolutionary particularities of each district, the footwear sector has figured in three major phases of development evolution and characteristics of the IDs (Tortajada *et al.*, 2005). The first, from the beginning until the mid-1970s, is characterized by intense increase in growth and exports generating the creation of companies and the mechanization of the manufacturing industry. Later, in the mid-1990s, periodic crises in the industry were triggered by reductions in international demand and rising prices of raw materials. This process in many cases generates reduction of the size of the companies in the sector and the outsourcing of part of the production, which promotes the development of the auxiliary industry. Since the end of the 1990s the sector has been restructured according to context, increasing the outsourcing of manufacturing, differentiating their products, and including factors such as quality and marketing. Finally, in the last few years the number of firms has decreased, especially those of smaller size. However, in this context there has been a significant increase in exports. As we can see, we find a series of common features in the evolution of the footwear industry in Spain. Nevertheless, focusing on the main IDs of footwear, we found certain specificities in the development and the current situation of each one, which we briefly highlight in Table 15.1. As Besussi and Sedita (2009) point out, IDs can react differently to the same external shocks and evolve differently according to their learning capabilities.

15.4.2   *Analysis of the measurement model*

In order to ensure that we obtained a proper measurement model we evaluated composite items' reliability and convergent and discriminant validity. First, we evaluated the reliability of the construct through the statistical alpha proposed by Cronbach (1951). All the constructs used were greater than 0.8, so we can presume that the reliability was high – cognitive proximity 0,898; pioneer orientation 0,954; management capabilities 0,940; marketing capabilities 0,882; technological capabilities 0,827; innovation differentiation 0,904; marketing differentiation 0,904; cost leadership 0,846; general performance 0,931. The convergent validity was evaluated through the average variance extracted (AVE). All the constructs exceeded the recommended value of 0.5 (Fornell and Larcker, 1981). Finally, for the analysis of discriminant validity we analysed correlations between variables, making sure that all of them were less than the value of the square root of the AVE. In addition, we checked that there were no multicollinearity problems in the model, checking the variance inflation factor was not greater than ten.

Table 15.1 Characteristics and evolution of the industrial districts

Almansa district: Its origin lies between the eighteenth and nineteenth centuries. In the district we find a high specialization in men's medium-range footwear and a strong export vocation. With the advent of mechanization in the production process, both the number of companies and their size increased. Subsequently, the restructuring of this district encouraged the emergence of an important auxiliary industry. Predominantly small and medium-sized enterprises, although there are various larger companies with brands of high reputation in the markets that have high marketing, technical and managerial capacities.

Arnedo district: Originating in the nineteenth century, this district's companies manufacture and market various types of footwear, although there is a stress on the safety footwear segment. The district is aimed at medium–high-range products and has an intermediate level of export. Its development was slow due to its lack of tradition. However, the relevance of this district in the Spanish footwear sector has been consolidated in recent decades. This district arose in companies that have oriented their skills and strategies to the development of new production lines focused on children's shoes and sports footwear for women.

Elche district: Here we find the origins of this industry in the nineteenth century, with the production of espadrilles. The production of this district is generalist, since it focuses on different types of footwear and is mainly aimed at the segment's average consumption. In this district there are companies with prestigious brands with different strategies and capabilities aimed at marketing, along with small businesses with own or outsourced marketing. Elche is leading the sector in the regions of the Vinalopó district. Its evolution is characterized by passing from an auxiliary industry, which still maintains a high weight, becoming an industry of footwear components capable of adapting to changes and making efforts in improving their capabilities and strategies oriented to innovation, quality and internationalization.

Elda district: Its origin is also around the nineteenth century. It is characterized by its specialization in manufacturing and distribution of upper–middle-range footwear for women and a strong export orientation. At the beginning of the century the incorporation of new machinery was significant and subsequently a growth of the auxiliary industry with leather factories occurred. The footwear district of Elda is the second in number of companies, after the Elche district. In recent years many of the companies in the district have reorientated their strategy to adapt to the new context, focusing more on product differentiation based on quality and marketing.

Villena district: The district has a later origin – at the beginning of the twentieth century – based on handicraft and has incorporated the process of industrialization at a more leisurely pace than the rest of the districts due to the strong presence of agricultural activity. This district specializes in high-quality shoes for men and children. The growth of the Elda district favoured the emergence of an auxiliary industry in Villena. In the final decade of the last century, with its restructuring process, new lines of production such as leather footwear were included, with a speciality in the infant range shifting to the textile industry in the area. In recent years companies and institutions have influenced the image of quality to improve their positioning, maintaining its strong export vocation.

Valverde district: The footwear industry emerged in this district during the nineteenth century, incorporating an artisanal activity that still maintains an important weight in the district. In this district general production prevails, although we found several companies that specialize in riding and country footwear, for a medium–high market segment. The weight of the shoe industry is lower than that of the mean, furniture and mining industries. There has been a significant drop in sales and a decline in exports since the beginning of the crisis in the district.

(*continued*)

Table 15.1 Characteristics and evolution of the industrial districts (*continued*)

Illueca district: The origin of the footwear industry in Illueca is related to the presence of tanneries since the seventeenth century, which were losing importance, giving way to the artisanal production of quality footwear. With the restructuring process various companies have encouraged the outsourcing of components and finished products, managing the distribution from the district. However, the companies have kept the manufacturing tradition based on the technical expertise coupled with an effort to reduce costs. In the last decade the ID has suffered a major fall, which has been evident in a reduction greater than one-third of the companies and more than half of the jobs linked to the footwear industry.

15.4.3   Determination of configurations

Once the variables had been typified, grouping of sample elements was conducted through cluster analysis, determining the OCs from the variables PO, CP, capabilities and strategies. The average values of the variables used to generate the conglomerates and the F test and Scheffé test results are shown in Table 15.2. The results obtained allow us to establish the following taxonomy of OCs:

Configuration 1: Pioneers with cognitive distance. This group of twenty-two companies presented the highest values for PO and negative levels of CP. These companies, which are the largest, tend to be the first to enter new markets with new products, paying little attention to the development of a culture and goals shared with contacts to access relevant information, making it difficult to obtain potential advantages of first entrant. Their capabilities are not adequate to compensate for this cognitive distance with their contacts and their strategic positioning is ambiguous, since it is not geared to achieve competitive advantages in costs or differentiation.

Configuration 2: Early followers with cognitive proximity. These forty-one companies, which also have a medium size greater than the mean of the sample, present a high PO, although less than the previous conglomerate, and have the greatest CP of all clusters. These companies are characterized by being early followers very close cognitively to their network of contacts. This homogeneity in aims, values and culture with contacts gives them access to valuable and innovative knowledge that is essential to attack the position of temporary leadership of the pioneer. In addition, these companies have greater managerial, marketing and technical capabilities linked to the development of a utility strategy (De Castro and Chrisman, 1995), which allows them to consolidate a position of leadership in the markets.

Configuration 3: Intermediate followers with high cognitive distance. These thirty-eight companies have the highest mean age, showing intermediate levels in the PO and a strong cognitive distance. They are companies with fewer resources derived from the understanding and the meaning that is shared with

Table 15.2 Cluster centres

Variables	Configurations					F	p	Differences between groups*
	C1 n = 22	C2 n = 41	C3 n = 38	C4 n = 40	C5 n = 25			
Pioneer orientation	**0,88**	**0,62**	**0,24**	**−0,67**	**−1,06**	**38,49**	**0,000**	**C1>C3,C4,C5** **C2,C3>C4,C5**
Cognitive proximity	**−0,35**	**0,78**	**−0,85**	**0,38**	**−0,32**	**25,03**	**0,000**	**C2>C5,C1,C3** **C4>C5,C1,C3**
Managerial capabilities	−0,22	0,94	0,20	−0,19	−1,36	44,53	0,000	C2>C3,C4,C1,C5 C3, C4, C1>C5
Marketing capabilities	−0,11	0,88	0,35	−0,37	−1,29	41,11	0,000	C2>C3,C1,C4,C5 C3>C4,C5 C1, C4>C5
Technical capabilities	−0,74	0,96	0,37	−0,05	−1,40	67,99	0,000	C2>C3,C4,C1,C5 C3>C4,C1,C5 C4>C1,C5 C1>C5
Innovation differentiation strategy	−0,06	0,86	0,40	−0,29	−1,43	50,61	0,000	C2>C3,C1,C4,C5 C3>C4,C5 C1, C4>C5
Marketing differentiation strategy	−0,27	0,97	0,36	−0,45	−1,16	44,46	0,000	C2>C3,C1,C4,C5 C3>C1,C4,C5 C1, C4>C5
Low-cost strategy	−0,70	0,97	0,34	−0,08	−1,35	59,89	0,000	C2>C3,C4,C1,C5 C3>C4,C1,C5 C4>C1,C5 C1>C5
Size	51,50	39,58	25,24	23,82	12,63	1,69	0,155	
Age	19,32	19,17	23,65	14,13	21,79	2,01	0,096	
Performance	−0,16	0,67	−0,03	−0,08	−0,76	10,22	0,000	C2>C3,C4,C1,C5 C3,C4>C5

Note: * $p < 0.1$.

their contacts, hindering their access to valuable knowledge. However, they present higher levels in their capabilities and develop balanced efforts to gain advantage in innovation, marketing and low costs. We consider that these companies can act as competitive early followers, taking advantage of the complementary nature of their capabilities and strategic positioning, and limiting the negative impact of the cognitive distance with their contacts.

Configuration 4: Late followers with cognitive proximity. This group consists of forty companies that have the lowest average age and tend to enter late into the markets using the CP to their contacts. This late-follower orientation may be due to the weakness of capabilities, especially managerial and marketing, and fragile strategic positioning. These companies can maintain only an acceptable level of efficiency as late followers, orienting their technical capabilities to limit their costs and taking advantage of the values and goals that are shared with their network of contacts.

Configuration 5: Late followers with cognitive distance. This group, which contains the twenty-five companies with smaller mean size, shows very late entry into the market and a cognitive distance with their contacts. This lack of norms and values shared with their network of contacts is aggravated by the weakness of their capabilities and strategic behaviour, making early market entry and a sustainable competitive position difficult.

In Figure 15.1 we show the position of each conglomerate based on the scores obtained at PO and CP.

Once we had identified and explained the taxonomy of companies, we explored differences in business performance by analysing the variations between conglomerates. We detected that the most competitive conglomerate would be number two since its companies achieve significantly higher levels of performance than the remaining four conglomerates. These results allow us to highlight the importance of the consistency between PO and CP, which complemented by the capabilities and strategies lead the companies to superior levels of performance.

15.4.4   Approximation to the distribution of configurations in each industrial district

When we analyse the percentage distribution of the clusters in each ID – Table 15.3 – we see that the majority of the OCs have a certain presence in all the IDs. We appreciate, therefore, that companies carrying out complementary competitive roles usually reside in the ID. However, when we explore the weight of the OC in each ID we observe that there are relevant differences that can be attributed to the development and characteristics of IDs.

First, the important presence of the most successful OC – early followers with cognitive proximity – is highlighted in the following ID: Almansa, Villena, Elche and Elda – 29.63 per cent, 28.57 per cent, 27.27 per cent and 20.59 per cent, respectively. These IDs are close geographically and communicate

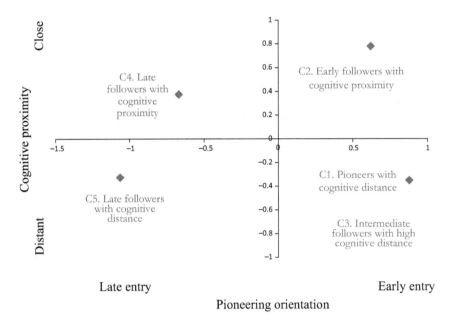

Figure 15.1 Organizational configurations.

Table 15.3 Distribution of configurations in each industrial district

	C1	C2	C3	C4	C5	Total
Almansa	0,00%	28,57%	28,57%	28,57%	14,29%	28
Arnedo	14,29%	14,29%	35,71%	14,29%	21,43%	14
Elche	11,11%	29,63%	18,52%	25,93%	14,81%	54
Elda	14,71%	20,59%	23,53%	29,41%	11,76%	34
Villena	36,36%	27,27%	18,18%	9,09%	9,09%	11
Valverde	0,00%	33,33%	16,67%	0,00%	50,00%	6
Illueca	12,50%	12,50%	12,50%	50,00%	12,50%	8
Others	30,00%	30,00%	30,00%	0,00%	10,00%	10

well with each other, which facilitates the exchange of resources and information. Therefore, these companies reinforce their skills and strategies with the cognitive and geographical proximity to take advantage of the opportunities generated by the pioneering companies. In the case of the IDs of Almansa and Elda, the specialization in a certain type of footwear – men and women, respectively – emphasizes CP with their contacts in the ID, which is also made clear by the presence of the group *late followers with cognitive proximity* – 28.57 per cent and 29.41 per cent. These companies are compensating their strategic weaknesses by means of cooperation with agents with shared values and goals. We also highlight the strong presence of the OC *pioneers with cognitive distance* in the ID of Villena – 36.36 per cent. In this case, the late origin of the ID and the relative youth and specialization of the firms encourage many of them to take the opportunity and the risk of launching new products in new markets. However, the lack of a network of contacts with culture and similar standards in the ID puts these companies at an intermediate level of performance. In the case of the ID of Arnedo we highlight the strong presence of the OC of *intermediate followers with cognitive distance* – 35.71 per cent. We believe that the development of the footwear industry by extension and displacement of other industries, the geographical remoteness of other footwear IDs and the generation of different lines of footwear have limited the development of a culture and common values. In this context, companies decide to imitate despite having solid strategic positioning. In the ID of Illueca it highlights the presence of *late followers with cognitive proximity* – 50 per cent. The enduring artisan tradition of footwear manufacturing and the geographic distance from major footwear IDs have led businesses to develop an imitator behaviour based on low costs, taking advantage of their technical capabilities. Finally, in the ID of Valverde we found a dichotomy in the presence of OCs. Thus, we can find *late followers with cognitive distance* – 50 per cent – which are the companies that get worse results, with *early followers with cognitive proximity* – 33.33 per cent, which is the most successful OC. In a geographical context far away from the main business concentrations of footwear companies, we find some undifferentiated companies that survive along with competitive innovative companies with high capabilities that share goals and culture.

15.5   Discussion and conclusions

With this study we have developed a configurational approach to the study of the strategic and relational heterogeneity in the context of the IDs. First, we have identified, from an inductive approach, a taxonomy of five OCs coexisting in the IDs by combining relations of cooperation and competition. In order to define the OCs, we start from two variables relevant to the field of IDs, such as pioneer orientation and cognitive proximity. Complementarily, we incorporate three types of capabilities – managerial, marketing and technical – and three competitive strategies – innovation differentiation, marketing differentiation and low costs – which have allowed us to analyse the internal coherence of the OCs.

We have also observed that there are significant differences in the OC's performance, which are justified by their internal coherence and their suitability to compete in the context of the IDs of the footwear industry. We highlight the role of the *early followers with cognitive proximity*, which is the most successful OC. The high levels of performance are explained by the high competitive potential, based on CP to agents that relates to the IDs, which give them access to relevant knowledge and enhance the strength of their skills and their hybrid strategies to follow and overcome the pioneer firms. This configuration maintains certain similarities with the technology gatekeepers identified by Hervás-Oliver and Albors-Garrigós (2014). Opposite to this successful OC, we put the *late followers with cognitive distance*, which is the OC that obtained the lowest levels of performance. In this case, we highlight the competitive weakness of these companies that adopt an imitator position because they cannot benefit from it due to the lack of interaction and values shared with agents of the ID, skills shortages and the lack of definition of their competitive strategies. The three remaining OCs have intermediate levels of performance, trying to compensate for their weaknesses with certain strengths. Therefore, the *pioneers with cognitive distance* face with a pioneer entry with innovative products in new markets the weakness of their relations with agents of the ID, capabilities and strategic position. By contrast, the late followers with CP adopt a clear role of imitators, compensating for their weakness to differentiate with their technical strengths and values shared with agents of the ID. Finally, the *intermediate followers with high cognitive distance*, although they do not share goals or standards with their contacts, can maintain competitive advantages as early followers to take advantage of their capabilities and their strategies.

This study has allowed us to explore the role of the OCs in the ID based on its evolution and characteristics. On the one hand, we have observed that in all the IDs we can find the great majority of the detected OCs, playing competitive complementary roles. On the other hand, the exploration of the distribution of the OCs in each ID allows us to detect a heterogeneous presence of the OCs which can be justified by aspects such as the origin and evolution of the IDs, the proximity and geographic connection between the IDs, the productive specialization or the competitive pressure.

We agree with Wang *et al.* (2014) on the need to overcome the approaches of density dependence which highlights that the members of a population are equivalent since each member assumes competition for the same scarce resources and with similar competitive actions (Baum and Amburgey, 2002). Indeed, we consider that geographical location determines the behaviour of the companies in the same industry (Wang *et al.*, 2014) overcoming the vision of the industry as homogenous (Klepper and Thompson, 2006). However, this study contributes to reinforce the competitive heterogeneity of the companies of an industry from several points of view. First, we observe that in an industry there are distinct OCs that compete and relate differently. Second, we observe that the internal consistency of configurations and the adaptation to the conditions of the environment generated mixed results. Third, we found that in the majority of IDs we can identify the main configurations, since they play different and complementary roles. However, we also appreciate heterogeneity in the presence of different OC in ID with different evolution and features.

With this study we contribute to connect the configurational approach (Miller, 1996) with the relevant work on ID (Becattini, 1990), which has been scarcely addressed in the literature (Camison and Molina, 1998). We believe that the combination of these theoretical approaches is adequate to get a better understanding about the evolution of competitive and relational heterogeneity in regional agglomerations.

We acknowledge several limitations in this study, some of which point to various future research opportunities. First, the study has an exploratory character. The inductive approximation to identify OCs makes it difficult to establish a typology with a strong theoretical support. However, we consider that the relevance of the chosen factors – PO and CP – has allowed us to extract a suitable taxonomy for approaching the competition and cooperation in the IDs. The incorporation of competitive strategies and capabilities in the definition of the OCs contributes to a better understanding about its internal coherence. Another limitation of the study is the small number of firms in some IDs. While the exploratory nature of the study does not allow us to generalize our conclusions, the results suggest that there is a competitive heterogeneity on the basis of the development of each district. This allows us to reflect and to suggest new investigations that deepen in competitive and cooperative roles played by companies in the IDs and how the evolution of each district modifies the presence of the OCs, its way of coopetition and its performance. Finally, the choice of a mature and traditional sector such as footwear limits the extension of the obtained results to other emerging or growing sectors. However, we consider that this sector is suitable for the study of the firms located in the IDs, since these are configured using the relationship of competition and cooperation which will strengthen over time. In any case, we consider it necessary to delve into competitive heterogeneity and evolution of clusters in emerging and growing industries from a configurational approach.

References

Bantel, K. (1998). Technology-based, 'adolescent' firm configurations: strategy indentification, context, and performance, *Journal of Business Venturing*, 13: 205–230.

Baum, J.A.C. and Amburgey, T.L. (2002). Organizational ecology, in Baum J.A.C. (ed.) *The Blackwell Companion to Organizations*, Blackwell Publishers, Malden, MA, 304–326.

Becattini, G. (1990). The marshallian industrial district as a socio-economic notion, in Pyke, F., Becattini, G., Sengenberger, W. and Loweman, G. (eds) *Industrial Districts and Inter-firm Co-operation in Italy*, International Institute for Labour Studies, Geneva, pp. 187–219.

Belso-Martínez, J.A. and Molina-Morales, F.X. (2011). The drivers of the open district development: a social capital approach, *Regional Science Policy & Practice*, 3 (2): 40–71.

Belussi, F. and Sedita, S.R. (2009). Life cycle vs. multiple path dependency in industrial districts, *European Planning Studies*, 17 (4): 505–528.

Belussi, F. and Sedita, S.R. (2012). Industrial districts as open learning systems: combining emergent and deliberate knowledge structures, *Regional Studies*, 46 (2): 165–184.

Bresci, S. and Lissoni, F. (2001). Knowledge spillovers and local innovation systems: a critical survey, *Industrial and Corporate Change*, 10 (4): 975–1005.

Cainelli, G. and De Liso, N. (2005). Innovation in industrial districts: evidence from Italy, *Industry and Innovation*, 12 (3): 383–398.

Camisón, C. and Molina, F.X. (1998). Configuraciones organizativas y desempeño: un análisis comparativo de diversos enfoques teóricos basados en una aplicación a las concentraciones de PYMES con base territorial, *Cuadernos de Economía y Dirección de la Empresa*, 2: 231–251.

Carbonara, N.; Giannoccaro, I. and Pontrandolfo, P. (2002). Suppy chains within industrial districts: a theoretical framework, *International Journal Production Economics*, 76: 159–176.

Chiarvesio, M., Di Maria, E. and Micelli, S. (2010). Global value chains and open networks: the case of Italian industrial districts, *European Planning Studies*, 18 (3): 333–350.

Covin, J.G.; Slevin, D.P. and Heeley, M.B. (2000). Pioneers and followers: competitive tactics, environment, and firm growth, *Journal of Business Venturing*, 15: 175–210.

Cronbach, L.J. (1951). Coefficient Alpha and the internal structure of test, *Psychometrika*, 31: 93–96.

De Castro, J.O. and Chrisman, J.J. (1995). Order of market entry, competitive strategy, and financial performance,*Journal of Business Research*, 33 (2): 165–177.

Dei Ottati, G. (1994). Cooperation and competition in the industrial district as an organization model, *European Planning Studies*, 2 (4): 35–53.

Fornell, C. and Larcker, D.F. (1981). Evaluating structural equation models with unobservable variables and measurement error, *Journal of Marketing Research*, 18: 39–50.

García-Villaverde, P.M., Parra-Requena, G. and Ruiz-Ortega, M.J. (2010). Capital social y comportamiento pionero: el papel mediador de las capacidades tecnológicas y de marketing, *Cuadernos de Economía y Dirección de la Empresa*, 45: 9–42.

García-Villaverde, P.M. and Ruiz-Ortega, M.J. (2007). Configuraciones organizativas en sectores dinámicos y hostiles: adecuación al contexto sectorial, coherencia interna y resultados, *Cuadernos de Economía y Dirección de la Empresa*, 32: 111–148.

Garrett, R.P., Covin, J. G., and Slevin, D.P. (2009). Market responsiveness, top management risk taking, and the role of strategic learning as determinants of market pioneering, *Journal of Business Research*, 62 (8): 782–788.

Grando, A. and Belvedere, V. (2006). District's manufacturing performances: A comparison among large, small-to-medium-sized and district enterprises, *International Journal of Production Economics*, 104 (1): 85–99.

Gupta, A.K. and Govindarajan, V. (1984). Business unit strategy, managerial characteristics, and business unit effectiveness at strategy implementation, *Academy of Management Journal*, 27 (1): 25–41.

Hervás-Oliver, J.L. and Albors-Garrigós, J. (2009). The role of the firm's internal and relational capabilities in Clusters: When distance and embeddedness are not enough, *Journal of Economic Geography*, 9 (2): 63–83.

Hervás-Oliver, J.L. and Albors-Garrigós, J. (2014). Are technology gatekeepers renewing clusters? Understanding gatekeepers and their dynamics across cluster life cycles. *Entrepreneurship and Regional Development*, 26 (5–6): 431–452.

Holling, C.S. and Gunderson, L.H. (2002). Resilience and adaptive cycles, in Gunderson, L.H and Holling, C.S. (eds) *Panarchy: Understanding transformations in human and natural systems*, Island Press, Washington, pp. 5–62.

Klepper S. and Thompson P. (2006). Submarkets and the evolution of market structure, *Rand Journal of Economics*, 37 (4): 861–886.

Krause, D.R., Handfield, R.B. and Tyler, B.B. (2007). The relationships between supplier development, commitment, social capital accumulation and performance improvement, *Journal of Operations Management*, 25: 528–545.

Krugman, P. (1991). *Geography and Trade*, MIT Press, Cambridge, MA.

Marshall, A. (1890). *Principles of Economics*, Macmillan, London.

Martin, R. and Sunley, P. (2011). Conceptualizing cluster evolution: beyond the life cycle model? *Regional Studies*, 45 (10): 129–131.

Menzel, M., and Fornahl, D. (2010). Cluster life cycles – dimensions and rationales of cluster evolution, *Industrial and Corporate Change*, 19 (1): 205–238.

Meyer, A.D., Tsui, A.S. and Hinings, C.R. (1993). Guest co-editors' introduction: configurational approaches to organizational analysis, *Academy of Management Journal*, 36: 1175–1195.

Miller, D. (1996). Configurations revisited, *Strategic Management Journal*, 17: 505–512.

Molina-Morales, F.X. and Martínez-Fernández, M.T. (2003). The impact of industrial district affiliation on firm value creation, *European Planning Studies*, 11 (2): 155–170.

Molina-Morales, F.X. and Martinez-Fernández, M.T. (2009). Too much love in the neighborhood can hurt: how an excess of intensity and trust in relationships may produce negative effects on firms, *Strategic Management Journal*, 30: 1013–1023.

Nahapiet, J. and Ghoshal, S. (1998). Social capital, intellectual capital, and the organizational advantage, *Academy of Management Review*, 23 (2): 242–266.

Porter, M. (1980): *Competitive Strategy: Techniques for analysing industries and competitors*, Free Press, New York.

Robinson, W.T. and Min, S. (2002). Is the first to market the first to fail? Empirical evidence for industrial goods businesses, *Journal of Marketing Research*, 39: 120–128.

Ruiz-Ortega, M.J., Parra-Requena, G. and García-Villaverde, P.M. (2013). Do territorial agglomerations still provide competitive advantages? A study of social capital, innovation and knowledge, *International Regional Science Review*, published online.

Shepherd, D.A. and Shanley, M. (1998). *New Venture Strategy. Timing, environment uncertainty, and performance*, SAGE Publications, Thousand Oaks, CA.

Short, J.C., Payne, G.T. and Ketchen, D.J. (2008). Research on organizational configurations: past accomplishments and future challenges, *Journal of Management*, 34: 1053–1079.

Simonin B.L. (1999). Ambiguity and the process of knowledge transfer in strategic alliances, *Strategic Management Journal*, 20: 595–623.

Spanos, Y.E. and Lioukas, S. (2001). An examination into the causal logic of rent generation: contrasting Porter's competitive strategy framework and the resource based perspective, *Strategic Management Journal*, 22: 907–934.

Tellis, G.J. and Golder, P.N. (1996). First to market, first to fail? The real causes of enduring market leadership, *Sloan Management Review*, 37 (2): 65–75.

Tortajada E.E., Fernández, L. and Ybarra, P.J. (2005). Evolución de la industria española del calzado: factores relevantes en las últimas décadas, *Economía Industrial*, 355: 211–227.

Tsai, W. and Ghoshal, S. (1998). Social capital, and value creation: the role of intrafirm networks, *Academy of Management Journal*, 41 (4): 464–478.

Wang, L., Madhok, A. and Xiao Li, S. (2014). Agglomeration and clustering over the industry life cycle: Toward a dynamic model of geographic concentration, *Strategic Management Journal*, 35 (7): 995–1012

Wiklund, J. and Shepherd, D. (2005). Entrepreneurial orientation and small business performance: a configurational approach, *Journal of Business Venturing*, 20: 71–91.

Wuyts, S., Colomb, M.G., Dutta, S. and Nooteboom, B. (2005). Empirical tests of optimal cognitive distance, *Journal of Economic Behavior & Organization*, 58: 277–302.

Yli-Renko, H., Autio, E. and Sapienza, H. (2001). Social capital, knowledge acquisition, and knowledge explotation in young technology-based firm, *Strategic Management Journal*, 22 (6–7): 587–613.

Zachary, M.A., Gianiodis, P.T., Payne, G.T. and Markman, G.D. (2015). Entry timing enduring lessons and future directions, *Journal of Management*, 41 (5): 1388–1415.

Zahra, S.A. (1996). Technology strategy and financial performance: examining the moderating role of the firm's competitive environment, *Journal of Business Venturing*, 11: 189–219.

Zahra, S.A., Nielson, A.P. and Bogner, W.C. (1999). Corporate entrepreneurship, knowledge and competence development, *Entrepreneurship: Theory and Practice*, 23 (3): 169–189.

16 Experiences of cluster evolution in the Brazilian ceramic tile industry

The accumulation of capabilities among local producers in a developing country

Renato Garcia and Gabriela Scur

16.1 Introduction

Recent analyses of the dynamics of industrial clusters are driving increasing attention to the main factors that affect the cluster's evolution. Several studies have presented strong empirical evidence on how industrial clusters emerge and grow over time (Audretsch and Feldman, 1996; Belussi and Sedita, 2009; Elola *et al.*, 2012), what makes them decline (Østergaard and Park, 2015) as well as renew (Vale and Caldeira, 2007; Hervás-Oliver and Albors-Garrigós, 2014). In general, there is strong recognition that the existence and the structure of industrial clusters can be understood only when analysing their evolution over time (Audretsch and Feldman, 1996; Lombardi, 2003; Menzel and Fornahl, 2009; Boschma and Fornahl, 2011; Ter Wal and Boschma, 2011).

Thus, it is possible to identify the main characteristics of the cluster evolution over time and the main driving forces behind their trajectories. In this context, the cluster life cycle model was presented in order to analyse its main features, in which conditions firms enter and exit the local system, as well as how the capabilities of the firms are developed (and sometimes converge). It also aims to analyse how internal and external inter-organizational linkages are established and how they disappear along the cluster life cycle (Menzel and Fornahl, 2009; Martin and Sunley, 2011).

The description and the main characteristics of the different stages of the cluster life cycle vary slightly according to each author and approach. However, all of them agree that there are distinct 'emergence', 'growth', 'maturity' and 'decline' phases, and that there are many ways to renew the cluster evolution (Hervás-Oliver and Albors-Garrigós, 2014).

In this way, recent analysis of industrial clusters has shown that the evolution of industrial clusters is tied into a path-dependence process (Martin and Sunley, 2006), in which the capabilities of local firms can evolve over time and affect the cluster evolution. In general, the evolution of industrial clusters is related to the evolution of the internal capabilities of local firms and the way they accumulate new knowledge (Hervás-Oliver and Albors-Garrigós, 2014).

The emergence and growth of industrial clusters is related to the creation and accumulation of new capabilities among local players, especially firms and local institutions. Yet the lack of capabilities among local firms to overcome technological and market disruptions is the key issue to explain the cluster decline (Østergaard and Park, 2015). In this scenario, it is important to note the role of technological gatekeepers, since they could be a very important channel to access external knowledge and spread it among local firms (Morrison, 2008; Hervás-Oliver and Albors-Garrigós, 2014).

This chapter aims to discuss the cluster evolution of the two major industrial clusters of the Brazilian ceramic tile industry in Santa Catarina and Sao Paulo. The Brazilian ceramic tile industry is the second largest in the world, just behind China, both in production and in consumption. The growth of the Brazilian domestic market in the last two decades, especially during the 2000s, has driven a substantial increase in local production, with positive effects in the two major Brazilian ceramic tile industrial clusters. The growth of local firms allows them to accumulate new technological capabilities, mainly through the interaction of the main technological gatekeepers. However, there are important differences in the interactive learning among firms from these two main industrial clusters.

The chapter discusses the Brazilian ceramic tile industry, presents the emergence of both industrial clusters, analyses their growth and maturity, and discusses the main characteristics of the accumulation of technological capabilities. Finally, concluding remarks and policy implications are presented. Before starting the discussion, it is important to present some brief methodological notes. Data presented in this chapter were gathered in a longitudinal study, which encompassed the collection of twelve years of secondary and primary data. Regular visits to the major agents were made in this period, including firms' representatives, technological centres, Brazilian trade fairs and the most important ceramic tile firms, machinery and glaze suppliers. In this way, main information was collected through regular visits to clusters' agents and even through informal talks with key players. Secondary data were also gathered from Brazilian and international ceramics magazines and journals. Finally, during 2015, semi-structured face-to-face interviews, lasting 2–3 hours, were conducted with fifteen key informants, in order to complement available data and reinforce the main results presented in this chapter.

16.2   The Brazilian ceramic tile industry

The Brazilian ceramic tile industry presented strong growth in recent decades. Total production increased from 172 million square metres in 1990 to 753 million square metres in 2010. In 2014, domestic firms manufactured 903.3 million square metres in a production capacity of 1,084 million square metres (Table 16.1).

Domestic production is largely directed towards the domestic market. Total physical sales reached 853.2 million square metres in 2014, in addition to

Table 16.1 Production, exports and domestic consumption of the Brazilian ceramic tiles industry (in millions of square metres)

Year	Production	Exports	Domestic consumption
1990	172.8	12.7	160.1
1991	166.0	13.9	152.1
1992	202.7	21.1	181.6
1993	242.9	25.6	217.3
1994	283.5	29.7	253.8
1995	295.0	29.4	265.6
1996	336.4	27.9	308.5
1997	383.3	29.6	353.7
1998	400.7	34.6	366.1
1999	428.5	42.6	385.9
2000	452.7	56.7	396.0
2001	473.4	59.5	413.9
2002	508.3	73.9	434.4
2003	534.0	103.5	430.6
2004	565.6	125.8	439.8
2005	568.1	113.8	454.3
2006	594.2	114.4	479.8
2007	637.0	100.7	536.3
2008	713.4	81.1	605.4
2009	714.9	60.4	644.5
2010	753.5	56.6	699.6
2011	844.3	60.1	774.7
2012	865.9	58.8	803.3
2013	871.1	63.3	837.5
2014	903.3	69.2	853.2

Source: Authors' own, based in Anfacer, SECEX.

69.2 million square metres of external sales. The huge growth of the ceramic tiles domestic market was higher than the growth of the Brazilian manufacturing industry. This discrepancy was due to a set of factors, such as the growth of the civil construction industry, the availability of natural raw material, especially clay, and the availability of energy, even with increasing costs and easy access to manufacturing technologies, both machinery and glazing materials. Macroeconomic factors were also important for this accelerated growth, such as the growth of Brazilian GDP, the advances in income distribution, the increased access to funding, especially for civil construction and building material, and a set of public policy measures to support civil construction.

Regarding the main technological characteristics of the ceramic tile industry, it is important to point out that the major knowledge base for innovation is mainly codified, and technological opportunities at the firm level are relatively low. As technological developments are strongly incorporated in machinery, equipment and other types of inputs, firms hardly obtain high profits related to technological innovation. Thus, firms' competitiveness is based on complementary assets, such as sales channels, customer services, brands and advertising.

It is worth pointing out the importance of international suppliers for the technical and technological development of the Brazilian ceramic tile industry, especially Italian machinery producers and Spanish glazing suppliers. Italian machinery producers played a very important role for the upgrading of technical and technological capabilities, since they were able to undertake an important learning process in terms of the manufacturing process of ceramic tiles, which allowed a substantial upgrade in standard. The role played by Italian machinery firms was crucial for the learning process (Meyer-Stamer *et al.*, 2004; Scur and Garcia, 2009). Meanwhile, Spanish glazing suppliers have also played a very important role. Interactions with Spanish firms enabled an important learning process in terms of product development (Meyer-Stamer *et al.*, 2004; Scur and Garcia, 2009). International suppliers, together with local technological centres, played the role of technological gatekeepers, and they provided the basic conditions for the upgrading of the Brazilian ceramic tile industry.

In terms of international linkages, the industry does not play a terribly important role in the global value chain. External sales of ceramic tiles from the Brazilian industry represent a share of around 8 per cent of domestic production, which was US$273 million in 2014. The most important markets are South America (which accounts for almost 50 per cent of total external sales), Central America (around 30 per cent) and the US and Canada (15 per cent). Therefore, Brazilian ceramic tiles' external sales are driven to supply regional markets and not to play a major role in the global value chain.

The Brazilian domestic market cannot be considered an open market for international competition. Purchases from international suppliers reached the amount of US$64 million, which represented around 10 per cent of physical domestic production in 2014. However, imports from international suppliers have increased significantly since 2003, when total foreign purchases was of US $1.7 million.[1] The most important international supplier for the Brazilian domestic market is China, whose share is almost 70 per cent of total imports, followed by Italy (share of 17 per cent) and Spain (share of 10 per cent). Furthermore, the average price of Italian and Spanish products in the Brazilian market is around 2.5 times higher than the average price of total imports. It is important to note that there are two main players responsible for the imports of ceramic products: the Brazilian ceramic tiles big firms, which purchase international products to complement their product lines, and some big Brazilian and foreign retail suppliers of building materials. In both cases, local producers or retailers are using the same sales channels used for domestic products to sell foreign ceramic tiles in the domestic markets.

Regarding the regional distribution of the production, it is possible to assure the most important regions, measured by the total employees in the ceramic industry.[2] In this way, the most important regions are those where

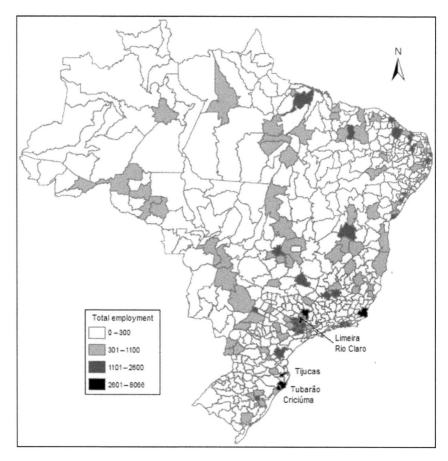

Figure 16.1 Regional distribution of production: total employees in the ceramic industry.

the bigger industrial clusters are located, Sao Paulo and Santa Catarina. The Santa Catarina cluster is located around the city of Criciúma, but it extends to an area of up to 200 km, in the city of Tijucas, where an important local big firm is located. It employs around 13,300 workers in the ceramic industry. The Sao Paulo cluster is located around the city of Santa Gertrudes and encompasses the micro-regions of Limeira, where Santa Gertrudes is located, and Rio Claro (see Figure 16.1). There are around 9,800 employees working in the manufacturing of ceramic products.[3] These two main clusters are responsible for a substantial share of the ceramic tile industry manufacturing.

Both of these industrial clusters present high specialization in the ceramic industry. The Locational Quotient of the Santa Catarina cluster is 7.4, while Sao Paulo's is 5.4.[4] Based on the high specialization of both clusters, even in regions with relatively highly diversified manufacturing industries, it is possible to assume that local producers can benefit themselves from Marshallian externalities, due to the high specialization in the manufacturing of ceramic tiles. In fact, it is possible to find the three characteristics of the Marshallian externalities (the so-called 'Marshallian Trinity'): labour market pooling, suppliers of intermediate inputs and knowledge spillovers (Meyer-Stamer *et al.*, 2004; Scur and Garcia, 2009).

16.3 Cluster evolution and capabilities in the Brazilian ceramic tile industry

A general claim in cluster analysis is that, at the general level, geographical proximity facilitates knowledge sharing, and consequently interactive learning and innovation. Thus, the analysis of cluster evolution should be carried out by examining the main ways in which local producers accumulate new capabilities through the interactive learning process. Learning could be a result of the interaction of both local agents – by the presence of local knowledge spillovers and extensive networks of producers that belong to the same institutional context – and non-local actors – which can be an important source of new knowledge and can disseminate it among local producers (Boschma and Ter Wal, 2007; Hervás-Oliver and Albors-Garrigós, 2014). Looking at non-local sources of new knowledge, technological gatekeepers can play a very important role for the evolution of industrial clusters since they can be active actors in the search for new knowledge and they can avoid lock-in at both firm and cluster levels (Morrison, 2008; Hervás-Oliver and Albors-Garrigós, 2014).

Based on these assumptions, the evolution of the Brazilian ceramic tiles clusters can be analysed by the identification of some stylized factors in order to characterize each stage of the cluster evolution. Thus, these stylized factors can describe the evolutionary path-dependent trajectory of industrial clusters (Belussi and Sedita, 2009). The cluster evolution approach is used to analyse the two most important Brazilian ceramic tile clusters, Santa Catarina and Sao Paulo.

16.3.1 The emergence

The emergence of the Santa Catarina cluster was due to the availability of coal, since large coalmines were located in the region and their ovens were originally used to manufacture rude ceramic products. Easy access to the coalmines was a chief factor for the emergence of the Santa Catarina ceramic tiles industrial cluster. The first products were manufactured in the 1950s and were very rustic, consisting mainly of bricks. During the 1970s, local production presented fast growth since local firms evolved to extract and manufacture non-minerals metallic products for use in civil construction. Most of the surviving big firms of the Santa Catarina cluster were founded in this period.

An important fact to mention is that in 1979, due to the lack of a local qualified workforce, one of the most important local firms still active nowadays created a technical school of ceramics. The school was funded integrally by this specific firm.[5] The establishment of the school played a very important role for the local cluster, since it was responsible for the creation of one chief local knowledge externality. The qualification of the local workforce fostered the accumulation of new knowledge capabilities, not only at the founder and funding firm but also for all local firms, reinforcing its role for the accumulation of new capabilities at the cluster level. Nowadays, the technical school still plays an important role in the supply of a qualified technical workforce.

After these initial stylized factors, a modern ceramic tiles industrial cluster arose. Some of the biggest firms today were created in this period, and the technical school catalyzed the initial process of accumulation of new knowledge capabilities. During the 1980s, local production quickly arose, due to the growth of local manufacturing firms, and specialized suppliers appeared to complement the local productive structure. However, it is important to mention that the production growth in this emergence stage was not followed by an increase in local production quality standards.

The origin of the Sao Paulo cluster is strongly associated with the availability of clay in the region, which was originally used to manufacture rustic products, such as roof tiles and bricks. However, from the 1980s onwards, local firms started to manufacture ceramic tiles, using the locally available raw material, specially directed towards low-income consumers in the domestic market. Local firms made huge investments both in the establishment of new facilities for manufacturing and in new machinery. In this period, rapid production growth was not followed by an increase in quality standards, which resulted in the manufacturing of poor quality ceramic tiles. During the 1990s, local firms experienced huge growth rates, due to the rapid increase of the demand for building materials in Brazil.

The availability of raw materials has been an important trigger factor for the growth of local producers. Due to its specific physical characteristics, the use of local clay in the manufacturing process requires little preparation. The region's clay does not require water for the milling process and because of this, the manufacturing process of the clay used by local firms is known as the 'dry process'. Moreover, the use of the local clay enables firms to reduce meaningfully operational costs, not only in the manufacturing process but also in their inventory. The local clay's specific physical characteristics have driven an important adaptation in the manufacturing process in order to support the use of the 'dry process'. To fit these requirements, local producers, with the support of the machinery industry, changed some manufacturing parameters and achieved success in the production of ceramic tiles using the dry process, which brought important productivity upgrades. One of the reasons for this success was the structural ceramic firms' capability in the management of the local raw material, even in the extraction and the milling process. The use of local raw materials allows important reductions in production costs (Table 16.2).

Table 16.2 Average costs of manufacturing of ceramic tiles in Brazil (base 100: water process)

	Dry process	Water process
Electricity	6.5	5.7
Thermal energy	18.4	19.3
Glaze materials	18.4	19.0
Natural raw materials	4.6	13.4
Packing	3.9	6.4
Direct labour costs	8.2	11.8
Indirect labour costs	3.4	4.0
Maintenance	5.1	7.8
Auxiliary materials	1.4	4.0
Others	10.1	8.6
	80.0	100.0

Source: Authors' own, based in Anfacer.

Another important trigger factor was the upgrading of the labour force qualification. Since there was not a local technical school, local firms started to hire qualified workers from further afield. These skilled workers came from other regions in the state of Sao Paulo, and even from the technical school in Santa Catarina. In fact, the 'first generation' of local firms' skilled workers came from the Santa Catarina ceramic tile cluster.[6] In addition, the Sao Paulo cluster was located closer to the main Brazilian consumer market, another factor that favoured the competitiveness of local firms, especially considering the high transportation costs for ceramic tiles.

16.3.2   Growth and maturity

After the emergence stage, local producers at the Santa Catarina cluster experienced huge growth in the 1980s. Investments in industrial processes allowed local firms to accumulate new capabilities, especially in manufacturing, which increased their quality standards. New products were designed, most of them based in the imitation of foreign products, especially Italian ceramic tiles.

However, at the beginning of the 1990s, local firms started to experience significant difficulties. First, macroeconomic restrictions in the first half of the 1990s hampered the growth of local firms. At the same time, firms from the Sao Paulo cluster appeared as new competitors by acting at the 'low-end' domestic market. The lower costs of the new rivals became a big challenge for firms of the Santa Catarina cluster, resulting in strong losses in their growth rates.[7]

The response of local firms from the Santa Catarina cluster was to foster managerial and technological upgrading. Regarding operations management, local firms tried to redefine their operational strategies by reducing management costs, eliminating non-profitable manufacturing lines, downsizing and outsourcing adjacent activities, such as clay extraction and enamelling. During the crisis of the 1990s, local firms decided to outsource activities that they had internalized earlier. The strategy of outsourcing helped local firms to focus on the manufacturing of ceramic tiles, with important positive effects in the accumulation of new technological capabilities. Local firms made considerable efforts to update their manufacturing process and product mix. They bought new foreign machinery (especially from Italy), which helped to increase productivity at the plant level and to add value to the mix of products. In addition, since frits and glaze materials activities were outsourced, firms strengthened interactions with local subsidiaries of foreign (especially Spanish) suppliers of glaze materials, in order to help them to upgrade products and the manufacturing process. In this way, the vertical disintegration of local producers was an important managerial strategy to foster innovation among firms from the Santa Catarina cluster. It allowed them to benefit from the ongoing development project of their main suppliers and to strengthen interactive learning through the creation of channels of communication and the exchange of information with main suppliers. In fact, vertical disintegration and the formation of networks of innovators were important tools in fostering and accelerating innovation among firms (Robertson and Langlois, 1995).

Local firms' strategy of focusing their product mix on high-value products meant abandoning the low-end market. Nevertheless, due to the low average income of most of the population, the huge Brazilian domestic market consists mainly of low-end ceramic tiles. For local firms, this strategy resulted in a noteworthy economy of scale losses and, as a result, the overthrow of local firms' profitability. Some of the local firms went bankrupt. Since then, the profitability of the big firms of the Santa Catarina cluster big firms has declined and remains in a decline today.

In addition, the financial and competitive problems of the Santa Catarina cluster local firms' have damaged their investment capacity and their ability to accumulate new technological capabilities. Local firms' financial problems prevented them from gathering resources to make the required investments in new manufacturing technologies, especially machinery and equipment, necessary to preserve their competitiveness.[8]

The growth of the Sao Paulo ceramic tile cluster dates from the beginning of the 1990s, when local firms made huge efforts to upgrade their manufacturing process through the accumulation of new technological and productive capabilities. In order to increase their market share and their profitability, local firms made significant investments in new machinery, in the upgrade of manufacturing processes and in the design of new products. It is important to note that environmental regulations and market conditions were also important drivers to these investments. Competitive advantages related to the production costs were key factors in boosting local firms' profits and in creating a huge capacity for investment in new technologies. After the second half of the 1990s, the increasing demand for low-end market ceramic tiles products in Brazil was another important factor for the growth upgrade of local firms.

Three main actors played important roles for the upgrade of local firms, as they acted as technological gatekeepers by keeping external knowledge, internalizing it and spreading it among local producers (Meyer-Stamer *et al.*, 2004; Scur and Garcia, 2009).

The first were the Italian machinery suppliers, which found big purchasers for their products in the Sao Paulo cluster. Italian machinery suppliers helped local firms to upgrade their operations as a requirement for the installation of modern and technologically updated machinery. Due to the specific characteristics of the local raw material, machinery suppliers were urged to adapt their equipment, which catalyzed an important process of interactive learning between machinery suppliers and local producers. Local firms had to upgrade all of the manufacturing process in order to meet the requirements of the new technology. Furthermore, machinery suppliers offered funding for new investment in capital goods, which brought down debt levels for local firms.[9]

The second key actors were the Spanish suppliers of glaze materials, who provided interactive learning processes related especially to product development and design of ceramic tiles. The Spanish suppliers played an important role in supporting local firms to upgrade their products. During the 1990s, suppliers of chemical inputs established local subsidiaries, which fostered face-to-face interactive learning with local producers. The glazing material suppliers not only sold their chemical products to local firms but also offered a combination of related products and services such as product concepts and manufacturing process assistance, which allowed the adaptation of new products and processes by applying them to local raw materials and market conditions. The glazing material suppliers also brought international market trends to local firms, which helped them to upgrade their production mix. At this time, the competitive advantages were in the middle and end processes such as presses, enamelling and burning phases, because of the impacts on aesthetic performance. This allowed the development of product differentiation such as a variety of sizes and silkscreens.

The third important actor was the Center of Technological Innovation in Ceramics (Citec/CCB), a local research and technological centre. The centre was created in 2002 through the installation of a quality lab at the local system, in order to render services of product certification for local firms. However, its activities went much further than the certification of products, since it acted as an active player to help firms upgrade their manufacturing process to reach the necessary requirements for certification. Moreover, the centre played a crucial role in internalizing and spreading new technological and scientific knowledge, since it established joint research contracts between Brazilian and foreign universities, fostering the acquisition and diffusion of new capabilities.

Thus, during the Sao Paulo cluster growth stage, local firms were able to learn through interaction with important technological gatekeepers, which allowed them to accumulate new capabilities. Local firms took advantage of their easy access to the huge Brazilian domestic market and were able to incorporate technological advances that were integrated in machinery and in materials.

16.3.3   Post-maturity and accumulation of capabilities

After the 1990s, there was an increase in rivalry among firms from both the Santa Catarina and the Sao Paulo clusters. The cost advantages of the firms of Sao Paulo allowed them to make high profits and sustain high-speed growth. Meanwhile, firms from the Santa Catarina cluster, mainly the big ones, were facing continuous financial problems. The rivalry with lower-cost firms, which forced a product price decrease, reduced local firms' profits. Nevertheless, the Santa Catarina cluster remains the biggest, and the continued growth of the domestic market during the 2000s has allowed all of its firms to grow in recent years.

Moreover, the scenario of increasing rivalry in the Brazilian domestic market underwent an important change during the 2000s. The Brazilian public policy to finance civil construction fostered a huge growth in the domestic market. Therefore, it was possible to accommodate firms' different market strategies, since most of them were able to find demand for their products. This was the main reason for the huge growth in sales and employment seen in both analysed clusters.[10]

Examining the Santa Catarina cluster, even with important managerial and operational restructuring, financial problems remained. Local firms tried to implement strategies to promote technological upgrading, but cash flow problems prevented them from making bigger investments in technological capabilities. In this way, the restructuring did not prevent the decrease of local firms' market share, mainly because firms from the Sao Paulo cluster expanded their sales specifically in the medium-price products market. Thus most of the Santa Catarina firms, mainly the largest ones, faced significant difficulties in accumulating new technological capabilities, since they had to reduce the purchase of new equipment, which weakened their linkages with the main technological gatekeepers. However, it is important to point out that local firms' main problem was their market performance and their higher manufacturing costs, but not their technical or technological capabilities.

Meanwhile, the accumulation of new technological and manufacturing capabilities among producers of the Sao Paulo cluster allowed them to grow in the low- and medium-price domestic markets from the 1990s. During the 2000s, the huge growth of the Brazilian domestic market reinforced their performance, which facilitated the financing of new investments in machinery and manufacturing processes, and the development and design of new products. In this scenario, local firms strengthened their linkages with foreign machinery suppliers, which led to continuous improvement in the manufacturing process, and glaze materials, which allowed them to upgrade the design of their products. These linkages strengthened the market performance of local firms, since they were able to upgrade their products, driving them to a high value-added market. One important example of the importance of local firms' accumulation of new capabilities was the development, with the assistance of the machinery suppliers, of a porcelain manufacturing process using the dry process. The fast diffusion of the inkjet technology among producers in the Sao Paulo cluster is another example.

Regarding the inkjet technology, it is important to consider the effects of this technological discontinuity, which came with the development of the digital full HD technology launched in the mid-2000s. The inkjet technology allowed firms to perfectly reproduce marble, wood, stones and wallpaper shapes through the use of high-quality printers. The new technology offered extraordinarily sharp image resolutions, fast line speeds and heightened productivity (Hervás-Oliver and Albors-Garrigós, 2014). Thereby, new niche markets could be achieved with high value added and new creations of exclusive brands. Besides the beauty and aesthetic proximity to any kind of material, other success factors are flexibility and the ease of creating new products. Firms need only a high-quality digital camera. When the development and marketing teams notice a new trend of colours and prints, they can take a picture and develop a final product based on a simple image. The diffusion of the inkjet technology among Brazilian firms started at the beginning of the 2010s, and rapid dissemination of this new technology among firms of the Sao Paulo cluster can be observed. Among those of Santa Catarina, however, the big firms' financial problems prevent a major diffusion of this new technology. Once more, it is possible to see that cash flow problems of Santa Catarina firms hinder the accumulation of new capabilities, even with the local presence of technological gatekeepers, which can spread these new capabilities among producers.

Technological regimes in the ceramic tile industry show that the main advances can be codified in machines, equipment and materials, and interactive learning between suppliers and producers could be the main way to accumulate new capabilities and knowledge. Since firms accumulate new capabilities by interacting with the main suppliers, the cluster analysis is based on the ways technological gatekeepers spread new knowledge among local producers of ceramic tiles. Meanwhile, firms with high technological capabilities do not necessarily have high appropriability of the benefits offered by technological advances, since profits are linked to the possession of complementary assets, such as operational management, production costs, brand names and access to market channels.

The analysis of the Brazilian ceramic tile cluster life cycle should be made considering the main characteristics of the sectoral technological regimes. Despite the fact that firms of the Santa Catarina cluster present higher skills and technological capabilities, they do not present higher economic performance and profits. The main reason can be found in the examination of the main capabilities of the firms of the Sao Paulo cluster. Its local firms do not have huge in-house technological capabilities, but there are three main factors that strengthen their economic performance. First, they are able to interact with the main local and non-local technological gatekeepers and learn from the knowledge bases that are exogenous at the firm level but were internalized at the cluster level by the main technological gatekeepers. Second, local firms present lower manufacturing costs related to easy access of the local clay, the main raw material used in the production of ceramic tiles – and technical problems related to the physical characteristics of the local clay have been progressively solved with the assistance of the machinery and input suppliers, reinforced by the local technical institution. Third, geographical proximity to the main Brazilian domestic markets allows them to reduce out-of-firm costs, such as transportation and logistics.

16.4   Final remarks and policy implications

The Brazilian ceramic tile producers' accumulation of technological capabilities is strongly linked with the set of externalities related to the agglomeration of producers in the two major clusters, Santa Catarina and Sao Paulo. The origin of both clusters is due to stylized facts related to the existence of natural resources. However, after the emergence stage, both clusters were able to accumulate new knowledge and new capabilities due to the presence of important technological gatekeepers, responsible for gathering external knowledge and spreading it among local actors. However, the accumulation of external knowledge and technological capabilities does not represent a guarantee for good economic performance. Technological regimes in the ceramic tile industry show that new technological advances are mainly embodied in machinery, equipment and materials, which facilitate its diffusion from suppliers to final producers. Thus, conditions of appropriability in this industry are linked to the possession of complementary assets, such as easy access to raw materials, brand names, operational management and market channels.

Analysis of the two major Brazilian ceramic tile clusters shows this characteristic clearly. The trajectory of the firms of the Santa Catarina cluster, especially the big ones, shows their capacity to accumulate new knowledge and technological as well as manufacturing capabilities. However, in the past twenty years, despite the huge growth of the Brazilian domestic market, firms have not presented good economic performance, which hampers their ability to accumulate funding for investment in new technological advances, such as the inkjet digital printer.

Firms from the Sao Paulo cluster, meanwhile, were able to learn from the interaction of the main technological gatekeepers, despite having accumulated much lower technological and manufacturing capabilities throughout their trajectory. Local firms were born leaner, which allowed them to reduce operational and manufacturing costs and, at the same time, accumulate knowledge through the interactive learning established with their Italian machinery suppliers, Spanish frits and glaze materials suppliers, and the local technological centre. In addition, firms have privileged access to local raw materialsand easy access to the main Brazilian domestic market.

Finally, in reference to policy implications, results of this research reinforce policy implications of previous studies (e.g. Hervás-Oliver and Albors-Garrigós, 2014). Several advances can be seen in policy making for the different stages of the cluster and the role of technological gatekeepers in fostering interactive learning and innovation among firms. In general, policy implications should be oriented to foster interactive learning and the accumulation of new capabilities among local producers. At the cluster level, due to the important role of the technological gatekeepers, policy should include measures to foster their activities. However, since technological accumulation occurs mainly at firm level, policy measures should encompass new ways to foster the upgrade of local firms' technological capabilities.

Notes

1 It should be mentioned that macroeconomic conditions in Brazil, especially the appreciated exchange rate until 2014, provided strong stimulus for firms to increase international purchase.
2 There are two methodological problems in this measure. First, data of regional production or gross sales revenue are not available in Brazil at the regional level, which implies the use of employment data. By using employment data, regional differences of productivity are not taken into account. Second, the employment data regarding the ceramic tiles industry at regional level include not only ceramic tiles but also structural ceramics, such as roof tiles, bricks and quarry tiles, which can overvalue the importance of the ceramic tiles industry.
3 Micro-regions is a Brazilian geographical aggregation similar to the EU NUTS 3.
4 Locational Quotient is an index used extensively to measure how concentrated a particular industry or cluster is in a given region compared with the nation. Here, Locational Quotients are calculated using employment data.
5 The school is still active and is named the Maximiano Gaidzinsky School, in honour of its founder, a local ceramic tiles entrepreneur.
6 It is worthy to highlight the role of the ceramic technical school of Santa Catarina for providing skilled workers for not only local firms but also firms located in other regions, such as Sao Paulo. In this way, the technical school provided, in the emergence stage of the Brazilian ceramic tiles industrial cluster, important externalities for the firms, both local and non-local.
7 For example, data from the local firms' association show that, in 1991, local firms' sales dropped around 30 per cent.
8 An example of the magnitude of the financial problems is the low speed of the diffusion of the ink-jet machinery, which will be discussed further on.
9 The over-appreciated Brazilian exchange rate during the second half of the 1990s helped local firms to finance the purchase of new foreign machinery.
10 Considering employment data from 2006 to 2013, both clusters presented very high growth rates: the Santa Catarina cluster grew at a rate of 5.8 per cent per year, while Sao Paulo grew at 5.2 per cent.

References

Audretsch, D. B. and Feldman, M. P. (1996). R&D spillovers and the geography of innovation and production. *The American Economic Review*, 86(3): 630–640.

Belussi, F. and Sedita, S. R. (2009). Life cycle vs. multiple path dependency in industrial districts. *European Planning Studies*, 17(4): 505–528.

Boschma, R. and Fornahl, D. (2011). Cluster evolution and a roadmap for future research. *Regional Studies*, 45(10): 1295–1298.

Boschma, R. A. and Ter Wal, A. L. (2007). Knowledge networks and innovative performance in an industrial district: the case of a footwear district in the South of Italy. *Industry and Innovation*, 14(2): 177–199.

Elola, A., Valdaliso, J. M., López, S. M. and Aranguren, M. J. (2012). Cluster life cycles, path dependency and regional economic development: Insights from a meta-study on Basque clusters. *European Planning Studies*, 20(2): 257–279.

Hervás-Oliver, J. L. and Albors-Garrigós, J. (2014). Are technology gatekeepers renewing clusters? Understanding gatekeepers and their dynamics across cluster life cycles. *Entrepreneurship & Regional Development*, 26(5–6): 431–452.

Lombardi, M. (2003). The evolution of local production systems: the emergence of the 'invisible mind' and the evolutionary pressures towards more visible 'minds'. *Research Policy*, 32(8): 1443–1462.

Martin, R. and Sunley, P. (2006). Path dependence and regional economic evolution. *Journal of Economic Geography*, 6(4): 395–437.

Martin, R. and Sunley, P. (2011). Conceptualizing cluster evolution: beyond the life cycle model? *Regional Studies*, 45(10): 1299–1318.

Menzel, M. P. and Fornahl, D. (2009). Cluster life cycles – dimensions and rationales of cluster evolution. *Industrial and Corporate Change*, 19(1): 205–238.

Meyer-Stamer, J., Maggi, C. and Siebel, S. (2004). Upgrading in the tile industry of Italy, Spain and Brazil: insights from cluster and value chain analysis. In Schmitz, H. (ed.) *Local Enterprises in the Global Economy: Issues of governance and upgrading*. Cheltenham: Edward Elgar Publishing, pp. 174–199.

Morrison, A. (2008). Gatekeepers of knowledge within industrial districts: who they are, how they interact. *Regional Studies*, 42(6): 817–835.

Østergaard, C. R. and Park, E. (2015). What makes clusters decline? A study on disruption and evolution of a high-tech cluster in Denmark. *Regional Studies*, 49(5): 834–849.

Robertson, P. L. and Langlois, R. N. (1995). Innovation, networks, and vertical integration. *Research Policy*, 24(4): 543–562.

Scur, G. and Garcia, R. (2009). Industrial clusters in the Brazilian ceramic tile industry and the new challenges for competition in the global value chain. In Belussi, F. and Samarra, A. (eds) *Business Networks in Clusters and Industrial Districts: The governance of the global value chain (regions and cities)*. London: Routledge, pp. 250–270.

Ter Wal, A. L. and Boschma, R. (2011). Co-evolution of firms, industries and networks in space. *Regional Studies*, 45(7): 919–933.

Vale, M. and Caldeira, J. (2007). Proximity and knowledge governance in localized production systems: the footwear industry in the north region of Portugal. *European Planning Studies*, 15(4): 531–548.

17 Understanding cluster evolution

Michaela Trippl, Marcus Grillitsch, Arne Isaksen and Tanja Sinozic

17.1 Introduction

The past two decades have witnessed an enormous scholarly and policy interest in regional clusters. A large body of work has focused attention on explaining why clusters exist and what the main characteristics of 'functioning' or fully developed clusters are. While there is a rich literature on existing clusters, relatively little has been said so far about how clusters emerge, change and develop over time. There is, however, a growing recognition of the need to develop dynamic perspectives to gain insights into long-term cluster evolution and change (see, for instance, Bergman 2008; Menzel and Fornahl 2010).

Popular approaches in this emerging field of research are different variants of the cluster life cycle (CLC) approach. In particular, the new generation of CLC models has enhanced knowledge of crucial factors that may trigger the rise and further development of clusters. However, these approaches suffer from several shortcomings, most notably rather deterministic views that preclude one from capturing the complexity and variety of cluster transformation that are evident from empirically grounded contextualised studies.

The aim of this chapter is to go beyond the CLC concepts and to contribute to a better understanding of the context-specific nature of cluster transformation. Based on an analysis of different strands of literature, alternative and possibly more convincing explanations of cluster change are explored. We provide a critique of the CLC approach by use of elements from the literature on industrial districts, innovative milieu and regional innovation systems.

The remainder of the chapter is organised as follows. Section 17.2 introduces the CLC concept. We discuss the conceptual arguments made by its main protagonists and elaborate on the limitations that surround this approach. In section 17.3 we review alternative schools of thought that have contributed – albeit under different labels – to cluster research. We analyse the literature on industrial districts, innovative milieus and regional innovation systems to find out whether these strands of literature can provide more promising insights into how clusters develop over time. Finally, section 17.4 outlines the contours of a context-sensitive approach to cluster change.

17.2   Review of the cluster life cycle approach

With the call for a more dynamic view on clusters, the CLC approach has recently gained increasing attention. The approach, however, is not new (for a review of the CLC literature, see Bergman 2008). It departs from the presumption that regional clusters go through different phases, often described as emergence, growth, sustainment, decline and possibly renewal. Various approaches to cluster life cycles exist, which differ in particular in their explanation of how new clusters emerge, and in the driving forces that explain the transition of clusters between the phases (Bergman 2008). In this section, we will focus on the currently most influential new CLC approaches of Menzel and Fornahl (2010), Ter Wal and Boschma (2011) and Martin and Sunley (2011).

The new CLC approaches have the merit of taking up recent developments in the literature on evolutionary economic geography, highlighting the importance of firm heterogeneity, related variety, the evolution of networks, and path-dependency for regional industrial change. The first model of Menzel and Fornahl (2010) focuses on firm heterogeneity and technological convergence or divergence through learning processes. Depending on these processes, they also acknowledge the possibility of alternative development paths. The contribution of Ter Wal and Boschma (2011) also underlines the importance of firm heterogeneity. In addition, they claim that clusters 'co-evolve with the industry to which they adhere, with the (variety of) capabilities of firms in that industry, and with the industry-wide knowledge network of which they are part.' (p. 929). Martin and Sunley's (2011) paper differs as cluster change is conceptualised through an adaptive cycle model, which does not privilege a specific development trajectory.

Menzel and Fornahl (2010) propose a clear distinction between cluster firms, firms in the same industry located elsewhere, and firms in other industries but located in the same region. While appreciating the role of interactions between these different types of firms, the institutional context and the industry life cycle, it is argued that firm heterogeneity and localised learning processes are the central factors explaining cluster change. Hence, the authors relate to recent work in evolutionary economic geography emphasising the importance of variety, i.e. firm heterogeneity for innovation and economic growth. What is more, their model exhibits parallels with the debate on related variety and proximity (Boschma 2005; Frenken *et al.* 2007). Menzel and Fornahl (2010) suggest that the development of technological relatedness between firms is a precondition for the emergence of a cluster while heterogeneity is considered as crucial source for the extension or renewal of development trajectories. Clusters begin 'in those regions where the knowledge bases of companies converge around technological focal points' (p. 231). Technological convergence underlying the momentum of cluster formation is shaped by, among other factors, interactive learning processes between heterogeneous firms in geographic proximity to one another. Firm heterogeneity can be increased through learning with non-cluster firms both locally and globally. This may bring in new knowledge to the cluster, shifting its thematic boundaries (Menzel and Fornahl 2010).

The first cluster phase is characterised by spin-offs, a small number of technologically diverse companies, a supportive science and skills base, and policy support 'which give the emerging cluster the potential to reach a criti-cal mass' (Menzel and Fornahl 2010, p. 225). In the second stage of the CLC, firms grow both in number and in size. The cluster becomes increasingly specialised, causing a more homogeneous knowledge base, a clearer cluster structure, and comes closer to the technological frontier. In the third stage, maturity, clusters are relatively stable and have dense firm networks. In this stage, clusters risk becoming homogenous, over-reliant on a single technological path, and thus locked-in and vulnerable to decline because their capacities for renewal have been exhausted. In such conditions, the cluster reaches its fourth stage of development, one of decline, its main features being firm closures, failures and lay-offs. In such conditions, declining clusters can be revitalised by an increase in technological heterogeneity via, for example, firms, skills or resources external to the cluster. Menzel and Fornahl's model suggests that localised learning dynamics and firm heterogeneity propel clusters through life cycles. Despite this dominant trajectory, the authors also open up for alternative trajectories. For instance, without technological convergence in the emergence stage, a cluster may never reach the growth stage. Also, by introducing heterogeneity in later stages, clusters can continuously renew themselves and do not necessarily need to decline. In sum, 'clusters display long-term growth if they are able to maintain their diversity' (Menzel and Fornahl 2010, p. 218).

Ter Wal and Boschma (2011) propose a framework where clusters co-evolve with firm capabilities, industry life cycles and networks. The authors emphasise the importance of variety as regards firm capabilities, which resonates well with the model introduced by Menzel and Fornahl (2010). In addition, the framework of Ter Wal and Boschma (2011) elaborates on the effects of networks for the evolution of clusters. However, the debate on how industry life cycles materialise in space dates back to earlier literature such as Storper and Walker's (1989) theory of geographical industrialisation.

Ter Wal and Boschma (2011) explain cluster evolution as interplay between cluster imminent factors (firm capacities and networks) and the evolution of the industry. Due to the high degree of uncertainty at early stages of an industry, a large variety of firm competences exists and networks are unstable. The emergence of clusters is initiated through pioneering firms introducing radical innovations. However, at this stage it is unclear which will be the dominant designs and successful firms creating a window of locational opportunity (Storper and Walker 1989). The probability of a new cluster, however, depends on regional branching processes, regional assets such as a qualified labour force and infrastructure, as well as new combinations facilitated through diversity. As clusters grow, Ter Wal and Boschma (2011) argue that several forces lead to stable core-periphery network patterns. These forces include the advantageous network position of pioneers, the higher likelihood of firms in weaker positions exiting the industry, and the importance of previously successful collaborations. The high degree of tacit knowledge at this stage makes physical proximity and social capital such as trust important, thus clustering becomes a distinct advantage for firms. Maturity relates to a saturation of markets and technological development potential leading to increasingly incremental and process innovations. Economies of scale and cost reduction increasingly matter, leading to a large number of firm exits. Being located at the core of the network, which often coincides with the location of the main clusters, facilitates survival. The endurance and stability of networks and clusters can have distinct disadvantages in the maturity stage because firm variety decreases, which may lead to cognitive lock-in, and the increasing codification of knowledge reduces the need for geographic proximity. Two possibilities, industry decline or renewal, are provided in the fourth stage of development. The cluster declines if no novel innovations are introduced. A new cycle may be started if cluster firms succeed in generating a new technological breakthrough. However, similar to the introductory stage, such technological breakthroughs will often be generated outside the cluster, leading to significant changes in the network structure. The degree to which clusters will emerge or renew themselves is partially uncertain because of the unpredictable nature of innovation (Ter Wal and Boschma 2011).

Both Ter Wal and Boschma's (2011) and Menzel and Fornahl's (2010) approaches argue for a life cycle model of cluster change underpinned by evolutionary processes, and create important theoretical linkages between previously disparate bodies of literature such as evolutionary economic geography, industrial and technological dynamics and cluster change. The combination of life cycle models with evolutionary processes is both a strength and a weakness of the two approaches. For example, conceptualising cluster change occurring along stages makes the search for outcome variables easy (e.g. firm entry during emergence, firm exit during decline). The combination of neo-Schumpeterian evolutionary concepts such as firm capabilities with sectoral change specificities (Klepper 1997) adds both depth and breadth to understanding the processes occurring within stages that lead to cluster change. However, it remains unclear how long each stage is supposed to last and why they should occur consequentially. It is likely that clusters can avoid steep falls in growth by institutional mechanisms such as labour laws and investment in research. Without an idea of how long the individual stages are, it becomes difficult to develop policy instruments to support the individual cluster stages, or indeed to define which stage a cluster is at. It must be noted that both Menzel and Fornahl (2010) and Ter Wal and Boschma (2011) emphasise the need for empirical testing, which may yield more substantive analytical arguments for extension or critique of the theoretical frameworks.

Compared with the previously reviewed models, Martin and Sunley (2011) introduce a framework of cluster evolution, which identifies besides the typical life cycle trajectory several other potential cluster trajectories. This is in line with the development of the path-dependence theory in evolutionary economic geography, where path-dependence does not imply historical determinism but is seen in relation to mechanisms propelling path creation and path destruction (Martin 2010; Simmie 2012). Following this logic, Martin and Sunley (2011) criticise the deterministic logic of life cycle approaches that carry biological connotations and imply 'some sort of "aging" process. But in what sense can clusters be thought of having 'lives' or 'ageing' or passing through 'life stages'?' (p. 1300). In their view, the trajectories of clusters are unpredictable, mainly because they consist of agents who learn, interact and respond to their perceptions about the current state and future development within the cluster and their environment. The authors propose thinking about clusters as complex adaptive systems and applying an adaptive cycle model. Comparable to traditional life cycle approaches, the adaptive cycle model describes four phases: i) cluster emergence, renewal or replacement; ii) cluster growth; iii) cluster maturation; and iv) cluster decline. In contrast to the traditional approaches, the adaptive system model allows for a variety of development trajectories. In their slightly modified version, Martin and Sunley (2011) identify six possible evolutionary trajectories. One follows the typical life cycle of emergence, growth, maturation, decline and eventual replacement. The notion of replacement strongly builds on the idea that existing resources are released and brought to new use. However, clusters do not necessarily need to move from a growth to a maturity stage. Particularly clusters with strengths in generic or general-purpose technologies, usually associated with high-tech industries, may continuously innovate and mutate. The heterogeneity of firms remains high due to ongoing intensive innovation activities. This is often linked to geographically open knowledge networks, i.e. while there might be a high connectedness within the cluster, firms have established interregional, sometimes global linkages, a feature that has been observed for high-tech clusters. Also, the future technological paths remain uncertain. This in turn requires a strong endowment with venture capital so that firms can embark on uncertain, radical innovation activities. Such clusters keep a high degree of resilience. In addition, Martin and Sunley (2011) illustrate that clusters may, for instance, fail to grow, be replaced and disappear, or stabilise after the growth phase even in mature industries.

17.3 Alternative approaches to cluster change

The CLC approaches suggest that cluster evolution should be seen as a sequence of prescribed stages. In this section we discuss alternative concepts, i.e. the literature on industrial districts, innovative milieus and regional innovation systems. These approaches share the conviction that there is more than one potential development path of cluster evolution. They thus offer a less deterministic view of cluster change and a more flexible and open framework to capture the variety of paths that clusters can follow.

17.3.1   Industrial district approach

The industrial district (ID) approach has its origins in Alfred Marshall's writings on the rise of localised industries and their long-term anchoring in districts. Marshall (1920) argued that the *initial localisation* of industries might have many sources, ranging from the availability of raw material, demand for goods of high quality or the immigration of people with specialised skills. Once an industry is spatially concentrated in a particular locality, a set of positive external economies of scale keeps it in place, including knowledge spillovers, the rise of supplier industries and labour market effects. Marshall also raised awareness of the potential dangers of such settings. He considered IDs that are dependent on one industry only as being extremely vulnerable, pointing to the risk of *crisis and decline* in case of changing context conditions such as, for instance, a fall in demand for its products or changes in technology.

Marshall's ideas were revitalised in the 1980s by a group of Italian researchers, who studied small-firm clusters operating in mature sectors (textiles, leather goods, furniture) in the Third Italy. This literature has enlarged one's understanding of the role of exogenous and endogenous factors in the rise of clusters. Changing external context conditions are viewed as essential for the *emergence and growth* of Italian IDs in the 1960s and 1970s. The end of the golden age of mass production, higher income levels, increasing demand for quality products and technological innovations provided a favourable context for the rise of IDs. The early growth of IDs, however, has endogenous sources also, notably the existence of a set of social–cultural factors that is territorially specific and deeply rooted in the history of Third Italy's regions (Isaksen 2011). These factors include long-standing traditions and competences in craft work, entrepreneurship and management of small firms, the prevalence of strong local identity and solidarity (providing the social underpinnings of local collaboration), and a tradition of family firms that are flexible towards market changes. Until the 1990s, many Italian IDs showed dynamic development.

The focus of recent contributions to the ID literature is primarily on major transformation processes that many Italian IDs underwent from the dynamic period until the 1990s. Several authors argue that these processes were mainly the outcome of changes in external context conditions (Rabellotti *et al.* 2009), particularly the spread of radical technological innovation, global changes in production systems and the internationalisation of the economy. Others scholars put more emphasis on endogenous factors, highlighting the erosion of factors that were critical for IDs' past success (Bianchi 1998).

Studies of Italian IDs have identified a variety of adjustment strategies of IDs and point to the existence of different development patterns (Rabellotti *et al.* 2009). Some IDs disappeared as a result of crises in their area of specialisation (e.g. textile districts in Lombardy and Veneto). In most cases, these districts were specialised in low-cost production and failed to compete successfully with manufacturers in newly emerging countries. In other IDs new specialisations emerged (quality upgrading within old sectors, rise of new sectors, increasing importance of the service sector). Some districts no longer show one of the key features of an ID, that is, the predominance of small firms. A process of 'hierarchisation' can be observed; leading medium-sized companies and groups of firms (Randelli and Boschma 2012) are now the most dynamic agents and key driving forces of structural changes (Rabellotti *et al.* 2009). A large body of work (see Belussi 2011 for a review) has dealt with new international strategies of ID firms. Increasing outsourcing of intermediate activities abroad and integration into global production networks have undermined one of the foundations of the past economic success of Italian districts, that is, deep specialisation along the production chain confined within the ID's geographical boundaries. IDs have transformed from previously relatively closed systems into more open ones as IDs are becoming increasingly integrated into innovation systems at higher spatial scales (Belussi 2011).

To summarise, the ID literature offers valuable insights into the genesis, decline and transformation of clusters. A key finding is that Italian IDs have not followed one development path but many (Belussi 2011; Rabellotti *et al.* 2009). Furthermore, the literature points to the complexity of changes that can be observed in the course of cluster evolution, ranging from changes in the economic specialisation, to the rise of new actors (emergence of business groups and leading firms that act as knowledge gatekeepers, new ethnic firms), changes in the composition of cluster actors (number and size of firms), new firms' strategies, new division of labour among firms, and a reconfiguration of internal and external economic and knowledge linkages. The Italian ID literature seems particularly useful for understanding change processes of clusters made up of small firms operating in traditional industries. One might, however, criticise that this literature is mainly empirically orientated, offering little in terms of conceptual progress as regards cluster evolution.

17.3.2 *Innovative milieu concept*

While there is no uniform definition for the innovative milieu concept, which was developed in the mid-1980s, one of its main advocates, Roberto Camagni (1995, p. 320) describes milieu as 'the set of relationships that occur within a given geographical area that bring unity to a production system, economic actors, and an industrial culture, that generate a localized dynamic process of collective learning and that act as an uncertainty-reducing mechanism in the innovation process"

A milieu, therefore, consists of formal and informal networks and interdependencies between economic actors in a region. This implies that actors are regionally embedded and, over time, build reputation, trust and shared expectations, underpinning knowledge exchange and facilitating regional collective learning. Collective learning is strengthened through joint projects and regional labour mobility. Consequently, collective learning brings about a shared knowledge base about technological and organisational solutions, usually in a specialised field (e.g. related to a technology or sector). In such a specialised field, strong regional input–output relationships are seen to be the core of a local production system (Maillat 1998).

The concept of innovative milieu is relevant for this chapter because it explicitly deals with change and evolutionary processes. 'A milieu is not unchanging, it is not defined a priori and once and for all. On the contrary, it constitutes a dynamic complex which in the course of time has had to change and evolve by means of a continuous process of resource creation, innovation and adaptation to external constraints' (Maillat *et al.* 1996).

Regional change and evolution are often described as a perpetual process of rupture and filiation, or break and continuity (Camagni 1995; Crevoisier 2004; Maillat 1998). The assumption is that local production systems and milieus have a tendency to reproduce themselves and thus exhibit a certain degree of inertia and continuity. Change results from the dynamic interplay between the existing milieu and local production system, capturing turbulences in the market and technological environment and collective learning processes based on the knowledge, skills, networks and expectations developed in the past. For such change processes, external linkages play an important role in identifying turbulences in the environment and in providing inputs to collective learning. Collective learning and innovation are required to maintain compatibility with the technical and market environment. In this way, collective learning leads to modifications of the milieu and the local production system, which are the new starting points for future changes. Finally, in order for an innovative milieu to prevail, integration processes are necessary to maintain its internal coherence. In the framing of change processes, some evolutionary thoughts such as path-dependencies can be identified (Crevoisier 2004; Maillat 1998).

The milieu concept also distinguishes factors that influence the above-mentioned change processes. Network linkages outside the region are such a factor and comprise, for instance, strategic alliances, or commercialisation agreements through which 'external energy' for innovation processes can be captured (Camagni 1995). The interaction logic within the milieu is another important factor. It refers to the capacity to interact and develop a collective response to external turbulences. This usually requires a long-term business rationale based on innovation as opposed to a short-term perspective based on rationalisation and cost-cutting. Also, it depends on whether regional consensus and shared visions exist. Ideally, by mobilising collective learning processes, the regional structure, organisation and technologies are upgraded and region-specific resources are created. In this process, leading actors that drive such processes play an important role (Maillat 1998; Maillat *et al.* 1996).

Research on innovative milieus has focused strongly on innovative growth regions and high-tech clusters, although there are also contributions dealing with the revitalisation of old industrial regions and conservative milieus. In summary, the milieu concept emphasises the role of innovation and regional adaptation to (external) changes in the technological and market conditions. Change is thought to occur through perpetual processes of rupture and continuity. However, it remains relatively vague as regards why, how and under which conditions key processes such as maintaining compatibility with the external environment or maintaining internal coherence lead to cluster growth or renewal and when they might fail. Also, the milieu concept has been criticised for a lack of clarity as regards terminology and for the difficulty in objectively measuring and comparing milieus of different regions.

17.3.3 Regional innovation systems

The ID concept and the milieu approach are key theoretical predecessors of the more recent regional innovation system (RIS) concept (Asheim *et al.* 2011). The RIS literature (Asheim 2007; Cooke 1992, 2001) devotes attention to the companies, cluster structures, knowledge providers and institutional set-up of a region, as well as to knowledge links within the region and to the external world. Like other innovation systems variants, the RIS approach conceptualises innovation as an evolutionary, non-linear and interactive process. The region is seen as a crucial level at which innovation is generated through knowledge linkages, clusters and the cross-fertilising effects of research organisations (Asheim and Gertler 2005).

RISs come in many shapes. Cooke (2004) distinguishes between entrepreneurial and institutional RISs and claims that the former offer excellent conditions for the development of high-tech clusters, while the latter provide a fertile ground for the evolution of traditional ones. Tödtling and Trippl (2005) draw a distinction between organisationally thin, fragmented and locked-in RISs and argue that each of these configurations is associated with distinct barriers to cluster development. These typologies are useful for analysing how the evolution of a cluster might be influenced by the RIS in which it is embedded. Indeed, there are strong reasons to assume that cluster change differs depending on the characteristics of the RIS.

The relation between RISs and cluster evolution is complex. According to the RIS approach, clusters form an integral part of RISs. The emergence, growth, maturity, decline and possibly renewal of clusters can, thus, be understood only if the specificities of the knowledge infrastructure, institutional set-up, cultural aspects and policy actions of a particular region are considered. Several studies suggest that the rise and early development of clusters are shaped by the configuration of the RIS. The emergence of clusters is likely to follow different routes, depending on historically evolved competences and pre-existing RIS structures. Conceptual and empirical work on the rise of high-tech clusters shows that RISs that already host dynamic high-tech clusters provide favourable conditions for the emergence of new ones, even if these newly emerging clusters are different from those developed earlier. Such RISs offer essential conditions, such as excellent research institutes, venture capitalists, a pool of highly skilled mobile workers and dense communication networks (see, for instance, Prevezer 2001). RISs that are poorly endowed with such structures, experiences and knowledge assets are likely to follow different paths. The rise of new (high-tech) clusters in such regions is less a spontaneous phenomenon but depends more on the inflow of external knowledge, expertise and market intelligence and a stronger role of policy. In addition, new cluster formation in such regions is inextricably linked to a transformation of the RIS that becomes manifest in the creation of a variety of organisations, processes of institutional (un)learning and socio-cultural shifts.

Then there are also scholarly contributions that deal with the renewal of traditional clusters. Much of this work is focused on old industrial regions, emphasising a strong relation between the rejuvenation of mature clusters and prevailing RIS characteristics, including their transformative capacities. It is argued that successful revitalisation of old clusters is influenced by the configuration of the RIS, such as structures, activities and orientation of knowledge providers, the role of regional policy agencies, the socio-institutional fabric, as well as the extent and nature of links. The presence or absence of favourable RIS structures and changes (transformation of the knowledge infrastructure, institutional innovations, policy-learning processes) can make a difference (Trippl and Otto 2009).

To summarise, the RIS literature emphasises that cluster development and change cannot be assessed independently from its context (i.e. the overall RIS). RISs can facilitate or hamper the development and change of clusters. Both the emergence of new clusters and the revitalisation of old ones are likely to show a different pattern, depending on the RIS in which they are embedded. Existing RIS structures and their transformation have an influence on how clusters change and which mechanisms of change dominate. Cluster evolution is thus a context-specific phenomenon that varies strongly between different types of RIS. However, the RIS approach is criticised for being primarily concerned with structural elements of the innovation system (Uyarra 2011). The importance of actors, such as entrepreneurs in universities and firms, for innovation performance are much less considered. Likewise, the role of uneven power among actors when it comes to prioritising tasks and resources in organisations in the innovation system seems to be absent in RIS studies (Uyarra 2011). Furthermore, RIS studies have often been snapshots focusing on the characteristics, and strengths and weaknesses, of particular well-developed systems, while the historical development of the systems is less reflected upon (Doloreux and Parto 2005).

17.4   Conclusions: towards a context-sensitive approach to cluster change

This chapter has sought to contribute to the development of a dynamic perspective in cluster research. We have argued that the CLC approaches – which have gained increasing visibility in recent reflections on cluster dynamics – are not uncontested. They provide a rather deterministic view, are indifferent with regard to regional and industrial context conditions as they aim to attain one general development path for cluster development, and suffer from biological connotations. We reviewed the literature on industrial districts, innovative milieus and regional innovation systems and examined whether these approaches allow for alternative views and a more profound understanding of how clusters evolve and change.

The review of the approaches has uncovered essential dissimilarities in their explanations of cluster change. An important difference 'dividing' the approaches concerns the dimensions of cluster dynamics that are highlighted. CLC approaches focus primarily on the characteristics and dynamics of firms, their capabilities and networks. The milieu approach, in contrast, emphasises socio-cultural aspects that shape clusters' internal interaction modes. Hence, it values institutional aspects of place-specificity higher than the CLC approaches. The ID concept stresses characteristics of the industry structure and also highlights the role of socio-cultural factors. The RIS approach emphasises the role of the region's organisational and institutional configurations, its overall industrial structure and knowledge exploration capacity as well as policy actions. It is argued that these structural features shape cluster dynamics. All approaches discussed in this chapter thus illuminate certain aspects of cluster change. Each of them highlights particular dimensions but pays less attention to others.

Then, as shown in section 17.3, the alternative approaches stress that clusters may not necessarily follow one path but many, i.e. they follow multiple path dependencies (Belussi and Sedita 2009). This highlights the need to carry out more empirical studies in the future that put cluster evolution into a comparative perspective. A possible route of further research is to distinguish between types of clusters and elaborate on their specific path dependent development. While not repeating the deterministic understanding in some CLC approaches, we nonetheless assume that different types of clusters, for example high-tech clusters drawing on scientific advances and traditional clusters based mostly on experience-based competence, have quite different driving forces of change. The search for one overarching theory of the emergence and evolution of clusters may therefore be misleading. It seems to be more promising to develop theoretical relevant categorisations of different types of clusters and examine the characteristics of their historical developments. This understanding implies that one task for further research on cluster evolution would be conceptual and empirical studies to outline typical, possible development paths for different types of clusters.

What, then, are distinguishing factors to identify clusters that follow comparable development paths? Ter Wal and Boschma (2011) focus on industry, firm capabilities and firm networks as key concepts to explain the development of clusters. Clusters in specific industries are affected by general market and technological development within these industries. Industrial classifications may include diverse activities, however. Different parts of industries may display different development dynamics, and clusters in similar industries may also reveal quite different path development. Belussi and Sedita (2009) demonstrate that firms in one footwear district in Italy diversified their products, which attracted some big luxury brands to the district, while firms in another Italian footwear district carried out a cost-led strategy and outsourced production to low-cost countries. This demonstrates that no one-to-one relationship between industry and cluster life cycles exists. Such a lesson can also be drawn from the empirical analyses of firms' innovation processes and strategies in thirteen European countries by Srholec and Verspagen (2012). These authors demonstrate that firms in individual industrial sectors use very different innovation strategies, for example with regard to inputs to and results of innovation activity. Most of the difference in firms' innovation strategy includes heterogeneity among firms within sectors; 'heterogeneity between firms will result from the process of strategy formation at the firm level' (Srholec and Verspagen 2012, p. 1248). This implies that industrial sectors do not display much about how clusters develop through their life cycles simply because no specific innovation strategies are prominent in individual sectors.

The empirically based categorisation of firms' innovation strategies by Srholec and Verspagen (2012) accords with the more analytical approaches of differentiated knowledge bases (Asheim *et al.* 2011) and innovation modes (Jensen *et al.* 2007). These approaches categorise firms based on their critical knowledge input in innovation processes and on how firms organise and conduct innovation activity. Isaksen and Karlsen (2012) demonstrate that firms within one regional cluster in mechanical engineering use different innovation modes, which indicates that innovation mode is more of a firm-specific activity than the characteristic of this specific cluster or industy. Other research demonstrates likewise that clusters dominated by analytical knowledge build upon, and develop, other formal and informal institutional structures than more traditional clusters based on synthetic knowledge (Asheim and Coenen 2005). For example, entrepreneurs have very different education and experience in the two types of clusters, firms are recruiting from different segments of the labour market, and firms draw on different kinds of external knowledge sources and develop new knowledge in different ways. Based on such arguments one should expect that clusters dominated by, for example, firms with a specific innovation mode share a number of common challenges and display some commonalities in their evolution.

The distinguishing factors to identify specific development paths of clusters have so far been studied at the industry and the firm level. While these factors are vital in analysing cluster evolution, our review of theoretical frameworks points also to the importance of the existing wider RIS structure for how clusters emerge and develop. The industrial district and innovative milieu approaches, in particular, also point to the importance of place-specific, social-cultural and institutional aspects for cluster evolution. Cusmano *et al.* (2015, p. 63) thus maintain that the entrepreneurial process in an Italian industrial district is largely influenced by 'Marshallian externalities, such as knowledge spillovers and the supply of "collective goods" at the territorial level'. 'Localized socio-institutional environments built over time in a path dependent way' (Strambach and Klement 2012, p. 1845) shape how firms use and create knowledge and innovate. The recent contributions on cluster evolution, however, hardly reflect on these context-specific factors as possible explanations as to why clusters follow different development paths (Trippl *et al.* 2015).

Based on the above discussion, the identification of diverse development paths of clusters should include a mix of macro factors (such as type of industry and industry life cycles), meso factors (the RIS structure including place-specific institutional set-ups) and micro factors (firms' knowledge bases and innovation modes). The relative importance of each factor and the mix of factors may differ among regions, but cluster evolution results from the dynamic interplay between macro, meso and micro factors. A similar multiscalar approach to analyses of cluster development is proposed by Santner and Fornahl (2014). Such an approach allows for a variety of potential path developments. Our contribution has been to elaborate analytically on the key factors in question. We suggest that future research should aim at exploring why and how the interplay of these factors affects cluster evolution in specific contexts, and consequently at identifying commonalities that allow grouping clusters according to the main factors driving their evolution. Hence, we also contribute by laying a sound foundation for comparative studies of cluster evolution and to make approaches to multiple path development of clusters theoretically informed so that these do not simply become empirically based exercises.

References

Asheim, B. (2007) Differentiated knowledge bases and varieties of regional innovation systems, *Innovation*, 20, 223–241.

Asheim, B. and Coenen, L. (2005) Knowledge bases and regional innovation systems: comparing Nordic clusters, *Research Policy*, 34(8), 1173–1190.

Asheim, B. and Gertler, M. (2005) The geography of innovation: regional innovation systems. In: J. Fagerberg, D. Mowery and R. Nelson (eds) *The Oxford Handbook of Innovation*, Oxford: Oxford University Press, pp. 291–317.

Asheim, B., Boschma, R. and Cooke, P. (2011) Constructing regional advantage: platform policies based on related variety and differentiated knowledge bases, *Regional Studies*, 45(7), 893–904.

Belussi, F. (2011) The new Marshallian districts and their process of internationalization. In: P. Cooke, B. Asheim, R. Boschma, R. Martin, D. Schwartz and F. Tödtling (eds) *Handbook of Regional Innovation and Growth*, Cheltenham: Edward Elgar, pp. 90–99.

Belussi, F. and Sedita, S. (2009) Life cycle vs. multiple path dependency in industrial districts, *European Planning Studies*, 17(4), 505–528.

Bergman, E. (2008) Cluster life-cycles: an emerging synthesis, in C. Karlsson (ed.) *Handbook of Research on Cluster Theory*, Cheltenham: Edward Elgar, pp. 114–132.

Bianchi, G. (1998) Requiem for the Third Italy? Rise and fall of a too successful concept, *Entrepreneurship & Regional Development*, 10(2), 93–116.

Boschma, R. (2005) Proximity and innovation: a critical assessment, *Regional Studies*, 39(1), 61–75.

Camagni, R. (1995) The concept of innovative milieu and its relevance for public policies in European lagging regions, *Papers in Regional Science*, 74(4), 317–340.

Cooke, P. (1992) Regional innovation systems: competitive regulation in the new Europe, *Geoforum*, 23, 365–382.

Cooke, P. (2001) Regional innovation systems, clusters and the knowledge economy, *Industrial & Corporate Change*, 10, 945–974.

Cooke, P. (2004) Integrating global knowledge flows for generative growth in Scotland: life science as a knowledge economy exemplar. In: J. Potter (ed.) *Inward Investment, Entrepreneurship and Knowledge Flows in Scotland – International Comparisons*, Paris: OECD, pp. 73–96.

Crevoisier, O. (2004) The innovative milieus approach: toward a territorialized understanding of the economy, *Economic Geography*, 80(4), 367–379.

Cusmano, L., Morrison, A. and Pandolfo, E. (2015) Spin-off and clustering: a return to the Marshallian district, *Cambridge Journal of Economics*, 39, 49–66.

Doloreux, D. and Parto, S. (2005) Regional innovation systems: current discourse and unresolved issues, *Technology in Society*, 27, 133–153.

Frenken, K., Van Ort, F. and Verburg, T. (2007) Related variety, unrelated variety and regional economic growth, *Regional Studies*, 41(5), 685–697.

Isaksen, A. (2011) Cluster evolution in P. Cooke, B. Asheim, R. Martin, D. Schwartz and F. Tödtling (eds) *Handbook of Regional Innovation and Growth*, Cheltenham: Edward Elgar, pp. 293–302.

Isaksen, A. and Karlsen, J. (2012) What is regional in regional clusters? The case of the globally oriented oil and gas cluster in Agder, Norway, *Industry and Innovation*, 19(3), 249–263.

Jensen, M. B., Johnson, B., Lorenz, E. and Lundvall, B. (2007) Forms of knowledge and modes of innovation, *Research Policy*, 36(5), 680–693.

Klepper, S. (1997) Industry life cycles, *Industrial and Corporate Change*, 6, 145–181.

Maillat, D. (1998) From the industrial district to the innovative milieu: contribution to an analysis of territorialised productive organisations, *Recherches Economiques de Louvain*, 61(1), 111–129.

Maillat, D., Léchot, G., Lecoq, B. and Pfister, M. (1996) Comparative analysis of the structural development of milieu: the example of the watch industry in the Swizz and French Jura Arc, Working paper 96–07, Institut de recherches économiques et regionals, Université de Neuchatel, Neuchatel.

Marshall, A. (1920) *Principles of Economics* (8th Edition), London: Macmillan.

Martin, R. (2010) Roepke Lecture in Economic Geography – Rethinking regional path dependence: beyond lock-in to evolution *Economic Geography*, 86(1), 179–192.

Martin, R. and Sunley, P. (2011) Conceptualizing cluster evolution: beyond the life cycle model? *Regional Studies*, 45(10), 1299–1318.

Menzel, M.-P. and Fornahl, D. (2010) Cluster life cycles – dimensions and rationales of cluster evolution, *Industrial and Corporate Change*, 19(1), 205–238.

Prevezer, M. (2001) Ingredients in the early development of the U.S. biotechnology industry, *Small Business Economics*, 17(1/2), 17–29.

Rabellotti, R., Carabelli, A. and Hirsch G. (2009) Italian industrial districts on the move: where are they going? *European Planning Studies*, 17(1), 19–41.

Randelli, F. and Boschma, R. (2012) Dynamics of industrial districts and business groups: the case of the Marche region, *European Planning Studies*, 20(12), 1961–1974.

Santner, D. and Fornahl, D. (2014) From here, from there, and from beyond: endogenous and exogenous factors triggering change along the cluster life cycle in a multi-scalar environment. Working papers on Innovation and Space #02.14. Philipps Universitet Marburg.

Simmie, J. (2012) Path dependence and new technological path creation in the Danish wind power industry, *European Planning Studies*, 20(5), 753–772.

Srholec, M. and Verspagen, B. (2012) The voyage of the Beagle into innovation: explorations on heterogeneity, selection and sectors, *Industrial and Corporate Change*, 21(5), 1221–1253.

Storper, M. and Walker, R. (1989) *The Capitalist Imperative. Territory, Technology, and Industrial Growth*, New York: Basil Blackwell.

Strambach, S. and Klement, B. (2012) Cumulative and combinatorial micro-dynamics of knowledge: the role of space and place in knowledge integration, *European Planning Studies*, 20(11), 1843–1866.

Ter Wal, A. and Boschma, R. (2011) Co-evolution of firms, industries and networks in space, *Regional Studies*, 45(7), 919–933.

Tödtling, F. and Trippl, M. (2005) One size fits all? Towards a differentiated regional innovation policy approach, *Research Policy*, 34(8), 1203–1219.

Trippl, M. and Otto, A. (2009) How to turn the fate of old industrial areas: a comparison of cluster-based renewal processes in Styria and the Saarland, *Environment and Planning A*, 41(5), 1217–1233.

Trippl, M., Grillitsch, M., Isaksen, A. and Sinozic, T. (2015) Perspectives on cluster evolution: critical review and future research issues, *European Planning Studies*, 23(10), 2028–2044.

Uyarra, E. (2011). Regional innovation systems revisited: networks, institutions, policy and complexity. In: T. Herrschel and P. Tallberg (eds) *The Role of Regions? Networks, Svale, Territory*, Malmö: Region Skåne, pp. 169–193.

Index

For Product Safety Concerns and Information please contact our EU
representative GPSR@taylorandfrancis.com
Taylor & Francis Verlag GmbH, Kaufingerstraße 24, 80331 München, Germany

www.ingramcontent.com/pod-product-compliance
Ingram Content Group UK Ltd.
Pitfield, Milton Keynes, MK11 3LW, UK
UKHW021016180425
457613UK00020B/949